Revitalizing Causalit

GW00775876

This book is a unique, cross-disciplinary collection of articles by philosophers, social scientists and social theorists who explore, at different levels of abstraction, what it means to invoke causal mechanisms, or powers, in the context of offering a causal explanation. Realism about causality is a compelling neo-Aristotelian alternative to the dominant Humean and Kantian approaches in philosophy and social science. Its proponents argue that causality is neither a misnomer for "constant conjunction" nor the exercise of a cognitive *a priori*, but rather is a matter of the powers that things have to affect other things.

The volume contains both new and previously published articles. It is distinctive in that it is an effort to give broad shape to the emerging challenge to the ontology implicit in positivism and post-structuralism alike. It will be of particular interest to readers of philosophy (metaphysics, philosophy of science, philosophy of social science), sociology, political science, and political economy, as well as to those familiar with critical realism.

Ruth Groff is a member of the political science department at the State University of New York.

Routledge studies in critical realism

Edited by Margaret Archer, Roy Bhaskar, Andrew Collier, Kathryn Dean, Nick Hostettler, Jonathan Joseph, Tony Lawson, Alan Norrie and Sean Vertigan

Critical realism is one of the most influential new developments in the philosophy of science and in the social sciences, providing a powerful alternative to positivism and post-modernism. This series will explore the critical realist position in philosophy and across the social sciences.

Also published by Routledge:
Critical realism: Interventions
Edited by Margaret Archer, Roy Bhaskar, Andrew Collier, Kathryn Dean, Nick
Hostettler, Jonathan Joseph, Tony Lawson, Alan Norrie and Sean Vertigan

Critical Realism
Essential readings
*Edited by Margaret Archer, Roy
Bhaskar, Andrew Collier, Tony Lawson
and Alan Norrie*

The Possibility of Naturalism
3rd edition
A philosophical critique of the
contemporary human sciences
Roy Bhaskar

Being and Worth
Andrew Collier

**Quantum Theory and the Flight from
Realism**
Philosophical responses to quantum
mechanics
Christopher Norris

From East to West
Odyssey of a soul
Roy Bhaskar

Realism and Racism
Concepts of race in sociological research
Bob Carter

Rational Choice Theory
Resisting colonisation
*Edited by Margaret Archer and Jonathan
Q. Tritter*

Explaining Society
Critical realism in the social sciences
*Berth Danermark, Mats Ekström, Jan
Ch. Karlsson and Liselotte Jakobsen*

Critical Realism and Marxism
*Edited by Andrew Brown, Steve
Fleetwood and John Michael Roberts*

Critical Realism in Economics
Edited by Steve Fleetwood

**Realist Perspectives on Management
and Organisations**
*Edited by Stephen Ackroyd and Steve
Fleetwood*

After International Relations
Critical realism and the (re)construction
of world politics
Heikki Patomaki

Capitalism and Citizenship
The impossible partnership
Kathryn Dean

**Philosophy of Language and the
Challenge to Scientific Realism**
Christopher Norris

Revitalizing Causality

Realism about causality in philosophy and social science

Edited by
Ruth Groff

 Routledge
Taylor & Francis Group

LONDON AND NEW YORK

First published 2008
by Routledge
2 Park Square, Milton Park, Abingdon, Oxon, OX14 4RN

Simultaneously published in the USA and Canada
by Routledge
270 Madison Ave, New York NY 10016

*Routledge is an imprint of the Taylor & Francis Group,
an informa business*

Transferred to Digital Printing 2009

© 2008 Edited by Ruth Groff

Typeset in Times New Roman by Keyword Group Ltd, UK

British Library Cataloguing in Publication Data
A catalogue record for this book is available from the British Library

Library of Congress Cataloging in Publication Data
Revitalizing causality: realism about causality in philosophy and social
science / edited by Ruth Groff.
    p. cm.
1. Causation. 2. Social sciences–Philosophy. 3. Critical realism.
I. Groff, Ruth, 1963–
BD541.R48 2007
122–dc22   2007029183

ISBN10: 0-415-37218-6 (hbk)
ISBN10: 0-415-56871-4 (pbk)
ISBN10: 0-203-93263-3 (ebk)

ISBN13: 978-0-415-37218-3 (hbk)
ISBN13: 978-0-415-56871-5 (pbk)
ISBN13: 978-0-203-93263-6 (ebk)

For Helen Splaver

Contents

x *Contents*

Contributors

Robert Albritton, York University, Department of Political Science, Emeritus. He writes on dialectics, political economy and subjectivity. His books and edited collections include: *Economics Transformed: Discovering the Brilliance of Marx* (2007); *Dialectics and Deconstruction in Political Economy* (1999); *A Japanese Reconstruction of Marxist Theory* (l986); *A Japanese Approach to Stages of Capitalist Development* (1991); *The Political Economy of the Present and Possible Global Future*, ed. with Bob Jessop and Richard Westra (2007); *New Socialisms: Futures Beyond Globalization* ed. with John Bell, Shannon Bell, Richard Westra (2004); *New Dialectics and Political Economy*, ed. with John Simoulidis (2003). Recent articles include: "Theorising Capital's Deep Structure and the Transformation of Capitalism," *Historical Materialism*, Vol. 12, No. 3; "Returning to Marx's *Capital*: A Critique of Lebowitz's *Beyond Capital*," *History of Economic Ideas*, Vol. XI, No. 3; "How Dialectics Runs Aground: The Antinomies of Arthur's Dialectic of Capital," *Historical Materialism* (2005); "Subjectivity in Capitalist Culture," *The Journal of Critical Realism* (2004); "Marx's Value Theory and Class Struggle: A Rejoinder to Lebowitz," *History of Economic Ideas* (2004).

Andrew Bennett, Georgetown University, Department of Government. He specializes in international relations and qualitative research methods. Forthcoming and recent works include: *Case Studies and Theory Development*, with Alexander George, MIT Press; "A Lakatosian Reading of Lakatos: What Can We Salvage from the Hard Core?" in Elman and Elman (eds.), *Progress In International Relations Theory: Metrics and Methods of Scientific Change* (2003); "Do We Preach What We Practice? A Survey of Methods in Political Science Journals and Curricula," with Aharon Barth and Ken Rutherford, *PS: Political Science and Politics* (2003); "Case Study: Methods and Analysis," in Smelser and Baltes (eds.), *International Encyclopedia of the Social and Behavior Sciences* (2001); *Condemned to Repetition? The Rise, Fall and Reprise of Soviet-Russian Military Interventionism 1973–1996* (1999).

Alexander Bird, University of Bristol, Department of Philosophy. He writes on the philosophy of science. He is the author of *Nature's Metaphysics: Dispositions, Laws, and Properties* (2007); *Thomas Kuhn* (2002); and *Philosophy of*

Science (1998). Recent articles include: "What is Scientific Progress?" *Noûs*; "Justified Judging" *Philosophy and Phenomenological Research;* "Selection and Explanation" in *Rethinking Explanation (Boston Studies in the Philosophy of Science* 252, eds. Persson and Ylikoski) (2006); "Looking for Laws" *Metascience* 15 (2006); "Potency and Modality" *Synthese* 149 (2006); "Unexpected A Posteriori Necessary Laws of Nature" *Australasian Journal of Philosophy* 83 (2005); "Laws and Essences" *Ratio* 18 (2005); "The Dispositionalist Conception of Laws" *Foundations of Science* 10 (2005); "Explanation and Metaphysics" *Synthese* 143 (2005); "Naturalizing Kuhn" *Proceedings of the Aristotelian Society* 105 (2005); "The Ultimate Argument Against Armstrong's Contingent Necessitation View of Laws" *Analysis* 65 (2005); "Antidotes All the Way Down?" *Theoria* 19 (2004); "Strong Necessitarianism: the Nomological Identity of Possible Worlds" *Ratio* 17 (2004); "Kuhn, Naturalism, and the Positivist Legacy" *Studies in History and Philosophy of Science* 35 (2004); "Kuhn and Twentieth Century Philosophy of Science" *Annals of the Japan Association for Philosophy of Science* 12 (2004); "Kuhn on Reference and Essence" *Philosophia Scientiae* 8 (2004); "Is Evidence Non-Inferential?" *Philosophical Quarterly* 54 (2004).

Anjan Chakravartty, University of Toronto, Institute for History and Philosophy of Science. He writes on philosophy of science and metaphysics. He is the author of *A Metaphysics for Scientific Realism: Knowing the Unobservable* (2007). Recent articles include: "Causal Realism: Events and Processes," *Erkenntnis* (2005); "Stance Relativism: Empiricism versus Metaphysics," *Studies in History and Philosophy of Science* (2004); "Structuralism as a Form of Scientific Realism", *International Studies in the Philosophy of Science* (2004); "The Dispositional Essentialist View of Properties and Laws," *International Journal of Philosophical Studies* (2003); "The Structuralist Conception of Objects," *Philosophy of Science* (2003).

Rachel Cooper, Lancaster University, Institute for Philosophy and Public Policy. She writes on the philosophy of social science and medicine, especially on issues concerning mental illness, the nature of disease, classification and natural kinds. She is the author of *Classifying Madness: A philosophical examination of the Diagnostic and Statistical Manual of Mental Disorders.* Recent articles include "Disease," *Studies in History and Philosophy of Biological and Biomedical Sciences* (2002); "Why Hacking is wrong about human kinds," *British Journal for the Philosophy of Science* (2004); "What's wrong with the D.S.M.?" *History of Psychiatry* (2004); "Can sociologists understand other forms of life?" *Perspectives on Science* (2004).

Howard Engelskirchen, Iowa State University, Department of Philosophy. He applies scientific realism to law and to capitalist social relations of production. He is a lawyer and a former professor of law, who now works within the discipline of philosophy. Recent publications include: "Why is This Labor Value? – Commodity-Producing Labour as a Social Kind," forthcoming in

Pearce and Frauley, *Critical Realism and the Social Sciences: Heterodox Elaborations;* "Powers and Particulars: Adorno and Scientific Realism," *Journal of Critical Realism* (2004); "Value and Contract Formation," in *Realism, Discourse and Deconstruction*, Jonathan Joseph and John Michael Roberts, eds. (2003); "Consideration as the Commitment to Relinquish Autonomy," *Seton Hall Law Review* (1997).

Ruth Groff, University at Albany, State University of New York (SUNY). She writes on the relationships between political theory, metaphysics and epistemology. She is the author of Critical Realism, Post-Positivism and the Possibility of Knowledge (2004). Her current project is entitled after Mechanism: The (Re)turn to Aristotle in Metaphysics, Ethics and Political Theory.

Stephen Mumford, University of Nottingham, Department of Philosophy. He writes on metaphysics and the philosophy of science, primarily on dispositions and laws. He is the author of *David Armstrong* (forthcoming, 2007); *Laws in Nature* (2004); *Powers: A Study in Metaphysics* (ed.) (2003); *Russell on Metaphysics*, (ed.) (2003); *Dispositions* (1998, 2003). Recent articles include: "Laws and Lawlessness," *Synthese* (2005); "Miracles: Metaphysics and Modality," *Religious Studies* (2001); "Realism and The Conditional Analysis of Dispositions: Reply to Malzkorn," *Philosophical Quarterly* (2001); "Normative and Natural Laws," *Philosophy* (2000).

Christopher Norris, Cardiff University, Department of Philosophy. He writes about a wide range of issues in epistemology, philosophy of language and philosophy of science. His recent books include: *On Truth and Meaning* (2006); *Epistemology: Key Concepts in Philosophy* (2005); *Hilary Putnam: realism, reason, and the uses of uncertainty* (2002); *Truth Matters: realism, anti-realism and response-dependence* (2002); *Quantum Theory and the Flight from Realism: philosophical responses to quantum mechanics* (2000); *Minding the Gap: epistemology and philosophy of science in the two traditions* (2000); *Deconstruction and the Unfinished Project of Modernity* (2000); *Resources of Realism: prospects for 'post-analytic' philosophy* (1997); *New Idols of the Cave: on the limits of anti-realism* (1997); *Against Relativism: philosophy of science, deconstruction and critical theory* (1997); *Reclaiming Truth: contribution to a critique of cultural relativism* (1996); *Truth and the Ethics of Criticism* (1994); *The Truth About Postmodernism* (1993).

Douglas V. Porpora, Drexel University, Department of Culture and Communication. He writes on topics ranging from the philosophy of social science to culture and international political economy. He is the author of *Transcendence: Critical Realism and God* (with Margaret Archer and Andrew Collier) (2004); *Landscapes of the Soul: The Loss of Moral Meaning in American Life* (2001); *How Holocausts Happen: The United States in Central America* (1990); *The Concept of Social Structure* (1987). Recent articles include: "The Caterpillar's Question: Contesting Anti-Humanism's

Contestations," *Journal for the Theory of Social Behaviour* (1997); "Are There Levels of Social Structure?" *Humboldt Journal of Social Relations* (1996).

Charlotte Witt, University of New Hampshire, Department of Philosophy. She writes on ancient philosophy, feminist theory and metaphysics. She is the author of *Substance and Essence in Aristotle* (1989, 1994); *Ways of Being: Potentiality and Actuality in Aristotle's Metaphysics* (2003); *Adoption Matters: Philosophical and Feminist Essays*, co-edited with Sally Haslanger (2005); *Feminist Reflections on the History of Philosophy*, co-edited with Lilli Alanen (2004); *Ancient Philosophy and Modern Ideology*, co-edited with Mohan Matthen, *Apeiron*, special volume, (2000); *A Mind of One's Own: Feminist Essays on Reason and Objectivity* co-edited with Louise Antony (1992, 2001). Recent articles include: "Feminist Interpretations of the Philosophical Canon" *Signs: Journal of Women in Culture and Society*, Vol. 31, No. 2 (Winter, 2006); "Analogy and Motion in Theta 6" in *Essays in Ancient Greek Philosophy*, Intercollege Press (2005); "Tragic Error and Agent Responsibility" in *The Annual Proceedings of the Center for Philosophic Exchange*, SUNY Brockport (20).

Acknowledgements

This book was conceived in Toronto, given shape in Milwaukee and completed in Williamstown, Massachusetts. Friends and family supported the project at every stage, for which I can only begin to express my full appreciation here.

I continue to owe my largest intellectual debt of gratitude to Richard Schuldenfrei and to Hugh Lacey, who introduced me to the problem of causality and to critical realism respectively, when I was an undergraduate at Swarthmore College. I also want again to acknowledge Ronnie Meyher, who first told the Bhaskar list about Irving Copi and Brian Ellis, and who as a result focused my thinking about critical realism on its metaphysical core.

I offer sincere thanks to the contributors of the collection for agreeing to be part of the book, and especially for their endless forbearance as various life events conspired again and again to delay its publication. Alan Jarvis of Routledge has been enormously patient in this regard.

Finally, I would like to give special thanks to Christopher Norris, for his generosity with respect to copyright permissions; to Anjan Chakravartty, for his invaluable philosophical and editorial advice; and to Paul Park and Noah Efron, for displaying exceptional team spirit.

Introduction

Realism about causality

Ruth Groff

Hume tells us that there is no such thing as natural necessity. What we call causality, he says, is a reification of our own subjective expectations regarding constant conjunctions. We expect that things that have come after other things in the past will continue to do so in the present and on into the future; "causality" is simply a misnomer for the feeling of anticipation that we experience in our encounters with the familiar. Doing away with the idea of natural necessity – an ontological move, albeit one forced upon Hume by his epistemology – ushers in the problem of induction. On what grounds, Hume and philosophers since have asked, may we justify predictions (fire, *ceteris paribus*, will burn paper next time too) and/or generalizations (fire always burns paper) if there are no necessary connections between things?

Hume's response was to say that there really is no way to justify our predictions and generalizations. If one is troubled by this response – either by the skepticism that it implies, epistemologically, or by the radical contingency that it presupposes, ontologically – but remains otherwise attracted to Hume's empiricism, one might try to solve the problem by asserting that the world just *is* ordered – that it contains regularities, given by laws, which sustain inferences from the present to the future and from the particular to the general. But this simply displaces the problem. For if Hume is right, then even if we "know" from experience that the world is ordered, we can only know that it has been ordered up until now. The problem of induction remains: we still have no grounds for thinking that it will be ordered the next time we check.

Kant undertook to solve the problem by saying that causality is a universal feature of reason itself. We cannot help, he said, but conceptualize the world, via the synthetic operation of the categories of the understanding, as being governed by necessary relations of cause and effect. We are saved, thereby, from radical contingency, epistemological as well as ontological. But it is not because the world is intrinsically structured by necessary connections. Rather, it is because we are incapable of experiencing the world in radically contingent terms, as Hume himself appreciated. Hume was right, then, to forswear the concept of natural necessity, wrong only to conclude that causality is therefore nothing other than a projected feeling of anticipation.

The contributors to this collection have in common with one another that they take issue with Hume, and by extension with Kant, on this issue. The unifying theme of the essays is support for an alternative position that I shall call "realism about causality." Realists about causality maintain that causality is connected to the display of things' dispositional properties: it is a matter of the powers that things have, in virtue of what they are, to affect other things, given what the other things are. Thus realists about causality think, *contra* Hume, that causal relations are relations of natural or metaphysical necessity, rather than of contingent sequence – and, further, *contra* Kant, that the necessity in question is given by properties inherent in the *relata* themselves, rather than by the synthetic operation of reason. From the perspective of realism about causality, then, to say "x caused y," or "x is the cause of y," is to express our common-sense conviction that there is something *about* x that made it be that y happened. It is not to say "Every time I observe x, y follows, and so now I expect y to follow." Nor is it to say "We cannot help but conceive of x-followed-by-y as a lawfully governed sequence." Rather it is to say, "x is such that it has the power to bring about y, other things being equal (and so will continue to do so in the future)."

This collection is an effort to give cross-disciplinary shape to the broadly neo-Aristotelian challenge to Hume and Kant that is mounted by those who are realists about causality, a challenge at the level of paradigm, we might even want to say. The "revitalization project," as Anjan Chakravartty calls it in Chapter 9, is at present being carried out by thinkers rooted in different academic disciplines, working at various different levels of abstraction, coming at the issue from a range of theoretical backgrounds, engaged primarily in specialized, relatively local debates. Academic life being as it is, it is often hard to see the forest for the trees. That philosophers engaged in argument about the nature of dispositions, and social scientists trying to determine the causal properties of macro-level phenomena such as value, are working within and upon the same emerging neo-Aristotelian framework may not be readily apparent, given the normal configuration of conferences, journals, and disciplinary associations. Nonetheless it is so.

II

It is worth clarifying what realism about causality does and does not commit one to philosophically. To begin, realism about causality should not be confused with causal theories of reference and/or with naturalist or evolutionary theories of knowledge. Realism about causality is neither a proposal about how language attaches to the world, nor an account of where beliefs come from, or why we might be justified in judging them to be reliable or sound. Rather, it is a theory about what causality is. It therefore bears upon causal approaches to semantic and/or epistemic issues, and it is perfectly consistent with them, but it does not entail them. Conversely, the position that ideas are grounded in our on-going causal interactions with the world leaves open the question of what causality is. It is consistent with realism about causality, but it does not imply it.

More difficult to parse is the relationship between realism about causality and scientific essentialism. Scientific essentialism is a realist position within metaphysics and the philosophy of science, the crux of which is the belief that things have essential properties, on the basis of which they fall into natural kinds, which kinds it is the aim of science to identify. Scientific essentialists are at odds not just with Hume and Kant, but with Locke, who argued that if there are natural kinds, they are unknowable. The position aligns its proponents instead with Aristotle, although scientific essentialism is held to be consistent with contemporary natural science – indeed, to offer an account of science that is superior to those advanced by empiricists and Kantians.

Now, the question is whether or not one may be a scientific essentialist without being a realist about causality, and/or vice versa. In practice the positions are often held simultaneously, with realism about causality figuring significantly in the articulation of scientific essentialism. And the combination is a coherent one. Still, it may be that the positions may be disentangled. To be a realist about causality, one must think that there are such things as dispositional properties – or, as Stephen Mumford would have it, just powers/dispositions *tout court*. It is not clear that this is a requirement of scientific essentialism. If it isn't, then in principle, at least, it might be possible to be a scientific essentialist without being a realist about causality. To be a scientific essentialist, meanwhile, one must at a minimum think that there are such things as essential properties of kinds of things. If Anjan Chakravartty is correct, however, and the dispositional properties of a thing are not necessarily those that are essential to it, then in principle, it would seem, one could be a realist about causality – attaching causality to the exercise of inessential powers – without affirming the kind essences defended by scientific essentialists.

Finally, realism about causality does not imply anything about how debates over physicalism, reductionism, and/or atomism ought to be decided. Realism about causality commits one only to the idea that causality is an expression of the powers that things have. Which sorts of things may be properly thought to have (or be) powers, and whether or not there are emergent ones, are not questions that are answered by the position. Accordingly, with respect to the social sciences, for example, there are proponents of realism about causality who maintain that it is only persons who may be regarded as "powerful particulars," as Harre and Madden put it in Chapter 4, and others – such as Engelskirchen, Albritton, and Porpora, in this volume – who think that social structures, for example, may also be bearers of powers.

Realism about causality does have important implications, however. One has to do with the treatment of scientific laws. If necessity is thought to derive from the nature of objects themselves, then causal laws are merely statements about the dispositional properties of things. Brian Ellis sets out this argument in Chapter 5. The standard alternative is to think of laws as themselves being efficacious in some sense: it is because they are in place that things are as they are. Realism about causality shows this to be backward. Laws register regularities *ex post facto*; they don't produce them. Stephen Mumford goes a step further, suggesting that if the causal work in question is being done by powers, then at the level of explanation the concept of laws is superfluous. Mumford and Ellis' positions are both consistent with realism about causality; the standard view is not.

Additionally, inasmuch as realism about causality commits one to the existence of powers or dispositions, it commits one to at least some degree of ontological realism. The powers that sustain causal relations are not thought to be conceptual posits, to use Quine's term; they are thought to be the real source of real effects. The ontological realism associated with the position is evident in the distinction – upon which realists about causality insist – between logical necessity (or possibility), given by the law of non-contradiction, and metaphysical necessity (or potentiality), given by what things are. Sellars, Harre and Madden, and Ellis, in this volume, all emphasize this point. Metaphysical necessity, it is worth noting, exercises greater ontological constraint than does logical necessity: if in virtue of what things are they act in certain ways and not in others, then radical ontological relativity, to reference Quine again, is off the table. Moreover, as a consequence of this foreclosure of *ontological* relativity, realism about causality also precludes relativism about knowledge – for if the world is not all possible ways, then all competing claims about it cannot be equally sound.

III

The volume is organized into three parts. The first part consists of a selection of key, previously published pieces, dating from 1929 to 2002, which I hope will come to be seen as touchstones in the development of realism about causality. We begin with two pieces by Roy Wood Sellars, "Critical realism and substance," published in the journal *Mind* in 1929, and "Causality and substance," which appeared in *The Philosophical Review* in 1943. The term "critical realism" was used by Sellars and others in the early twentieth century. Although it is suggestive, it does not link him directly to contemporary critical realists – or them to him. In "Critical realism and substance," Sellars cautions that in our thinking about the world, "logical structure must not be identified with ontological structure," as he puts it.[1] Taking Locke as his target, Sellars argues that the idea of a substance that is the bearer of qualities that are separate from it is simply a reification of the abstraction involved in thought. Real things are ontologically unified. They have attributes – Sellars uses the term "characteristics" – but their attributes are features of them as determinate objects, not ontologically distinct "qualities" to be predicated of them.[2] Knowledge, Sellars suggests, is a grasping, in thought, of the characteristics of things: "the determinations of reality are translatable into universals," he writes.[3] It is things, however, that exist, not "peculiar unions of form and matter."[4] Sellars takes even Aristotle to not be clear enough about this. In "Causality and substance," Sellars says that his aim is to "induce the category of causality to disclose more about itself by putting it in its ontological context."[5] Here his argument is that the empirical basis for the concept of causality is not the repeated feeling of expectation generated by the observation of constant conjunctions, but rather the developmental awareness of ourselves as intentional, embodied creatures – creatures that act upon, and are acted upon by, determinate things. This is a line of argument echoed by Rom Harre and E. H. Madden in *Causal Powers*, published several decades later.

Part I also includes work by Irving Copi, Harre and Madden, and Brian Ellis. Copi, primarily a logician, published "Essence and accident" in *The Journal of Philosophy* in 1954. In it he argues, modestly if radically, for something very much like scientific essentialism: Locke, he suggests, turned out to have been mistaken to think that real essences cannot be investigated empirically. Moreover, he observes, even if one were to say that we organize the world into categories that reflect our own interests (i.e. into kinds based on nominal rather than real essences), is precisely the identification of the real essences of things.[6] Harre and Madden's *Causal Powers: A Theory of Natural Necessity*, Chapter 1 of which is re-printed here, appeared in 1975. They begin with the declaration:

> There can be no doubt that the Humean conception of Causality and its linear descendant, the Regularity Theory, must be wrong. To accept either of these doctrines is to be forced in the long run to admit the irrationality of science and to acknowledge the impossibility of accounting for the common-sense view of the world.[7]

They go on to defend the idea that causality is a way of talking about the productive or generative capacities of what they call "powerful particulars," and to set out both the dynamic, realist ontology that such a view involves – including a defense of real essences – and the model of science that it sustains.[8] Brian Ellis, finally, is a well-known contemporary proponent of scientific essentialism. Reproduced here is "Powers and dispositions," Chapter 4 from his recent book *The Philosophy of Nature: A Guide to the New Essentialism*. In this chapter Ellis contrasts the ontology of Humeanism – what he calls "the dead world of mechanism" – with that of scientific essentialism.[9] Ellis holds that things have intrinsic dispositional properties – that is, ways of behaving that are given by the nature of the things themselves. In Ellis' view, a thing's dispositional properties define it as being the kind of thing that it is; dispositional properties are thus, from this perspective, essential properties (a claim that Anjan Chakravartty challenges in Chapter 9). Different kinds of things, Ellis suggests, themselves figure essentially in different kinds of causal processes.[10]

Part II of the volume contains new articles related to debates within metaphysics and the philosophy of science, as well as a previously published article by Christopher Norris that touches on issues in the philosophy of language. The section opens with Norris' piece, an argument to the effect that from Quine on, "the agenda of current debate with regard to issues of causal explanation still tends to be set by those . . . kinds of . . . argument that take a lead from Hume in denying the existence – or at any rate the knowability – of real-world operative causal forces, powers, or dispositions in nature."[11] Norris is rightly critical of the anti-realist metaphysics of Quine, Kuhn, and Putnam (in all but his earliest work), among others. In the context of the present volume, Norris' article may be read in part as an illustration of the way in which, after the linguistic turn, debates over the nature of causality are expressed within analytic philosophy as debates concerning the nature of reference. As noted above, the questions involved are not actually the same ones.

Next, Charlotte Witt frames the realist challenge by undertaking to specify which if any aspects of Aristotle's thinking may usefully be appropriated by present-day realists about causality. Stephen Mumford follows with a close analysis of the relationship between powers, dispositions and properties. Mumford argues that powers and dispositions are in fact the same, and that they are constitutive of properties. He goes on to highlight certain important features of the powers-based ontology that he defends – e.g. that it has a "holistic quality," and also that powers may be internally related to one another – concluding with the proposal that "causation may then turn out to be something like the shifting about of powers," and that, if so, laws of nature become philosophically superfluous.[12] Anjan Chakravartty then makes the case that we ought to pry apart the concepts of causal powers and essential properties. "One may well account for causal behavior in terms of causal powers," he writes, "but powers need not constitute anything resembling essences."[13] Distinguishing between essence kinds, membership in which is determined by "a set of intrinsic properties which are individually necessary and jointly sufficient," e.g. electrons, and what he calls cluster kinds, "groups whose members may have *no* distinguishing properties in common," e.g. a given biological species, Chakravartty observes that things that are members of cluster kinds are not thereby precluded from having causal powers.[14] He concludes that "powers explain behaviors regardless of whether they are necessary for membership in a particular class of thing."[15]

With the last two articles in this section, the discussion becomes less general. Alexander Bird takes on the issue of emergent properties, specifically those of evolved organisms. He defends the position that such properties are "genuine, natural properties," ontologically irreducible to the physical phenomena upon which they supervene.[16] Finally, Rachel Cooper argues that none of the common objections to natural kinds in relation to psychological phenomena are persuasive. "Given that there are plausible candidates for psychological kinds," she concludes, "we should thus accept that there are natural kinds in psychology."[17]

Part III contains new articles related to meta-theoretical debates within social science. Doug Porpora starts off the discussion by showing that the seemingly unshakeable attachment to empiricism of most American sociologists leads them to handle the concept of causality either badly or not at all – and sometimes both. At best, the "3rd variable model" that is often used to distinguish between spurious and significant correlations can be seen to rely, for whatever theoretical force it carries, upon the concept of a genuinely causal mechanism – a concept at odds, Porpora observes, with the over-all program.[18] Andrew Bennett, in turn, recommends that the identification of causal mechanisms be the explicit objective of political and other social scientists. He defines causal mechanisms as "ultimately unobservable physical, social or psychological processes through which agents with causal capacities operate … to transfer energy, information, or matter to other entities."[19] A causal agent thereby "changes the affected entity's characteristics, capacities or propensities in ways that persist unless and until subsequent causal mechanisms act upon it."[20] Bennett goes on to consider whether or not emergent, macro-level phenomena may play a role in explanations based on causal mechanisms (his answer is a guarded yes) and to recommend that different types of mechanisms be combined into what he calls "typological theories," which can provide for richly textured explanations.[21] Bennett, it is worth noting, holds out the possibility that realism about causality may be able to be squared with a Humean metaphysics, though this is not the focus of the article.

Rob Albritton and Howard Engelskirchen each add a significant empirical component to the conversation by offering, in addition to meta-theoretical argumentation, substantive analyses of aspects of capitalism. Albritton, using the terms "dialectical causality," "structural causality," and "historical causality," suggests that capitalist crises are caused by different kinds of causal mechanisms, operating at different levels of abstraction, as he puts it. Dialectical causality refers to the mechanism that is capitalism's "inner logic," considered "in the abstract and in general."[22] Here – in my words rather than Albritton's – we are talking about the essential dispositional properties of capitalism as a unique mode of production – as, we might want to say, a social kind. Structural causality refers to the ways in which the powers of the essential mechanisms of capitalism are mediated through "political or ideological extra-economic" mechanisms, themselves efficacious but non-essential features of capitalism at different "phases" of development.[23] Historical causality, meanwhile, refers not to a qualitatively different kind of mechanism, but rather to *particular instances* of – and with an emphasis upon the role of agency in – the confluence of the effects of political and/or extra-economic mechanisms and the effects of the on-going exercise of capitalism's essential dispositional properties. In considerations of historical causality, the fact of change and the specificity of concrete phenomena come to the fore. I have put an ontological spin on Albritton's presentation – which, as noted above, has empirical as well as theoretical content – but I believe that doing so helps to situate his piece within the volume. Last, but certainly not least, Howard Engelskirchen offers a trenchant, neo-Aristotelian reading of Marx's treatment of value, arguing that "the labor that produces the product in the commodity form is itself form determined."[24] The labor that produces value is organized in a specific way: it is undertaken by producers working independently of one another, and it therefore yields products that must be exchanged. It is this fact, Engelskirchen maintains, that is the real essence of value, establishing the commodity form of labor as a social kind.

I am especially pleased that there are so many evident connections between pieces in the volume, beyond the authors' shared commitment to realism about causality. Bennett and Albritton, for example, both make the point that reference to different kinds of mechanisms is required to explain complex, concrete phenomena. Meanwhile, something like Chakravartty's distinction between causal powers and essential properties is implicit, it seems to me, in Albritton's view that capitalist crises are caused not only by the essential dynamics that constitute capitalism's "inner logic," but also by contingent features of capitalist societies. Engelskirchen and Cooper, *contra* Ellis, agree that the language of natural kinds may be extended beyond natural science. Porpora and Bennett offer similar critiques of the deductive-nomological model of explanation in the social sciences. Bird and Engelskirchen both regard at least some emergent properties as being ontologically irreducible to the physical processes that support them. Engelskirchen builds on Witt's comments by showing what a contemporary neo-Aristotelian explanatory account might look like. And Albritton's and Engelskirchen's discussions of capitalism both, it seems to me, illustrate Mumford's point that powers may be internally related to each other, thereby precluding the adequacy of an atomist ontology.

There are also points of disagreement. Most striking is Bennett's suggestion that Hume's notions of spatial contiguity and temporal succession may be able to animate the concept of a causal mechanism. But there are others as well: neither Harre, in his subsequent writings on the issue, nor Ellis think – *contra* Albritton, Engleskirchen and perhaps Porpora – that social structures can be causal mechanisms – or, to put it differently, that social structures exhibit emergent dispositional properties. Indeed, Harre is leery of the very idea of a social structure. Ellis is committed to kind-essences, but in contrast to Engelskirchen does not admit social kinds. Mumford and Chakravartty, meanwhile, are committed to dispositions, but not to kind-essentialism – and Bennett may well fit this description at the macro-level. Finally, it is not clear that Bird's argument for the existence of emergent properties of biological phenomena commits him to holism with respect to social phenomena, or that Cooper's defense of psychological kinds commits her to affirming the existence of sociological kinds, as Engelskirchen in particular does explicitly. That there are disagreements such as these amongst contributors is a strength of the present volume, it seems to me.

Let me conclude by saying a word about how this collection of articles fits into the burgeoning literature surrounding critical realism. In my view, realism about causality forms the ontological core of critical realism, a species of scientific essentialism advanced by Roy Bhaskar in the mid-1970s and 1980s. Yet only two or three of the contemporary contributors to this volume would be likely to identify themselves as critical realists – though most if not all are friendly to the position. I have shaped the collection in this way because I believe that as interest in critical realism continues to grow internationally, the approach ought to be brought into closer contact with – and ideally integrated into – larger, directly relevant neo-Aristotelian currents within metaphysics and the philosophy of science. Thus I regard it as useful, for general readers as well as for the critical realist audience, to see that realism about causality crosses not just disciplinary boundaries, but also the boundaries of what, for lack of a better term, I will call intellectual genre. For those who would like to better familiarize themselves with Bhaskar's version of the case for realism about causality, I recommend his first book, *A Realist Theory of Science*.

It is an exciting moment in which to be involved in the revitalization project, as these articles show. Enjoy.

Notes

1 Roy Wood Sellars, "Critical realism and substance," *Mind*, New Series, Volume 38, Number 152 (October 1929), p. 477.
2 Sellars (1929), pp. 475–477.
3 Sellars (1929), p. 479.
4 Sellars (1929), p. 481.
5 Roy Wood Sellars, "Causality and substance," *The Philosophical Review*, Volume 52, Number 1 (January 1943), p. 1.
6 Irving M. Copi, "Essence and accident," *The Journal of Philosophy*, Volume 51, Number 23, American Philosophical Association Eastern Division Papers to be Presented at the 51st Annual Meeting, Goucher College, December 28–30, 1954 (November 11, 1954), pp. 706–719.
7 Rom Harre and E. H. Madden, *Causal Powers: A Theory of Natural Necessity* (Totowa, New Jersey: Rowman and Littlefield, 1975), p. 1.
8 Harre and Madden (1975), p. 5; pp. 1–26 for full discussion.
9 Brian Ellis, *The Philosophy of Nature: A Guide to the New Essentialism* (Montreal and Kingston: McGill-Queen's University Press, 2002), p. 60.
10 Ellis (2002), esp. p. 67.
11 Christopher Norris, *On Truth and Meaning: Language, Logic and the Grounds of Belief* (London and New York: Continuum International Publishing Group, 2006), p. 41.
12 Stephen Mumford, "Powers, dispositions, properties," in *Revitalizing Causality: Realism About Causality in Philosophy and Social Science*, edited by Ruth Groff (London: Routledge, 2008), pp. 139–151.
13 Anjan Chakravartty, "Inessential Aristotle: Powers without essences," in Groff (2008), pp. 152–162.
14 Chakravartty, in Groff (2008), pp. 152–162.
15 Chakravartty, in Groff (2008), pp. 152–162.
16 Alexander Bird, "Causal exclusion and evolved emergent properties," in Groff (2008), pp. 163–178.
17 Rachel Cooper, "Are there natural kinds in psychology?" in Groff (2008), pp. 179–191.
18 Doug Porpora, "Sociology's causal confusion," in Groff (2008), pp. 195–204.
19 Andrew Bennett, "The mother of all 'Isms': Causal mechanisms in political science," in Groff (2008), pp. 205–219.
20 Bennett, in Groff (2008), pp. 205–219.
21 Bennett, in Groff (2008), pp. 205–219.
22 Robert Albritton, "Marxian crisis theory and causality," in Groff (2008), pp. 220–241.
23 Albritton, in Groff (2008), pp. 220–241.
24 Howard, Engelskirchen, "On the clear comprehension of political economy: Social kinds and the significance of Section 2 of Marx's Capital," in Groff (2008), pp. 242–259.

References

Brian Ellis, *The Philosophy of Nature: A Guide to the New Essentialism*, Montreal and Kingston: McGill-Queen's University Press, 2002.
Christopher Norris, *On Truth and Meaning: Language, Logic and the Grounds of Belief,* London and New York: Continuum International Publishing Group, 2006.
Irving M. Copi, "Essence and accident," *The Journal of Philosophy*, Volume 51, Number 23, American Philosophical Association Eastern Division Papers to be

Presented at the Fifty-First Annual Meeting, Goucher College, December 28–30, 1954 (November 11, 1954), pp. 706–719.

Rom Harre and Madden, E. H., *Causal Powers: A Theory of Natural Necessity,* Totowa, New Jersey: Rowman and Littlefield, 1975.

Roy Wood Sellars, "Critical realism and substance," *Mind*, New Series, Volume 38, Number 152 (October 1929), pp. 473–488.

Roy Wood Sellars, "Causality and substance," *The Philosophical Review*, Volume 52, Number 1 (January 1943), pp. 1–27.

Part I
Key formulations

1 Critical realism and substance*

Roy Wood Sellars

Critical realists are in the stimulating position of being forced to reanalyse many categories which idealism had too hastily thrown into the discard. In recent writings I have tried to show that knowledge of genuinely external, or transcendent, objects is possessed by the human mind and have pointed to the mechanism which mediates such direct knowledge. Such direct knowledge, I have argued, rests upon the cognitive, or revelatory, value of discriminated contents which function within the act of cognition. The critical realist differs from the naïve realists chiefly in two ways: (1) he is aware of the mechanism making knowledge possible and not, as the naïve realist, only of the result; and (2) he is led by reflexion to revise the content of knowledge, that is, *the object as thought*. Such a theory of knowledge may be said to lie between naïve realism and representative realism, for it asserts, with the first, the directness of knowing and, with the second, the contents and processes which mediate this direct knowing. Its insight comes from a more careful study of the conditions and claims of knowing than was possible in the seventeenth century. Now, may not this alteration in theory of knowledge involve a new approach to the category of substance? Instead of rejecting substantial things—as the idealist was led to do—may we not accept them and interpret them without landing in any self-contradiction?

In the present paper I wish to study the category of substance in the light of modern science and critical realism. As a physical realist I believe in *physical systems* (ordinarily called things) which exist independently of our knowing them and which have specific characteristics. From the very beginning I want to dissociate this return to substance from Cartesian dualism. I can see no *a priori* reason why certain evolved physical things, such as human organisms, should not have mental properties and include psychical processes. Such, as is well known, is the thesis of emergent, or evolutionary, naturalism. But more of this particular point later.

The elimination of substance as a category began with idealism. The first step was the rejection of physical substance. Leibniz and Berkeley may be said to have inaugurated this development. And then came empiricism and phenomenalism

*Source: *Mind*, New Series, Vol. 38, No. 152. (Oct, 1929), pp. 473–488.

with a like attack upon spiritual substance. Something of a compromise on this latter was symbolised by the adoption of the term subject by the idealism of the nineteenth century.

When we look over this movement, we soon realise that it was motivated by two lines of argument which reenforced one another, *viz.*, (1) an epistemological motive and (2) a logical motive. The first cast doubt on genuinely external, or transcendent, objects, while the second sought to point out contradictions in the very idea of such realities. I shall argue that this whole development had only a partial validity. Because of an inadequate epistemology, possibilities were ignored which must again be brought to light. It is my present purpose to explore these possibilities. While I have indicated them in my books, I have apparently done so in such a terse fashion that they have been misunderstood or ignored.

I

Locke is a convenient point of departure. I believe that it can be maintained that Locke's theory of substance was somewhat of a parody of even the Medieval doctrine. As is well known, Locke formulated his position in such a way as to leave substance, or matter, a hidden core supporting adjectival entities called primary qualities. This construction was open to the objections, advanced by Berkeley, which we shall shortly study. Is substance unknowable? Is it something hidden by its very nature from cognition? Does it support entities which can be called qualities and which are really extrinsic to it? I shall try to show that this whole formulation is vicious and unnecessary. The physical realist believes in physical systems having definite knowable characteristics. Is this belief vulnerable to Berkeley's arguments? In other words, can we think external physical things without falling into logical absurdities?

We may call external things physical systems and consider them substantial or substantive. What do we mean by this? Surely several things. We consider them existents which are continuants and not dependent upon something else like mind or deity for their existence. This means that we hold them to be self-existent. Such self-existence does not imply self-sufficiency in the sense that they are unaffected by their surroundings. Surely self-existence does not involve isolation of the sort affirmed in extreme pluralism. Physical systems are concrete bodies in definite commerce with other physical systems. And commerce presupposes existence rather than creates it.

With this frank physical realism in mind let us for a moment return to Berkeley's criticism of Locke's formulation. Locke had set up a *substratum* spread under accidents. Notice that we have spoken of *things* having characteristics. We have not as yet set up any theory as to what characteristics are nor as to how things possess them. That we shall do shortly. In the *Three Dialogues between Hylas and Philonous*, Philonous suggests that this substratum is something in its own nature entirely different from its accidents. Hylas replies: "I tell you, extension is only a mode, and Matter is something which supports modes. And is it not evident the thing supported is different from the thing supporting?" And Philonous: "So that something *distinct from*, and exclusive of, extension is supposed to be the substratum of extension?" Clearly, this leads to the difficulty of conceiving the relation between matter (substance) and its primary qualities if they are thus external to each other.

But we must ask whether this construction is necessary. Is the relation of its characteristics to a physical thing to be thought of as a relation between an unknowable substratum and the accidents it supports? It is obvious that we must determine the nature and the reach of knowledge, on the one hand, and the relation between an object and its determinate nature, on the other hand, before we can go farther. In what follows I shall try to reanalyse the whole situation and keep in mind both the ontological categories and the cognitive approach to those categories. Surely characteristics are not adjectival entities supported externally. When properly interpreted they are *intrinsic* to the thing known. The thing is the reality and includes its nature seamlessly. It is our thinking which distinguishes between a thing and its characteristics and is easily misled into a false separation between the two on the ontological side. We reify that about the object which we can discern and are then, perhaps, led to the idea of a substratum to support these reifications. I shall argue that we must at one and the same time give up this kind of a substratum and this kind of qualities. We must think more delicately and carefully.

II

Let us disregard Locke and come back freely to the deliverances of our own knowing. Can we then harmonise our cognition with the ontology which it seems to set up?

To me it is a demand of knowing that the object known be of a *determinate nature*. It is a that-what. But Locke's construction is a parody of this demand. The determinate nature of an object is intrinsically inseparable from the object and not stuck on it externally in some incomprehensible fashion. Here we are face to face with ontology. It is evident that characteristics are not entities and do not need support. Their relation to their object is far more intimate than that. They are elements of the nature of the object. But even this way of putting it is not penetrative enough. We must not think of the nature of an object as in any way distinct from the object. The object is a *determinate object*. Thus when we say that a physical thing is extended we do not mean that there is some substratum which possesses an adjectival entity called extension but simply that the thing is correctly thought of *as extended*. It is that kind of a determinate object. To say that a thing has a definite structure does not mean that there is a substratum which owns an entity called structure but simply that the thing is intrinsically structured. And so on. This means that we must not be controlled by grammatical forms or by metaphors, but that we must seek to clarify our actual thought of objects.

This analysis signifies that when we speak of that-what or things with determinate natures we really mean determinate objects. As we shall see, our unavoidable cognitive approach to objects tends to make the nature of objects, that which we know about objects, stand out almost in abstraction from the object.

It is to avoid this epistemological abstractness that we must stress ontologically the fact that the reality is a determinate object in determinate relations with other objects. I would hold, then, that the categories of object and the nature of the object are mutually implicatory. The reality is the determinate thing. But our knowledge picks out the determinations of the determinate thing and abstracts them, for it is the only way we can think the object. Thus, unless we are on our guard, our inevitable cognitive approach tends to introduce a dualism into the object which ontologically does not exist. We speak of a thing (subject of the judgement) which has properties (predicates of the judgement). But we should penetrate beyond this logical form to reality as thought as against the mechanism of our thinking it. Logical structure must not be identified with ontological structure.

Now if this basic reality of a determinate object, a that-what, is once granted, we can reject at once the scheme which dominated representative realism of the Lockian type and animated Berkeley's dialectic. 'Support' and 'inhere in' and 'spread under' are clearly totally misleading metaphors for this basic and ultimate unity. The determinate nature of an object is not something distinct in any fashion from the object. The object and its nature, or characteristics, are intrinsically one. In knowing its characteristics, we know the object; and this is the only way we can know it. And, for the physical realist, the object is a physical system of a definite sort. We must not think of the object as retreating from its characteristics into a sort of majestic aloofness; nor must we think of an inner core as unknowable and an outer shell as knowable. To know a physical system is to know it as extended, massive, structured, behaving, etc. That is the way the object manifests itself and that is the way the object is in itself.

If this analysis holds, Locke committed the sin of separating the object (physical system) and its nature so that the object becomes a something-I-know-not-what back of its nature as a complex of primary qualities which are, as it were, hypostatised into entities which must be supported. Knowledge is given the deceptive goal of a substratum which cannot be known and which yet cries out to be known. But if this substratum has no determinate nature, is it even a possible object of knowledge? And if it has no determinate nature and is, therefore, not a possible object of knowledge, is it not, as Berkeley argued, a complete fiction?

Surely, the only way of intellectual salvation is to see that the attempt to change the nature of an object into a set of entities called accidents, or qualities, is to distort the intrinsic and unique identity of a thing and its characteristics. In fact, I am reluctant to use the term relation in this connexion for I have found that philosophers have constantly been misled by it. It seems to me, rather, that when we speak of the characteristics of a thing we are making a logical distinction which involves no existential separateness.

III

Since I am at present engaged in a constructive analysis, I shall disregard the history of the distinction between a substance and its accidents, only registering my conviction that this distinction is a mistake. It is truer to our actual thinking to speak of a thing and its characteristics. And even here we must not be misled by language. A thing is not separate from its characteristics, nor are characteristics separate from the thing. The characteristics of a thing are that about a thing which can be cognitively grasped.

There are, then, two errors to be avoided. We must not reduce a thing to its characteristics because the reality is a determinate thing. And we must not rob a thing of its determinate nature and thus make it an unknowable. Idealism has always tended to make the first mistake, while agnosticism has made the second. We must move with more delicacy than have these positions. We know things. What, then, does knowledge grasp? Idealism and neo-realism tend unavoidably to identify the that with the what. Existence disappears into its characteristics. The object passes into knowledge without a remainder. It is against this that the critical realist protests. Knowledge is knowledge, and yet it is never the actual equivalent of the object. It reveals the object, and yet it is other than the object. We cognitively grasp the nature of the object but, in so doing, we get the nature as an abstraction. No literal part of the object gets into our minds. It is, as it were, the ghostly outline, or form, of things which we grasp. To realise this is to understand what human knowledge of external things is. It inevitably falls short of *being* itself. And yet it is knowledge. This means that we must not expect of knowledge what knowledge cannot give. It is a revelation of the structure, relative quantity and behaviour of objects; but the objects as realities are structured, massive, energetic; they play a role in the economy of nature; they exist.

To appreciate our knowledge of things is at the same time to understand what knowledge can never be. Being is always other than knowledge. To know a thing is not to be it. It is a cognitive grasping of the determinate nature of an object, these determinations being translated into human formulae of measurements and patterns and possibilities. In this sense, it is a genuine vision of the nature of the object, that is, of the object as a determinate thing. But such a vision presupposes the object's existence, presupposes that there is a realm of being.

I am quite aware that this epistemology which stresses the peculiar nature and reach of knowledge breaks sharply with immanentist traditions. It is, however, inseparable from a frank physical realism. We interpret things in terms of logical ideas which reveal their characteristics or determinations. We believe that physical systems are extended, measurable, structured, active. But this does not mean that things are equatable with a complex of universals. Sense-data and universals are immanent, are intrinsic to the act of cognition; while characteristics are as transcendent as physical things themselves. It is in this fashion that an adequate epistemology harmonises with ontological demands.

IV

For my form of critical realism, knowing is an interpretation of the object, a peculiar grasping of its characteristics or determinations in terms of, and by means of, logical ideas held before the attention in the complex act of cognition. These logical ideas are intrinsic to the mental act which is a brain-mind act resting on the activity of the whole organism. It is a postulated revelation of the nature of the object and this turns out to be pattern, that is, constitution, composition, behaviour, all presented at the scientific level of cognition in terms of the results of measurement. What we know about things is a kind of abstraction, a sort of ontological form, the logical outline of things.

We are now in a position to discuss the age-old question of *universalia in re*. I would distinguish sharply between universals and characteristics or determinations. Universals, like all logical ideas, seem to me to be always *in mente*. That is, they are intrinsic to the complex act of cognition by means of which the object is known. It is the characteristic of the object that is *in re*, as constituting its determinate nature. Thus universals are *in re* only in a Pickwickian sense as cognitively revealing the specific characteristics which are intrinsic to things. In knowledge they are so one with the characteristics which they reveal that we do not at the moment distinguish them and give them their proper locus. And yet as soon as we step from epistemology to ontology we must do so or else get into all sorts of unreal problems. Because universals are logical tools for revealing the characteristics of things the statement that universals are in things is an ellipsis for saying that we know the characteristics of things in terms of universals. And this cognitive union expresses an ultimate correspondence between them which makes the ellipsis almost justifiable. The determinations of reality are translatable into universals. It is for this reason that we can speak of the physical world as having a logical structure. It is, if you will, a touch of anthropomorphism, and yet an unavoidable one. And since the critical realist maintains that the object *with the assistance of the subject* controls this logical structure in the mind, it is an anthropomorphism which calls attention to man's oneness with the world.

Yet ontologically the characteristics of a thing are as transcendent as the thing itself and one with it. They are also as specific as the thing of which they are the characteristics. Each specific characteristic is sustained by the object and is seamlessly one with it. In this fashion the critical realist assigns universals to epistemology and characteristics to ontology.

This distinction between universal and characteristic seems to me to clear up many points which have hitherto involved confusion. It rids us of the temptation to postulate entities of a timeless sort called essences (Santayana and Drake) or eternal objects (Whitehead) with their ingressions and embodiments. To speak of essences as embodied in objects is to resort to a misleading metaphor. And yet, unless the distinction between universals and characteristics is made, universals must be *in re* or else agnosticism follows. I would also suggest that this distinction does justice to the motives underlying Stout's distributive theory of universals. It is the specificity of characteristics that Stout—if I mistake not—has in mind.

In this analysis I am, I presume, nearer to Aristotle than to Plato. In fact, I am very much of an anti-Platonist even though I recognise to the full the contributions of Plato to an adequate theory of knowing. But while I am nearer to Aristotle than to Plato, I dissent from Aristotle in my conception of *ontological form*. I would take a step still farther from Plato, a step still nearer naturalism and to the intrinsic unity of form and matter. Being is always formed being. There is no being without form and no form apart from being. But more of this later.

This distinction between universals, as intrinsic to the act of cognition, and characteristics as intrinsic to the object known enables us to deal with another of the puzzles of thought, the problem of individuality. Idealism has tended to conceive an object as a complex of universals. This led to the difficulty of differentiating one thing from another. The realist, on the other hand, appealed to a stuff which, united with universals, would give individuality. The stuff of a thing was the principle of individuality. But this stuff was unknowable and also the nature of the union was scarcely thinkable. We may say that physical realism has always been handicapped by this apparently unescapable dualism. Let us see whether critical realism can avoid it. Do we know one element of reality and are we ignorant of another element? Or do we know an object in knowing its characteristics?

It is readily seen that, once we clearly distinguish between universals and the specific characteristics of an object which they cognitively reveal, this traditional problem takes on a new and solvable form. A physical system is not a peculiar union of a stuff and universals. Instead, it is an organised whole with determinate characteristics expressive of what it is. In knowing these characteristics, we know the physical system. But, unless we are very careful, cognition, which knows the object in terms of its characteristics, leads us to abstract and reify the characteristics and thus to introduce a dualism in the object. It has been our thesis, instead, that ontological form is intrinsic to the object. The reality is a formed, or determinate, stuff. Knowledge reaches to things and illuminates them; and yet there is a plus to things which must not be ignored. We are here confronted by one of the most delicate problems of thought. *It is the question of the precise grasp of knowledge.* It grasps objects after its own nature; we do know objects. And yet this grasping is always other than a being of the object. The abstracted form of an object is a shadow, an outline. The reality is the formed object. In this sense, cognition enables us to know an, object, and yet such knowledge is other than being. The physical realist believes that ontology rejects as inadequate and mistaken a purely logical realism.

V

But before I study the category of being in more detail I would like to say a few more words about universals and their role in cognition. I shall be very brief and concern myself with the relation of universals to sense-data and to the specific characteristics of things.

First, how can two objects be known by means of the same universal? My reply is, *that specificity does not involve uniqueness.* The roundness of one pea is existentially as specific as the roundness of another pea, both being expressive of the metabolism of the pea in the pod. This specific characteristic is intrinsic to the kind of physical system, to its energies, to its line of growth. Yet this fact does not preclude the similarity of results. Hence, they can both be correctly enough revealed by the same logical idea, sense-datum at the perceptual level, universal at the explicit, judgmental level. Let us remember that it is things that we compare primarily and not universals; this is because cognition is directed first at things. And this is why we speak of two things as alike when they are revealed by the same universal. We have every reason to accept the world as it is known. And this world of ours is known as containing many similar things. And once we distinguish between logical ideas functioning in acts of cognition and specific characteristics intrinsic to objects, this otherness involves no contradiction. We do not have to speak even of the same universal embodied in different matter. Our epistemology must harmonise with the necessities of ontology. And by this distinction between universals and specific characteristics we have shown how this is possible.

We should note that universals grow up in the mind in the process of knowing objects. They are moulded upon that activity, and universals take final form in judgement with its use of language. Here we have a high level of symbolisation and generalisation. All this tends to make us forget that in specific acts of cognition these universals are nearly always specified to fit specific data. This shape is never quite like that shape; this colour is seldom the exact shade of that other. In strict universals we stress what may be called a *type* which covers and permits variations. These variations are the instances.

For this reason it has seemed to me best to speak of logical ideas or logical discriminations to cover both sense-data and universals. I would hold that such logical ideas reveal the characteristics of objects and are so used in interpretative cognition. Logical ideas may be sensory or they may be conceptual. In both cases their function is the same in cognition. And it is out of primitive logical ideas that universals in the strict sense arise and it is upon them that they rest. There is this much truth in the distributive theory of universals. And yet this theory reflects still more a confused sense of the specificity of characteristics in the object known.

We are at last ready to handle the problem of substance constructively. Our point of departure is this, that we know individual physical things in terms of their specific characteristics and that these are not entities supported by an unknowable substratum, but the outline, or form, of the thing disclosed to cognition and standing out abstractly as a consequence. We also realise that knowledge has the reach peculiar to its nature. It grasps the characteristics of things but cannot participate in their being. This ultimate thing knowledge can never do. It is as near to an external thing as we can get. But to know a thing is not to be it. Knowledge falls short of existence. And, finally, let me point out that, contrary to Dr. Bosanquet's dialectic, the critical realist regards the existent as a that-what and never a mere that.

VI

From the beginning, then, we can reject the Lockian construction as false and misleading. A clearer idea of characteristics shows us that they are not entities to be externally supported by a substratum. It is the whole determinate thing which exists. Characteristics taken by themselves are abstractions.

But if characteristics taken by themselves are abstractions, what is it that exists? How shall we conceive existence? We are on the track of the meaning of such terms as stuff, matter, physical reality, content of being. What do these terms stand for? To answer this question we come back again to the context of cognition.

The act of cognition is the expression of ourselves as existents and is directed toward another existent. Both the known and the knower are realities. Now in going back to the level of naïve realism we quickly note our sense of existences, that is, of something as real as ourselves to which we must adjust ourselves. This sense of reality is, I am sure, coexistent with any specific knowledge. It furnishes the context of it. Things are as real as we ourselves are. *All this involves no intuition of being but merely our sense of reality*, something which grows up in us on adequate psychological grounds. It has been abundantly proven that our sense of external existence grows up in us step by step with our sense of our own existence and *vice versa*. Thinghood is, accordingly, a category which has a normal development in human thought. It develops step by step with our knowledge of the nature of these existents which surround us.

Now I should hold it a great mistake to assume that our sense of reality involves any intuition of the content of existence. It is much more an attitude with correspondent meanings. The nuclear ingredient in our thought of thinghood is this sense of external existence. It furnishes the sheet-anchor of knowledge but is not itself an element of knowledge. Rather is it a presupposition of knowledge with which knowledge must harmonise. Hence it is not a predicate in the ordinary sense, a fact which both Hume and Kant realised and which is often today expressed by the saying that we cannot define existence. The most we can do is to point out the experience and indicate its psychological foundations.

Now this affirmation of an object, this sense of external things, is the context of cognition. From the time of Aristotle it has been recognised. The subject of a judgement symbolises an individual thing which is interpreted by predicates.

Individual things are, then, existents. They are substantives. Here we have the ultimate fact which all knowing presupposes and develops. It seems to me that, in philosophy, the terms, matter, stuff, content of being, etc., have but reflected this ultimate situation. They have stood for being existence, what exists. None of these terms should be taken to imply any particular scientific theory of the content of being. Matter in the philosophical sense may be variously interpreted—according to the prevailing knowledge—as inert stuff, energy, electricity, waves in ether. But in each case it presupposes this more basic meaning of that which exists. And clearly, if critical realism is right, the characteristics of being must conform to our tested knowledge. Being must be capable of organisation to form physical systems capable of various kinds of behaviour.

Today our knowledge of the external world proclaims that that which exists is active and system-forming. The kind of matter that Berkeley rejected as unable to cause ideas is no longer believed in. We conclude that that which exists is known as regards its characteristics. It is not an unknowable substratum supporting accidents. Knowledge is directed at things and is an interpretation of them, but it does not deny, rather does it presuppose, their self-existence. This means that things have a kind of reality that predicates can never have. Knowledge is a vision of the characteristics of things, but things exist. And this is why we feel that a thing cannot be reduced to its characteristics taken abstractly. To ignore this is the mistake of idealistic rationalism. And there is a kind of logical realism to which Mr. Russell frequently succumbs and commits the same mistake. Another way of putting what I am driving at is this. The specific characteristics of things are not entities but distinctions in the nature of things; and these distinctions are translated into universals or logical ideas in our mind. Now when these logical ideas are taken apart from the reference of cognition in which they reveal the specific characteristics of things they are mere logical contents sustained by the mind yet having no concern with existence. Those who forget their cognitive use forget existence.

Now because we, the knowers, are also existents, this sense of existence is deepened by our feeling of our own activities and purposes. This is the reason why voluntarism—when properly understood—has always checked extreme rationalism. Voluntarism has expressed a fuller sense of reality than external cognition alone could grant us. Of course, this does not mean that we must naïvely read into nature at the inorganic level our feelings and volitions, as analogical panpsychism has tended to do.

I have argued, then, *that cognition has an existential context* expressed in such a category as thinghood or existence. As I understand it, all the critical realists are at one here. Thus Strong speaks of a sensibly mediated intent, Santayana of animal faith, myself of an interpretative affirmation. We respond to the things which are stimulating us at the level of perception.

But there has been much misunderstanding of a phrase we have used. I have said, for instance, that we cannot intuit the stuff of things. What does this mean? It is simply a way of calling attention to the nature of our actual knowledge of objects. In knowing, we grasp interpretatively the characteristics—for instance, the structure, relative size and mass, the ways of behaving—of things; but we cannot literally get over to, and absorb or sample, the things themselves. We know objects, but we cannot be them or have them materially in our minds. Thus this expression was not meant as a declaration of agnosticism but as an indication of the nature of human knowing as mediated by logical ideas.

Naïve realism, because it accepts sensory qualities, is led to what I might call an inspectional view of knowing. It seems that we are aware of the literal surface of things. Now the critical realist is led to refine the predicates in terms of which we think things until this surface-quality is relinquished. In this it is one with science. Knowing finally turns out to be a grasping of the structure, composition, relative sizes, connexions and behaviour of things rather than of sensory qualities. Thus all temptation to a literal inspection of things vanishes. We assuredly know objects, but we now better realise what knowing is and what it grasps. We may say that, after its kind, human knowing has no fixed limits. It can explore and decipher the characteristics of physical systems as far as man's patience and technique will carry him. But such knowledge cannot transform itself into something else. It can never become the equivalent of being. Self-existence, or substantiality, is the ontological context which knowing presupposes.

What, then, are characteristics? And what is their relation to physical systems? I think that it is best to follow the detailed categories of thought as this is directed to things. We think things as structured, extended, behaving, massive. Surely we must regard these categories as giving us specific insight into the very nature of things. These determinations are not stuck on a blank substratum; they arise out of, and are intrinsic to, determinate things. And we cannot get nearer to things than their determinations or nature. Being is a that-what.

VII

In this concluding section I wish to examine very briefly three things: (1) the distinction between primary and secondary qualities; (2) the position of panpsychism and (3) the substitution of the category of event for that of substance.

I should hold that there is no good reason to retain—and many reasons against retaining—what I should call sensory, qualitative predicates in our thought of external things. These must be taken up into a more critical judgement which brings out the fact that they are functions of many conditions and cannot be so reformulated that they give insight into the external object. The external event with which colour, e.g. can be correlated seems of the nature of an electronic vibration.

Size, shape, structure and behaviour predicates seem to be not sensory in a qualitative sense so much as formal and relational. Critical realism points out that such predicates are revelatory of the characteristics of things but need refinement and development before we accept them as adequately interpretative of things. This development is carried through by science. A critical predicate gives not an intuition of the absolute size of an object—an ideal that perception at first suggests—but a ratio which is yet significant for the object.

It seems to me that we must distinguish between the characteristics of an object, which must be specific and intrinsic, and the terms in which we formulate and estimate those characteristics. To say that an object is five feet long is a very indirect way of getting at the size of an object, and yet it must give us something of the nature of a revelation of the actual size of the object. It must enable us to think the object clearly. I have argued in many places that the so-called primary qualities are really those characteristics of objects which are in some measure reproducible in our mind in an abstract way. Thus the pattern of things is reproducible in different media. The *form,* of the cause can appear in the effect, whereas passive qualities would have no way of reproducing themselves.

It should be noticed, then, that I would not speak of *primary qualities* but of intrinsic characteristics.

I might point out in this connexion that the essence wing of critical realism, while they have usually asserted their belief that colours and flavours are not a part of the essence of the object, have never clearly explained why this class of essences are never embodied in objects. In other words, they have never gone far into the logic of science. Perhaps it is because of this that many younger thinkers are following Whitehead instead.

We come now to panpsychism and neutral monism. It will be recalled that I denied the necessity of starting with ontological dualism. It has always been my argument that the knowledge gained by the so-called objective sciences— those sciences depending upon the facts of perceptual observation—was limited to the characteristics so revealed. In other words, I denied that such knowledge participated in the content of being. But, so I have held, in consciousness we are literally on the inside of being in the case of our brains. *Consciousness is a qualitative dimension of being characteristic of this high level of emergent evolution.* I have called this the double-knowledge approach to the mind-body problem.[1]

It is, I think, fair to point out that Mr. Russell has adopted this position lately without, apparently, any awareness of my priority. I would also point out that this position cannot be connected with the neutral-monism view because the epistemology is entirely different. Mr. Russell has been swinging to my form of critical realism and away from the view that sensations are neutral entities having an external status, as in his *Analysis of Mind*. His old view was, of course, a development of James's radical empiricism.

The older panpsychism was analogical and agnostic. It was reared on a theory of unknowable things in themselves. Recently Strong and Drake have devised a doctrine which makes sentience an almost unknowable mind-stuff (but how does it deserve the name sentience?) while consciousness with its contents are *appearances*. 'All the data of consciousness', writes Drake, 'are mass-effects, products of "fusion"'. It is an ingenious doctrine of motor reaction which leads to the strange awareness of what is not there. *There is a fusion which is an illusory fusion, and not a cerebral integration.*

I have great admiration for the ingenuity of the doctrine. But I myself believe in actual integration with intrinsic, emergent novelties. All levels of the psychical seem to me to be such intrinsic novelties, of the nature of a qualitative dimension within the brain-mind. As to the content of being at lower levels, I have no first-hand information. Thus my theory of knowledge excludes any form of naïve materialism.

It is important to note that the Drake-Strong doctrine of essences, which are not mental but are appearances somehow intuited, goes with their theory of consciousness as against mind-stuff. I, on the other hand, hold that logical ideas are discriminations within the act of cognition intrinsic to the cerebral response, which is, itself, a part of the whole organic response to the object.

Last of all, I come to the doctrine of events. Why substitute this category for that of a substantial system within which events occur! I must confess that the motives of Russell and Whitehead seem to me connected with a rejection of the permanent core, or substratum, view. I certainly would not hold matter to be changeless. I would introduce the notion of activity into the very heart of being. And yet I still feel that the term event does not furnish a suitable category for such *systems* as minerals and organisms. Where is the idea of system, of organisation? And Russell still seems to me to want to identify things with logical constructions. At heart, he is not yet a frank physical realist.

In a recent review in *Mind* of my book, *The Principles and Problems of Philosophy*, Miss Stebbing took occasion to say that she did not quite understand my view of substance. This article is meant as an explanation.

Notes

1 Sellars, *Evolutionary Naturalism*, ch. xiv.; *Aristotelian Society Proceedings*, 1922–3. *Critical Realism*, ch. ix.

2 Causality and substance*

Roy Wood Sellars

It is my wish in the present paper to induce the category of causality to disclose more about itself by putting it in its ontological context. Such a procedure should be suggestive in these days when categories and ontology are somewhat at a discount.

It will be noted that I employ the term ontology rather than metaphysics, since the latter term seems to be easily misleading because of its verbal associations. People have the tradition of thinking of metaphysics as something beyond physics in a theological sort of way; and they have, of course, good Aristotelian and Thomistic and even idealistic precedent for such a perspective. But the naturalist is concerned with being or existence and he considers physics as a basic empirical science about being, chiefly at the inorganic level. It concerns itself with primary constituents, properties and laws. It follows, of course, that, if the physicist were equally concerned with the clear apprehension of categories, he would be an ontologist also.

The dividing line is a matter of degree, for there are capable philosophical physicists. And yet I am persuaded that the interpretation of such categories as matter, space, time, and causality, requires the deepening and supplementation which epistemology and ontology alone can contribute. All of which amounts to saying that the philosophical approach is distinctive and unavoidable.

The reason for this belief will, I hope, become evident in the details of the argument of this paper, which, in the main, will be of the nature of an attempt to integrate epistemology and ontology. However, I permit myself at this point the suggestion that the common tendency to take the theory of relativity as an ontological principle illustrates what I have in mind. Equally relevant is the fact that science can be given operational and positivistic translations as well as the more realistic ones which the majority of scientists probably entertain as an extension of common sense. I would hold, then, that science requires a philosophical completion, not as regards facts and theories, but as regards *categorial setting*. Of course, scientists are invited to pass their criticisms upon this attempted philosophical supplementation, for I do not think that there is anything very esoteric about it. It reflects not much more than an intellectual division of labor.

*Source: *The Philosophical Review*, Vol. 52, No. 1 (Jan, 1943), pp. 1–27.

I shall use the term physical realism as an indication of my position. It is, I may point out, a shortened expression for critical realism and evolutionary naturalism taken together. Thus it symbolizes the integration of epistemology and ontology of which I have spoken. Physical realism is a post-Humian position. Much of its effort has had to do with the escape from subjectivism and phenomenalism.

As a physical realist it is my thesis that scientific knowledge, that is, empirical, and not formal or purely mathematical, knowledge, is highly probable knowledge or disclosure about what exists, and that its facts and theories inexorably involve an ontology for their reference and philosophical meaning. This view does not, of course, imply that any particular science need greatly concern itself about this philosophical completion, but that the culture of the time cannot and will not ignore it. Modest as a philosopher must be in this age of science and technology, I would, nevertheless, suggest that the development of science as a whole is affected by its basic assumptions. It is doubtful that science is as completely self-sufficient as it was led in the nineteenth century to regard itself.

The position adopted here signifies that *being* (what exists) has categorial characteristics which are disclosed in the categorial meanings operating in sense-perception, self-awareness, and the sciences, and that it is the job of basic philosophy to apprehend them and to clarify them. It will, perhaps, be remembered that, in my book, *Evolutionary Naturalism*, I argued that categorical meanings have a natural, empirical origin and an ontological reference and significance. While recognizing the value of Kant's stress upon categories as against Hume's scepticism, I criticized his extreme innatism and his phenomenalism. I still regard this contrast as basic and fruitful. In other words, I am not one of those who would throw common-sense categories away in a nonchalant fashion as do those who have the virus of logical apriorism in their veins. I simply regard myself as more adequately empirical than Hume's atomism and sensationalism permitted him to be and far more so than those who hover between sensationalism and conventionalism.

In my opinion, then, knowledge, being, and the categories, are both causally and formally connected. They are reciprocally elucidating. *Being* without categorial characteristics is scarcely thinkable; and in knowledge-claims, being is characterized through categorial meanings. In this fashion all three are tied together. So much in the way of perspective.

I

The category of causality furnishes an excellent illustration of the dangers confronting conceptual apprehension as a result of an inadequate philosophical context. It is well known that Hume rejected its ontological setting and sought to reconceive it in a subjective and phenomenalistic setting. So taken, causality was reduced to a weak form having something to do with experiential sequences and expectations. Hume was forced to this reduction because he found himself unable to give either it or substance an empirical foundation and so refused to fall back on what rightly seemed to him an obscurantist type of rationalism.

The critical realist would suggest that at least one root of the difficulty was the confusion of acts of cognition with the occurrence of sensations and images, which, after all, but furnish some of the raw material for denotative and depictive acts. However that may be, both substance and causality were really dismissed together, although something weaker which was of the nature of succession in experience was given the name of causation. It was this shift which I have spoken of as taking causality out of its ontological context. I do not deny that a new emphasis, reflecting the newer developments in science, also entered, that temporalism and contingency received overdue recognition. But I do claim that it is really doubtful whether the category of causality remained after this removal of the ontological context.

What, in the main, I shall try to do is to reverse Hume's action and, while retaining temporalism and contingency, give causality once more its ontological setting. By so doing, it will again be linked with physical systems conceived dynamically and relationally; and, through this linkage, it will be tied in with such categories as substance, activity, time, space, tendency, potentiality, and emergence.

In my opinion it is only in this fashion that scientific knowledge can be given a philosophical completion, that is, can be harmonized with what seem to me basic ontological categories. As I have already indicated, I am quite aware that many contemporary thinkers of distinction do not feel this need. That is the continuing Humian note. But I do, for reasons which I hope to make clearer as I proceed.

The critical realist—for whom empirical knowledge is a mediated affair—recognizes that science is likely to contain some measure of *epistemic translation* in its facts and laws. Thus the past does not exist in nature while it is dated and described in human knowledge. There is something hypothetical in laws in so far as they set up conditions. I suggest that such terms as space-time, change, event, probability, and fact, can only be properly accounted for and understood in the light of an adequate ontology. It is only those who identify empirical knowledge with a direct intuition of reality and do not grasp the manipulations and comparisons involved who are surprised by this descriptive *spreading out* which emphasizes chronologies, predictions, facts, and laws. Let it be remembered that neither the past nor the future exists and it will be realized that the actual cannot be reduced to a mere present *event*. At least, so it seems to me; and that is one reason why I am led to explore such categories as substance and potentiality. These must, however, be so conceived that they harmonize with modern scientific knowledge.

It is not too much to say that many of the paradoxes of philosophy and much of the misunderstanding of the nature of such things as moral decision result from this refusal to correlate scientific knowledge with ontology. Thus causation has been thought of as a push by a non-existent past and moral choice has been conceived, curiously enough, as an *event* succeeding other events and not, more deeply, as an *activity* of the whole organic self. This contrast between event and activity seems to me intriguing. May it not in some measure correspond to the different perspective of scientific knowledge and ontology? Why so many philosophers should ignore such fascinating topics is a marvel to me. But, so long as epistemology and ontology are ignored or kept from their fruitful interaction by positivism and pragmatism, such will be the case.

By linking causality with substance, taken in a dynamic or activistic sense, I shall be led to distinguish between transeunt causality, immanent causality, and emergent causality. These distinctions will be situational in character but also qualitative. I shall attempt to give the notion of emergence a rational ontological ground. It is my thesis that the ontological categories are intrinsically related and that each fades to the extent it is taken from its connection with the others. The ontological situation, as I see it, is analogous to what the logicians call entailment. It is as though substance were a superordinate category which found implication and expression in subordinate ones such as causality, activity, potentiality, space, and time. In other words, these subordinate categories are adjectival in nature and *expose* the dynamic and structural nature of substance. Certainly, one reason for the historical desiccation of the category of substance was its abstraction from these subordinate categories. Only in this fashion did it become "something I know not what" or the reflection of the subject-predicate form. Even the idealist's substitution of self or person for it represents in part this desiccation. We shall, in fact, see that self-awareness is a significant source of the proper apprehension of the category of substance, though it must be taken in the context of emergence or evolutionary naturalism.

Since Hume—and that is one of his recognized glories—no discussion of causality can get intelligently under way without attention being paid to the epistemic side. How do we apprehend this category? And why, and by what right, do we apply it both to ourselves and the things around us? Kant drove these further questions home.

Now I take all categories, from the epistemic side, to be gradually apprehended concepts grasped within experience. And I further suppose such apprehension not to be arbitrary but to be based upon traits of cognitional and conational, or practical, experience. Both of these activities concern themselves, I would hold, with self and things rather than with sensations and feelings. Here is where *denotative realism* makes a profound difference to epistemic analysis. For many reasons, some of which were connected with his views of space and time, Kant turned his back upon physical realism and embraced a phenomenalism for which knowing was a kind of constructing. Hence, though he was even more aware than Hume of categorial meanings, he did not give them realistic significance.

II

The resources of both genetic and analytic psychology would be required for any adequate psychological verification of the categorial meanings with which I am concerned. All I can do here is to indicate the perspective which, it seems to me, any epistemic study of causality and substance must emphasize.

It is not sufficiently recognized that Hume admitted the presence and operation of instincts and beliefs with respect to both things and selves. "It seems also evident that, when men follow this blind and powerful instinct of nature, they always suppose the very images, presented by the senses, to be the external objects, and never entertain any suspicion that the one are nothing but representations of the other." Both here and with respect to the self we find his rational principles at war with his natural beliefs.

But his rational principles turn out upon examination to reflect assumptions which are highly doubtful. These lead him to turn his back upon denotative symbolism and explicit judgment with the use of thinghood as a category and to embrace in a mood of resigned scepticism a radical empiricism of atomic sense-impressions and images, a radical empiricism which has ever since appealed to many as toughminded, through it is really very artificial and tenderminded.

To make a long story short, I would hold that the field of the individual's experience is dominated by denotative reference in both sense-perception and self-awareness, and that these two directions develop together and are of genetic assistance to each other. The individual's attitudes and interests help to give body and objectivity to their objective or *Gegenstand*, and it is for this reason that sensations are caught up into a perceptive form and seem the very surface of the objective not-self which the embodied self is concerned with. All this seems to me genetically and epistemically natural, and I am persuaded that critical realism has shown that it can be epistemologically developed in such a fashion that empirical knowledge turns out to be of the nature of judgmental assertions about denoted, but not intuited, objects in the environment of the organic self.

But into the purely epistemological aspect of the question I do not wish to enter, for I have written about it almost *ad nauseam* and with too little stimulating criticism on the part of fellow philosophers. What I desire to do here is to call attention to the corresponding mechanism and categorial form of self-awareness. In place of the stream-of-consciousness psychology I would put a thing-and-self psychology dominated by directions and categorial meanings. It seems to me, in short, that sense-perception and self-awareness must be taken as co-ordinate and mutually implicated. As I see it, the tension of felt attitudes has a double direction, one outward and the other inward. In its outward direction it gives body to sensations and helps to put them into a perceptive form which is deepened by memories and expectations. But in its inward direction there is a corresponding development of subjectivity, or selfness, also deepened by memories and anticipations. Desires and hopes and fears play about this subjective counter-reference. It is in this fashion, I believe, that the form of self-awareness develops step by step with the form of sense-perception. What deepens the one deepens the other also. But feelings, organic sensations, and desires, constitute the psychical material taken up symbolically and cognitively in this self-reference much as visual and touch sensations are taken up into objective perceptual form. As I shall try to show, in both cases reflection emphasizes reference and denotation and queries intuition of the object. We shall find, indeed, that intuition has more to say for itself in the case of self-knowledge than in the case of external perception. However, ontological questions of the relation of substance to its momentary activation will appear in connection with the equivalence of feeling to the enduring organic self.

Before I go further I should like to point out that explicit categorial meanings like those of thinghood and selfhood are subjects of reflective examination only in philosophic thought. Yet that they are apprehended and verbalized long before cannot be doubted. It is quite evident that such meanings emerge from biologically founded patterns. As factors they are operative in the life of the lower animals. Such meanings are relational and directional in character and are, I suppose, carried by feelings, sensations, and images. I would not take these latter terms atomistically but on a background of attention and action giving continuity and compresence with transition.

What I wish to stress is that categorial meanings emerge and operate in this fashion and that what may be called a *conceptual apprehension* of them presupposes this prior status. Otherwise it would be artificial and without foundation. We perceive things and are aware of the self long before we apprehend with any clarity what things are and what the self is. One aim of the present study is to stimulate such clarified apprehension which, since Hume's dampening scepticism, has not been any too evident. My thesis is that the conceptual apprehension of categories presupposes the empirical presence of categorial meanings in the operative forms of sense-perception and self-awareness. Here is where realistic empiricism differs from Humian empiricism. And yet, as we say, Hume acknowledged these meanings but did not see how they could be given a rational explanation in terms of his psychological and epistemological assumptions. Critical realism breaks with these assumptions in the fashion I have indicated.

III

It is tremendously important that the status of the organism in self-awareness be correctly grasped. I take it to be empirically correct to speak of the embodied self or the organic self. Certainly I have no intuition of the self as distinct from the organism. And it seems to me clear that Cartesian dualism is a theory resting upon assumptions which evolutionary naturalism undercuts. I refer here both to the doctrine of emergence and to the double-knowledge approach to the mind-body problem.

Let us look at our actual experience in self-awareness. Is it not a fact that, guided by organic sensations and feelings, we experience ourselves to be in some sense *in* the body? There is a diffuse localization in the body as against other perceived things set over against it. Psychologists have pointed out this nuclear basis and the attachments and deepenings which it acquires in the awareness of desires and aversions and in the localization of eye-movements and muscular activities. But why do more than refer to these well known facts? The self at what one might call the sensuous level is noted through, and by means of, such subjective, intra-bodily localized, data. All this is a matter, not of theory, but of experiential distinctions. It is only later for theory that the mind and the realistically conceived body, or organism, must be integrated anew in answer to dualistically formulated ontological conceptions.

We are concerned here with the awareness of self. And the primary self seems to me to be denoted and symbolized through subjective, psychical material localized within the body. I take it that memory and anticipations play much the same supplementary role here as they do for our perception of thinghood. The self tends to be thought of as indwelling and *more than the passing feelings* which are states or expressions of it. The correspondence with sense-perception is fairly complete. In both directions there is the same development of meanings of endurance and capacity. The body may well help to mediate this double development, since the awareness of the body is fairly constant. I am convinced that I could move my body if I would. The self retreats in some measure from the muscular integument and we think of the latter more as an instrument of the self we are aware of. It is in this sense that we seem to ourselves to look out through the eyes and feel with the hands.

But into the subtle details of the conceptualization of the self we cannot here enter. Social intercourse has much to do with this development of desires, actions, and thoughts, which do, quite literally, develop the self upon its biological base. But the point I wish particularly to make is that, without the primary self-awareness we have discussed above, the concepts of the self could secure no existential reference and attachment. I find that pragmatists like Mead and Dewey have never sufficiently grasped this fact because they were not sufficiently interested in epistemology and ontology. They never clearly distinguished between the concept of the self and the self. And to the physical realist this distinction is basic.

The point I wish now to make is that the self is never something given alongside of the feelings and desires through which it is disclosed any more than an external thing can be something given alongside of the sense-data. In both cases the denoted object is something apprehended through data and categorial meanings. Hume was on a false search. As I see it, the difference between inorganic things and the self is at least twofold: (1) a difference in capacities, and (2) the self is in some fashion integral to the human organism whose capacities are somehow its capacities. To make a long story short, I see every reason to believe that the organism is the self, not something-I-know-not-what located in liver, heart, or brain. It is the activities and operations of the organism that we apprehend through our feelings and concepts. We may be said to pass from a sensuous to a conceptual apprehension of the self, *apprehension being a directed awareness through concepts.*

IV

It is in this fashion that I argue for a realistic empiricism as against phenomenalistic empiricism. It is evident that such realistic empiricism gives a foundation for ontological categories, for it asserts that categorial meanings develop in both sense-perception and self-awareness and that these meanings are conceptualized and mediate the conceptual apprehension of the categorial characteristics of our world.

Now I take substance to be a category to whose full conception all our knowledge of self and things is necessary. It is to me analyzable in the sense that any adequate conceptual apprehension of it involves such meanings as endurance, activities, potentialities, causality, etc. As I see it, such conceptual apprehension is mediated by all relevant knowledge of a generic sort. I doubt that the category of substance excludes even space and time when these are grasped as categorial meanings and not merely equated with scientific measurements. In short, substance is an abstract, but internally complex, concept, and to brush it aside as a mere projection of the subject-predicate linguistic form seems to me the height of absurdity.

In order that we may keep our promised integration of epistemology and ontology let us try to see how this approach to substance through both self and things affects the interpretation of this category.

It is clear that we must distinguish between the generic characteristics of substance and the specific characteristics which distinguish one level of nature from another. I take it that new capacities emerge which are yet compatible with the generic ones of endurance, potentiality, dynamism, and causal capacity. And it is my hypothesis that organization is the clue to such emergence. I shall have more to say of this point later when I study emergent causality.

At present I am primarily interested in clarifying the difference between the knowledge of self and the knowledge of things. I have argued that the categorial meanings apprehended in the concept of substance develop in the situation where we pass back and forth between sense-perception and self-awareness. There is control and countercontrol, action and reaction. It is likewise clear that the body itself helps in this linkage of the two. The body is a thing as well as the embodiment of the self.

For each individual there is an ultimate epistemological difference, which he assumes for other selves, that is, that he is outside of other things and can only get revelatory messages from them while he is participating in the activity of its own body-self. It is the organic self which desires, feels, judges, makes decisions. The data used in knowing the self are expressions of its activity. Nowhere else in nature has the individual the same privileged position. And, of course, it is rationally quite understandable. We should, therefore, expect the inorganic world to be more opaque in the sense that we are limited in its case to the kind of descriptive knowledge disclosed by sensory data. The result is what I called an epistemological translation, or spreading out, especially marked as regards scientific space and time, and a tendency to feel a trifle bewildered by the category of substance itself. It is not surprising, therefore, to find that even causality shares an analogous fate and, with it, the rational basis of induction. It is, I believe, the strategic role of philosophy to emphasize the significance of a naturalistic approach to the organic self. Here we are dominated by the thought of an enduring, highly organized, and active substance which we are and by the conviction that our experiences of feeling, thinking and deciding are one with, and expressions of, such substantial activities. Here is the perspective of empirical realism as against phenomenalism. My break with Hume should now be evident. It is at once epistemological and ontological; and the two are inseparable though distinguishable. It rests on the thesis that empirical knowledge involves a directed claim to disclose a world which is conceptually apprehended as substantial. Because Hume ignored, or rejected, this framework and thought of knowledge as an affair of sensory givenness, his treatment of substance and causality was inevitable.

Let us now turn to the epistemic side of causality. Here, again, I would argue that the categorial concept rests upon a categorial meaning which emerges in experience.

Of late there has been a rise of interest in the subjective source of this category. Ewing, Broad, Stout, Pratt, Swabey, and Parker, have argued for an awareness of causal relatedness in the individual's experience. The epistemic side of the problem is concerned with the experiences in self-awareness and sense-perception which develop into this type of categorial meaning which can then be more and more conceptualized. In large measure it is a genetic question and involves the growth in awareness of the self's doing and suffering. But such awareness is integrated with the perception of things as affecting us and of ourselves as handling and moving things. I take it that our feeling of ourselves as pervading the organism has much to do with the growth of these relational meanings. But as desire, memory, and decision, constitute larger elements in the thought of the self, such experiences as the direction of the attention, trying to remember a name, making a moral choice, seem to me to be regarded as disclosing the self as active. It is not, I suppose, that we intuit a conational element as such, but that we are led to think the self as active and as disclosed in these relational experiences. In short, activity seems to me to be a categorial meaning developing around primary self-awareness. Once this level is reached we are convinced that the self has something to do with the movement of the eyes or the use of the various bodily organs even though we can trace no continuity between volition and action. The important point to bear in mind is that we do not claim to know the self exhaustively and to intuit just how it operates. So far as I can see we have nothing more than the apprehension that the self is operating and expressing itself and that we are consciously on the inside of this operating, consciously participating in it. For instance, to use Dr. Ewing's example, we can note how we react to the thought of the death of a friend; and we are convinced that this reaction gives us knowledge of our character and disposition. We think the self through what we believe to be a set of relevant experiences bearing upon the self.

Now I have not the space to go into the details of this deepening awareness of the self as active, which I take to be the basis of the growth of the categorial meaning of causality. Suffice it to point out that the position I am advocating does not hold to any intuition of force or energy as these terms are used in physical science. We should not expect to intuit how our muscles are innervated nor should we expect to see necessary connections in nature. Rather am I pointing out that we are led to deepen our conception of the self as a substance, that is, an enduring unity having dispositions and capacities, by this additional category of causal activity. Substance, dispositions, capacities, activity, doing and suffering, what are all of these but supplementary concepts? That we have such concepts and use them in our conceptual apprehension of the self there seems to me little doubt. I am simply arguing that these concepts rest upon categorial meanings developed around sense-perception and self-awareness but more dominantly around the latter.

It would scarcely be fair not to mention Whitehead's appeal to the mode of causal efficacy as against the mode of presentational immediacy. I can appreciate his motive and agree with what may be called his subjective emphasis. My divergence lies chiefly in my stress upon the operation of the category of selfhood. It seems to me that the categorial meaning of causal activity develops from experiences of the sort indicated above as they are used to interpret a substantial self which can do things. I can and do attend to things; I have desires and make a choice; I have capacities and dispositions. All this becomes the more explicit the more conceptually selfconscious we are. That is, the more the awareness of the bodily self is deepened and supplemented by the consciousness of what are usually spoken of as mental operations and moral decisions. My argument is that the organism *is* the substantial and active self so known.

It is surely not surprising that a self which feels itself continuous with muscular sensations and able to control their coming through imaged decisions should interpret kinesthetic sensations symbolically as effort and resistance. We regard our muscular activity as an extension and prolongation of the activity of the self even though we detect no connective bond between decision and the later kinaesthetic sensation. Self-knowledge is not complete physiological knowledge, though it should not conflict with it. And I see no reason to deny that imaged decisions do control muscular movements. In other words, Hume demanded too much. What alone I am arguing for is the growth of the categorial meaning of causality within experience as tied up with the awareness of the self as active and controlling, on the one hand, and as suffering and being controlled, on the other. All this seems to me to emerge in the setting of self and things. I do not see how sensationalism as such could give a nucleus for the development of such intertwined categorial meanings.

Under these conditions it is not surprising that muscular sensations become, as I said, symbolic of action, passion, and direction, both spatial and temporal. In this fashion causality gets its extra-bodily extension and application. I learn that I can not only move my body but the things around it. And I soon learn instrumental routines outside the organic self which I can set going. Laws of nature are in the offing.

I have suggested that kinaesthetic sensations and even feelings take on *causal symbolism* and give solidity and volume to our thought of causal operations. So far as I can see, they do not do more than this but readily become indicative of the measurements of effort and resistance attached to them by science. It is merely another case of our sensations becoming symbolic through their integration with categorial meanings. Just as I tend to take a colored patch to be the surface of the thing to which I am attending and toward which I am moving, so I take the muscular sensations as expressing my causal effort. In neither case does a critical level of knowing project *sensory qualities into things*. These must find a locus in the self as organism; and that, as we saw, is the mind-body problem.

Now the import of my whole argument is to the effect that the categorial meanings of substance and causality develop together in connection with the awareness of self and things. Such is their setting; and conceptual apprehension of the categories should not violate this mutual involvement. If philosophy violates this setting, substance becomes inert, merely linguistic, and mythological, a parody for positivists to scorn; and causality, abstracted from it, likewise turns into something unempirical and undiscoverable. Both epistemic and epistemological acumen are needed to handle categories.

V

Let us apply these conclusions to Humianism or what I have called phenomenalistic empiricism. It is obvious that I have been seeking to push beyond Kant's compromise answer to Hume. Kant knew we employed categories, but he did not trace their epistemic source to categorial meanings emerging in sense-perception and self-awareness. As I see it, both his psychology and his epistemology were inadequate. And yet he was so clearly on the right track. Our thinking is dominated by these categories. All we need to do essentially is to realize that conceptual thinking of this sort arises upon the apprehension of categorial meanings developed in the operations of sense-perception and self-awareness. The further epistemological task is to elicit a *denotative realism* which moves from naive to critical realism. Phenomenalism then gives way to a physical realism with the apprehended categories rightly applied to *existence*.

A basic ontological question arises at this point and must at least be mentioned. Hume rightly saw that the idea of existence must take its departure from actual existence, in his case from impressions and ideas. I should suppose that existence is here of the nature of an acknowledgment arising from the recognition of the contrast between presence and absence. It is a notorious fact that people whose organic sensations are strongly modified get a feeling of unreality, of nonexistence.

I am strongly of the opinion, then, that in psychical matters the assertion of existence is tautological. Existence is not a property of such an event but is the event itself. And as we note the sensation, or the feeling, fading we become conscious of something ceasing or going out of existence.

But, as a realist, I am of the opinion that we have in this case to do with events which must ultimately be conceived as activities of the organic self. Let us, therefore, try to understand what existence means as applied to the self and to external things. I take it to be evident that, just as the category of substance applies to both, so will the meaning of existence. Now in self-awareness we think the self as that which *discloses itself* in such subjective experiences as feeling-attitude, desire, and moral decision, and at the same time *expresses itself* in such experiences. The result is that existence is automatically assigned to the self as inclusive of them. To say the self exists is to say that it is continuous with these subjective experiences. But that is not all, for the self has a different categorial status from them. It is an object of knowledge which is regarded as enduring, active, and the subject of capacities, habits, and aptitudes. The self for each knower has the special status of being *continuous with* the subjective experiences which form the point of departure for self-awareness, so that self-knowledge cannot be an affair of hallucination, even though elements of illusion may enter. This situation it is that helps to make reflexive knowledge or self-knowledge possible. I know myself; and in this fact I cannot be mistaken though I may be mistaken in the particular specific concepts used. We have, I hold, valid reflexive knowledge of the self.

But into the details of self-knowledge I cannot here enter. Suffice it to say that the self is sensuously known through subjective experiences which are intrinsic to the activities of the organic self and in a more conceptual way through concepts based on categorial meanings. The result is that the concept of existence emerges from these categorial meanings to adjust itself to substance. It is the very nature of things and selves to exist unless they cease to exist. To assign existence to them is tautological. The problem is not to find existence but what exists. And one point of departure for each one is the organic self sensuously known through subjective experiences.

Here, again, the primary task was to raise Hume to the level of denotative realism. For Kant this position signifies that the sharp distinction between the empirical self and the transcendental ego breaks down just as that between the phenomenon and the thing-in-self does. Had Descartes not been so certain that mind and matter are alien to each other, his analysis might well have been similar.

We must give a nod at least in the direction of external existence. It is obvious that we must distinguish between the grounds for our belief in external things and the question of the kind of existence we assign them. Even idealists are not solipsists. And yet the two problems are intertwined.

The main grounds for external existence are those operating in sense-perception and in overt action involving handling and pushing and being pushed. Once begun, these motives are supplemented by conceptual thought, which explains intercourse, travel, communication, events, etc., in terms of a physical world. But it seems to me quite clear that the categorial meaning stems primordially from the consciousness of being affected in sense-perception and in the complex experiences of doing and suffering. The critical realist argues that, in sense-perception, sensations are used as natural signs of objects because of the reaction of the organic self to and through these sensations. Introspection can, I think, note the feeling of being startled in the case of unexpected and intense sensations. In sense-perception there is an integration of this feeling of being affected with the supplementary factor of felt attitude and response. The process of interpretation adds itself in terms of memories and expectations and, I have argued, the self thus denotes a *counterexistent* with which it feels itself to be confronted. Judgment and its asserted facts flow in to build upon this inception. Now, as I see it, the generic kind of existence assigned to these counterexistents is substantive and like that of the organic self.

It is in terms of this thick perceptual form with its categorial meanings that visual and tactile sensations tend to be regarded as helping to constitute the very surfaces of objects. Their marginal status with respect to the subjective experiences which chiefly dominate self-awareness and their function as guides to attitude and behavior assist in the development of this interpretation which gives rise to naive realism. It is *as though* the very existence of the external thing were given.

There are all sorts of gradations as in hearing, smelling, and tasting. But the general mechanism is of the sort indicated.

Another relevant topic is that of the *quid juris* of the external application of the categories of substance, causality, and existence, what Kant called the transcendental deduction. The divergence between Kantianism and critical realism on this point turns around the identification by the latter of thing with thing-in-itself and of empirical self with the transcendental self. We should not speak of phenomenal objects and phenomenal selves. And it is important to note that these categories arise from, and are demanded by, the organic self. The alternative here is, so far as I can see, a wilful agnosticism, or phenomenalism, which refuses to do justice to our actual knowledge-claims.

Kant undertook to show that without these categories science would be impossible. I would also add common sense to science. Both our cognitive forms and our action presuppose them. And I see no reason to believe that our categories are arbitrary. Instead I have attempted to show that they are conceptualizations of categorial meanings which clearly have an empirical and existential origin. In the manner indicated above we do extrapolate them. And the more we integrate the self with the organism—an identification which, in my opinion, the recognition of the social expansion of the concept of the self does not militate against—the more inevitable such extrapolation seems, since the existential extension is from the organism to its environment. It is a fact that we tend to regard ourselves as causal substances within a more inclusive world. This mode of thought is, according to the argument developed here, both natural and rational and does not, contrary to Kant, meet with antinomies. The alternative would seem to be such categoriless perspectives as positivism and pragmatism, which rest mainly upon a kind of stubborn rejection of epistemological and ontological analysis, a rejection motivated by certain phobias, loyalties, and inadequate concepts.

There can be little doubt that Cartesian dualism with its *supposed intuition that body could not think* had something to do with the burden of this extrapolation-problem. With the recognition of the artificiality of Cartesian dualism it becomes natural to extend categories beyond man just because we now think of him as continuous with nature. And, in so doing, we affirm in a more sophisticated way what man has always done and what philosophy had done from Aristotle to Kant. However, due attention must be given to the idea of levels of causality and substance in order to escape false anthropomorphism. There are clearly evolved kinds of substances with emergent causal modes. Again, man should not expect to intuit causal routines outside himself but must develop and apply criteria. And this is but what science does.

In concluding this epistemological section I would stress the thesis that the principle of causality makes the discovered routines in nature rationally comprehensible and gives a foundation to induction. And it is important to connect causality with substance in order to deepen the latter by absorbing processes, activities, powers, and potentialities. Only in this fashion can a basis be given to the nomic form "*would be q* if it were p" as against the purely factual form "is q if p."

VI

I shall now pass to a study of the categorial setting of science. What I shall be primarily concerned with will be a grounding of scientific concepts in ontological ones under the guidance of the above epistemological and ontological analyses.

The category of substantivity has no similitude to the pictorial eleatic conception of matter of the nineteenth century. We must recognize that our knowledge of physical entities is very abstract; and yet that there is nothing in its texture which conflicts with duration and agency and extensity, primary requirements of substantivity. It is in terms of these requirements that scientific concepts of space, time, quantity, and causality, can be rationally understood and what I have called their *descriptive spreading out* comprehended. Duration and agency disclose themselves in our experience in terms of time. And the operations of remembering, anticipating, and dating, spread out our knowledge of *events*, which are cognized facts about activities in nature. We recognize that events are not themselves realities but presuppose the agency, or activity, of that which durationally exists. Many of the paradoxes of time could have been avoided had this ontological basis for time been grasped. The present in contrast to the past and the future is only more actual in the sense that it refers to the actual activities of enduring substances. *It does not then mean a stretch of time but the source and basis of time.* Such is the only meaning I can give to the haunting sense of an absolute now. Does it not express our belief that the universe, as substantial, is a field of coexistential activities? But science develops concepts in relation to techniques of measurement; and so scientific time without a categorial setting has no meaning to assign to absolute simultaneity. The theory of relativity expresses the discovery of this fact. This analysis illustrates what I mean by a philosophic supplementation of science by giving it a categorial setting.

Now much the same sort of operation must be applied to causality, as used in science, to make it ontologically adequate. It is clear that the past cannot push the present, rather that the activity of an agent in its relation or field brings something to pass. Moral decision does not represent a push from a no-longer-existing past. It is an act of self-decision, of moral agency. We must be on our guard, as I have indicated, against a static epistemic spread or else we confuse knowledge with being. What, then, do causal laws mean? *Factually*, a routine in nature; *nomically*, the potency for a determinate kind of activity.

Developments in modern physics are obviously away from eleaticism and from the kind of transeunt causality characteristic of the so-called mechanical view of the world. In field-theory transeunt causality seems to me to be a phase of the immanent causality of the field. And yet physical substances, such as electrons and protons, indicate a center of activity of a dominantly relational sort. It is only as these combine to secure a new wholeness and substantiality that immanent causality begins to emerge as something more localized and specific to be set over against transeunt causality. In a very real sense these become correlatives.

It is at the level of atoms and molecules that the idea of emergence gains its first definite applicability, though there are hints in physics of the emergence of matter from energy. But what is really implied by emergence? Surely, in order to become rational, it must secure an ontological status and be linked with substance and causality. To me it seems most plausible to connect it, as evolutionary naturalism does, not with natural piety but with causality. The fact of emergence must be explained in terms of the synthetic rise of higher-order substances or functionally unified continuants. We must take relations and organization seriously as characteristics of nature. What Professor Savery calls concatenism, which is a kind of effective togetherness, gives a better categorial context than does the atomism of purely external relations, whatever the latter may mean.

Suppose we put it in this fashion: emergence is an expression of an emergent causality which should be conceived as an activity of synthesizing upon the basis of a prior level of transeunt and immanent causality. As a term it points to the transition from transeunt to immanent causality, for it refers to the operations which make possible a higher level of substance and immanent causality. It is concerned with the genesis of what Locke called "real essences" and I would prefer to call complex constitutions. Transeunt causality involves a receiving from outside, immanent causality an activity dominantly internal, emergent causality the process of integration into a new whole. There is, so far as I can see, nothing mysterious and unfactual about such an interpretation.

What follows? The Aristotelian must relinquish his fixed natural kinds and his eternal forms together with his vitalistic apparatus of potency and act. Activity must be intrinsic to a substance as a whole and not to some postulated factor in it. And it must pass along the lines of relations and organization. It is foolish to create abstracta called universals and then seek to project them into nature. The *ratio essendi* is the reverse. Ross suggests that Aristotle was moving in a more Ionic direction in the later books of his *Metaphysics*. I think he would have moved still further in that direction were it not for his teleological astronomy and his unwillingness to think in evolutionary terms. What we need today is a materialization of Aristotelianism. I shall have something more to say about this when I come to discuss *functional teleology*.

It was along these lines I was thinking in *Evolutionary Naturalism*. With all due respect for those great thinkers, Lloyd Morgan and S. Alexander, it has been my conviction that the first was too phenomenalistic in his epistemology and so was induced to fall back in his ontology on an Activity with a capital A. Substantialism would have avoided this separation. Activity would have been of the material substances themselves. And emergence could not escape a mysterious air in S. Alexander just because he had no substance in which emergent causality could operate. New qualities just emerged as factually as new colors apparently quiver into being in the sky. No; I believe that empirical realism and evolutionary substantialism alone show promise of making the idea of emergence rational.

It is clear that the fact of emergence must be distinguished from the ground of emergence much as the fact of evolution is distinguishable from the method of evolution. And here it seems to me that two basic points must be noted. The first may be stated thus: New properties do not emerge; what emerges are new substances. The second point concerns the kind of unity brought about by emergent causality and finding expression in immanent causality.

Strictly speaking, of course, properties do not emerge; it is the newly constituted substance which does so. Properties are not adjectival entities which float around mysteriously or come from nowhere in a mysterious fashion, nor are they entities stuck on to an inert substratum as Locke at his worst suggested. Properties are laws to the effect that, if certain conditions be fulfilled, certain facts can be noted. Thus water is *such that* it will boil under specified conditions. Science seeks to understand such a property by attention to the energy-structure of the molecule. Properties must express the *constitution* of the substance or complex of substances of which they are properties. Locke, quite obviously, had something like this in mind when he talked of real essences. His epistemology was not realistic enough and his ontology too obscure.

What, then, shall we mean by the constitution of a substance? It is clearly something which can emerge through that kind of activity we have called emergent causality. In one direction it points toward genetic potentialities; in the other, toward a unified, or concatenated, togetherness. The active economy of a substance expresses its constitution; and its constitution depends upon the unified togetherness of its constituents. Once grant an active, or dynamic, nature to substance and it follows that we must think in terms of equilibria, wholeness, and dominance.

As I see it, immanent causality must be correlated with a type of togetherness in which causality is in some degree under the control of the constitution of a substance. In this situation a part-whole relation is asymmetrical with a whole-part relation. There is, so far as I can see, no *a priori* way of determining the tightness of the unity involved in higher-order substances. The economy here is so definitely temporal as well as spatial. It is interesting to note that what is apparent at the level of organisms has been shown by physics to apply, in terms of included rhythms, to the microscopic world. Such an outlook signifies the inseparability of activity and duration in substance. And we should expect that a higher-order substance would have rhythms of a longer temporal span than the included ones. How could it be otherwise? To deny it would be to deny the existence of the constituted unity of the new whole.

What I am driving at is that a higher-order substance must have both spatial and temporal unity. Without both we would have but atomism. Another point: the temporal unity is inseparable from the spatial constitution, and the spatial constitution, not being inert, depends upon the temporal rhythms. Only as space and time are taken in this fashion are they compatible with the underlying durational activity of a substance. The general economy of a substance demands the essential inseparability of structure and function. It seems that biologists have long realized this fact, which, I think, must be extended downward to simpler substances.

Here, again, I would suggest that ontology throws light upon, and supplements, epistemology. To the extent that science neglects the categorial setting of its facts it is in danger of a thinness in its interpretation. Its theoretical structure is unable to give meaning to its facts. A materialistic substantialist like myself feels that scientific knowledge about substances in their relations gets added meaning when we grasp it as knowledge about the economies of such substances in their spatial and temporal dimensions. In the strict sense physical time is always local and reflects a durational rhythm. And such rhythm is determined by the economy and constitution of the enduring substance. Such is the source and basis of time. Only by such an approach can, it seems to me, the traditional paradoxes be escaped. We get a sense of on-moving durational activity unattainable by mere eventism.

VII

Materialistic substantialism differs from Aristotelian substantialism in its stress upon relations, upon emergence, and upon enduring constitution. It does not look upon form as either artistically imposed or vitalistically presupposed. Hence it is more Ionic and refuses to dichotomize a substance into form and matter, actuality and potency. And yet it is grateful to the Stagirite for the suggestive handling of change and continuity. I take it, also, that only in terms of enduring substances with dynamic constitutions expressible in economies can we understand powers, aptitudes, habits, and dispositions. All this becomes empirical and obvious at the level of human beings. To human nature, or the constitution of human beings, belong powers and aptitudes. And so complex is its economy that aptitudes may remain latent or may be developed. Again, the direction of the economy of a human being may activate a disposition or leave it dormant. Only in terms of emergence and complexification can this be understood. The self is no simple thing but involves an involution of organization within organization. Both external and internal knowledge indicate such a complicated pattern of endurance.

For any emergent view consciousness or togetherness-in-experiencing is of critical importance. This primary fact must be approached both genetically and functionally.

The functional interpretation, while tremendously significant, does not seem to me particularly baffling. From this point of view consciousness must be conceived as a qualitative dimension of the activity of the self expressive of, and significant for, the functional togetherness of the brain-mind. It would seem that here—and here alone—do we have *empirical verification of functional wholeness*. At least, this is the case if we take James's introspection as truer than Hume's form of mental atomism. And I take it that psychology has been moving in this direction. Since emergent causality implies both substantial and functional wholeness, we have here a confirmation of the theory. And, as I have so frequently pointed out, here by the very nature of the situation can the individual have some measure of inside information about a high-level substance. There is nothing about external knowledge, which is very abstract and descriptive, which conflicts with this quite obvious fact. I feel that consciousness must be correlated with the activity of a very complicated and enduring substance. It is for this reason that we all tend to think of it as an illumination rather than as a substance. Here we have a basic categorial problem. It is intrinsic to an activity and is isomorphic with it; but the activity is itself an expression of the activated substance. It is the old question of the inseparability of structure and function in the economy of any system. It is my opinion that we must take endurance and accumulation seriously and always regard the mind-brain as that which furnishes the matrix and medium of consciousness. In this fashion I am too much of a substantialist to be a panpsychist.

The genetic, or evolutionary, approach to the fact of consciousness turns for me on the above status of consciousness. Quite clearly, it is to be correlated with rather complicated functions. And it is something which appears and disappears with the passage from latency to activation. By its very nature we have nothing to contrast it with. It stands to me as an indication that *being* always has an intrinsic nature, that it is *not* qualitatively vacuous, to use Whitehead's term. The best our reason can do—it seems to me—is to ground consciousness in this basic qualitativeness of all substance. Here is its emergent potentiality. We cannot inspectively trace it in a genetic way, for the last term alone is open to inspection. But I can see no reason to assume a complete discontinuity. Consciousness, as I see it, is adjectival, expressive, intrinsic to functional activity. If emergent causality signifies the generation of higher-order substances we must expect basic novelties.

I must turn in conclusion to the question of teleology. My logical path is already indicated. An enduring wholeness with an immanent causal economy implies the rejection of eleatic mechanism. Science is already moving away from pictorial notions based on molar happenings. The field, relations, tensions, equilibria, become relevant terms. But evolutionary substantialism would emphasize immanent causality as the locus of anything akin to purpose.

It is important to get rid of dominance by mensurational time and to stress what I have called the source and basis of time. The more there is of immanent causality, the more important in the economy becomes functioning and its expression, order. It will be recalled that I asserted that all agency is durational like substance itself; that is, there are no mathematical instants in nature, no such existential discontinuity as Descartes supposed. It follows that any subsystem has its native durational rhythm. Wholeness must be conceived as temporal as well as spatial. The nature of a high-order substance involves activities so related that one spreads into another. It is this ordered packing of tendencies, habits and dispositions like an organic spring that accounts for ordered and integrated behavior. Purpose can be understood only on the background of durational organization. Events flow out from such an economy much as music takes its origin from a record, only here the connection is brought about externally by means of a needle sliding from one indentation to another.

What I am arguing for is a teleology of self-direction rather than a teleology of finalism, a teleology intrinsic to an economy which is both spatial and temporal. In such immanent causality traditional ideas of pushes from the past or pulls from the future are transcended. A high-order substance makes its own time in terms of its economy. In all this I am not forgetting that such immanent causality must be adjusted to the play of transeunt causality, for the organism must act in relation to its environment. But to the extent there is self-direction there is escape from blindness and chance. As I see it, the brain-mind is an organ for the highest type of self-direction.

Let me now state in conclusion some of the principles which any philosophy of nature should explore:

1 The category of causality must be put in its ontological context, which is that of substantive being both endurant and spatial.
2 Properly understood, categories involve one another.
3 Aristotelianism must be profoundly modified by a shift which replaces a vitalistic form by an immanent organization.
4 Realistic empiricism with the recognition of categorial meanings represents a more adequate epistemology than phenomenalistic empiricism.
5 Relativity is epistemic and not ontological.
6 The basis and source of time is activity within and between enduring substances.
7 There are three main types of causality, transeunt, emergent, and immanent.
8 Properties by themselves do not emerge but higher-order substances do.
9 Consciousness is the only "natural isolate" we can be acquainted with. It shows that *being* has a qualitative dimension.
10 Immanent causality is self-directional. Mind is the highest level of such functional, self-directional teleology.

3 Essence and accident*

Irving M. Copi

The notions of essence and accident play important and un-objectionable roles in pre-analytic or pre-philosophical thought and discourse. These roles are familiar, and need no elaboration here. Philosophers cannot ignore them, but must either explain them or (somehow) explain them away. My interest is in explaining them.

If they are taken seriously, the notions of essence and accident seem to me most appropriately discussed within the framework of a metaphysic of substance, which I shall accordingly assume. The account of essence and accident that I wish to set forth and argue for derives very largely from Aristotle, although it is not strictly Aristotelian. Where it differs from Aristotle's account it does so in order to accommodate some of the insights formulated by Locke in his discussion of "real" and "nominal" essences. My discussion is to be located, then, against the background of a substance metaphysic and a realist epistemology. The theory of essence and accident to be proposed seems to me not only to fit the demands of the general philosophical position mentioned, but also to be consistent with the apparent requirements of contemporary scientific development I wish to begin my discussion with some historical remarks.

The earliest Western philosophers were much concerned with change and permanence, taking positions so sharply opposed that the issue appeared to be more paradox than problem. If an object which changes really changes, then it cannot literally be one and the same object which undergoes the change. But if the changing thing retains its identity, then it cannot really have changed. Small wonder that early cosmologists divided into warring factions, each embracing a separate horn of their common dilemma, the one denying permanence of any sort, the other denying the very possibility of change.

Aristotle discussed this problem in several of his treatises, bringing to bear on it not only his superb dialectical skill but an admirable, common-sense, dogged insistence that some things do maintain their identity while undergoing change. To explain the observed facts he was led to distinguish different kinds of change.

*Source: *The Journal of Philosophy*, Vol. 51, No. 23, American Philosophical Association Eastern Division: Papers to be presented at the Fifty-First Annual Meeting, Goucher College December 28–30, 1954. (Nov, 11, 1954), pp. 706–719.

A man does retain his identity though his complexion may change from ruddy to pale, or though he may move from one place to another. He is the same man though he become corpulent in middle life or his sinews shrink with age. In these types of change, called *alteration, locomotion, growth*, and *diminution*, the changing thing remains substantially or essentially what it was before changing.

Another type of change, however, was admitted to be more thoroughgoing. To take, for example, an artificial substance, we can say that if a wooden table is not just painted or moved, but destroyed by fire, we have neither alteration, locomotion, growth, nor diminution alone, but *substantial* change. The characteristic mark of substantial change is that the object undergoing the change does not survive that change or persist through it, but is destroyed in the process. The ashes (and gas and radiant energy) that appear in place of the burned table are not an altered, moved, or larger or smaller table, but no table at all. In substantial change its essential property of being a table disappears.

It seems clear that distinguishing these different kinds of change involves distinguishing different kinds of attributes. The basic dichotomy between substantial change and other kinds of change is parallel to that between essential attributes or *essences*, and other kinds of attributes, which may be lumped together as accidental attributes or *accidents*. (Here we diverge rather sharply from at least one moment of Aristotle's own terminology, in ignoring the intermediate category of "property" or "proprium.")

Of the various bases that have been proposed for distinguishing between essence and accident, two stand out as most reasonable. The first has already been implied. If we can distinguish the different kinds of change, then we can say that a given attribute is essential to an object if its loss would result in the destruction of that object, whereas an attribute is a mere accident if the object would remain identifiably and substantially the same without it. This basis for distinguishing between essence and accident, although helpful heuristically, is not adequate philosophically, for it seems to me that the distinctions among these kinds of change presuppose those among the different kinds of attributes.

The other, more satisfactory basis for distinguishing essence from accident is an epistemological or methodological one. Knowledge of the essence of a thing is said to be more important than knowledge of its other attributes. In the *Metaphysics* Aristotle wrote: "… we know each thing most fully, when we know what it is, e.g. what man is or what fire is, rather than when we know its quality, its quantity, or its place…."[1] It is the essence that is intended here, for a subsequent passage explains that: "… the essence is precisely what something *is*…."[2] It is perhaps an understatement to say that Aristotle held knowledge of essence to be "more important" than knowledge of accidents, for he later says explicitly that: "… to *know* each thing … is just to know its essence…."[3] And if we confine our attention to scientific knowledge, Aristotle repeatedly assures us that there is no knowledge of accidents at all,[4] but only of essences.[5]

Aristotle was led to draw an ontological conclusion from the foregoing epistemological doctrine. If some attributes of objects are epistemologically significant and others are not, the implication is that the former constitute the real natures of those objects, whereas the latter can be relegated to some less ultimate category. I must confess that I am in sympathy with the realist position which underlies and justifies such an inference, but to expound it in detail would take us too far afield.

As a biologist Aristotle was led to classify things into genera and species, holding that things belong to the same species if and only if they share a common essence. In remarking this fact we need not commit ourselves to any position with respect to the systematic or genetic priority of either logic or biology in Aristotle's thought. He aparently believed these species to be fixed and limited, and tended to ignore whatever could not be conveniently classified within them, holding, for example, that "the production of a mule by a horse" was "contrary to nature,"[6] a curious phrase. Some modern writers have tended to regard this shortcoming as fatal to the Aristotelian system. Thus Susan Stebbing wrote: "Modern theories of organic evolution have combined with modern theories of mathematics to destroy the basis of the Aristotelian conception of essence...."[7] It seems to me, however, that the fixity of species is a casual rather than an integral part of the Aristotelian system, which in its broad outlines as a metaphysical framework can be retained and rendered adequate to the most contemporary of scientific developments. A not dissimilar objection was made by Dewey, who wrote that: "In Aristotelian cosmology, ontology and logic ... all quantitative determinations were relegated to the state of *accidents*, so that apprehension of them had no scientific standing. ... Observe by contrast the place occupied by measuring in modern knowledge. Is it then credible that the logic of Greek knowledge has relevance to the logic of modern knowledge?"[8] But the Aristotelian notion of essence *can* admit of quantitative determination, as is suggested by Aristotle himself in admitting ratio as essence.[9] Hence I do not think that this criticism of Dewey's can be regarded as any more decisive than that of Miss Stebbing.

Having set forth in outline an Aristotelian philosophy of essence and accident, I propose next to examine what I consider to be the most serious objection that has been raised against it. According to this criticism, the distinction between essence and accident is not an objective or intrinsic one between genuinely different types of attributes. Attributes are really all of the same basic kind, it is said, and the alleged distinction between essence and accident is simply a projection of differences in human interests or a reflection of peculiarities of vocabulary. Let us try to understand this criticism in as sympathetic a fashion as we can.

The distinction between different kinds of change, on this view, is subjective rather than objective. We happen to be interested, usually, in some attributes of a thing more than in others. "When the thing changes, we say that it persists through the change provided that it does not lose those attributes by whose possession it satisfies our interests. For example, our interest in tables is for the most part independent of their colors. Hence that interest remains satisfiable by a given table regardless of any alteration it may suffer with respect to color. Paint a brown table green, and it remains substantially or essentially the same; the change was only an accidental one. If our interests were different, the same objective fact would be classified quite differently. Were our interest to lie in *brown* tables exclusively, then the application of green paint would destroy the object of our interest, would change it substantially or essentially from something which satisfied our interest to something which did not. The implication is that attributes are neither essential nor accidental in themselves, but can be so classified only on the basis of our subjective interests in them. Dewey stated this point of view very succinctly, writing: "As far as present logical texts still continue to talk about essences, properties and accidents as something inherently different from one another, they are repeating distinctions that once had an ontological meaning and that no longer have it. Anything is 'essential' which is indispensable in a given inquiry and anything is 'accidental' which is superfious."[10]

The present criticism lends itself easily to reformulation in more language-oriented terms. That we regard a table as essentially the same despite alteration in color or movement from place to place is a consequence of the peculiar nature and limitations of our vocabulary, which has a single word for tables, regardless of color, but lacks special words for tables of different colors. Suppose that our language contained no word for tables in general, but had instead—say—the word "towble" for brown table and the word "teeble" for green table. Then the application of green paint to a towble would be said to change it essentially, it might be argued, for no towble would remain ; in its place would appear a teeble. Or if there were a single word which applied indiscriminately to tables and heaps of ashes, say "tashble," with no special substantive denoting either of them univocally, then perhaps the destruction of a table by fire would not be regarded as an essential change. That which appeared at the end of the process would admittedly be in a different state from what was there at the start, but it would still be identifiably the same tashble. C. I. Lewis regards the difference between essence and accident to be strictly relative to vocabulary, writing: "Traditionally any attribute required for application of a term is said to be of the essence of the thing named. It is, of course, meaningless to speak of the essence of a thing except relative to its being named by a particular term."[11]

I think that for our purpose these two criticisms can be regarded as variants of a single basic one, for the connection between human interests and human vocabulary is a very intimate one. It is an anthropological and linguistic commonplace that the concern of a culture with a given phenomenon is reflected in the vocabulary of that culture, as in the several Eskimo words which denote subtly different kinds of snow. In our own culture new interests lead continually to innovations in vocabulary; and surely it is the decline of interest in certain things that leads to the obsolescence of words used to refer to them.

Both variants of this criticism were formulated long ago by Locke, and developed at considerable length in his *Essay*. Locke paid comparatively little attention to the problem of change, but where he did discuss it his treatment was very similar to Aristotle's. Thus we are assured in the *Essay* that: "... an oak growing from a plant to a great tree, and then lopped, is still the same oak; and a colt grown up to a horse, sometimes fat, sometimes lean, is all the while the same horse...."[12] The oak "... continues to be the same plant as long as it partakes of the same life..."[13] and the identity of animals is explained in similar terms.

Personal identity is explained in terms of sameness of consciousness.[14] If we ignore the Cartesian dualism implicit in that last case, and if we are not too critical of the reappearance of the term "same" in the explanation of *sameness*, we can recognize these answers to be the Aristotelian ones, for according to Aristotle the soul is the principle of life,[15] the life of a plant is the nutritive soul,[16] that of an animal its sensitive soul,[17] and that of man his rational soul,[18] these souls constituting the substantial forms or essences of the respective substances.[19] On the other hand, in his brief discussion of identity as applied to non-living things, Locke construes it very strictly to apply only to things which "… vary not at all.…"[20] But the following passage has a characteristically Aristotelian flavor: "Thus that which was grass today, is tomorrow the flesh of a sheep; and within a few days after becomes part of a man: in all which, and the like changes, it is evident their real essence, i.e. that constitution, whereon the properties of these several things depended, is destroyed, and perishes with them."[21]

Despite this partial similarity of their views, the bases for distinguishing between the essential properties and other properties of a thing are very different for Locke than for Aristotle. For Aristotle, the distinction is twofold: first, the essential properties of an object are those which are retained by it during any change through which the object remains identifiably the same object; and second, the essential properties of an object are most important in our scientific knowledge of it. For Locke, on the other hand, the *real* essence of a thing is a set of properties which *determine* all the other properties of that thing.[22] Since all other properties depend on its real essence, *any* change in an object entails a change in its real essence. Hence for Locke the essential properties of an object are *not* retained by it during any change. This view is very different from Aristotle's, on which the accidents of a thing are not bound to its essence but can change independently of it. The epistemological difference is equally striking. Whereas for Aristotle all scientific knowledge is knowledge of the essence, for Locke there is *no* knowledge of the real essences of things.[23]

Locke was more interested in what he called "nominal essences," which are more nearly analogous to the Aristotelian notion of essence. Our idea of a particular substance, according to Locke, is a complex idea composed of a number of simple ideas which are noticed to "go constantly together," plus the notion of a substratum "wherein they do subsist."[24] A general or abstract idea of a sort or species of substance is made out of our complex ideas of various particular substances that resemble each other by leaving out "that which is peculiar to each" and retaining "only what is common to all."[25] Such an abstract idea *determines* a sort or species,[26] and is called a "nominal essence,"[27] for "every thing contained in that idea is essential to that sort."[28]

The properties contained in the nominal essence of a thing can be distinguished from the other properties of that thing on the same basis as that on which the Aristotelian essence is distinguished from accidents. In the first place, a particular substance of a given species can change with respect to some property whose idea is *not* included in the nominal essence of that species, and will continue to be recognizably the same thing; whereas it must be regarded as a quite different thing if it changes with respect to some property whose idea is included in the nominal essence.[29] And in the second place, the nominal essence is more important in knowledge than other properties. To have knowledge of a thing is to know what *sort* of thing it is, and to know the nominal essence is to know the sort. Locke says, moreover, that the leading qualities of a thing, that is, the most observable and hence, for Locke, the most knowable, are ingredient in the nominal essence.[30] Finally, it is argued in the *Essay* that knowledge of nominal essences is required if we are ever to be certain of the truth of any general proposition.[31] Since Locke's nominal essences play so similar a role to that of Aristotle's essences, Locke's arguments intended to prove their subjectivity and relativity to human interests and vocabulary can be interpreted as applying to Aristotle's notion as well as his own.

One fairly minor difference should be noted before going on. Since Locke's nominal essences are abstract *ideas*, they are immediately subjective in a way that Aristotle's essences are not. But that difference is not decisive, for substances may well have objective properties that nominal essences are ideas *of*, or objective *powers* that correspond to them exactly.[32]

Locke urges that essences are subjective in a less trivial sense. Since they are "inventions"[33] or the "workmanship"[34] of the understanding, different persons in fashioning abstract ideas which they signify by the same term can and do incorporate different simple ideas into them. Acts of choice or selection are involved here, and people do make different choices, as proved by the disputes that so frequently arise over whether particular bodies are of certain species or not.[35]

That essences are relative to vocabulary is argued by Locke in terms of an example: "A silent and a striking watch are but one species to those who have but one name for them: but he that has the name watch for one, and clock for the other, and distinct complex ideas, to which those names belong, to him they are different species."[36]

That the "... boundaries of species are as men, and not as nature, makes them...,"[37] proved by the verbal disputes already referred to, is explained by the fact that since we have "... need of general names for present use..."[38] we "... stay not for a perfect discovery of all those qualities which would best show us their most material differences and agreements; but we ourselves divide them, by certain obvious appearances, into species...."[39] Nominal essences are made for *use*, and different intended uses or interests will determine different essences. Even the *noticing* of similarities between distinct particulars is relative to our interest in them, so our selection of simple ideas for inclusion in a nominal essence is relative to such interests. These determining interests are not scientific, for as Locke observed, "... languages, in all countries, have been established long before sciences."[40] The situation is rather that the terms of ordinary discourse "... have for the most part, in all languages, received their birth and signification from ignorant and illiterate people...."[41] And for the purposes or interests of those practical people, the properties selected by them as essential to the objects they deal with are adequate enough. For "Vulgar notions suit vulgar discourses; and both, though confused enough, yet serve pretty well the market and the wake."[42]

Now do these arguments succeed in establishing that the distinction between essence and accident is subjective rather than objective, that is, relative to human interests and vocabulary!

I think that the objections are not utterly destructive of the Aristotelian doctrine, although they do call attention to needed modifications of it. Locke's ease, it seems to me, depends upon his distinction between real and nominal essences, and his belief that real essences are unknowable. But his doctrine that real essences cannot be known flows from two peculiarities of his philosophy, which I see no reason to accept. One of the bases for his belief that real essences are unknowable is his view that the only objects of our knowledge are the ideas that we have in our minds.[43] Locke's other basis for his belief that real essences are unknowable is his doctrine that experiment and observation yield only "... judgment and opinion, not knowledge...."[44] Here the term "knowledge" is reserved for what is *certain*.

I would reject these two doctrines on the following grounds. The first of them, that knowledge is only of ideas, is the germ of scepticism. Locke's premises lead necessarily to Hume's conclusions, and the partial scepticism we find explicitly set forth in Locke is but a fragment of the complete scepticism that Hume later showed to be implicitly contained there. It seems to me that if a philosophy denies the very possibility of scientific knowledge, then so much the worse for that philosophy. As for reserving the term "knowledge" for what is certain, that usage has but little to commend it. It seems more reasonable to accept the results of experiment and observation, although probable rather than demonstrative, as knowledge nonetheless.

It must be admitted that the doctrine of the unknowability of real essences was not an unreasonable conclusion to draw from the relatively undeveloped state of science in Locke's day. For chemistry, at least, if we can believe what is said of it in the *Essay*, was in a very bad way in the seventeenth century. Locke tells us of the "sad experience" of chemists "... when they, sometimes in vain, seek for the same qualities in one parcel of sulphur, antimony or vitriol, which they have found in others. For though they are bodies of the same species, having the same nominal essence, under the same name; yet do they often, upon severe ways of examination, betray qualities so different one from another, as to frustrate the expectations of very wary chemists."[45]

Contemporary science, however, presents a quite different picture. Locke characterized the (allegedly unknowable) real essences of things as the "... constitution of their insensible parts; from which flow those sensible qualities, which serve us to distinguish them one from another...."[46] Now modern atomic theory is directly concerned with the insensible parts of things. Through the use of his Periodic Table, interpreted as dealing with atomic number and valency, "... Mendeléev was enabled to predict the existence *and properties*..." of half a dozen elements whose existence had not been previously known or even suspected.[47] And other scientists have subsequently been able to make similar predictions. Modern science seeks to know the *real* essences of things, and its increasing successes seem to be bringing it progressively nearer to that goal.

It must be granted that Locke's distinction between real and nominal essence is a helpful one, even though it is not absolute. The construction of nominal essences is usually relative to practical interests, and the ordinary notion of the essence of a thing is relative to the words used in referring to it. I think that Locke (and Dewey and Lewis) are correct in that contention. Surely different interests lead different people to classify or sort things in different ways, and thus to adopt different nominal essences, the more permanently useful of which receive separate names in ordinary language. Thus it is that: "Merchants and lovers, cooks and taylors, have words wherewithal to dispatch their ordinary affairs...."[48]

The distinction, however, is not absolute. Not every interest is narrowly practical. The interest of the scientist is in knowledge and understanding. The scientist desires to know how things behave, and to account for their behavior by means of explanatory hypotheses or theories which permit him to predict what will occur under specified conditions. He is interested in discovering general laws to which objects conform, and the causal relations which obtain among them. The scientist's sorting or classifying of objects is relative to this interest, which is not well served by classifying things on the basis of properties which are either most obvious or most immediately practical. It is better served by classifying things in terms of properties which are relevant to the framing of a maximum number of causal laws and the formulation of explanatory theories. Thus a foodstuff and a mineral source of aluminum, common salt and cryolite, are both classified by the chemist as sodium compounds, because in the context of modern chemical theory it is this common characteristic which is most significant for predicting and understanding the behavior of these substances. In the sphere of scientific inquiry, the distinction between real and nominal essence tends to disappear. The scientist's classification of things is intended to be in terms of their *real* essences. And here, too, the process is reflected in vocabulary, not necessarily or even usually in that of the man in the street, but rather in the technical jargon of the specialist.

The essences which science seeks to discover, then, are real essences rather than nominal ones. Since the arguments for subjectivity or relativity to interest or vocabulary were concerned with nominal rather than real essences, they simply do not apply to real essences as either Locke or Aristotle conceived them.

In one passage of his *Essay*, though, Locke does make the further claim that even a real essence relates to a sort and supposes a species.[49] But on Locke's own account of real essence, the real essence of a particular must be that set of its properties on which all of its other properties depend. And that can be investigated independently of any sorting or classifying we may do—although once its real essence is discovered, that will determine how we should classify it scientifically if the occasion for doing so arises.

At this point let me indicate the direction in which I think the Aristotelian doctrine of essence and accident might well be modified. Aristotle definitely held that there could be no scientific knowledge of accidents,[50] but contemporary science would admit no such limitation. It seems to me that both Locke's and Aristotle's views about unknowability should be rejected. Contrary to Locke, I should hold that real essences are in principle knowable, and contrary to Aristotle,

I should hold that non-essential or accidental properties can also be objects of scientific knowledge.

It seems to me also that neither Locke nor Aristotle gives a satisfactory account of the relationship between essence and accident. For Locke, all (other) properties of a thing depend on its "real constitution" or real essence;[51] but it is not clear whether the dependence is supposed to be causal or logico-deductive. The former is obviously the more acceptable doctrine. Aristotle, on the other hand, held that some properties of a thing, namely, its accidents, do not in any way depend upon its essence. I think that Locke's view, understood as asserting a causal dependence of accident on essence, is the more plausible one, and that the Aristotelian doctrine ought to be so modified as to accord with that of Locke in this respect.

Now if both essences and accidents are scientifically knowable, on what basis are they to be distinguished from each other! I suggest that the epistemological or methodological distinction is still valid. For example, common salt has many properties, some more obvious than others, and some more important than others relative to different practical interests. The scientist singles out its being a compound of equal parts of sodium and chlorine as its essential nature. In doing so he surely does not mean to imply that its chemical constitution is more easily observed than its other properties, or more important to either cook, tailor, merchant, or lover. He classifies it as sodium chloride because, within the context of his theory, that properly is fundamental. From its chemical formula more of its properties can be inferred than could be from any other. Since the connection is causal rather than logical, the inference from essence to accident must make use of causal law premises or modes of inference as well as strictly logical ones. Hence to derive conclusions about *all* accidental properties of a substance, we should need to know both its real essence and all relevant causal laws. That is an ideal toward which science strives, rather than its present achievement, of course. To the extent to which one small group of properties of a substance can serve as a basis from which its other properties can be causally derived, to that extent we can be justified in identifying that group of properties as its real essence. This view, it should be noted, is in agreement with Aristotle's doctrine that the definition of a thing should state its essence,[52] and that definition is a scientific process.[53]

There is a certain relativity implied in this account, although it is quite different from those previously discussed. Our *notion* of what constitutes the real essence of a thing is relative to the science of our day. Centuries hence, wiser men will have radically different and more adequate theories, and their notions will be closer approximations than ours to the real essences of things. But it will still be the real essences of things that are destined to be known by Peirce's ultimate community of knowers.

There is one other and more radical sense of accident that I would agree to be relative. Bach separate science is concerned with only some of the properties or aspects of things which it studies. Those left out will be accidental relative to the special science which ignores them. They will not be derivable from what that science considers to be the real essences of those things, although a different special science might be much concerned with them, and even include them in *its* notion of the thing's real essence. But as (and if) the sciences become more unified, no properties of a thing will be wholly accidental in this sense, and all will be causally derivable from the real essence.

In closing, I should like to refer once again to the topic of change. If all of a thing's properties depend on its real essence, then it would seem to follow that every change is an essential one. In my opinion, that unwelcome conclusion can be evaded in two ways. In the first place, with respect to common-sense, practical usage, our ordinary sortings will continue to be based on nominal rather than real essences, so that changes can continue to be classified as accidental or essential in the traditional way. And in the second place, with respect to scientific usage, we can say the following. The real essence of a thing will consist very largely of powers or, in modern terms, dispositional properties. An essential change in a thing will involve the replacement of some of its dispositions or powers by other dispositions or powers. But a change which is non-essential or accidental would involve no such replacement; it would rather consist in differently actualized manifestations of the same dispositional property or power. Unfortunately, lack of space prevents an adequate development of this suggestion.

Notes

1 1028^a 37–1028^b 2. Quotations are from the Oxford translation.
2 1030^a 1.
3 1031^b 20.
4 1026^b 4; 1027^a 20, 28; 1064^b 30; 1065^a 4. Cf. also *Posterior Analytics*, 75^a 18–22.
5 75^a 28–30.
6 1033^b 33. But cf. 770^b 9–13.
7 *A Modern Introduction to Logic*, p. 433.
8 *Logic: The Theory of Inquiry*, pp. 89–90.
9 993^a 17–20.
10 *Op. cit.*, p. 138.
11 *An Analysis of Knowledge and Valuation*, p. 41.
12 Bk. 2, Ch. 27, §3.
13 *Ibid.*
14 Bk. 2, Ch. 27, §8, §9, §10, §16, §17, §23.
15 *De Anima*, 402^a 6, 415^b 8.
16 432^a 29, 434^a 22–26; cf. also *De Plantis*, 815^b 28–34.
17 432^a 30.
18 *Politics*, 1332^b 5.
19 *De Anima*, 412^a 20, 412^b 13, 415^b 10.
20 Bk. 2, Ch. 27, §1.
21 Bk. 3, Ch. 4, §19. But cf. Bk. 3, Ch. 6, §4, §5.
22 Bk. 3, Ch. 3, §15.
23 Bk. 3, Ch. 3, §15, §17, §18; Ch. 6, §3, §6, §9, §12, §18, §49; Ch. 9, §12; Ch. 10, §18.
24 Bk. 2, Ch. 23, §1.
25 Bk. 3, Ch. 3, §7.
26 Bk. 3, Ch. 3, §12.

27 Bk. 3, Ch. 3, §15.
28 Bk. 3, Ch. 6, §2.
29 Bk. 2, Ch. 27, §28.
30 Bk. 3, Ch. 11, §20.
31 Bk. 4, Ch. 6, §4.
32 Bk. 2, Ch. 23, §7.
33 Bk. 3, Ch. 3, §11.
34 Bk. 3, Ch. 3, §12, §13, §14.
35 Bk. 3, Ch. 3, §14; Ch. 6, §26, §27; Ch. 9, §16; Ch. 10, §22; Ch. 11, §6, §7.
36 Bk. 3, Ch. 6, §39.
37 Bk. 3, Ch. 6, §30.
38 *Ibid.*
39 *Ibid.*
40 Bk. 3, Ch. 6, §25.
41 *Ibid.*
42 Bk. 3, Ch. 11, §10.
43 Bk. 2, Ch. 1, §1.
44 Bk. 4, Ch. 12, §10; cf. also Bk. 4: Ch. 3, §28.
45 Bk. 3, Ch. 6, §8.
46 Bk. 3, Ch. 3, §17.
47 J. D. Main Smith, in the *Encyclopaedia Britannica*, 14th Edition, 1947, Vol. 17, p. 520
    (my italics).
48 Bk. 3, Ch. 11, §10.
49 Bk. 3, Ch. 6, §6.
50 1064^b 30–1065^a 25.
51 Bk. 3, Ch. 3, §18.
52 91^a 1, 101^b 21, 38.
53 1039^b 32.

4 Conceptual and natural necessity*

Rom Harre and E. H. Madden

I The plot

Fundamental assumptions of the Humean theory

There can be no doubt that the Humean conception of causality and its linear descendant, the Regularity Theory, must be wrong. To accept either of these doctrines is to be forced in the long run to admit the irrationality of science and to acknowledge the impossibility of accounting for the common-sense view of the world. Why has the Humean point of view continued over many centuries to attract adherents among intelligent men? The answer must surely lie in there being certain assumptions in the Humean way of thinking whose full range of consequences have never been fully examined. Just as the tiniest error in navigation may lead to a landfall even on the wrong continent, so the acceptance of apparently innocuous principles can lead to doctrines which, if accepted, would render intellectual life as we practise it, and the world as we conceive it, impossible. But for some of those for whom the Regularity Theory and its associated doctrines in philosophical logic and the philosophy of science make up an attractive point of view, these dire consequences hold no terrors. For them the construction of a conceptual system capable of accommodating the actual intellectual practices of science, and in which the known character of the world can be satisfactorily and systematically described, are not reasonable ambitions. To such a one this book can offer little. But if an adherent of the Regularity Theory and its siblings is troubled by the continual revelation of disparities between what that theory claims ought to be the case in science and nature, and what actually obtains, then we are confident that in joining us he has nothing to lose but his dogmatic scales.

The Humean or Regularity Theory of causality rejects the concept of natural necessity and offers an allegedly better theory of the world supposedly forced on everyone by inescapable argument. What we need to do to establish the propriety of the conceptual system that embraces both common sense and science, the view

*Source: Rom Harre and E. H. Madden, *Causal Powers: A Theory of Natural Necessity*, Totowa, New Jersey: Rowan and Littlefield (Basil Blackwell), 1975 (pp. 1–21).

that causes produce their effects and can be known to do so, is to show that the arguments adduced by Humeans are not inescapable. In a sense the Regularity Theory cannot be refuted, since no one would wish to deny that there are regularities in causal productions. The issue is whether there can be any good grounds for claiming anything more. And since neither science nor common-sense knowledge could possibly work the way they do if causation were no more than regular precedence, the critic of the Regularity Theory need do no more than expose the partiality of the grounds by which the theory is supported. Then the way is clear for positive construction of a system of concepts better adapted to the expression of common-sense and scientific knowledge.

We identify two fundamental assumptions of the Humean point of view, one having to do with the nature of philosophy itself, the other an assumption about the very nature of the world as we experience it. One can hardly imagine assumptions more fundamental than these. Together they lead inexorably to the Humean position. Throughout the book we shall be showing why each must be abandoned.

Since Hume, it has been assumed by philosophers in the empiricist tradition that the philosophical analysis of any non-empirical concept must be a formal explication, and that any residual features of the concept must be capable of analysis in terms of its psychological origins. The effect of this assumption has been to lead philosophers to suppose that their task is to provide an analysis of key concepts and relations wholly in terms drawn from formal logic, since relations of necessity are, on this view, fundamentally logical relations. The ambition of Humean philosophers, as of any other school, is to provide a suitable analysis of most of the concepts with which we ordinarily make sense of the world. They are, then, in the same business as any other school of philosophy, investigating such concepts as cause, law and the like. But what tends to be offered by this school, as a philosophical analysis of some concept, is a specification of the logical form of the statements in which the concept is manifested. But most important distinctions just cannot be made out by this method.

The assumption that there is an exclusive dichotomy between the formal and the psychological is, in our view, an error of enormous consequence. We shall maintain that the most important meta-scientific concepts with which philosophy deals, such as cause, law, explanation, theory, evidence, natural necessity and the like, have not been shown to be capable of adequate characterisation in wholly formal terms. We hold that adequate accounts of those concepts which are neither purely formal nor simply psychological can be achieved by attention to the third element in our intellectual economy, namely the content of our knowledge, content which goes beyond the reports of immediate experience. We shall show in a wide variety of cases that the concepts with which we are concerned, and particularly the concept of causality, can be adequately differentiated, the rationality of science defended, and the possibility of the world preserved only by attending to certain general features of the content of causal propositions by which they can ultimately be distinguished as having a conceptual necessity, irreducible either to logical necessity or to psychological illusion. In this way we resolve many of the problems which the tradition has bequeathed us.

There is a second assumption involved in the Humean tradition, an assumption about the world as we experience it. It is assumed without examination that the world as experienced can with equal facility be conceived as a system of things or as a flux of events, and that the latter assumption contains all that is present in the former without its allegedly unwarranted assumption of continuity. The ontology of science is then restricted to a world of events. The origin of this notion is obscure, but its immediate source in modern philosophy derives from Hume's opening remarks in the *Treatise* and the *Enquiry*, in which he passes from a theory about experience, namely that it comes in atomic impressions, to a view about the experienced world, namely that it too comes in atoms, but of course its atoms are events.

The assumption of the independence of successive events, and of co-existing properties, is a related and equally fundamental feature of the Humean point of view usually assumed along with the epistemological atomism explicitly advocated by Hume. It is assumed that if a material thing undergoes a sequence of changes, thus generating successive events, that these events are absolutely independent one of another, that is, that no matter what the structure of the previous succession had been, it is possible that the thing could take on any property whatever in the future. Similarly, it is assumed that no matter what properties a body has, it could, for all we can know, at any time take on simultaneously any other properties whatever. The only constraint we can maintain upon hypotheses of possible sets of co-existing properties is that deriving from the distinction between determinates and determinables in that under a given determinable only one determinate can be had at any one given time. Thus, if a thing is coloured, it can only be red, not both red and green. And this constraint upon determinates is no more than a reflection of the restrictions deriving from the principle of contradiction. A thing cannot be both red and green because the assertion of both 'red' and 'not red' of the same object at the same time is a logical contradiction.

The independence of successive events and of co-existing properties reflects a corresponding doctrine of the independence of predicates. The possible predicates of a thing can, on the Humean view, come under no other constraint than that derived from the distinction between determinables and determinates. So that if any given logical subject is known to have truly been both red and not red, this is only possible if these predications are different in time. Indeed, time might be thought to be generated by the necessity to accommodate the contingency that the same logical subject has truly predicated of it two contradictory predicates. Thus, if the only constraint upon predication is the principle of non-contradiction, we are driven to accept the doctrine of the independence of predicates. This chimes in with the underlying ontological theory of the independence of properties, which is itself a consequence of the epistemological and ontological priority assigned to events.

Throughout this volume we will be arguing against all aspects of the Humean atomistic and independence claims and in contradistinction attempting to establish an alternative analysis which makes sense of science and common sense. We think it established by the psychology of perception that Hume's doctrine of impressions is, as a matter of fact, false as an account of our experience of the world, and we hope to show that its philosophical sibling—the doctrine that the world as experienced can be adequately conceived as a sequence of atomistic and independent events—must also be rejected. We shall show that it is possible to conceive of a world of things whose interactions produce the flux of events. The system of things, of ultimate and derived individuals, is the permanent structure of the universe. Since we try to preserve the structural integrity of the universe, we are in no need of a cement to stick it together.

A conceptual system capable of expressing the scientific idea of the world as experienced

Our most central idea is that of the powerful particular. We show how in terms of that notion the citation of the presence of a particular has explanatory force. We develop a concept of natural necessity that, we claim, characterises the relation that holds between the nature of a particular and the occasion for the exercise of any of its powers, on the one hand, and the manifestation of that power in observable effects, on the other. Our conception of causality is deliberately in keeping with one of the commoner ways in which this concept is employed. In this sense, causation always involves a material particular which produces or generates something. But what may be singled out as the cause may be an event, a state of affairs, or even in certain contexts, a material substance. We acknowledge that there are occasions where it makes sense to single out the event that releases a power as the cause of that power's manifestation. There are other situations where it seems proper to refer to the particular and the event together as the cause. The latter case will prove especially useful in the analysis of many a causal nexus. But in any specific application of the notion of causality, the crucial element, we argue, the presence of which makes the action *causal*, is a powerful particular. According to this point of view, the conceptual analysis of causal notions must clearly be drawn from a wider ontology than events. Events can only be identified as having a role in a causal relation, in fact, if they can be shown either to stimulate a suitable generative mechanism to action, or to be the clearance away of impediments to the activity of a powerful particular already in a state of readiness to act. These particulars are to be conceived as causal agents, and in the course of the book we show how the concepts of causal power and causal agency can be constructed in a wholly non-anthropomorphic way.

The location of causal power or potency in things and materials need not be conceived as the attribution of occult and mysterious properties but can be given a quite unproblematic basis in the chemical, physical or genetic natures of the entities involved. The combining power or valency of a chemical atom is located in its electronic constitution and structure, and the power to resist shearing forces which a metal may have is located in its crystalline form. The re-emphasis upon the nature of things leads to a reintroduction of the concept of natural kind, exemplified in such ideas as the genotype of an organism or the subatomic structure of the atoms of an element. For us, those things and materials will be most fundamental for which we may maintain, as an empirical hypothesis, that their natures are identical with their powers. We show how the physicists' concept of the field of potential is adapted to this role.

It is through the application and development of the concepts of power, nature and generative mechanism that we show that a variety of rational constraints upon logical possibility can be constructed so as to limit our expectations as to what patterns of events are likely to be identified and what ensembles of properties the things and materials of the world are likely to manifest. From these constraints we devise a theory of natural necessity. This modality turns out to be neither a mere reflection of logical necessity nor a roundabout way of referring to empirical contingency. With the help of the concept of natural necessity—an analysis of which runs throughout the book—we dispose not only of the crucial Humean argument that in principle there can be no natural necessity since a conjunction of a description of a cause with a denial of the description of its usual effect is never self-contradictory, but also show why it is legitimate to talk about the actual perception of the action of causal powers.

Using our concepts, we systematically resolve the galaxy of epistemological problems notoriously derivative from the Humean point of view. By basing rational expectations of the future course of events upon knowledge of the natures of powerful particulars we come to see just how far we are entitled to expect inductive evidence to support our conclusions about a world in which, were our reasonable expectations defeated, we would be directed to look for changes in the natures of the things and materials involved. While natures are preserved the world must go on in its usual way.

The natural necessity in the world is reflected in a conceptual necessity in discourse about the world. Predicates are bound into ensembles by virtue of the joint origin of the properties they ascribe to things, in the natures of those things. When we think there is a natural necessity between manifested properties and hypothesised dispositions, that is, a real connection via the nature of the thing, then we are entitled to make a conceptual link, incorporating the power or tendency to manifest the property within the concept of the thing or substance.[1] And, similarly, the production of an effect by the powerful particular involved in a causal production licenses us to treat *some* appropriate description of a causally productive set-up as conceptually incorporating a description of its usual effect. But since which effects a causally efficacious set-up produces have to be discovered *a posteriori*, there must have been some description under which the causal set-up was conceptually independent of the effect. But diachronically a conceptual link is established that may, though it need not, and usually does not, involve all the descriptions under which a causally efficacious set-up may fall. In this insight we find the groundwork for a resolution of all those problems which have their origin in unthinking assumptions of the absolute independence of empirical predicates. Among the problems which can be dealt with in this way is the problem of the status of the contrapositive instance as evidence for a law, as well as the problem of the contingently time-dependent predicate which is the basis of Goodman's new riddle of induction.

We conceive our world to be an interacting system of powerful particulars. The patterns of events and ensembles of properties which they produce in their interaction upon one another give rise to the multitudinous phenomena of the world we experience. Our system provides, we believe, a thorough-going alternative to the world view and conceptual system that has dogged philosophy and interfered with science since the end of the eighteenth century.

It will even now be evident to the reader that our differences with the Humean or positivist tradition are deep. Not only are we repudiating the ontological assumptions of that tradition, but we are also going so far as to repudiate even the conception of philosophy which underlies that tradition. In our view the task of a philosopher is to devise and critically assess conceptual schemes in the service of some overall vision of the world. In this perhaps we do share common ground with the Humean, but the regularity theorist's vision of the world is so mean a thing that one can barely acknowledge it as having that status. It is partly, we suppose, a matter of the paradigm exemplars which one envisages in examining the viability of one's conceptual scheme. When we think of causality and action we look to such images as a springtime plant forcing its way upwards towards the light, as the pulsing, surging movement of the protoplasm within an amoeba, of a flash of radiation as a positron and an electron meet, of the enormous flux of electromagnetic radiation from a star, of the mobility and imaginative control of his own actions exercised by a human being, of the potent configuration of a magnetic field. For us, a billiard table is relevant to philosophy only in so far as it is conceived of as surrounded by the players, and embedded within a gravitational field.

II Conceptual and natural necessity

Conceptual necessity in statements of causality

Our fundamental contention is that the necessity that is such a striking feature of the conceptual relation between the predicates descriptive of events, things and states of affairs as causes and the predicates descriptive of their usual effects, as it is unreflectingly understood, matches a natural necessity in the relation between the states, powers and natures of those physical systems which in fact constitute the universe. In this chapter we undertake the task of exactly locating these concepts in preparation for the detailed analyses to come.

That there is a conceptual necessity involved in statements descriptive of causal relations can be brought out fairly easily. A certain colourless fluid can come under several, logically independent descriptions. By a pair of logically independent descriptions we mean two descriptions for which there are no known principles in accordance with which propositions attributing either could imply one attributing the other. But when this fluid comes under the description 'acid', part of the meaning of that description is the dispositional predicate 'can turn logwood solution red'. This may, for example, be because we have good empirical reason for thinking that the presence of an acid in dilute solution, under suitable conditions, is sufficient to turn logwood solution red. Thus we can say the acidity of the liquid is the cause of the colour change of the indicator. In this situation the predicates 'acid' and 'can turn logwood solution red' are no longer logically independent, and the causal hypothesis 'Acid solutions turn logwood solutions red' no longer a mere empirical generalisation.

One must be careful to maintain the proper grammatical form of causal statements in the course of the analysis. A causal statement relates, for example, a common noun and a predicate by a verb of causal activity. Thus: 'Acid solution *turns* logwood solution red'. One would already have conceded the Humean analysis if one treated such a proposition as having the form: 'If acid is present then logwood solution turns red'. Clearly to achieve this form the transfer of the verb of causal activity from its place as a main verb, the subject of which is the powerful particular, the acid in that solution, to a passive qualification of effect has deprived it of its sense of activity, the sense it had in the original statement. The argument offered, for example by Davidson, to support the view that causal statements relate pairs of propositions, is clearly a *petitio*, since the analysis only conveys conviction provided the Humean theory, denying activity to the acid, is assumed all along, for only on that theory can the neutralisation of the active force of the main verb be justified.

The test for whether a relation of meaning has developed between two descriptions is to ask how someone, using the predicates, would react if on some specific occasion dilute acid was mixed with logwood solution and this time the mixture failed to change colour. It seems clear to us that it would never be rational to claim both that those conditions were in fact usually sufficient to produce the colour change, and that though they had been fully present on this occasion, it just happened that no effect was produced. We believe that the concept of causality is such that the rational response to the failure of the usual conditions to produce their expected outcome may take either of two forms.

1   We admit that our original ideas as to what were the true causal conditions were faulty and, in abandoning the generalisation about the effect of acid solutions on logwood, we abandon any putative conceptual necessity between 'acidity' and 'the power to change the colour of logwood solution'.
2   Alternatively we can preserve the conceptual relation between the predicates by the claim that something had gone wrong in the aberrant case.

There are three possible hypotheses as to something going wrong on a particular occasion which would account for the deviance and preserve the necessary relation of the predicates. All three involve the *nature* of the solution under test. We might have been mistaken as to the nature of the reagent added in one of three possible ways. We might have poured the reagent out of the wrong bottle, say carelessly mistaking the caustic soda bottle for that containing dilute sulphuric acid. Or we might have picked up the bottle we had used for previous demonstrations but unbeknown to us the nature of the reagent within it had changed. It had, perhaps, attacked the glass and so been neutralised. We would say that it was no longer acidic, and so, necessarily, had lost its power to change the colour of logwood solution. Or thirdly, that though there was some acid present, and no other substance than the solvent, the solution had been so diluted that the concentration of hydrogen ions was insufficient to bring about the change.[2] This case introduces the important concept of a threshold of action. All the conditions, powerful particulars and so on may be present, and of the required nature, but the level of activity can be insufficient to bring about the action. This is the case of not pushing quite hard enough to overturn the stone, or of the pan being not quite warm enough to melt the butter.

The reasoning behind this anecdote is something like this. If the solution does not turn logwood red in the conditions in which it is usually effective, it has lost the power to do so. If it now lacks the power to do so this may be either because it has changed its chemical composition in some relevant way or because the proper threshold of activity has not been reached. In short, if it does not turn logwood red, and we have no reason to believe it has been diluted beyond the minimum effective concentration, it *cannot* be an acid. The ground for this inference is the conceptual necessity of the relation that obtains between 'acidity' and 'the power to turn logwood solution red'. In a science in a fairly advanced stage of development, the conceptual necessity would be further backed up by chemical explanations of the powers of acids.

So the failure of a normally efficacious substance to produce its usual effect is, in the absence of any indication of trouble in the surrounding conditions, explained either by the substitution of a substance of a different nature, or by a change in the nature of the original substance, or by the failure of that substance to reach the threshold level of activity.

It is worth pointing out that the conditions for action are not usually intensionally related to the powerful particulars which produce the action, that is, they form no part of its meaning. So the relation between the obtaining of those conditions and the coming to be of the effect *is* Humean. This fact may be another source of the Regularity Theory, since if the central role of the powerful particular is overlooked, and the effect is considered only in relation to the conditions of its action, that relation is extensional.

So far we have seen how causal hypotheses seem naturally to involve conceptual necessity, but the question immediately arises whether this necessity is only stipulative and conventional in character or whether it mirrors something about the nature of physical systems. The latter, we shall proceed to argue, is clearly the case if we take our ordinary ways of thinking seriously.[3] We shall show that there is no compelling reason to depart from them.

Natural necessity in causal production

To see that the conceptual necessity involved in relations between the predicates involved in causal hypotheses reflects the natural necessity of the upshot of the activities of physical systems, consider the case of a suction pump. Let us say that the pressure of the air on the reservoir and the partial vacuum in the cylinder of the pump are the conditions the obtaining of which are jointly sufficient for raising the water up the pump and out of the spigot. Ordinarily we would say that the atmosphere has the ability or power to push the water up the cylinder, which manifests itself when there is no counteracting pressure, and that the water has the liability, or disposition, to be pushed up the cylinder in the absence of air. This power or ability of the atmosphere, in turn, would be explained by referring to the nature of the atmosphere. The atmosphere is a blanket of air around the surface of the earth. Air has weight and so exerts pressure, and the farther down in the blanket of air the greater the weight of the air above, and so the greater the pressure, etc.

While the power or ability of the atmosphere to raise water is understood by referring to its nature, such reference does not explain away the power. A Reliant Scimitar GTE has the ability (is able, has the power) to do 125 mph., and this ability is explained in terms of its having six cylinders, a certain kind of fuel pump, etc.—that is, in terms of the nature of the car.[4] But such explanations in terms of the nature of the car do not lead to the elimination of the notion of 'power' in the description of the car as a potent thing, since that power is specified in terms of an effect which is not part of the description of the nature in virtue of which the power is possessed. 'Power', 'ability' and 'nature' are intimately interwoven and any effort to assign ontological priorities among them is as futile as trying to assign priorities among the concepts of particulars, properties and relations. The ineliminability of 'power' and 'ability' shows up again on the most fundamental level of explanation. At that level one can do no more than ascribe powers to individuals identified purely referentially, since there is no further level in which the nature that helps explicate that power could be found. Confining ourselves to classical physics, we would say, e.g. that the masses of the earth and the atmosphere have the power of attracting each other, but we do not know anything in the nature of the masses that explains that power.

The ineliminable but non-mysterious powers and abilities of particular things, then, are the ontological 'ties that bind' causes and effects together and are what the conceptual necessity of causal statements reflects.[5] The atmosphere *has* the power to raise the water, though it will not produce an effect unless the partial vacuum in the cylinder exists. The earth has the power of attraction which is manifested when the barn collapses, though this effect would not have occurred unless the centre beam had been removed. Furthermore, reference to the same power is equally effective in the explanation of the non-occurrence of any of certain classes of events, which the Regularity Theory must countenance as possible. It is not just a matter of fact that barns don't float off their foundations, it is, in ordinary circumstances, impossible. And that impossibility is derived from the fact that the heavy barn is in still air, within a uniform and stable gravitational field.

An important aspect of this concept of power is that it catches what might be called the strong sense of potentiality or potency, namely, 'what would happen, as a matter of course, if interfering conditions were absent or taken away'. As long as there is air in the cylinder of the pump the power of the atmosphere to raise the water is frustrated; and as long as the centre beam is intact the attraction between barn roof and earth is kept in check. But as soon as the air is removed, or the beam rots, the operation of these powers, whose constancy in the given set-up is ultimately a product of the basic structural nature of our universe, comes into play. They finally produce the effect which had been held in abeyance by interfering conditions.

For us, efficient causes comprise both the presence of stimuli which activate a quiescent individual and the absence or removal of constraint upon an individual already in a state of activity. There is an argument upon which we ourselves do not put much weight, that the latter case, if admitted as involving a genuine form of efficient causality, is itself sufficient to rebut the Humean Regularity Theory, since it is impossible to specify a regularity in terms of the regular absence of the antecedent condition, while the powerful particular to which one must refer in explanation of the causal action *was* present all along, with many other states of affairs than the final effect.

Conceptual and natural necessity in descriptions of substances

In the case of concepts used to refer to material substance, the conceptual necessity involved in causal hypotheses creeps in, in addition to the conceptual necessity built into any concept whose analysis into component predicates has definitional force. Take, for example, the apparently non-causal concept 'copper'.[6] For the scientist this term refers to something having the properties of malleability, fusibility, ductility, electric conductivity, density 8.92, atomic weight 63.54 and atomic number 29. All but the last of these properties are dispositional, ascribing powers and liabilities to the substance and hence already have a force over and above the attribution of manifest properties. But since the properties set out above serve to specify what a substance has to be, and to be capable of doing to be copper, if an entity lacked any of these properties it would not properly be called 'copper'. The ascription of that material identification to that sample at any given time necessarily implies the presence of a cluster of properties, each member of which is a necessary attribute of the substance. The reason for this latter necessity is clear. All the dispositional properties whose manifestations make up the nominal essence are explicable by reference to *the* atomic structure and hence, via that structure, connected with each other. Thus, if any of those dispositional properties were not manifested by some reddish metal, the whole conceptual framework implicit in the scientific concept of 'copper' would be vitiated and the ascription of the concept 'copper' would fail since the other properties of the linked cluster would have to be denied it. Again, this conceptual necessity, far from being merely the reflection of a stipulative definition, has important ontological implications, in that it is, in principle, possible that the atomic structure might be investigated independently of any one of the dispositional properties in the above 'definition'.

The passivity of the definitional dispositions in this example is of no significance. A concept such as 'malleability' refers to a capacity to undergo rather than an ability to do, while 'conductivity' refers to a disposition to react in certain ways under given conditions rather than a power to act in certain ways when the occasion arises. Yet the dispositional properties of malleability, fusibility and conductivity are just as much explained by the atomic structure of copper as the power of the atmosphere actively to raise water is explained by the nature of the atmosphere. Capacities just as much as powers, what particulars or substances are liable to undergo as well as what they are able to do, are explained by reference to what the thing is in itself.[7]

What particulars are liable to undergo and what they are able to do are determined by their natures since they are manifestations of their natures—and hence to talk about particulars remaining the same and yet lacking their usual capacities and powers is at once to assert and deny that a certain object or sample of material has a given nature. If we had compelling reason to believe that a certain entity had existed continuously for a certain time, during which it ceased to be malleable, then we could correctly conclude that since it had different capacities and powers at the end from those it had at the beginning of the period, it must have undergone a change in nature. We would be forced to conclude that it was no longer the particular copper it was before. It is physically impossible for a substance to act or react incompatibly with its own nature. It is not impossible for an object or sample to act and react differently at one time rather than another. But in general it *cannot* do so under the same circumambient conditions and be deemed to have remained the same substance. In short, the relation between what a thing is and what it is capable of doing and undergoing is naturally necessary. It is this natural necessity that the conceptual necessity of the ensemble of powers and liabilities ascribed by the use of a term like 'copper' reflects.

There seems, however, to be an immediate problem with this view, since some individuals do gain or lose certain capacities or powers but do not thereby lose their identity. They still have the same nature.[8] A drug may lose its effectiveness over a period of time, photographic paper will not make prints after a while, and a person may lose his capacity to remember names; but the drug, paper and person do not thereby lose their identities. This is only a *prima facie* problem, however, since such changes in powers and capacities occur in the ambit of theory which explains them. The overall theory provides a justification for the assumption of the invariable and hence continuously identical nature of an entity which continues constant throughout *certain* changes. Such a concept as 'same paper' refers to the cellulose backing rather than light-sensitive coating. Such an explanation of continued identity presupposes the nature of some relatively 'fundamental particulars', for example, chemical atoms, which are fundamental in the sense that their natures are taken as unchanging and explain the self-identity of those less fundamental particulars which are held to be identical through certain changes of powers and liabilities.

III The place of necessity in explanation and the non-necessity of worlds

The relative necessity of explanatory theories

Now let us turn our attention briefly to a preliminary analysis of the nature of scientific explanation and see what implications it has for the concept of causal necessity. Recall again the example in which the power of the atmosphere is cited in explanation of the rising of water in the cylinder of a pump. The necessity that the water will rise in the cylinder is relative to the truth of gravitational theory, we say, because that theory plus information to the effect that there is a partial vacuum in the cylinder, explains why the water *rises,* rather than, say, turns purple. If anything else than the water's rising could have happened, given our account of the set-up, we would not have succeeded in explaining why it did that rather than anything else. Conversely, we have good reason for believing that gravitational theory is true because it is indirectly and independently established by the various particular events and circumscribed laws that it conceptually unites. Hence, the necessity in a body of knowledge follows from what must be the case if the most general theory of causal efficacy in that body of knowledge is true, and we have good reason in this case for believing that gravitational theory is true.

A fundamental theory defines a world

It does not follow, however, that a general theory which explains all sorts of particular cases of causal efficacy, such as gravitational theory, is necessarily true in the sense that its meaning entails its truth. Gravitational theory is not necessarily true in that sense though its necessity in *this world* derives from the fact that it is sufficiently fundamental to be in part definitive of the nature of this world. But a world defined by our contemporary fundamental theories is not the only possible physical framework. Rather the point is that given some general theory specifying the fundamental causal powers and thereby laying down the general lineaments of a world, the necessity of certain effects can be inferred. Such effects are 'hypothetically necessary' in the sense that, given the specification of the causal powers of the things and substances of the world, the denial of statements describing these effects of those powers, when the environment allows them to be exercised, would be inconsistent with the natures of those things ascribed to them on the basis of the theory.

That the world as we conceive it, our world, is contingent

Even though this universe is not the only possible one, the unification of disparate phenomena brought about by a theory which is general enough to be taken as a specification of a universe suggests the hypothesis that that universe *is* the actual one, though, that the necessary character of the world so specified describes our world must be found out *a posteriori.* The adequacy of the theory in the sense of its power to unify disparate phenomena can be taken to mean that it reflects the nature of *this* universe. In so far as such a theory is adequate, it has the kind of conceptual necessity that reflects physical or natural necessity, since a change in the physical universe would involve a change in the nature of the particulars of that universe. Supposing such a change to occur, there would be a new universe with a new nature, described in a new adequate theory, etc. So there is a necessity corresponding to the nature of the actual, though this necessity does not imply that the actual is itself necessary in the sense that the denial of its existence would be self-contradictory.

Thus we depend upon just the same formal framework as the most ardent logicist for identifying the presence of necessitation by the appearance of an inconsistency. But we claim that what we have thus identified is a conceptual relation which is a reflection of a real relation of necessitation between a particular thing endowed with the power to produce an effect in virtue of its nature, in the absence of constraint and when properly stimulated.

IV The scientific use of the distinction between real and nominal essence

A distinction between two ranges of essential properties is required by any theory purporting to give an account of natural science which preserves its main outlines. There are those properties the manifestation of which are necessary to a thing or sample of substance being of a certain kind. We follow Locke in calling this the nominal essence of a thing or substance. We hold that nominal essences are fixed, and can be known *a priori* by an examination of the meaning given to general sortal terms in a natural science, though we acknowledge that that meaning has a history, a fact to which we shall pay considerable attention. The only empirical question relevant to nominal essences, *at some moment in time*, is whether there are any things or samples of substances falling under them. Populations change, and nominal essences cease to be exemplified in anything real. Of course, which nominal essences we think worth espousing is a product of a diachronic process of conceptual construction, guided by what properties we observe to go together, and which of these can usefully serve the practical requirements of criteria for the identification of sorts and kinds.

But the task of natural science is to investigate the nature of a thing or substance, and to test hypotheses as to the constitution of that thing or substance. The result of such investigations are *a posteriori* discoveries that, for example, the real essence or chemical nature of diamond is a tetrahedral crystal of carbon atoms. That this is the nature of diamond explains its manifest properties, and *provides the ground for the choice of criteria of individuation and identity of diamonds*. A substance continues to be diamond only while it has that nature; just as a population only continues to be rabbits while each member has just so many chromosomes, and just such a genetic inheritance. A more widely known example of the operation of the distinction between real and nominal essence in practical life is the substitution of chromosome counts for anatomical examination in determining the sex of an athlete.

Natural science still uses the distinction just as Locke set it out: 'For it is the real constitution of its insensible parts, on which depend all those properties of colour, weight, fusibility, fixedness, etc. which makes it to be gold, or gives it a right to that name, which is therefore its nominal essence'.[9] Yet, if we wish to preserve the distinction between real and nominal essence, we must note that definitions of nominal essence are very different in kind from definitions of real essence, despite a common logical form. It is clear that a statement which asserts that a substance or thing must manifest certain properties in order to be identified as a thing or substance of that sort can be laid down *a priori*. In short, that copper has the properties by which we recognise it as such is clearly an *a priori* truth, though 'copper' has an etymology, and a conceptual history. But once we have abandoned the idea that knowledge of the natural world is confined wholly to the surface appearances of things, their manifest properties and the flux of such ontologically simple things as events, changes in their manifest properties, we are obliged to conceive of another kind of definition, namely that of the real essence of things. Science, it is plain, is concerned with real essences, at least as much as it is concerned with nominal. It is part of the scientific investigation of copper to try to discover in what way it differs as a structure of sub-atomic 'particles' from other chemical elements. It turns out that there are structural differences in terms of which the various chemical elements can be differentiated and the differentia which appear in the nominal essence explained.

If this is the case, and it plainly is in chemistry, then the definitions which express the real essences of substances are to be discovered *a posteriori* and cannot be laid down *a priori*. We have to discover by an experimental technique, under our general theory of the nature of materials, what is the real essence of a particular metal or of any other chemical element. In a similar way, we can distinguish between the phenotypical specification of a natural species, in which anatomical and physiological features are used to differentiate members of that species from categories of other living creatures, from the real essence or genotype of the species which can be discovered only *a posteriori*.

It is plain that the epistemological distinction between our knowledge of each kind of essence rests upon an indisputable and rather simple historical fact, that is, that we can learn to differentiate one subject from another, successfully, without knowing at that time the underlying structure or nature of the entity which will explain the regular appearance of the differentia which we use, as it were, in the natural state. Chemistry and genetics provide the necessary underpinning to our assumptions about the viability as differentia of what predicates appear in nominal essences.

Now none of this can be found in the logical structure of definitions. From a logical point of view all definitions look exactly alike, that is, they contain a logical subject and a set of predicates which are attributed of necessity to that subject. Only by paying attention to the differing empirical status of the several predicates involved can we distinguish adequately between the kinds of definitions that appear in the natural sciences. The more adequately the co-presence of an ensemble of manifest properties is explained in terms of the nature of a thing or substance, the more inclined are we to treat the corresponding predicates as part of the meaning of the term we use for the thing or substance. Thus there is a diachronic process by which relations of meaning between predicates are established, and change.

It is worth noticing that one of the effects of making the distinctions we have made in this section is that the concepts of necessity and contingency are detached from those of the *a priori* and the *a posteriori*. It is our contention that such simple examples as the history of the study of the chemical elements shows that we are required to employ the notion of an *a posteriori* discovery of necessary relations both between properties and correspondingly between predicates in order to make sense of that history. Whether there can be *a priori* knowledge of contingent matters of fact is a matter upon which we have no opinion. We do not make any use of that notion in the course of this book.

V The modes of necessity

In the system we are constructing we recognise four modes of necessity, two conceptual and two natural. We believe that the concept of necessity is univocal, that its sense is always the same but that the contexts of and grounds for its application are very various. In each major context there are appropriate grounds for attributions of necessity. We recognise the differentiated grounds and univocal sense of the concept by speaking of 'modes' of necessity.

The meaning of an attribution of necessity

To attribute necessity to items as various as a condition, an outcome or effect, the truth of a statement, a conclusion, is, we contend, to indicate that within the relevant context no alternative to that condition, outcome, truth-value or conclusion is possible. In each context there are certain appropriate grounds upon which such a judgement is made. For instance, in the case of the outcome of a physical process, the grounds are our knowledge of the natures of the powerful particulars which are the productive agents of the effect and of the conditions within which they are then operating. In the case of the truth-value of a statement, the grounds are our knowledge of the logical form of that statement.

'Possibility' we define by reference to the range of stales, truth-values, etc. expressed in the consequent clauses of the conditionals, assertoric or counter-factual, true of some system of particulars, in virtue of the natures of those particulars. Thus, from the chemical nature of dynamite we infer 'If detonated it will explode'. Exploding then, is a possibility for dynamite. If our knowledge of its nature and the conditions of a particular sample shows that that is the only possibility, then if the antecedent is realised, it *must* explode. (If the wall is a sheer face ten metres high and there is only one break in its circumference, then an invading army without ladders or cannon, *must* enter the city there.)

The distinctions between modes of necessity

Modes of necessity attributable a priori

When the logical form of a statement is offered as the grounds for the judgement that it cannot but be true we have logical necessity. When the conditions for a rational being having knowledge of the nature of a world are offered as the grounds for the judgement that such a world must have certain characteristics, we have transcendental necessity. These modes of necessity have some colour of universality about them, though we believe transcendental necessity to be a more stringent concept than logical necessity since it is not the case that a rational being could have knowledge, or even exist, in all possible worlds. For a strict Humean, logical possibility and the possibility of experience are in perfect match. Both these modes of necessity can be attributed *a priori*, since the grounds for an attribution of logical necessity are the logical forms of statements, and the grounds for the attribution of transcendental necessity are the meanings of such concepts as 'experience', 'rational being', 'world' and the like.

Modes of necessity attributable a posteriori

When the natures of the operative powerful particulars, the constraining or stimulating effect of conditions and so on are offered as the grounds for the judgement that a certain effect cannot but happen, or cannot but fail to happen, we have natural necessity. When the probability of its happening falls within a certain range, we have the natural necessity of a range or function of probabilities. This is clearly attributable to the outcomes of the action of a system of particulars only *a posteriori*.

When the discovery of natural necessity is used as the basis for the inclusion or exclusion of the appropriate predicate in the meaning of a concept of a kind of particular, then that that kind of particular has the property or power to produce the effect so attributed is conceptually necessary. The development of the meaning of a concept is a diachronic process, absorbing or excluding predicates in response to discoveries about the natures of things and substances and the conditions for their activity or inactivity. Thus the mode of necessity for a component of meaning cannot be decided by the fact that it is revealed by a synchronic conceptual analysis, since reference to the history of the concept is necessary to determine how far it has developed its meaning in response to empirical discovery. We are unable to offer a clear cut boundary condition to differentiate some cases of transcendental necessity from some cases of conceptual necessity. For example, we do not think one can decide at all readily how far the concept of time reflects the temporal experience of mankind and how far its form and content are transcendentally necessary to a world capable of being understood by any rational being.

In each mode we recognise, we have attributed necessity to an entity, state or property; to a statement, outcome, nature of a world or thing and so on. But philosophers speak too of certain relations being necessary, particularly entailment, a relation between propositions. We are convinced that this use of the apodeictic modality is appropriate only in the case of logical necessity where it is the statement of the entailment that cannot but be true. Notoriously, the conclusion of most splendid entailments are only too often themselves false. But in the other modes, it is, for example, the inherence (presence within) of a property that is necessary, not the relation between that property and the thing, whatever that might be, though, of course, the proposition which states that the object has that property is, or may be, conceptually necessary.

The inter-relations of the modes

What of the relations between these modes of necessity? Clearly, whatever is logically necessary must be reflected in a corresponding transcendental necessity. But there are a great range of transcendental necessities which are not reflected in any logical necessity. For example, that no thing may be in two places at once clearly depends upon current relations between the concepts of thing, space and time, and is certainly not a property of all logically possible worlds.

Though our discovery of the natural necessity of the production of some effect by a system of powerful particulars is a common ground for the incorporation of the power to produce that effect in the concept of those particulars, we may hold to conceptual necessities which are groundless in reality, and there are certainly many natural necessities which, being so far unknown, could not be reflected in meanings. And since our knowledge of natural necessities is *a posteriori*, we may be mistaken about them and have incorporated meanings into our conceptual system in response to wholly or partly mistaken ideas about some natural process. For example, in its original meaning, the word 'malaria' reflected a mistaken view as to the nature of the productive process of the disease.

VI The true history of 'Copper'

We have argued that in the two contexts of natural necessity, the inherence of essential properties in a thing or substance and causal production, *a posteriori* discoveries about the natures of things and the means of causal production are in certain conditions reflected in the establishment of meaning relations between the corresponding predicates. The conditions under which this occurs relate the two contexts. When discoveries about the nature of a thing or substance explain and justify our holding that certain properties are its nominal essence, that is, are the set of properties by which we recognise it as a thing of a certain kind, then the diachronic process of meaning development creates a genuine conceptual necessity. And when the discoveries about the means of causal production make clear the role of the appropriate powerful particular in that production, and the nature of that particular enables us to claim the necessity of just such an outcome of the productive process, then the concept of that particular can legitimately be allowed to come to include the power to produce just those effects.

However, convincing this account may be as a possible theoretical account of the origin of necessary connections between empirical concepts, in order to establish it we must show that it makes sense of an actual case of conceptual development. So we turn to an account of the actual history of a substance concept, 'copper'.

As Crosland points out,[10] the metals seem to have been first distinguished by their sensible qualities, and their 'names' were little more than succinct expressions of their nominal essences, there being no theory according to which hypotheses as to real essences could be devised. 'One of the Aryan words for copper, "roudhos" is said to mean red'. Even sonority could be used as a distinguishing quality as in Geber's use of the term *plumbum stridens* for tin, which creaks when bent.

The first clear case of a theory about the nature of metals affecting metal terms appears 'in medieval alchemy where the relationship between the metals and the planets was so intimate that the names of the planets were used as synonyms for the names of metals.... Occasionally the names of metals were entirely replaced by the names of planets'.[11] Thus in the works of Origen, copper appears as 'Mars'. The later, more common name 'Venus' for the metal seems to derive from the guardianship which that goddess was supposed to exercise over Cyprus, the island from which copper, 'aes cyprium' gets its English name. It is perhaps entertaining to note that Boerhaave, mistakenly supposing that natural necessity followed from conceptual necessity, and not, as we insist, the other way round, took the occurrence of O, the symbol for gold, in ♀ the Venus symbol, to show that copper contained gold.

One of the clearest statements of a hypothesis as to the real essence of copper is to be found in the works of Paracelsus, where he says:

> Copper is generated of a purple sulphur, a redish salt, and a yellow mercury. These three colours if they be mingled among themselves, then Copper is produced. But Copper doth contain in itself its female, that is its dross or refuse; which is separated by Art, and the body reduced, then the male doth appear. But this is the nature of them both, that the male doth not suffer itself again to be destroyed, and the female doth not any more send forth dross or scorias, and they are different in their fusion and malleability, as Iron and Steel differ. And also if this separation be used, either of them being severed into its nature, there do arise two Metals, different one from another in essence, species, kind and propriety. And further saith, that though commonly the male and female go together, yet they ought to be separated.[12]

Webster, writing in 1671, and quoting Paracelsus, offers the following account of copper, which gives first its nominal essence and then a brief description of its real essence in Paracelsian terms, together with the empirical evidence in favour of that hypothesis.

> Aes or Copper (which was so called from the Isle of Cyprus, where it was first gotten in great plenty) is a metallick body, participating of a fuscous or darkish redness, being ignible, and fusible, and is as the mean betwixt Gold and Silver; and is generated of *Argent vive,* impure, not fixt, earthy, burning, red, not clear, and of such a sulphur, it wants fixation, purity, and weight.
>
> And *Casalpinus* tells us that it differs from both Gold and Silver because it does not bear the trial of fires as they do, but is universally burnt; from whence it is noted to contain much of combustible exhalation, for above the metals it yieldeth a sulphurous smell and flame.[13]

Wilson's description of 1709 is on identical lines. '*Venus* or *Copper* is a metalline Body, Foul, Imperfect, and Generated of an Impure *Mercury;* Its Sulphur is Earthy, Combustible, and of an obscure Red, it wants Fixation, Purity and Weight, but if handled by an Expert Artist, is of great use both for Internal and External Médecines'.[14]

But by 1796, confidence in the chemical theories that had allowed the development of hypotheses about real essences had all but evaporated. Nicholson's definition is of the nominal essence only. 'Copper', he says, 'is a metal of a peculiar reddish brown colour; hard, sonorous, very malleable, and ductile, of considerable tenacity, and of moderate specific gravity'.[15] And in the first half of the nineteenth century, the situation remained substantially the same, Dalton's atoms being generally taken non-realistically. Thomson's immensely influential *System of Chemistry* of 1817, after providing a general classification of the elements into simple supporters of combustion, simple incombustibles and simple combustibles, on the basis of a rather feeble caloric theory, slid back into a nominal essence account:

1   This metal is of a fine red colour, and has a great deal of brilliancy. Its taste is styptic and nauseous, and the hands, when rubbed for some time on it, acquire a peculiar and disagreeable odour.
2   It is harder than silver ...
3   Its malleability is great ...
4   When heated to ... 1450 °F it melts ...
5   Copper is not altered by water ...[16]

Even in 1855, still four years before Cannizaro's memoir, purely nominal essence accounts are given:

Copper possesses several excellent properties, which have rendered it an exceedingly useful metal.

a   It is ductile ... *strong* and *tenacious* ...
b   It *fuses with difficulty* ...
c   When exposed to air, it *suffers from rust much less* than iron ...
d   It is tolerably hard ...
e   With zinc, tin and nickel, it forms very useful *alloys* ...
f   It is precipitated from its solutions by the galvanic current ...
g   It yields with oxygen and several acids ... a beautiful green and blue colour, of various application in painting.[17]

But by 1872, with the atomic theory thoroughly established in chemistry, a brusque but adequate reference to real essence appears:[18]

COPPER

	symbol	weight
Atom	Cu	63.5/Density = 8.9

coupled with a traditional outline of the nominal essence of the metal: 'Copper is the only metal of a red colour. It is highly malleable and ductile, and an excellent conductor of heat and electricity', since at that time, the causal relations between the two essences were unknown.

In 1972, so fully articulated is the corpus of theory and observation, including both real and nominal essences and all the chemical and physical reactions of the metal, that Cotton and Wilkinson content themselves with a purely real essence exegesis of the concept of copper: 'Copper', they say, 'has a single electron outside the filled 4d shell but cannot be classed in Group I, since it has little in common with the alkalis'.[19]

There are thus a multiplicity of explications of the concept 'copper': as a red, easily worked metal; a mixture of sulphur, mercury and salt; a collection of atoms each sixty-three and a half times the weight of a hydrogen atom; and, finally a collection of atoms each with a definite and identical internal structure. It is our view that these explications disclose substantially different meanings of the concept, limited by a core of identity in the nominal essence, and the changes so disclosed are the product of *a posteriori* discoveries as to the nature of copper.[20]

Notes

1 S. L. Godlovitch was helpful on this point.
2 Our attention was drawn to this case by S. L. Godlovitch.
3 Cf. Sterling Lamprecht, *The Metaphysics of Naturalism*, Appleton-Century-Crofts, New York, 1967, 129–45.
4 M. R. Ayers, *The Refutation of Determinism*, Methuen, London, 1968, 84 ff.
5 Lamprecht, *op. cit.*, 141.
6 Professor Ducassc's favourite example.
7 For an analysis similar to ours, of power, capacity and liability statements, see D. M. Armstrong, *A Materialist Theory of the Mind*, Routledge and Kegan Paul, London, 1968, 86.
8 M. R. Ayers, *op. cit.*, 84–9.
9 J. Locke, *Essay Concerning Human Understanding*, III, 3, 18.
10 M. Crosland, *Historical Studies in the Language of Chemistry*, Heinemann, London, 1962, 68.
11 *Ibid.*, 80.
12 Paracelsus, *De Mineralibus*, 1, 349.
13 J. Webster, *An History of Metals*, London, 1671, 235.
14 G. Wilson, *A Compleat Course of Chymistry*, London, 1709, 64.
15 W. Nicholson, *The First Principles of Chemistry*, London, 1796, 217.
16 Thomas Thomson, *A System of Chemistry*, London, 1817, 442.
17 J. A. Stöckhardt, *The Principles of Chemistry*, London, 1855, 296–7.
18 G. Wilson, *Inorganic Chemistry,* London and Edinburgh, 1872, 399.
19 F. A. Cotton and G. Wilkinson, *Advanced Inorganic Chemistry*, Wiley, New York, 1972, 903–4.
20 This point has been greatly clarified by W. I. Matson, 'How Things Are What They Are', *The Monist*, 56 (1972), 234–49. An early version of this theory is due to Whewell, *The Philosophy of the Inductive Sciences* (1847), Johnson Reprints, London and New York, 1967, vol. I, ch. 2, sect. 4.

5 Powers and dispositions*

Brian Ellis

Introduction

Essentialism presents a view of reality that is very different from that of any kind of passivism. Essentialists believe that:

a   inanimate matter is not passive, but essentially active;
b   the actions of things depend on their causal powers and other dispositional properties;
c   dispositional properties are genuine properties, and intrinsic to the things that have them;
d   the essential properties of things always include dispositional properties;
e   elementary causal relations involve necessary connections between events, namely between the displays of dispositional properties and the circumstances that give rise to them;
f   the laws of nature describe the ways that members of natural kinds are logically required (or are necessarily disposed) to act, given their essential natures and
g   the laws of nature are metaphysically necessary, because anything that belongs to a natural kind is logically required (or is necessarily disposed) to behave as its essential properties dictate.

These are all highly controversial theses that are anathema to most philosophers. Those I call "Humeans" would argue that:

a   inanimate matter is essentially passive, never intrinsically active;
b   things behave as they are required to by the laws of nature;
c   the dispositional properties of things (including their causal powers) are not real properties, and are never intrinsic to the things that have them;
d   the essential properties of things never include any dispositional ones;
e   causal relations are always between logically independent events;

*Source: Brian Ellis, *The Philosophy of Nature: A Guide to the New Essentialism*, Montreal and Kingston: McGill–Queen's University Press, 2002, Chapter 4.

f the laws of nature are universal regularities imposed on things whose identities are independent of the laws and

g the laws of nature are contingent, not necessary.

Evidently, many of the disagreements between essentialists and others hinge on their different conceptions of dispositional properties. Essentialists believe that there are genuine dispositional properties in the world, which are inherent in the things that have them. Passivists do not believe this, and are reductionist about dispositional properties. That is, they say that such "properties" are not real properties, and may be reduced to non-dispositional (i.e. categorical) properties and laws of nature. The root cause of this disagreement can be traced back to an even more fundamental one about the sources of power and activity in the world.

The dead world of mechanism

From the perspective of seventeenth- and eighteenth-century mechanism, the objective world is not intrinsically active. It is a world, according to Burtt, that is "hard, cold, colourless, silent, and dead; a world of quantity, a world of mathematically computable motions in mechanical regularity" (1932: 237). Descartes, Locke and Newton certainly believed something like this, as did most of their eighteenth-century followers. For Descartes, the essence of matter was just extension. It occupied space, and therefore had essentially only the attributes of things *vis-à-vis* their extension in space: shape, size and so on. For Boyle, Locke and Newton, the qualities inherent in bodies were just the primary qualities, namely number, figure, size, texture, motion and configuration of parts, impenetrability and, perhaps, body (or mass). If things with the same primary qualities were nevertheless different, then this difference must be due to differences in the primary qualities of, spatial relations between, or motions of, their elementary parts.

The qualities by which things are known to us are the qualities of experience: their colour, taste, warmth, odour, feel and so on. These qualities are known to us by the sensory ideas to which they give rise. Locke calls the powers that produce these sensory ideas the "secondary qualities". According to Locke (1690), these powers are not really inherent in the objects as they are in themselves. In themselves, the objects of experience have only the primary qualities. Nor can the sensory ideas be supposed to resemble, in any way, the powers of the objects to induce them in us, for these powers must be supposed to be grounded solely in the primary qualities of the insensible parts of these objects, which are of an altogether different character from any of the ideas they furnish.

Locke distinguished two kinds of powers: active and passive. The active ones are the powers of things to *make* changes; the passive ones are the abilities of things to *receive* changes (Locke 1690: 234). God, he supposed, had only active powers. Inanimate things, he speculated, may have only passive ones. If this is right, then created spirits, such as ourselves, would be the only things to have both active and passive powers. When we exercise our free will in some voluntary action, we certainly display an active power, according to Locke. Hence, there is no doubt, he thought, that human beings, *qua* created spirits, have active powers. But also, when we perceive anything we display our capacity to be affected by it. So it is evident that, *qua* created spirits, we also have passive powers.

The question of importance in the present context is whether active powers exist in inanimate nature. What Locke believed about this is a question of scholarship that need not concern us. But certainly a great many seventeenth- and eighteenth-century mechanists did believe in the complete passivity of inanimate nature. If one object seems to affect another, for example crash into it and so cause it to move, then what is involved is not so much an *action* on the part of the first body as a *passion*. As Locke explained:

> A Body at rest affords us no *Idea* of any *active Power* to move; and when it is set in motion it self, that Motion is rather a Passion, than an Action in it. For when the Ball obeys the stroke of a Billiard-stick, it is not any action of the Ball, but a bare passion: Also when by impulse it sets another Ball in motion, that lay in its way, it only communicates the motion it had received from another, and loses in it self so much, as the other received; which gives us but a very obscure *Idea* of *active Power*, which reaches not the Production of the Action, but the Continuation of the Passion.
>
> (1690: 235, original emphasis)

Perhaps the mathematician Leonhard Euler adequately represents mid-eighteenth-century views on causal powers. In his *Letters to a Herman Princess* (1795), written in the early 1760s, he addressed at length the question of what kinds of powers exist in the world, and what their sources are (Vol. 1, 295–340). He argued, as Locke had speculated, that the powers existing in inanimate nature are all essentially passive. Indeed, he thought that the powers necessary for the maintenance of the changing universe would turn out to be just the passive ones of inertia and impenetrability. There are no active powers, he argued, other than those of God and living beings. Consequently, if the mechanist's world-view is correct, the myriad changes that we see occurring around us must all be consequential upon the inertial motions of things, and their mutual impenetrabilities. The so-called forces of nature, for example gravitational attraction, may describe the ways in which things are *disposed* to behave *vis-à-vis* each other. There is no doubt that things are disposed to accelerate towards each other as the laws of gravity and motion require. But the source of that disposition, he argued, is not an attractive force emanating from the bodies, or just a natural tendency of bodies to move according to the dictates of some pre-established harmony, as Leibniz believed, but an impulsion of one thing towards another produced by some kind of tension in the ether. When the nature of this process is fully understood, Euler supposed, the planetary motions, and gravitational accelerations generally, would all be seen to be the passive consequences of inertia and mutual impenetrability.

Plausible as some of the mechanists' arguments for this conclusion may have been, it is to be argued here that this is a radically incorrect view of the nature of reality. The real world is essentially active and interactive. It is not passive, as the old mechanists believed, and the neo-mechanists of today also believe. It is dynamic. And its dynamism stems from the existence of genuine causal powers in things, both active and passive. Locke, Euler and the other mechanists of the period all believed in the essential passivity of nature. But they were wrong, or so I shall argue. The inanimate world is not passive, as they believed. Material things do have causal powers, which, in appropriate circumstances, they will exercise; and these causal powers are real occurrent properties of the things in question.

Scientists today certainly talk about inanimate things as though they believed they had such powers. Negatively charged particles have the power to attract positively charged ones. Electrostatic fields have the power to modify spectral lines. Sulphuric acid has the power to dissolve copper. The question we have to consider in this chapter is what is the source of these powers? The old mechanist view was that *things* do not *themselves* have causal powers. The powers lie outside them. They are contained in the forces that act externally on things to change their states of motion or aggregation.

Forces as external to objects

The mechanists of the seventeenth and eighteenth centuries all believed in the mechanical nature of change. That is, they thought that all changes must ultimately be just changes of position, or changes in the states of motion of things. If a thing changes shape, for example, then its parts must change their positions in relation to one another. If it explodes, then its parts have been caused somehow to become rapidly separated, and consequently move rapidly away from each other. If a thing changes colour, it was supposed, then this too must ultimately be due to some change in the arrangement of its parts. And similarly for any other change that might occur. The elementary parts of things were all thought to be rigid and unchanging, and to be distinguished from each other only by their shapes, sizes and the like. But these ultimate constituents of matter, they thought, could not change. So all changes, it was supposed, must consist of only changes in the arrangements or motions of these most elementary things.

Forces were postulated as elementary causal links between things for the purpose of explaining the changes that take place. The forces were not, however, thought to change the elementary things themselves, but only how they move or are arranged, for the identities of the elementary things were considered to be independent of the forces that operate on them, and the forces were always thought to be external to objects on which they directly impinge. So the picture was one of intrinsically rigid bodies being pushed or pulled around by the forces of nature acting on them. Even the forces of cohesion, which hold the parts of bodies together, were considered to be really external. They might be internal to the bodies themselves, but they are external to the parts of the bodies on which they directly operate.

Given this conception of reality, it is clear that the forces are the sources of all power and order in the world, and that these are supposed to exist externally to the things they affect, just as in the divine command theory. Thus passivism is a natural consequence of mechanism. Change the forces, or change the laws of nature so that new forces may come to act between things, and the same elementary things will be disposed to behave in different ways. The dispositions of things must therefore all depend ultimately on the underlying structures of the elementary things of which they are composed, and on the laws of nature that determine what forces there are, and how they operate on these most elementary things. This, with perhaps a few concessions to modernity, is the doctrine known as "categorical realism".

Mechanists assumed the identities of things to be independent of any forces they may be said to generate. Indeed, the most widely accepted view was that inanimate things could not generate any forces at all, for that would imply that they had active powers, which, by their inanimate nature, they could not possess. Yet things do at least appear to have some active powers, and various kinds of forces (e.g. gravitational, electric and magnetic) were recognized. Consequently, the natural philosophers of the period all used the language of active causal powers quite freely in their descriptions of inanimate nature, even it they believed that these powers were ultimately not active, but passive. If pressed, they would say that the powers were not really inherent in the objects that seemed to possess them, but were dependent on their ultimate constitutions, and on the laws of nature, which were universally supposed to be external to them.

For these reasons, causal powers, and forces generally, were regarded as occult. Hume went so far as to deny that there existed in nature anything other than the regular patterns of behaviour that explanations in terms of forces were intended to explain; and when we speak of causes, he said, it is really only to such regularities that we can be referring.

Consequently, propositions attributing causal powers to things have long been regarded with suspicion. And this suspicion applies not only to active causal powers (those which are not obviously dependent on the actions of God or man), but also to the passive ones, for the two go together. For every passive causal power – that is, power to *receive* change – which is ever exercised by anything, there must be an active causal power – power to *make* changes – to which it is responding. Consequently, if one kind of power is suspect, then so is the other. If the power to produce a change is no more than an invariable disposition of something to behave in a certain way in certain circumstances, then the power to receive change can be no more than an invariable disposition of something to respond in a certain way in these circumstances. But such invariable dispositions are not thought to be real properties of the things in question. The real properties are just the underlying structures to which the laws of nature may be supposed to apply.

Dispositions and causal processes

Information about the dispositions of things tells us about what they are likely to do, or how they are likely to react, in various kinds of circumstances. It is, therefore, information about how things affect, or are affected by, things. Most dispositions that are discussed in the literature are concerned with causal relations between two or more things, although there are some dispositions, such as that of a radioactive substance to decay, that are not. Water-solubility, toxicity and brittleness are often cited as examples in the literature. Each of these dispositions is concerned with a kind of causal process, and may be identified with a kind of causal power or capacity or liability, depending on point of view, and on what role in the process it is seen as having. Thus, if something is water-soluble, then it has the capacity to dissolve in water. If it is toxic, then ingesting it may well cause one to become ill or die. If it is brittle, then, if it is given a sharp shock, or otherwise handled roughly, it is liable to shatter or snap. Each of these is a disposition of something to act or react in a certain kind of way. It is also a disposition that can be expected to be displayed in certain kinds of circumstances. The circumstances in which a disposition would be displayed are called the "triggering" circumstances.

The distinctions between causal powers, capacities, propensities, liabilities and so on, which appear to name different species of dispositions, are difficult to make, and of doubtful philosophical significance. What we think of as a causal power occupies the role of driving force in a causal relation. But many dispositions that we think of as causal powers might equally well be regarded as capacities (a term that is more or less neutral between activity and passivity), or even as liabilities. If causal powers are dispositions to affect other things in certain kinds of ways, then liabilities are dispositions to be affected by other things. If something is brittle, for example, then it is liable to break. But not all causal processes are as straightforwardly directed as some of these standard examples suggest, and in many cases it is much more natural to think of the causal processes involved as causal interactions, where each participant may be thought to be both active and reactive. Water-solubility, for example, is as much a power as a liability. It can be thought of as the power of the substance to dissolve into the water. Or, equivalently, it can be regarded as a liability to be dissolved by it. Clearly, both solute and solvent have some kind of causal power or capacity in relation to the other, even though there is no clear direction of causal influence.

This much is all more or less common ground, but philosophers disagree strongly about how the dispositions of things are to be explained, for they have different theories of causation; and how one thinks about dispositions depends largely on how one thinks about causal relations. For Newtonians, and other mechanists, a causal relation is one that is mediated in a certain way by the action of forces between two states of affairs. Therefore, given this conception of causation, the dispositions of things must depend on what forces exist, and how they act. If the laws of nature were different, and different forces consequently existed, then the dispositions of things would also be different. For Hume, and for all latter-day Humeans, an instance of causation is just an instance of a universal regularity of some kind. Therefore, if the laws of nature were different, and the regularities that existed were consequently different, the dispositions of things would no longer be the same. For essentialists, however, the dispositions of things depend on the intrinsic causal powers or capacities of their most basic constituents, and on how these constituents are arranged. Consequently, the dispositions of things cannot be varied, except by changing their constitutions in some way, so that they cease to be things of the kinds they are.

The kinds of dispositions that are named in English, and in other languages, often refer to clusters of causal processes that are grouped together by us as having similar effects. For example, many different kinds of things may be said to be fragile, and this dispositional term may he applied to almost anything that is easily destroyed or broken. Thus we have fragile vases, parchments, spiders' webs, ecosystems and personalities. But no one imagines that things of these diverse kinds have a genuine common property of fragility. There are, in fact, many different properties or structures that make for fragility, and they are mostly very different from one another. This being the case, it is implausible to suppose that the predicate "… is fragile" names a real property. In general, one must always be careful not to be too influenced by the occurrence of a common name. A common name may signify a common reason for interest, or a similar evaluation of something. But it is not, in itself, good evidence for the existence of a common property.

But not all dispositions of the kinds that we can name in our language are like fragility. Many of them are due to genuinely similar properties. Acids, for example, have something in common in virtue of which they are acidic. Alkalis have something in common in virtue of which they are alkaline. Electrons have something in common in virtue of which they have the same power to generate electromagnetic fields. In each case, the things classified together as being of the same kind are so classified because they have the same or similar causal powers. All electrons have the same capacity to generate electromagnetic fields. All acids have a similar capacity to supply protons in chemical reactions.

Essentialists argue that these causal powers are genuine properties, or kinds of properties. The charge on an electron, they say, is a genuine property of the electron, and not a property that it happens to have just because of its non-dispositional properties, and what the laws of nature happen to be. The acidity of a solution, they say, is a genuine property of that solution, and acidity in general is a kind of property that is shared by many different substances. Moreover, acidity is not a property that could be changed just by changing the laws of nature. For the same substances, they would argue, would be acidic in any world in which they might exist. Essentialists call such properties as charge and acidity "dispositional properties", because they are properties whose identities depend on what they dispose their bearers to do.

The dispositional properties that exist in nature are all associated with natural kinds of causal processes. To say that an object has a specific dispositional property is to say that it is intrinsically disposed to participate in natural causal processes of the kind that are associated with that specific property. To say that is has some generic dispositional property is just to say that it is intrinsically disposed to participate in causal processes of the generic kind associated with that generic property. It is plausible, therefore, to think of a dispositional property as a relationship (of potential instantiation) between an object (its bearer) and a natural kind of process (the kind of causal process involved in its display).

In classical Greek metaphysics, properties were thought of as universals that are instantiated in the things that have these properties. In modern essentialist metaphysics, dispositional properties are dynamic universals (i.e. natural kinds of processes) that are potentially instantiated in the things that have these dispositional properties. But more on this later.

Categorical and dispositional properties

There is an important distinction in the literature between categorical properties and dispositions. Categorical properties are thought of as properties that things may have independently of how they may be disposed to behave: they are considered to be essentially non-dispositional. Dispositions, on the other hand, are supposed to be essentially dependent on how things are disposed to behave in various possible circumstances. So there is, apparently, a sharp distinction between the two kinds of properties. However, it is not entirely clear which properties are dispositional and which are not, for every property must be capable of manifesting itself to us in some way or other; otherwise we could never know about it. It is easier to say what categorical properties are not, than what they are, for whatever they are, they are not causal powers or capacities of any kind, because causal powers and capacities are all essentially dispositional. That is, their identities depend on the kinds of circumstances in which they would be displayed, and how they would be displayed in each of these kinds of circumstances. The categorical properties, on the other hand, are thought to be properties of a different kind, which are intrinsically different from each other, and whose identities depend on *what* they are, rather than on how they dispose their bearers to behave. The Lockean primary qualities of shape and size, for example, and also the various structural properties of things, are often cited as examples of categorical properties.

The so-called categorical properties all have this at least in common: they are readily imaginable. Things having these properties can always be pictured or drawn, and if different colours are used for different substances, then complex structures of atoms or molecules of different kinds can also be represented in our imaginations. So it is easy to think that such structures might exist independently of any patterns of behaviour by which they might be known. Dispositions, on the other hand, cannot be pictured, except in action. There are not enough visually distinguishable colours in the rainbow for us to use a distinctive colour for each distinct dispositional property.

Categorical properties are also, in a sense, multi-dimensional. All of the exemplary categorical properties may be pictured as structures in two or more dimensions. Other properties, such as refractivity, elasticity, magnetic permeability, heat capacity, torsion modulus and the like, which cannot be so pictured, are generally considered to be dispositional. Because these properties are one-dimensional, the differences between them do not depend on any *imaginable* differences between states of affairs. Pictures of things differing from each other in respect of these various properties might all *look* exactly the same (although the view through two things of different refractive index might look a bit different).

We might be able to distinguish between them in our imaginations by using some colouring or shading conventions. But this would clearly be highly artificial. One may be inclined to suppose that the same must be true of all intensive magnitudes. But temperature differences may clearly be regarded as categorical differences, since the different states of agitation of the molecular structures are easy enough to picture.

The distinction between dispositional and categorical may thus appear to be very superficial, for what is able to be pictured or imaginable is hardly what counts in ontology, and if this were the only basis for the distinction, then there would not be much of a case for it. However, there are independent reasons for thinking that structural properties are different from non-structural ones. First, there are "block structures". Block structural properties are properties that depend on relations between things that have identities independently of these relations. They are properties that exist if and only if the constituent things exist and are related in the appropriate ways. A molecular structure, for example, is a block structure. It exists if and only if the constituent atoms of this structure exist and are related in the appropriate manner for this molecular structure. Moreover, these atoms themselves have block structures that exist if and only if there are subatomic particles that are related in the manner appropriate for atoms of these kinds. Now these block structural properties are clearly not just dispositional. It may be true that an atomic or a molecular structure of a given kind exists if and only if there is some atom or molecule that is disposed to behave in a certain way in appropriately specified conditions. But this is not what makes it an atom or molecule of this kind. Its essence is structural, not dispositional. It is, of course, only from the behaviour of an atom or molecule that we can infer its structure. But the structure exists independently of its disposition to behave in this way.

Secondly, there are intrinsic structures. These are the structures of fields, of the quantum vacuum, of space-time and so on. These structures are not made up of parts that are capable of independent existence, as the block structures are. Nevertheless, there is a clear sense in which they are structures, for they are all spatiotemporal distributions of (statistical) causal powers (in the broad sense in which this term is here being used). To take a classic example, the electromagnetic field, which is described by Maxwell's equations, is an intrinsic structure of electric and magnetic potentials. A knowledge of these equations, and of the boundary conditions of a given field, enables us (in principle) to determine the magnitudes, directions and spatiotemporal distributions of electrical and magnetic forces that would operate in this field. But the parts of this structure are incapable of existing independently of it. And the same is true generally of all intrinsic structures. They are dispositional property structures.

It is reasonable to accept, therefore, that there is an important distinction between categorical and dispositional properties, although this view is not generally shared by essentialists. The categorical properties are structural, I want to say, in one or other of these two senses, and their essences are not dispositional. The dispositional properties are not structural, however, and their essences lie in the dispositions they sustain.

However, if this is the correct basis for the distinction between categorical and dispositional properties, then the categorical properties in nature must all be ontologically dependent on the dispositional ones, and on the spatial, temporal or other relations that may exist between things whose essential properties are purely dispositional. In other words, the basis for the distinction between categorical and dispositional properties implies that dispositional properties and structural relations are ultimately fundamental.

Categorical realism

Probably the most widely accepted theory of dispositions is "categorical realism", for this is the only theory of dispositions that passivists can readily accept. Categorical realists believe that the fundamental properties of nature are all categorical, and that the dispositional properties of things all supervene on their categorical ones. The dispositional properties, they argue, all depend on the laws of nature, which tell us how things in nature are naturally disposed to behave. The things themselves, they say, must be entirely neutral about this. They cannot, by their own natures, be required to act in one way rather than another, because it is the prerogative of the laws of nature to determine how they must behave. On the other hand, the things in nature cannot be entirely lacking in properties, unless one can believe in "bare particulars". So the intrinsic properties of things in nature must all be categorical. They cannot have any dispositional properties essentially.

It is plausible to suppose that categorical realists take this position on dispositional properties mainly because an ontology of primitive dispositional properties must be incompatible with passivism, for to believe that the most fundamental properties in nature are dispositional rather than categorical is to believe that things in nature are essentially active and reactive. It is to accept an ontology of causal powers, capacities and propensities, rather than one that is passive, as Locke's and Hume's ontologies were.

But the reasons for belief in categorical realism are really much more complicated than this. It is not just a one-step inference from passivism, for categorical realism is just one aspect of a very large complex of more or less consistent views about the nature of reality – one that has been thoroughly investigated by philosophers over the centuries, and holds a special place in Western philosophy. It is the established metaphysic of our culture. It embraces the whole system of beliefs described at the beginning of this chapter, and many others besides. It is the metaphysical position that I call "Humeanism", not because Hume invented it, but because he probably did more than anyone else to articulate it.

One aspect of Humeanism that is important in this context is its strong commitment to the contingency of the laws of nature: to the thesis that these laws could have been other than they are. This is now generally known as the "contingency thesis". The contingency thesis has a very long history, for it was already implicit in the divine command theory that was widely accepted in the Middle Ages. If God makes the laws of nature, as theists of those times generally believed, then God can unmake them, or change them. They are, after all, supposed to be at His command. Indeed, if God could not change the laws of nature at will, then He could not perform miracles either, and to say that would be heresy.

The contingency thesis is not, however, basically a theological doctrine, and it easily survived both the scientific revolution of the seventeenth century and the Enlightenment of the eighteenth. With the exception of Leibniz, every Western philosopher of note in this era believed in the contingency of laws of nature, and most philosophers today still do. Philosophers then and since have disagreed about the nature of causation, and hence about causal laws. Some, whom I call Newtonians, believed that all causes are mediated by forces. But the causal laws were still held to be contingent, for what forces there are was said to be a contingent matter. Thus, the contingency thesis about the causal laws just became a contingency thesis about the forces acting. God might not be able to change the way in which a given force acts, but He could surely bring other forces into play, or remove any of the ones that were already operative. Other philosophers, most notably Hume and his followers, thought that forces were unintelligible entities that contributed nothing to our understanding of causation. There are no forces, he argued, nor any other necessary connections in nature, but only some regular sequences of events. Properly understood, he said, causal laws are nothing more than universal regularities of some kind, and causes are just instances of such regularities. These Humean theses are known as the "regularity theories" of laws and of causation.

Categorical realists mostly operate in this tradition, although new and much more interesting theories of laws and causation have recently been developed, and defended along with categorical realism. All of them, however, accept the contingency thesis. Categorical realists are thus agreed that dispositions depend on the causal laws of nature, and that these laws are all contingent. Therefore, they argue, it is possible for the causal laws, and hence the dispositions of things, to be different from what they are. In some worlds (such as ours), for example, ethylene freezes at a lower temperature than water. But, say the categorical realists, there must be other possible worlds in which ethylene freezes at a higher temperature. Therefore, they would argue, the disposition of ethylene to freeze at a lower temperature than water must be world-dependent. It must depend on what the laws of nature happen to be in the world in question. And the same, they would say, must be true of all dispositions. If something has a certain disposition in this world, then, necessarily, there is another possible world in which it (or its identical counterpart) does not have this disposition. What is brittle here might well not be brittle there. Hence, the identity of a thing cannot depend on its dispositions; it can only depend on its categorical properties. The dispositions of things cannot be of their essence, because all dispositions depend on what the laws of nature are, and these laws are all contingent and extrinsic to the things on which they operate.

If the dispositions of things may thus vary from world to world, depending on what the laws of nature are for the different worlds, then, we must ask, what grounds them in the specific things? What makes one thing have a given disposition while another lacks it? Presumably, each disposition has some kind of basis in the things that have it. Presumably, one disposition could depend on others. But, ultimately, the categorical realists say, the manifest dispositions of things must be grounded in the categorical properties of the things that have them. Otherwise, their existence would be inexplicable. A metaphysical wedge is thus driven between the dispositions of things and the real properties of the things that have them. Given that the laws of nature are contingent, the relationship between a given disposition and the categorical properties that are supposed to ground it must also be contingent, and hence the grounding properties and the disposition must be ontologically distinct from each other. If this is right, then we are free to associate dispositions with categorical bases according to how the laws are in each possible world, thus ensuring that objects that are disposed to behave in a particular way in a given world are said to have the dispositions that correctly describe their behaviour.

The main arguments in favour of the categorical realist's claim that dispositions need categorical bases are that they are needed to explain the continuing existence of, and also the differences between, dispositions that are not currently (and perhaps never have been, and never will be) manifested. These are the "continuing existence" and the "difference" arguments.

The continuing existence argument is this: (1) Dispositions continue to exist unmanifested. (2) The fact that dispositions continue to exist unmanifested needs explanation. (3) The continued existence of a disposition would be explained if it had a purely categorical basis, for the continued existence of such a basis needs no explanation. (4) The continued existence of a disposition cannot be explained in any other way. Therefore, (5) dispositions must ultimately have categorical bases. There is, however, no good reason to believe that dispositional properties cannot be fundamental, and therefore capable of existing and continuing to exist unmanifested. The fact that dispositional properties cannot be pictured, as categorical properties can be, is no good reason to think that they cannot exist fundamentally. On the contrary, there is every good reason to believe that the most fundamental properties in nature are causal powers, capacities and propensities, and the fact that we cannot picture them is irrelevant.

The difference argument is more interesting. It is the argument to the effect that if two things differ in respect of any of their dispositions, they must also differ in respect of at least one of their non-dispositional properties. Otherwise, the difference would be inexplicable. The argument is interesting because its premise seems quite plausible. If two things differ in respect of any of their dispositions, then surely there must be a difference elsewhere that would explain this difference. But why must it be supposed that the only possible explaining difference is one of categorical properties? Why could the explaining difference not be one of dispositional properties? Unless one is already of a mind to think that the only real properties are the categorical ones, the difference argument has no force. One could accept that there must be some other difference, but deny that this difference must be categorical.

It is true, of course, that dispositions need to be based in reality. They must always be grounded in real properties. The only question concerns the nature of these real properties. Categorical realists say that the only real properties are the categorical ones. Essentialists take the view that the real properties – for example, causal powers, capacities or propensities – may be dispositional. That is, they are dispositional realists. The question is, then, whether the main arguments for categorical realism are persuasive. I think not, for both arguments rely on the assumption that real properties are able to be visualized or represented in our imaginations. But this is an assumption for which there appears to be no justification. No unidimensional properties, and surely there are many, are going to be able to be visualized in the sort of ways that shape, size or structures are. There are just differences of degree for such properties, and the only way in which they could possibly be pictured would be by adopting some convention (e.g. of shading or colouring) to do so. But why should that count against them? On the contrary, it is much more plausible to suppose that the most basic properties are the underlying quantitative ones that dispositional realists believe in. And these, by their nature, cannot be represented directly in our imaginations.

If the arguments in favour of categorical realism are weak, those in favour of dispositional realism are fairly strong. First, there is the argument from science. The most fundamental things that we know about all have causal powers or other dispositional properties, and, as far as we know, they only have such properties. Of course, it could be that they have structures that we do not know about, which are somehow responsible for their dispositional properties, but there is nothing that suggests that this might be so, and there is even less reason to believe that the causal powers or propensities of the most basic things in nature are ontologically dependent on these supposed underlying structures. On the contrary, block structures are not ontologically primary, since they are dependent on the existence of their parts, and intrinsic structures are spatiotemporal structures of dispositional properties.

Second, there is the argument from the nature of the laws of nature. The laws do not merely describe the behavioural regularities of things that are characterized by their categorical properties alone. On the contrary, the laws of nature appear more often to be concerned with properties that are not structural. There are no known laws of nature that are concerned with the shapes or sizes of things, and those that are concerned with block structures are dependent on the dispositional properties of their component parts. Most laws of nature, it seems, are concerned with quantitative dispositional properties such as mass, charge, magnetic field strength, moment of inertia, specific heat, energy density, potential energy, half-lives or how the various forces of nature would operate to affect things. Or, at a more fundamental level, the laws of nature are concerned with what causal interactions are possible, with what probabilities they would occur, and what quantities would be conserved in these interactions. Dispositional concepts thus occur essentially in the laws of nature, as far as we know them. Therefore, laws of nature of the sort that categorical realists would need to effect their ontological reductions of dispositional properties simply do not exist. There are no known regularities of behaviour that are specific to things of a given shape or size, for example, or to the members of the extensions of any other categorical property. In chemistry, there are laws that plausibly just describe how substances of various kinds interact, but these laws do not express mere regularities. On the contrary, they make use of precisely the kinds of dispositional concepts that categorical realists seek to reduce. That salt dissolves in water, for example, or that hydrogen is exploded by a spark in oxygen to form water, are laws that, perhaps more plausibly than most, are just statements of regularities. But the laws that underlie these regularities are dispositional, for what has to be explained in these cases is the *solubility* of salt in water, or the *potential* for hydrogen and oxygen to combine explosively to form water.

Third, there is the ontological regress argument. Whenever a causal power is seen to depend on other properties, these other properties must always include causal powers, for the causal powers of things cannot be explained, except with reference to things that themselves have causal powers. Structures are not causal powers, so no causal powers can be explained just by reference to structures. For example, the existence of planes in a crystal structure does not by itself explain the crystal's brittleness, unless these planes are cleavage planes: regions of structural weakness along which the crystal is disposed to crack. But the property of having such a structural weakness is a dispositional property that depends on the fact that the bonding forces between the crystal faces at this plane are less than those that act elsewhere to hold the crystal together. Therefore, the dispositional property of brittleness in a crystal depends not only on the crystal's structure, but also on the cohesive powers of its atomic or molecular constituents.

However, cohesive powers are causal powers. They are the forces that bind things together. For a crystalline structure, these forces are presumably electromagnetic, and therefore depend on the dispositions of charged particles to interact with each other in the sorts of circumstances that exist inside a crystal. To explain the distribution of the cohesive forces existing in such circumstances, the structure of the crystal must be described in some detail. But this description will not by itself do anything to explain the cohesion of the parts of the crystal. To do this, it is also necessary to say what energy states are occupied by the structure's various constituents, and to specify their dispositions to resist being prised out of their respective positions. So cohesive powers have to be explained in terms of other causal powers. And there never seems to be any point at which causal powers can just drop out of the account.

An analysis of dispositions

What, then, are dispositions and dispositional properties? I have so far used these terms fairly loosely and intuitively. Let us now try to be a little more precise. When I speak of the dispositions of things, I am talking about how these things will, or be likely to, behave in various kinds of circumstances. I am not diagnosing the causes of this behaviour. But when I speak of the dispositional properties of things, I am talking about what I believe to be genuine properties, rather than just behavioural tendencies: properties that I take to be of the nature of causal powers or capacities of some sort.

Dispositional properties are attributed to things in order to explain their manifest dispositions: to explain how things will, or be likely to, behave in various kinds of circumstances. Such explanations are easily parodied, for they often appear to be trivial. The manifest disposition of takers of a given drug to go to sleep following its ingestion is only trivially explained by saying that the drug is a soporific. Nevertheless, this is a genuine explanation, and it is not the only possible one. The drug taker might believe the drug to be a soporific, when it is only a placebo, and the disposition to sleep might well be caused by this belief, rather than by the nature of the drug that is taken. The dispositional properties of things cannot, therefore, be defined behaviouristically, and ought not to be identified with the dispositions they are postulated to explain. The manifest, behaviouristically describable dispositions of things might have many different causes (as the case of the placebo soporific illustrates).

A natural kind of process that is a display of a given dispositional property has a real essence. In the case of any simple causal process, this real essence will be a dispositional property, and the scientific problem will be to specify precisely what this properly is. The manifest dispositions of things are likely to be symptomatic of the processes in which they are involved, and often the best explanation of a disposition will be just that there is an underlying dispositional property that is directly responsible for it. But sometimes the best explanation will turn out to be much more complex. Perhaps several different kinds of processes are involved in producing the dispositions that are to be explained. The causal processes that are involved in the detailed explanation of a given disposition will all have the same kind of structure. Each will be characterizable by the kind (or kinds) of circumstance C that *would* trigger or initiate the action, and the kind (or kinds) of outcome(s) E that *would* (or would with probability p) result, *provided that there were no interfering or distorting influences*. The qualification is required because processes rarely occur in isolation, and what is actually observed will often be the combined effect of many different processes occurring simultaneously.

Real dispositional properties thus ground natural kinds of causal processes. But like all natural kinds, these natural kinds of causal processes exist independently of our systems of classification. Natural processes that appear to be of the same kind may turn out to be essentially different, and kinds of processes that appear to be very different may be just different species of the same kind. Refraction through a prism, and diffraction from a grating, produce very similar outcomes. Nevertheless, they are essentially different kinds of processes. One results from the refractivity of a medium, the other does not. On the other hand, many of the most important discoveries in science result from identifying apparently very different kinds of processes as species of the same generic kind. Newton, for example, showed that the apparently different kinds of processes of falling towards the earth and orbiting the sun are essentially the same. Similarly, Lavoisier showed that respiring, rusting and burning are all essentially processes of oxidation. Malcolm Forster (1988) talks of discovering a common cause in these and similar cases. But perhaps these discoveries would best be described as discoveries of sameness of essential nature.

Natural kinds of processes may be either causal or stochastic (i.e. probabilistic). An example of a natural kind of stochastic, process is β-decay. β-decay is essentially the spontaneous emission of an electron from the nucleus of an atom resulting in an increase by one of its atomic number. It is a process that occurs independently of human concerns, and it has its own essential nature. To specify a kind of stochastic process such as this, it would appear to be sufficient to say what happens when it occurs, and how probable it is that it will occur within a given time interval. The properties responsible for stochastic processes generally are known as "propensities". But not all propensities are quite like β-decay, for there are other kinds of stochastic processes that do not occur spontaneously, but have to be triggered in some way. However, the focus of this book is not on propensities of either of these kinds, but rather on dispositional properties whose laws of action are deterministic, and that are, therefore, much more straightforwardly of the nature of causal powers.

The main difference between the analysis of dispositional properties that is proposed here and its more traditional rivals lies in the semantics of dispositional terms used to refer to them. Dispositional terms may be defined operationally by specifying the conditions for saying that something has, or does not have, a given disposition. But dispositional properties cannot be so defined. Dispositional properties, if they exist, have essential natures, and it is the business of natural science, not of semanticists, to discover and describe these natures. Consider the situation that existed before the chemical composition of water was known. At such a time, the term "water" might well have been defined in terms of the manifest characteristics of water. And this definition might have served reasonably well to pick out the same substance on each occasion of its use. But water is a natural kind of substance, and its essential nature could only be discovered by scientific investigation. When it was, and the essential nature of water then became known, any nominal definition of the term "water" would naturally have been superseded by the real definition of water as H_2O. The situation with dispositional terms and dispositional properties is similar. If a dispositional term reliably picks out the members of a natural kind of causal process, then there is a further question: what is the essential nature of this kind of process? It is then the job of natural science to describe the dispositional property that grounds processes of this kind. This is not a question that can be settled by appealing to the conventions of language, for real dispositional properties exist as distinct entities, prior to any nominalist or operationalist definitions of the terms we might use to refer to them.

This analysis of dispositions has some distinct advantages over more traditional theories. First, it explains why dispositions bear special relationships to subjunctive conditionals.[1] Dispositional properties support subjunctives because their existence entails that certain kinds of natural processes would occur in certain kinds of (possibly idealized) circumstances to the objects that have these properties. The subjunctive conditionals simply spell out these implications. Second, it explains why dispositional properties can be mocked or frustrated, for circumstances can often be manipulated to make an object appear to have a dispositional property that it does not have, or appear not to have a dispositional property that it does have.

Third, it explains why genuine dispositional properties can often be obscured. They can be obscured because different processes can occur in the same thing at the same time, so that the effect of any single dispositional property being triggered may well be obscured by the effects of other dispositional properties that are being simultaneously manifested.

An attractive feature of this analysis is that it leaves dispositional properties to be identified and explicated rather than defined operationally. And the process of explication is not philosophic, linguistic or lexicographic. It is a posteriori and scientific.

Notes

1 A subjunctive conditional is a conditional proposition (i.e. an "if … then …" proposition) in the subjunctive mood. It is thus a proposition that says what *would* happen if certain conditions *were to be* fulfilled, or what *would* have happened, if certain conditions *had been* fulfilled. Often such conditionals are asserted in the belief that the relevant conditions either have not been, or will not be, fulfilled.

Part II
Realism about causality in philosophy

6 Meaning, truth, and causal explanation*

The 'Humean condition' revisited

Christopher Norris

I

The belief expressed by Quine's famous quip that 'the Humean condition is also the human condition' is one that as yet shows little sign of relaxing its grip on mainstream analytic epistemology and philosophy of science, despite various recent developments which would seem to point in a radically different direction.[1] That is to say, the agenda of current debate with regard to issues of causal explanation still tends to be set by those familiar kinds of sceptical (e.g. positivist or empiricist) argument that take a lead from Hume in denying the existence – or at any rate the knowability – of real-world operative causal forces, powers, or dispositions in nature. Of course there is a crucial distinction to be drawn between full-strength ontological and scaled-down epistemological versions of the sceptic's claim. On the one hand are ranged those old-guard 'orthodox' Humeans (by now perhaps rather few) who would reject any realist of objectivist notion of causality, while on the other can be found subscribers to the lately ascendant, more moderate or revisionist view.[2] According to this we can have no demonstrative proof or knowledge of physical causes even though, by the same token, we have no good reason to deny that they exist and exert their various capacities or powers quite apart from our knowledge (or lack of it) concerning them. Thus scepticism is held within decent, scientifically reputable bounds and can also be made out to comply with the single most basic tenet of philosophic realism, that is, the objectivist claim that truth might always exceed the scope and limits of humanly attainable proof or verification.

Hence perhaps the emergence of this 'new' reading of Hume at just the time when old-style logical empiricism (along with its sceptical upshot) had lost credibility owing to various widely influential attacks from the causal-realist quarter.[3] No doubt its demise was also much hastened by Quine's famous demolition-job which purported to show that the whole programme was based on a pair of residual 'dogmas' – the analytic/synthetic distinction and the idea of scientific statements or predictions as testable one by one against likewise discrete items

*Source: Christopher Norris, *On Truth and Meaning: Language, Logic and the Grounds of Belief*, London and New York: Continuum, 2006, Chapter 2.

of empirical evidence – which failed to hold up under critical scrutiny.[4] In its place, Quine proposed, we should adopt a naturalized epistemology that takes its lead from the physical sciences, along with a thoroughly holistic approach to issues of truth, meaning and interpretation which responds to recalcitrant empirical data by allowing truth-values to be redistributed across the entire 'fabric' or 'web' of received scientific belief. At the limit, conceivably, this might entail giving up certain axioms of classical logic – even bivalence or excluded middle – in the interests of conserving well-attested empirical data, such as quantum superposition or wave/particle dualism.[5] Or again, if we want to conserve some especially powerful or well-entrenched physical theory in the face of anomalous empirical findings, then this might require that we reject the presumed self-evidence of perceptual warrant, as for instance by putting the anomalies down to defects in our measuring instruments or limits on our powers of technologically enhanced observation. All this Quine takes as nothing more than a straightforward consequence of the twin principles comprising the so-called 'Duhem-Quine thesis', namely the under-determination of theory by evidence and the theory-laden character of observation statements.[6] Thus any decision about which items of belief to retain and which to revise or give up is primarily a matter of 'pragmatic convenience' – of simplicity, conservatism, maximal coherence with the current range of beliefs-held-true – rather than (as the logical empiricists supposed) a matter of applying certain well-defined methods and protocols for valid, i.e. truth-conducive reasoning on the evidence.

In which case, according to Quine, we have no choice but to push right through with this holistic conception and acknowledge that a naturalized epistemology along the lines that he proposes must also entail an outlook of full-fledged ontological relativity. Such questions as the realist might wish to phrase in objective-sounding terms – 'Do x's exist?', 'Is y a natural kind?', 'What exactly are x's properties, attributes, microstructural features, causal dispositions?', and so on – should rather be treated as questions that arise (and that receive some definite answer) only relative to this or that conceptual framework or ontological scheme. Hence Quine's famously provocative claim that the issue of 'existence' as regards such a diverse range of candidate objects as mathematical sets or classes, centaurs, Homer's gods, or brick houses on Elm Street is one that cannot be settled except by reference to the various systems of belief within which they play or once played a role. Such items are selectively 'imported' into some given scheme as more or less convenient working posits whose reality – along with the truth-value of any statements concerning them – is decided solely on pragmatic grounds, or as a matter of what works best for this or that scheme-relative purpose. Quine is perfectly willing to acknowledge that his own strong preference, 'qua lay physicist', is for the kinds of entity that figure in the discourse of our current best theories in natural science, and not for such objects as centaurs or Homer's gods. He is also – surprising as it might seem – a realist about mathematical entities, and indeed expresses strong Platonist leanings in that regard.[7] However any charge of inconsistency here is briskly set aside by Quine's pragmatist avowal that science (physics especially) provides the most convenient way yet discovered of 'working some structure' into the otherwise inchoate flux of sensory experience. Moreover hypotheses concerning the existence of mathematical objects – right up to the highest-level abstractions of set-theory – are so deeply entrenched within present-day scientific theory and practice as to justify our counting them among the range of well-attested putative realia. All the same, whatever his own inclinations, Quine is adamant that any ontological privilege granted to atoms, numbers, or sets as distinct (say) from centaurs or Homer's gods is something they enjoy only in virtue of belonging to a favoured conceptual scheme.

Thus the question arises as to whether Quine's physicalist outlook – his subscription to a naturalized epistemology that favours such baseline behaviourist posits as our reflex responses to the 'constant bombardment' of incoming sensory stimuli – should itself be taken as just one scheme among the many currently on offer. So likewise with those various 'intensional' items like meanings, thoughts, modalities, propositional contents, attitudes, and so forth, that Quine seeks to purge from philosophical discourse so as to maintain a strictly extensionalist remit and avoid all the well-known problems about quantifying into opaque (i.e. modal or belief-related) contexts.[8] This follows directly from his frontal attack on the two last 'dogmas' of logical empiricism, since – as Quine makes clear – that argument has to be pushed right through to the point of embracing on the one hand a thoroughgoing naturalized, science-led approach which treats the process of belief-formation in purely behaviourist terms, and on the other a wholesale contextualist doctrine of truth, meaning and interpretation which places no limits – no ultimate logical or empirical constraints – on the revisability of any beliefs thus formed. Only thus, he argues, can epistemology assume its rightful place as a sub-branch of the natural sciences whose job it is to explain how the 'meagre input' of sensory promptings to which various subjects are exposed somehow gives rise to their 'torrential output' of hypotheses, predictions, observation statements, scientific theories, and so forth.[9] What drops out completely on Quine's account is the idea of knowledge and progress in the sciences as coming about through a process of increasing conceptual grasp and causal-explanatory depth. That is to say, he pushes the consequences of Humean scepticism to their furthest (and, one may think, their rationally insupportable) extreme even though his argument in 'Two Dogmas' starts out from the rejection of Hume's dichotomy between empirically warranted 'matters of fact' and analytic or a priori 'truths of reason'.

No doubt Quine's essay latched on to some deep-laid problems with that whole way of thinking about issues in epistemology and philosophy of science that had begun with Hume, received a more elaborate (yet scarcely less problematical) treatment in Kant, and thereafter remained as a source of unresolved tensions and aporias in the project of logical empiricism.[10] From a causal-realist standpoint these can be seen to have resulted from a failure (or refusal) to recognize scientific progress as providing adequate warrant for the claim that science must in general be on the right track with regard to those various objects, properties, structures, causal dispositions, and so forth which alone make it possible to explain the manifest achievements of science as anything other than a downright miracle.

Such is the case for convergent realism – along with inference to the best, most rational explanation – advanced by those philosophers who have worked their way through and beyond the antinomies bequeathed by that whole previous chapter of developments.[11] Thus we have Quine to thank for bringing this situation about, that is to say, for showing how downright impossible was the Kantian attempt to overcome Hume's sceptical impasse by embracing a hybrid outlook of 'transcendental idealism' on the one hand and 'empirical realism' on the other.[12] Certainly 'Two Dogmas' did more than any other work to emphasize the kinds of dead-end predicament that thinking was sure to encounter if it started out from any version, no matter how elaborately qualified, of the basic Humean dichotomy.

Nor does there seem much hope of success for latter-day revisionist Kantians, like John McDowell, who propose that we reclaim what is valid in Kant's arguments by simply dumping all that otiose 'transcendental' apparatus (as well as all the talk of a noumenal reality beyond phenomenal appearances) and hanging on to his cardinal insight concerning the strictly inseparable roles of 'spontaneity' and 'receptivity' in every act of conceptually informed and empirically warranted knowledge.[13] For, as I have argued elsewhere, this switch of preferential idioms does nothing to prevent the old dichotomy from cropping up yet again, despite and against McDowell's regular cautions – taking a lead from 'Wilfrid Sellars – that we should not think of those roles as 'even notionally' separate.[14] Indeed its residual grip on his thinking – as likewise on that of the logical empiricists before him, whatever their determination to expunge all traces of Kantian 'metaphysics' from the discourse of epistemology – is evident in numerous passages where McDowell strives to repress or circumvent such dualist modes of thought. 'If we restrict ourselves to the standpoint of experience itself, he urges, then

> what we find in Kant is precisely the picture I have been recommending:
> a picture in which reality is not located outside a boundary that encloses
> the conceptual sphere ... The fact that experience involves receptivity
> ensures the required constraint from outside thinking and judging. But since
> the deliverances of receptivity already draw on capacities that belong to
> spontaneity, we can coherently suppose that the constraint is rational; that
> is how the picture avoids the pitfall of the Given.[15]

What emerges most strikingly here is the fact that any claim to move beyond the Humean-Kantian dilemma will need to do more than repeat Kant's arguments against Hume in a scaled-down, naturalized, or 'detranscendentalized' form which nonetheless conserves their basic commitment to a notion of the teal as in some sense epistemically constrained or subject to the scope and limits of human cognition. Thus the above passage, like many in McDowell, makes a tortuous, quasi-Hegelian attempt to transcend the subject/object dualism ('reality is not located outside a boundary that encloses the conceptual sphere'), while also following Sellars in its claim that such problems can best be got over by renouncing the empiricist 'Myth of the Given' and accepting that every item of perceptual experience is *always already* conceptually informed.[16]

Of course this idea falls square with Quine's twin theses – taken up from Duhem and embraced by Thomas Kuhn along with many others – concerning the underdetermination of theory by evidence and the theory-laden character of observation statements.[17] Where they differ is in Quine's hard-headed physicalist conclusion chat this spells the end of any attempt, like McDowell's after him, to reclaim the epistemological ground – the normative or justificatory 'space of reasons' – which Kant laid down as the *sine qua non* of any adequate theory of knowledge. The logical empiricists roundly rejected such claims in keeping with their programmatic drive to wean philosophy off its addiction to bad old Kantian-idealist habits of thought, and thus restore it to a properly serviceable adjutant, role *vis-à-vis* the methods and procedures of the natural sciences. Yet, as Quine made clear, that programme still preserved just those elements of Kant's philosophy (chief among them the distinction between analytic truths and matters of empirical warrant) which continued to exert a grip on their thinking despite their claim to have cut epistemology down to size by excluding all notions of a priori knowledge or appeals to the supposed self-evidence of certain apodictic truths. Indeed it is on just this point, so the story goes, that the 'two traditions' split off during the early twentieth century. That is to say, the majority of analytic (chiefly Anglophone) philosophers set out along a logico-linguistic path that steered well clear of such swampy metaphysical ground while 'continental' (i.e. post-Kantian mainland-European) thinkers pursued the alternative path that led from Husserlian phenomenology to various later – and, as the analytic types would have it, equally misguided since 'subjectivist' or 'psychologistic' – movements of thought. That this story is a massive simplification amounting to downright travesty is a case that I have argued at length elsewhere, along with other recent revisionist commentators.[18] What if signally fails to grasp, in brief, is first the extent of that residual Kantian influence which runs right through the analytic tradition from the logical empiricists to a thinker like McDowell, and second the fact that continental thought has itself produced a range of approaches (among them Husserl's writings on logic and mathematics and the French critical-rationalist school in philosophy of the natural sciences) which must themselves be counted 'analytic' on any but a narrowly parochial or partisan usage of that term.[19]

II

Still my point here is not to engage in yet another large-scale redrawing of the intellectual map. Rather it is to comment on the peculiar turn of thought – almost (one is tempted to say) a return of the philosophical repressed – whereby Kantian themes have continued to set the agenda of much analytic debate. With the logical empiricists they are mostly present in a covert or unacknowledged way, while in McDowell they take the form of a selective, quasi-naturalized or non-'metaphysical' reading of Kant that inherits all the problems outlined above (including those remarked upon by Quine) and moreover yields up any claim to conserve that normative dimension which for Kant could not possibly be redeemed except through the appeal to transcendental modes of reasoning. Hence, I would suggest, the extraordinary impact of Quine's 'Two Dogmas', managing as it did – perhaps in ways that went beyond his conscious intent – to encapsulate the various dilemmas facing philosophy of language, logic, and language at just that critical stage. What his essay brought out with maximal force was the dead-end predicament of a mode of thought – epitomized in logical empiricism – which failed to break with the most problematical aspects of Kantian epistemology and yet gave up on the hope sustained by other ('continental') thinkers that there might be some alternative way to redeem that project. So there is good reason for the widespread view that 'Two Dogmas' marked the crucial point of transition where analytic philosophy in its first, more assertive and confidently problem-solving mode gave way to those various later developments for which the phrase 'post-analytic' serves as a somewhat vague and catch-all but nonetheless apt description. Thus Quine's is the name most often invoked by thinkers of a broadly ecumenical mind who would advise that the best way forward from these problems with the legacy of old-style analytic philosophy is one that combines his doctrines of theory-ladenness, under-determination, and meaning-holism with a strong-descriptivist or depth-hermeneutic approach that breaks entirely free of that tradition.[20] Only then, so the argument runs, can thinking transcend the deep-laid antinomies of Kant's critical project and their latter-day upshot in the impasse that Quine so shrewdly locates in the discourse of logical empiricism.

However Quine's alternative, more radical (minus-the-dogmas) version of empiricism turned our to harbour problems of its own, among them a marked normativity-deficit or failure to provide adequate criteria for rational theory-choice – and a consequent inability to explain our knowledge of the growth of scientific knowledge.[21] That is to say, by adopting this science-led (physicalist and behaviourist) approach to epistemological issues it left no room for those normative values of truth, rationality, logical warrant, falsifiability under pressure of conflicting evidence, and so forth, that are basic to the very enterprise of science or any other reputable branch of enquiry. After all, it was just Quine's point that no strongly held belief, theory, or prediction need be thought of as falsified by the empirical evidence just so long as there remained the option of adducing some 'auxiliary hypothesis' or background premise that might instead be revised (or abandoned) so as to save appearances. And again, no empirical observation need be taken as decisive evidence against this of that cherished theory just so long as the appearances might be ascribed to some perceptual distortion, erroneous measurement or (at the limit) hallucinatory experience on the part of an otherwise well-placed observer. But in that case nothing remains of the idea that knowledge accrues – and can reliably be known to accrue – through certain well-tried procedures of empirical observation, inductive warrant, rational conjecture, hypothesis-testing, and inference to the best (most empirically adequate and theoretically cogent) explanation. To be sure, Quine is perfectly entitled to assert, on his own holistic and framework-relativist terms, that these procedures can all play a variously weighted role in the kinds of pragmatic adjustment between competing methodological claims that define what counts as 'rational' theory-choice once epistemology has managed to break with the two last dogmas of empiricism. However this doctrine – that such choices, 'where rational, are pragmatic' – is one that conspicuously fails to explain why certain rationally motivated choices of one theory over another should have laid claim to something more in the way of justificatory and causal-explanatory warrant than other possible choices. Thus, to take Quine's favoured examples, it would leave us very largely at a loss to account for the sorts of decisive paradigm-shift 'whereby Kepler superseded Ptolemy, or Einstein Newton, or Darwin Aristotle'.[22] That is to say, those classic 'revolutions' in scientific thought would have to be treated – as Kuhn was quick to argue very much in the Quinean spirit – from an ontological-relativist standpoint that allowed no appeal to the kinds of causal or depth-explanatory theory which were ruled out on strict empiricist (ultimately Humean) grounds.[23]

I think the best way to read 'Two Dogmas' is as an exercise in the genre of *reductio ad absurdum*, whatever its original (intended) purport or the question as to whether Quine might himself have been disposed to endorse such a reading. (That he did come around – some four decades on – to moderating certain of its central claims is a different matter though certainly of interest in this regard.)[24] My point is not merely to belabour the problems with old-style logical empiricism and likewise with Quine's radical-empiricist critique of that position. Rather it is to draw the fairly obvious conclusion that Quine so conspicuously failed to draw, i.e. that this entire chapter of developments in mainstream analytic (and 'post-analytic') philosophy amounted to little more than an update on Humean sceptical themes. Thus Quine's version of naturalized epistemology coupled with his doctrine of full-fledged meaning holism ran into a dead-end precisely on account of its refusal to acknowledge the validity of arguments to the best, most adequate (rationally grounded) causal explanation. Of course I am by no means alone in reaching this verdict, one that has been argued with considerable force by Wesley Salmon and other defenders of a causal-realist epistemology against what they see as the stalled enterprise of empiricist and post-empiricist approaches in philosophy of science.[25] Just as telling is the way that thinkers like Hilary Putnam have remained partially in thrall to the strictures of that now presumptively *depassé* movement of thought even while claiming to have moved beyond it in various decisive respects. Putnam is perhaps the most interesting case, since he started out – in his essays of the late 1960s and early 70s – as a strong advocate of causal realism in epistemology and philosophy of language and then backed away from that position through successive attempts to reformulate his thinking in framework-relativist, 'internal-realist', pragmatist, and other such scaled-down compromise terms.[26] Thus Putnam's progress took just the opposite direction to that other main tendency in the wake of Quine's 'Two Dogmas', namely a widespread recognition that the only way forward from the impasse of old-style logical empiricism was to break with Hume's sceptical legacy and – in Salmon's pithy phrase – to 'put the "cause" back in "because"'.[27]

I have written elsewhere about the various stages by which, as I see it, Putnam was led to give up on his early realist approach through an over-emphasis on problem areas (such as the philosophy of quantum mechanics) which in truth required no such drastic shift in his basic ontological commitments.[28] Without repeating that argument in detail it might be useful to summarize the basic points since they offer so striking a contrast with the case that I am presenting here, i.e. my thesis that causal realism and inference to the best explanation represent the only viable alternative to the kinds of dilemma thrown up by logical empiricism. Thus it is, I would suggest, a curious inversion of priorities that leads Putnam to argue from certain as-yet unresolved anomalies in these relatively specialized branches of enquiry to the conclusion that there must be something wrong – 'metaphysically' over-committed – about any form of scientific realism that involves an objectivist ontology and a commitment to the idea of truth-values as potentially transcending our utmost means of proof or verification. All the more so, to repeat, since his own early work provided such a range of strong and resourceful arguments for adopting precisely that position as a counter to various sceptical or anti-realist modes of thought. Indeed it is among his great virtues as a thinker always willing to revisit and revise his previous beliefs that Putnam has responded with an almost seismographic sensitivity to every challenge raised against realism during the past four decades and more. Thus his work has successively registered the impact of (1) logical empiricism with its sceptical (Humean) outlook as regards causal explanation; (2) Quine's radically 'naturalized' approach to epistemological issues, along with his under-determination thesis and doctrines of full-scale meaning-holism and ontological relativity; (3) arguments such as those involving the paradoxes of classical set-theory, Gödel's incompleteness-result, and the Löwenheim-Skolem theorem which he rakes to pose enormous problems for an objectivist understanding of logic, mathematics, and the formal sciences; (4) quantum mechanics on the orthodox (Copenhagen) as well as on various alternative accounts; (5) Dummett-style anti-realism and other such logico-semantic updates on old-style verificationist themes; (6) Wittgenstein's reflections (amplified by Kripke) on the issue as to just what can ultimately count as our standard of correctness in 'following a rule'; and (7) – as a fairly constant refrain – the pragmatist challenge to objective (i.e. non-practice-based) conceptions of truth, knowledge and enquiry.[29] So the chief lesson to be drawn, Putnam thinks, is that henceforth any viable defence of realism will have to make terms with this predicament and acknowledge the extent to which truth is always, inescapably a function of our various interests, priorities or discipline-specific modes of reasoning. To suppose otherwise – in 'metaphysical'-realist fashion – is to leave the door wide open to scepticism by adopting an objectivist. view from nowhere that collapses under the least pressure from arguments of just that sort.

Most recently Putnam has fixed his sights on the fact – value distinction, which he considers just another unfortunate consequence of that old way of thinking – from Hume to the logical empiricists – which sets up a strictly impossible ideal of objectivity and truth, and then proceeds (through a typical pattern of sceptical over-reaction) to deny the rationality of value-judgements or the basis for endorsing a whole vast range of everyday-commonsense beliefs.[30] That is to say, he thinks that the only way to counter such arguments is to accept a sensibly scaled-down 'realist' position which yields no hostages to sceptical fortune in the manner of those other, less cautious realist types who allow – indeed require – that there is always potentially a gap between objectivist truth and knowledge to the best of our epistemic capacities. Putnam now rejects his own middle-period 'internal realist' view, i.e. that one can keep truth in the picture but only when conceived as internal (or relative) to some particular framework of enquiry or motivating programme of research.[31] That approach now strikes him as surrendering too much ground to the kinds of sceptical or 'strong'-constructivist approach that would see nothing more in the notion of truth than a merely honorific or place-filler term that equates, for all practical purposes, with 'true by the lights of this or that community' or 'good in the way of belief'. All the same he is still far from reverting to the argument, so forcefully expressed in the writings of his first decade, that there exist certain objects and natural kinds, along with their intrinsic properties, structures, and causal dispositions which may always quite possibly transcend our best powers of epistemic grasp but which nonetheless determine the truth-value of any well-formed statement, prediction or hypothesis we may venture concerning them.

On that early-Putnam objectivist and causal-realist account scientific knowledge can be thought of as reliably 'truth-tracking' just to the extent that it manages to pick out such items and to manifest a steadily increasing grasp of their distinctive, defining, or depth-ontological attributes. Thus the (act that our criteria for kind-membership have changed very often beyond recognition – e.g. from surface or phenomenal features of items such as 'acid', 'gold' and 'water' to more precise specification in terms of their subatomic, atomic or molecular structure – is no good reason to suppose (in Quinean-Kuhnian fashion) that these changes involve so drastic a shift of theoretical and ontological commitment as to rule out any prospect of meaningful comparison in point of scientific accuracy or causal-explanatory power. Rather what this shows, according to early Putnam, is that we now possess a better, more adequate knowledge of just those objects (along with their defining or constitutive properties) that were once picked out on the basis of a largely intuitive and in some cases – such as that of iron pyrites or 'fool's gold' – an unreliable or downright fallacious method of identification. Thus one might expect the recent, 'third-period' Putnam who has recoiled from the framework-relativist idea of truth as 'internal' to some given investigative framework or conceptual scheme to accept at least a qualified version of the outlook adopted in his first-period writings. All the more so since he is now even keener to disown any remnant of the old positivist distinction between matters of empirically verifiable fact and issues of an ethical or sociopolitical nature which supposedly belong to a separate realm – whether one of 'emotive' pseudo-statements or Hare-type categorical prescriptives – that offers no hold for assessment in rational-evaluative terms.[32]

This is just the point of Putnam's attack on the fact/value dichotomy, as argued most forcefully in his recent essays on the work of the economist and moral philosopher Amartya Sen.[33] His admiration for Sen's work is mainly on account of its refusal to accept the kind of orthodox thinking that draws a sharp distinction between means and ends, or questions that can properly be treated in terms of instrumental (e.g. rational-choice) theory and issues that involve some ethical component – some ultimate value – beyond reach of any such method. Putnam sees this as just another bad relic of the same misbegotten habit of thought that Quine so effectively demolished in his attack on the two last dogmas of logical empiricism. Thus he cites with approval the remark of another economist-philosopher, Vivian Walsh, that '[t]o borrow and adapt Quine's vivid image, if a theory may be black with fact and white with convention, it might well (so far as logical empiricism could tell) be red with values. Since for them confirmation *or* falsification had to be a property of a theory *as a whole*, they had no way of unravelling this whole cloth'.[34] That is to say, if their programme came unstuck – as Quine argued – on its failure to make good the distinction between analytic and synthetic statements (or Humean 'truths of reason' and 'matters of fact') then along with it went the likewise untenable and yet more pernicious distinction between factual or verifiable statements on the one hand and ethical or evaluative judgements on the other. In which case 'the moral is clear', Putnam writes: 'when we are dealing with any important value disagreement, we assume that facts ate irrelevant at our peril', since '[n]o convincing reason can be given for the *logical* irrelevance of facts to value judgements, even if we accept the positivist conception of what a "fact" is'.[35] Thus Quine serves Putnam as a stalking-horse for his attack on the fact/value dichotomy and – following from that – his case for the rational accountability of judgements that the positivists either consigned to some realm of 'emotive' pseudo-statement or else treated as forms of prescriptive utterance likewise devoid of cognitive, rational or truth-evaluable content.

However this serviceable aspect of Quine's thought turns out to have sharp limitations when it comes to Putnam's mote substantive proposals for the way that philosophy should go once freed from the various dilemmas thrown up in the wake of logical empiricism. After all, Quine's 'solution' swung over so far towards a radical-empiricist (i.e. behaviourist.) theory of knowledge-acquisition – a theory devoid of normative or rational-evaluative constraints – as to leave it a mystery how scientific progress could ever have come about, or how we could ever have adequate warrant for claiming to know (on rational, evidential or causal-explanatory) grounds that genuine progress had occurred.[36] Such was the upshot of a naturalized approach which insisted that philosophy should stick to its role of under-labourer *vis-à-vis* the physical sciences and not fall prey – as had happened so often since Kant – to delusions of epistemological grandeur. Putnam is clear enough that this leaves all the really important questions unanswered, among them (not least) the question as to just what constitutes knowledge as opposed to present-best belief, or truth as opposed to '"truth" by the lights of this or that currently accredited expert community'. Such questions cannot possibly find an answer if one takes it, like Quine, that the only route from 'raw' sensory stimuli to the vast proliferation of theories, hypotheses, covering-law statements, and so forth is one that involves nothing more than a process of *ad hoc* pragmatic 'adjustment' and a consequent readiness to ditch any item of belief – whether at the logical 'core' or the empirical 'periphery' – that threatens to obstruct that process. What this amounts to is an emptying-out of all those normative criteria of truth, rationality, evidential warrant and inference to the best (most adequate and powerful) explanation which would otherwise offer a means of avoiding the logical-empiricist impasse. That is to say, it leaves epistemology and philosophy of science with no real work to do save that of remarking how great is the gap between the 'meagre input' of sensory stimuli to which human enquirers are exposed and the 'torrential output' of linguistically articulated theories and beliefs which they somehow manage to generate despite that drastically impoverished database.

Hence Noam Chomsky's well-known critique of Quine, pointing out that no such radical-empiricist approach could begin to explain the human capacity for acquiring and manifesting a whole range of cognitive skills, among them our native competence in language and our ability to frame and test various kinds of rationally formed conjecture, in the natural sciences and elsewhere.[37] Indeed it was largely by way of response to this then-dominant strain of Skinnerian behaviourism in psychology, epistemology and linguistics that Chomsky first developed his theory of transformational-generative grammar, along with his strongly rationalist stance with regard to philosophy of mind.[38] His case against Quine draws much of its force from his 'poverty of the stimulus' argument, i.e. Chomsky's claim that human powers of linguistic expression and rational belief-formation cannot possibly be described or explained by any theory that would treat them in terms of a crudely reductive stimulus-response psychology. Putnam raises similar objections, albeit from a different philosophical angle, when he remarks on the lack of normative criteria for rational, progressive or knowledge-conducive theory-choice in Quine's approach to these matters. Thus:

[h]is answer to those who want a more realistic epistemology, an epistemology that concerns how real scientists manage to select real theories on real data, is the famous, 'Why not settle for psychology?' What many of his readers have missed is that when Quine said this he *meant* it. 'Naturalized epistemology' in Quine's sense means the *abandonment* of epistemology. 'Psychology' (which for Quine always means Skinnerian psychology) is all the epistemology we want or need. This is evasion of the epistemological question with a vengeance![39]

One can readily assent to these criticisms of Quine – as also to Chomsky's kindred range of objections – while nonetheless doubting whether Putnam's later stance on the realism issue leaves him strongly placed to sustain them. That is to say, it is not clear that the case for some plausible (i.e. scientifically and philosophically adequate) version of realism can be made to convincing effect while backing off as far as Putnam does – in his post-1980 writings – from the basic realist principles of objectivity, truth as verification-transcendent, and inference to the best causal and rational explanation.

Indeed Putnam's early approach to these matters was in many ways better equipped, from a realist viewpoint, than Chomsky's resolutely internalist (or rationalist) outlook with regard to epistemological issues. Thus Chomsky has come out very firmly against any notion of external reference-fixing – such as that proposed by Kripke or early Putnam – that would (as he sees it) amount to just a slightly more sophisticated version of old-style Skinnerian behaviourism.[40] Hence Chomsky's stress on the native (internal) capacity of the human mind to acquire and manifest modes of rational thought – just as it constructs well-formed grammatical sentences – through a faculty (or 'competence') whose workings can be specified in formal or structural terms, and which depends not at all on 'external' stimuli as supposed by theorists from Skinner to Putnam. His objections to externalism range all the way from 'poverty of the stimulus' (that is, *contra* Skinner, the claim that human infants exhibit a power of acquiring complex grammatical structures far beyond anything available in their formative linguistic environment) to the moral or ethico-political case that behaviourism drastically underrates the capacity and entitlement of human beings to think for themselves and not be subject to Skinnerian techniques of operant conditioning or social control.[41] This is why Chomsky argues strongly against the Kripke-Putnam causal theory of reference-fixing, a theory, in his view, that threatens the interests of human autonomy, rationality and freedom of conscience by placing sharp limits on the scope for exercise of our innate rational and moral-evaluative powers.[42] Thus, on his account, issues of reference or real-world context dependence had best be shunted off into the realm of pragmatics, rather than brought within the stricter remit of theoretical linguistics or cognitive psychology.

However, as I have argued at length elsewhere, this requirement is itself such as to impose a fairly drastic restriction on the scope of those disciplines and, above all, their ability to address the kinds of philosophical question that arise with regard to language in its wider (everyday, scientific, informational, and social-communicative) functions.[43] If these are regarded as merely 'pragmatic' concerns that exert no significant claim on the interest of linguists or cognitive psychologists then there is a problem about Chomsky's larger project. Thus it becomes hard to see how Chomsky can justify his case for the alignment of a rationalist, i.e. anti-behaviourist and non-empiricist theory of mind with an ethics and politics premised on the ability of human subjects to arrive at truth – and to resist the pressures of conformist ideology – through the exercise of factually well-informed critical judgement. Moreover, one may doubt that Chomsky's aims are well served by his adopting so extreme a version of the innatist (Cartesian) hypothesis that explains human knowledge and communicative grasp in terms of a priori concepts, ideas or powers of rational understanding, for this leads him not only to postulate (in my view) an implausibly large and multifarious range of such ideas but also to cut away some crucial load-bearing structures that are needed in order to make good his claims for the inherently rational and truth-oriented character of human thought, at least when not deflected from its aim by the effects of mass-indoctrination or 'manufactured consensus'.[44] Quite simply, without an adequate theory of reference that establishes the link between word and world – or well-formed, truth-apt statements and that which renders them objectively truth or false – we are lacking a basic component in linguistics, epistemology, and philosophy of mind, as well as a crucial enabling premise of ethics, politics and the social sciences.

III

Thus Chomsky's powerful arguments against Skinnerian behaviourism and Quinean radical empiricism are far less convincing when extended to his case against the causal-realist or externalist theory of reference developed by Kripke, early Putnam, and others. That is, it signally fails to acknowledge the crucial difference between a behaviourist account of operant conditioning which leaves no room for normative criteria of rational theory-choice and an account of reference-fixing which, on the contrary, rebuts any such charge since it explains how rival theories can pick out the same kinds of object and describe or explain them more or less adequately – despite large divergences of paradigm, theory or 'conceptual scheme'. Putnam is very good at making this point through a range of shrewdly chosen examples where acceptance of Quine's ideas about 'ontological relativity' or Kuhn's doctrine of 'incommensurable' paradigms must lead to an outlook of extreme scepticism with regard to the very possibility of scientific knowledge, progress or truth. Such is indeed the inevitable upshot if we don't take it that scientists were basically talking about 'the same thing' when they advanced from describing *gold* as a 'yellow, malleable metal that dissolves in weak nitric acid' to defining it as 'metallic element with atomic number 79'; or from thinking of *water* as 'liquid stuff that falls as rain, fills up lakes, boils and freezes at certain temperatures, quenches thirst, has useful cleansing properties', and so forth, to assigning it the molecular structure H_2O; or again, from identifying *acids* by their sour taste in dilute form to picking them out by their property of turning litmus paper red, and then – through a further advance in knowledge – defining 'acid' as 'proton-donor',[45] The crucial point here is that reference is fixed by just that property or structure that intrinsically distinguishes, say, genuine *gold* from a look-alike substance such as 'fool's gold' (iron pyrites), or genuine *water* from its Twin-Earth substitute with molecular constitution XYZ. For if we take the alternative, descriptivist view that 'sense determines reference' – i.e. that whatever we refer to *just is* anything that satisfies our present-best range of identifying features or attributes – then it is hard to place limits on the scope for Quinean ontological relativity or to draw the line short of wholesale Kuhnian paradigm-relativism.

There is no room here for a full-scale account of the various detailed arguments that early Putnam brings up in support of his causal realist approach. Sufficient to say that it explains (1) how reference may be at least partially conserved across episodes of even quite radical theory-change; (2) how early usages of terms such as 'gold', 'water' or 'acid' can be thought of as truth-tracking of 'sensitive to future discovery'; (3) why scientific knowledge therefore manifests a pattern of intelligible progress despite what thinkers like Kuhn would see as its sharply discontinuous, paradigm-relative, and hence non-cumulative history to date; and

(4) why the causal-externalist account of reference fixing – Putnam's claim that meanings 'just ain't in the head' – is the only one that makes adequate sense in scientific as well as in logico-semantic or modal terms.[46] The point about modality has to do with the Kripke/Putnam case that assertions such as 'water = H_2O' or 'gold = metallic element with atomic number 79' are examples of *a posteriori* necessary truth, that is to say, statements whose truth-value holds necessarily in our own and in all worlds compatible with outs in the relevant (physical) respect while clearly in no sense a priori since they must have been found out by some empirical means. However the fact that reference is 'fixed' in this way – sometimes by a range of kind-specific microstructural (e.g. subatomic, molecular, or chromosomal) features that, may as yet be unknown entails absolutely no restriction either on the everyday usage of 'gold' or 'water' as genuine referring expressions or (still less) on our cognitive powers of discovering such features through a process of further investigation. On the contrary: it is a chief virtue of the causal theory of reference that it allows for relative stability of sense across episodes of theory change – even in the case of such contested terms as 'mass', 'element', 'atom', 'electron' or 'gene' – while making full room for those normative values (of rationality, empirical warrant, falsifiability, theoretical scope, explanatory power, and so forth) that are conspicuously lacking in Quine's radical-empiricist or Kuhn's paradigm-relativist accounts.

Thus, *pace* Chomsky, there is nothing in the causal theory that would lay it open to the charge of ignoring, discounting or drastically under-rating the capacity of human enquirers to exercise their powers of jointly creative and critical-reflective thought in forming and testing rational conjectures with regard to the nature and structure of physical reality. Rather (I would suggest) it is the one approach that does justice to our best intuitions concerning the objective (verification-transcendent) status of scientific truths, the possibility of progress (but also of error or uneven development) in our knowledge of them, and also the fact that we can offer a rational, i.e. non-miraculist account of how such knowledge accrues.[47] Nothing could be further from the kind of reductively physicalist theory of belief-acquisition that does service for 'epistemology' in Quine's treatment of these issues. Indeed it is just this lack of adequately specified normative or justificatory criteria that impels Quine to adopt what might seem the very opposite kind of position, that is, the holistic (scheme-relativist) approach according to which physical objects are merely so many 'posits' imported into this or that ontological scheme so as to make some provisional sense of incoming stimuli or sensory data. What links these two otherwise disparate theses – radical empiricism and radical holism – is, ironically enough, just the same problem that Quine so acutely diagnosed in the discourse of Carnap and other thinkers who inherited the old Humean/Kantian dichotomy between 'truths of reason' and 'matters of fact'.[48] To be sure, Quine is sceptical – famously so – as concerns the possibility of fixing that distinction on valid, substantive or non-circular grounds. However there is still a conspicuous gap, in normative terms, between Quine's starkly behaviourist account of belief-acquisition and his holistic view of theory-change as a process whose sole criterion of 'rational' warrant is the appeal to what best fits (i.e. what involves least conflict) with our existing framework of belief. This shows the extent to which post-empiricist – more precisely: post-logical-empiricist – approaches have inherited the same kinds of dilemma that characterized previous attempts to cut epistemology down to size, or to treat it as a sub-branch of the natural sciences with no proper warrant to adjudicate in such matters. Or again: it brings out the strange ambivalence that typifies claims (whether by Quine or the logical positivists) to espouse a Lockean 'under-labourer' role *vis-à-vis* physical science while nonetheless staking their own authority on just this special kinship with a method conceived as having no need of such merely 'philosophical' support.

Hence, as I have said, the peculiar Quinean mixture of extreme modesty as regards the normative or rational-evaluative content of his project with an attitude of high 'scientific' disdain for any approach to epistemological issues that would claim something more in the way of adjudicative warrant. For it is precisely this double manoeuvre – putting philosophy very much in its place as compared, with the natural sciences but also, by the same token, asserting its own scientific credentials – that creates all the problems with Quinean naturalized epistemology. Chief among them, to repeat, is the normativity deficit which cannot but result from an outlook of radical empiricism coupled with an equally radical conception of meaning-holism. Hence his idea, of empirical statements (along with 'laws of nature' and the axioms of classical logic) as always potentially revisable should this seem the best, most conservative, or least disruptive way of maintaining coherence across the entire fabric of beliefs currently held true. In which case it can hardly be said that Quine's arguments have been misunderstood or put to wrong use by those – such as Kuhn, Rorty, and a whole assortment of cultural relativists, linguistic constructivists, and 'strong' sociologists of knowledge – who take him to have shown beyond doubt that realism is simply not a live option in epistemology and philosophy of language.[49] Rather they are drawing the valid implication from a set of claims which, if jointly true, would indeed put an end to the prospect of explaining how we could ever acquire knowledge of an objective, mind-independent reality that wasn't just a construct of our various languages, conceptual schemes, Kuhnian paradigms, and so on. Still one can legitimately turn the question around and ask – as the realist surely will – whether a theory that goes so clean against the evidence of scientific progress to date (thus effectively denying our knowledge of the growth of knowledge) must have left the rails at some point. All the more so when, as in Quine's case, that theory also raises large problems for the idea of translatability between natural languages, or – as with Kuhn – for the claim that we can mostly compare and contrast rival scientific hypotheses in point of their empirical adequacy, predictive power or rational and causal-explanatory warrant. For there is good reason (scientific as well as philosophical) to conclude that such a theory is demonstrably on the wrong track and is thus better treated as a salutary instance of *reductio ad absurdum* rather than a genuine, credible challenge to our well-tried methods of scientific discovery or knowledge-acquisition.

That is to say, Quine's problem is just that – a problem induced by his own, highly distinctive (not to say idiosyncratic) approach to these issues – and not one that should be seen as posing such a strictly unavoidable challenge. Nor is the problem convincingly resolved by those, like Donald Davidson, who detect a residual third 'dogma' of empiricism in Quine's embrace of the scheme/content dualism, and who therefore urge that we abandon such talk along with its unwelcome consequences, such as ontological relativity and the problem about translating between different schemes, languages or conceptual frameworks.[50] The trouble with any attempted solution along Davidsonian lines is that it comes down to yet another version, albeit more carefully disguised, of the same old dualism that afflicted in Quine's (on the face of it) radically monistic approach. Thus Davidson's attack on the idea of 'conceptual schemes' again yokes an outlook of downright 'commonsense' empiricism – whence his talk of 're-establish[ing] unmediated touch with the familiar objects whose antics make our sentences and opinions true or false' – to a generalized (Tarskian) theory of truth, meaning and interpretation coupled with a wholesale 'principle of charity' that imputes rationality and truth pretty much across the board.[51] From this point of view, '[i]f we can produce a theory that reconciles charity and the formal conditions for a theory, we have done all that could be done to ensure communication'.[52] And again, '[g]iven the underlying methodology of interpretation, we could not be in a position to judge that others had concepts or beliefs radically different from our own'.[53]

Thus it follows, according to Davidson, not only that we can (*contra* Quine, Kuhn, Whorf and company) have reasonable confidence in our ability to translate across different languages, paradigms, or 'conceptual schemes' but also that other people (like ourselves) must be 'right in most matters' since we and they could otherwise have no such background of shared understanding. For given that truth (or the attitude of holding-true) is basic to all interpretation of meanings and beliefs, and given moreover that we cannot make a start in that process without presupposing a large measure of convergence on truth across various cultures, languages, and individual speakers, therefore it is nonsensical to think that different 'conceptual schemes' might carve things up in such drastically different ways as to render translation or comparison between them strictly impossible. However it is a big and very questionable jump from Davidson's strong point about the conditions of possibility for linguistic understanding to his notion that this leaves us no choice – if we want to understand others – but to count, them 'right in most matters'. For this is to conflate the two distinct claims, (1) that getting a handle on their meanings and beliefs requires chat we possess and also assume them to possess the basic attitude of holding-true, and (2) that their various holdings-true, like ours, must moreover be largely justified, warranted or borne out by the way things stand with the world since we should otherwise be pretty much back to square one as regards mutual comprehension. The first claim is highly persuasive and is further backed up by Davidson's point that conceptual-scheme relativists often go wrong by over-stressing the semantic aspects of language – i.e. the fact chat different speech-communities have different vocabulary ranges or lexical resources – and under-stressing those logico-syntactic components (quantifiers, connectives, devices for conjunction, disjunction, negation, and so forth) which any language must possess in order to function as an adequate means of communication. But the second claim is apt to look a lot less convincing if one reflects that many people – including entire cultural and indeed scientific communities – have very often been wrong about various deeply held convictions in the past and no doubt still are with regard to some likewise well-entrenched items of belief.

This is where Davidson's theory falls down, that is, in its claim that we should *always* seek to maximize the imputed truth-content of utterances, statements, observations, theories, hypotheses, and so forth on the assumption that we couldn't even start to make sense of what their advocates had in mind except by thus enlarging the range of communal beliefs-held-true. For this is to reverse the natural order of epistemological and linguistic priorities, or – in a typically Davidsonian phrase – to 'get the matter backwards'. It is also where the Kripke/ early Putnam theory of truth, meaning and reference can be seen to provide a more adequate account *both* of how knowledge is conserved and advanced across episodes of even 'revolutionary' theory-change *and* of how successive theories can be truth-tracking – along with their constituent referring terms – despite such periodic upheavals. There is now quite a sizeable literature in history and philosophy of science, as well as philosophical semantics, that has set out to describe particular, well-documented cases of this process at work.[54] Among them are some striking instances – such as the atomist hypothesis or conceptions of mass from Newton to Einstein – where a certain range of theoretical beliefs and associated object-terms can be shown to have undergone decisive transformations of content and yet to have maintained a certain continuity of reference throughout their history to date. Thus Hartry Field makes a strong case that if one takes the three nowadays well-defined operative senses of 'mass' – rest-mass, inertial mass, and relativistic mass – then one can specify the stages through which that concept has evolved without any need for Kuhnian talk of radical incommensurability.[55] So likewise with 'atom' from its ancient Greek speculative origins to the latest theories of subatomic structure, and even with a term like 'electron' that was first introduced in order to denominate whatever it was that produced a certain remote luminescent effect, and thereafter underwent a whole series of often quite drastic redefinitions. In such cases, so the causal theory goes, there is an initial act of reference-fixing (an 'inaugural baptism', in Kripke's colourful phrase) which ensures a sufficient degree of continuity over subsequent applications of the term, no matter how remote from what its first users had in mind.

Putnam, as we have seen, fills out the picture through a range of examples, ingenious thought-experiments, and counterfactual scenarios designed to support his claim that semantic externalism of this kind – as opposed to the erstwhile dominant descriptivist-internalist account – is the only approach that can resolve those problems thrown up by the doctrines of Quinean ontological relativity and Kuhnian paradigm-relativism. His argument is strengthened – rendered more plausible – by Putnam's idea of the 'linguistic division of labour', that is, his allowance that non-experts can successfully refer to *gold* or *water* without the least knowledge of their subatomic structure or molecular constitution just so long as there are experts around who could, if required, pick out genuine from look-alike samples of the kind.[56] Or again, in his own case, the professed inability to distinguish beeches from elms doesn't mean that any allusion to either sort of tree on Putnam's part must be either mistaken, hopelessly vague, or referentially void.[57] What saves the situation for these non-expert types is the communal sharing of knowledge whereby cognoscenti of various ilk – physicists, chemists, biologists or arborologists – stand more directly in the causal line of epistemo-linguistic transmission and are always on hand to deliver a verdict in borderline or disputed cases. These latter may range all the way from straightforward instances of classificatory correction (as when children or ill-informed adults discover that whales are mammals, not fish) to more specialist disputes where the expert is called in to decide, say, whether a piece of the semi-precious stone jade – adequately so described for most purposes – belongs to one or other of the two distinct natural kinds *nephrite* or *jadeite*. Thus the Kripke/Putnam causal theory of reference has the signal advantage (as against its descriptivist rival) of explaining both how knowledge accrues through progressively more adequate, e.g. microstructural or depth-explanatory theories and why such advances can be thought of as a matter of communal know-how even if relatively few people have access to the relevant special expertise. Also, as I have said, it gets over the problem – one that lies in wait for descriptivist theories when pushed to their ultimate conclusion – of just what should *count* as an advance in knowledge if scientific theories and their object-terms are construed as radically paradigm-relative and hence as strictly incommensurable one with another.

No doubt there are issues to be raised concerning various aspects and possible shortcomings of the causal theory. Thus some would argue that it fails to account for the manifold ways in which the reference of terms can be modified, extended, refined, or – on occasion – radically transformed through the impact of contingent historical or socio-cultural factors which provide little purchase for that theory (at least in its pure-bred form) since they create so large and disruptive a kink in the postulated 'chain' of transmission. In such cases there looks to be a crucial role for some alternative approach that takes due stock of the extent to which the reference of object-terms is indeed dependent on the range of descriptive criteria or identifying attributes that enable us to pick out this or that candidate item according to our best current knowledge.[58] What seems fairly cleat – after much discussion – is the need to devise a hybrid theory which combines the best features of the 'old' descriptivist account with those elements of the Kripke-Putnam approach that offer a solution to the chief problems with that account. Chief among them are its inability to explain our knowledge of the growth of scientific knowledge and the ease with which it slides into a wholesale paradigm-relativist view devoid of substantive rational or causal-explanatory content. However the desired outcome is not to be had from any theory (such as Davidson's) that goes some way towards exposing the aporias and self-refuting arguments of Quinean-Kuhnian talk about 'conceptual schemes' but which stops well short of embracing a causal-realist position.

IV

Davidson famously makes this point on grounds of the performative self-contradiction that scheme-relativists run into when attempting (impossibly, on their own terms) to describe how far and in just what respects the various schemes must be thought to differ. Thus:

> Whorf, wanting to demonstrate that Hopi incorporates a metaphysics so alien to ours that Hopi and English cannot, as he puts it, 'be calibrated', uses English to convey the contents of sample Hopi sentences. Kuhn is brilliant at saying what things were like before the revolution using – what else? – our post-revolutionary idiom. Quine gives us a feel for the 'pre-individuative phase in the evolution of our conceptual scheme', while Bergson tells us where to go to get a view of a mountain undistorted by one or another provincial perspective.[59]

So far as it goes – that is to say, within the limits of an argument based on logico-linguistic and broadly pragmatic considerations – this makes a strong case against the 'very idea' of a conceptual scheme, along with its kindred cultural-relativist or linguistic-constructivist claims. On the other hand it doesn't go anything like far enough if one wants to adopt a realist stance according to which the truth-condition for any given conjecture, prediction, hypothesis or well-formed (truth-apt) statement is that it satisfy the basic requirement of corresponding precisely to the way things stand with regard to this or that objective, real-world state of affairs. Anti-realism in its currently most influential form works on just the opposite set of premises. These are (1) that 'objectivity' in this sense is by very definition beyond our utmost powers of cognitive or epistemic grasp; (2) that truth therefore cannot exceed our best capacities of proof, ascertainment or verification; and (3) that we had thus better leave off talking of truth, objectively or realistically conceived, and plump for the more workable conception of assertoric warrant or 'truth' as epistemically constrained, i.e. as coterminous with the scope and limits of human investigative thought.

This argument has been pushed furthest by those, like Michael Dummett, who make out a case on logico-semantic and ultimately metaphysical grounds that statements of the so-called 'disputed class' (those whose truth-value we cannot decide by any means at our disposal) must: be thought of as simply not belonging to the class of candidates for truth or falsehood.[60] Thus unproven (maybe unprovable) mathematical statements such as 'Goldbach's Conjecture is true' or empirically unverifiable claims such as 'there exists a duplicate solar system in some remote, radio-telescopically invisible region of the expanding universe' must be treated as neither true nor false, rather than as having some objective truth-value that pertains to them despite our inability to find it out.[61] However it is also close kin to the idea espoused by 'constructive empiricists' like Bas van Fraassen that empirical adequacy, rather than truth, is what science should properly aim at since to assert anything more – such as the truth, realistically construed, of statements concerning recondite items like atoms, electrons or remote astrophysical bodies – is to stray beyond the bounds of plain observational warrant and hence yield unnecessary hostages to sceptical fortune.[62] That is to say, we are better off rejecting realism with respect to such putative objects and treating them rather as useful, instrumentally convenient posits which earn their keep simply by virtue of figuring importantly in our present-best (so far unfalsified) scientific theories.

Van Fraassen sometimes pushes this doctrine pretty hard, as for instance by arguing that whatever we can see through some fairly basic piece of observational technology (e.g. an optical microscope or telescope) counts as sufficiently 'real' for constructive-empiricist purposes, whereas whatever requires the use of advanced equipment such as an electron-microscope or radio telescope must be counted an artefact of technologically enhanced observation and hence inadmissible on just those stipulative terms. However this involves him in some wiredrawn (not to say absurd) passages of argument. Thus, for instance, it follows that a claim to have truly perceived the moons of some remote planet by an astronaut close up enough to see them through a low-resolution optical telescope is epistemically more reliable than the finding of earthbound astronomers equipped with the latest, most highly sophisticated observational technology. Or again, we are better placed as regards any issue concerning the existence (or reality) of objects on whatever physical scale by deploying optical devices, no matter how primitive, that involve only a stepwise increment to our basic, unaided perceptual powers rather than high-tech devices which interpose all manner of complex instrumentation between us human observers and the various entities concerned. So in the case of objects too tiny, remote, fast-moving, short-lived, or otherwise elusive to show up without the use of advanced electronic equipment we had best take the sensible constructive-empiricist line and remain studiously non-committal as regards their objective reality. Moreover, this means that such talk of relatively 'primitive' or 'advanced' prosthetic devices is talk that must be thought to beg the whole question as to just what we see – whether an object or an artefact of observation – when we look through an electron microscope or radio-telescope.

Thus it follows that we are metaphysically out on a limb if we assume that things have moved on since the time of Galileo or Robert Hooke and that we are now on firm epistemological ground in asserting the objective truth (as opposed to the merely instrumental utility) of statements concerning such items as electrons, atoms, molecules, chromosomes or remote astrophysical bodies. Much wiser to avoid these excess ontological commitments and not go in for what van Fraassen scornfully describes as the realist's false display of courage in such matters. For if reality *just is* the sum-total of our evidence for it when construed in terms of empirical adequacy, rather than objective truth, then the realist stands neither to gain nor to lose anything worth having by taking this merely notional extra risk. After all, 'it is not an epistemological principle that one might as well hang for a sheep as for a lamb'. And again:

> [i]f I believe a theory to be true and not just empirically adequate, my risk of being shown wrong is exactly the risk that the weaker, entailed belief will

conflict with actual experience. Meanwhile, by avowing the stronger belief, I place myself in the position of being able to answer more questions, of having a richer, fuller picture of the world ... But, since the extra opinion is not additionally vulnerable, the risk is – in human terms – illusory, and *therefore so is the wealth.* It is but empty strutting and posturing, this display of courage nor under fire and avowal of additional resources that cannot feel the pinch of misfortune any earlier.[63]

This is why constructive empiricism requires 'a resolute rejection of the demand for an explanation of the regularities in the observable course of nature, by means of truths concerning a reality beyond what is actual and observable, as a demand which plays no role in the scientific enterprise'.[64] Causal realism might look good by comparison with empiricism or instrumentalism in so far as one endorses this deluded idea that there is something over and above the warrant of straightforward empirical evidence that decides the truth-value of our statements, predictions or explanatory hypotheses quite apart from that evidence itself. Yet it one takes a sceptical view of such claims then it will look much more like a faith position with little to commend it bar a vague and wholly unjustified sense of taking additional risks for greater rewards.

Van Fraassen's is basically a refined update on the Mach-inspired positivist doctrine that we are entitled to carry on talking about atoms and suchlike invisible entities in so far as they play a useful role in our various scientific theories and just so long as we don't take the further (ontologically extravagant) step of assuming their existence as a matter of objective, knowledge-independent truth. What this rules out – in the name of parsimony, commonsense, and philosophic hygiene – is any version of the argument from inference to the best causal and rational explanation that would justify realism with respect to those entities precisely on the grounds of their playing that not merely useful but *strictly indispensable* role. Besides, there is something odd about a theory that reduces truth to the limits of perceptual or empirical verifiability, and this in turn to the scope of unaided (or minimally enhanced) human observation. Hence the objection of some critics – Paul Churchland among them – that van Fraassen's is a protagorean doctrine which, if consistently applied, would indeed make 'man the measure' and thus turn its back on all those advances in scientific knowledge that have come about precisely by discounting or rejecting the plain self-evidence of the senses.[65] (Churchland makes the point rather nicely by imagining an 'arboreally rooted' philosopher, one Douglas van Firssen, whose notion of reality encompasses nothing beyond his drastically limited purview.) Besides, there is a strong case to be made that we understand enough about the working principles, design, and construction of various present-day advanced observational technologies to more than offset what van Fraassen regards as their inherently complex and hence perceptually unreliable character. For there seems little virtue in an argument that would attach more weight to the result of observations conducted through Galileo's telescope and interpreted according to the then current state of optical theory than to results achieved with modern instruments, however complex, whose design incorporates just the sorts of knowledge that enable us the better to allow for any possible distortions, artefacts, interference-effects, and so forth.

Moreover it is hard to maintain any version of empiricism, 'constructive' or otherwise, which ignores the sheer amount of cognitive processing involved in even the simplest, most basic forms of perceptual experience. Such, after all, is the chief lesson of just every research-programme in cognitive psychology and neuro-science over the past two decades and more.[66] On the one hand these findings might be taken to support the Quinean-Kuhnian idea that observations are always, inextricably theory-laden and theories always under-determined by the best empirical evidence. On the other – and I think more plausibly – they may be taken to support just the opposite conclusion. Such is the realist and causal-explanatory claim that scientific progress most often comes about through a complex interplay of empirical observation and theory which can itself be tracked through a careful application of historico-philosophical analysis and which therefore involves no such premature (scepticism-inducing) conflation of realms. That is to say, it still leaves ample room for explaining the advancement of knowledge in terms that allow for the theory-laden character of even the most basic observation-statements but which nonetheless account for that advancement precisely by adducing the cumulative nature of the various changes thus brought about in our state of theoretical-informed observation. Thus, for instance, it is wrong to conclude – like Kuhn on the basis of Quinean radical empiricism plus wholesale ontological relativity – that there is ultimately no distinguishing in point of rational warrant between Galileo versus Aristotle on swinging stones, or Lavoisier versus Priestley on the process of combustion, or Darwin versus the advocates of preformationism on the nature and development of species.[67] What counts most decisively in favour of the latter and against the former hypothesis in each case is its greater extent of empirical warrant and also its far superior degree of theoretical and causal-explanatory power. Theory-ladenness is no more a threat to our knowledge of the growth of scientific knowledge than the fact of our dependence, when advancing such claims, on ever more complex and sophisticated forms of technologically enhanced observation. In both cases we have good warrant for supposing such knowledge to be adequately grounded, whether by appeal to our existing stock of empirical evidence and developed theoretical understanding or – closely allied to that through the range of accumulated scientific know-how embodied in those various technologies.

At any rate there is no need to go along with the Quine-Kuhn thesis in its full-fledged version, i.e. the radically holistic and paradigm-relativist claim that observations are always theory-laden and theories always underdetermined by the best empirical evidence. For this is to ignore the fairly obvious point that *some* very basic observations – those that are not subject to dispute between rival hypotheses or paradigms – can be counted theory-neutral for all practical scientific purposes, while *some* basic theoretical commitments hold firm across a range of otherwise divergent or conflicting claims with regard to that evidence. Of course there is no reverting to the old Baconian-inductivist idea of the quest for scientific knowledge as a patient but largely random accumulation of raw, theoretically untainted empirical data which somehow produce a whole range of valid hypotheses, laws and predictions. On the other hand it is just as wrong – and equally at odds with the record of scientific progress to date – if philosophers swing to the opposite reactive extreme and take for granted (after Quine) the absolute impossibility of distinguishing the empirical from the theoretical content of any given hypothesis. For this argument quickly leads, via Kuhn, to those varieties of thoroughgoing cultural-relativist or social-constructivist approach that likewise trade on the under-determination and theory-ladenness doctrines in order to controvert the very notions of scientific reason, objectivity or truth. Hence the frequent setting up of a straw-man 'positivist' opponent who is supposed to believe, like Bacon, that the advancement of knowledge requires nothing more than a passive gathering of facts or empirical data which can simply be relied upon to speak for themselves once laid out in perspicuous fashion. Actually this does nothing like justice to Bacon's account of inductive method, let alone to the work of those logical positivists or empiricists (like Carnap) whose attempt to uphold some version of the observation/theory dualism – along with that between empirical 'matters of fact' and logical 'truths of reason' – was the chief target of Quine's 'Two Dogmas' and a good many subsequent critiques.[68] Still, as I have said, there is a sense in which those thinkers laid themselves open to attack in so far as they followed Hume in adopting a sceptical or studiously nescient attitude with regard to any kind of realist epistemology that went beyond the empirical evidence or purported to account for that evidence in causal or depth-explanatory terms. This left them no adequate line of defence when confronted with the charge pressed to such powerful effect by Quine – that their programme ran aground on the failure to justify its own most basic premise, namely the existence of a sharp, substantive, and non-circular distinction between the empirical content and the logical structure of scientific theories. For if one thing is clear from the history of debate on this topic from Hume to Quine it is the fact that scepticism will always win out, on its own favoured terms of engagement, so long as the issue is framed in such a way as to exclude or disallow any ultimate appeal to causal, explanation as the grounding rationale of a realist ontology and epistemology.

Moreover, I would suggest, the prospects are not much better for responses to Quine, Kuhn, *et al.* which seek to maintain the priority of truth (or the attitude of holding-true) as a counter to paradigm-relativist talk of variant conceptual schemes, but which still go along with the linguistic turn at least to the extent of supposing that such issues can only be resolved in logico-semantic terms. This is Davidson's ruling idea throughout his entire body of work on truth, meaning and interpretation, despite his occasional guarded hints – most often under pressure from critics of a realist bent – that the Tarskian formal theory of truth requires a more substantive specification if it is not to invite charges of redundancy or vacuously circular definition.[69] Like Tarski, he is at times strongly drawn to endorsing some version of the correspondence-theory in order to make up this deficit, yet prone to espouse a safer (less 'metaphysically' committed) position when confronted with the various well-known objections to that theory mounted by Quine, Putnam, Rorty, and others.[70] Thus Davidson opts for a coherence theory of truth but one that supposedly avoids any wholesale scheme-relativist outcome by building in a truth-based theory of meaning, belief, and communicative uptake.[71] This latter provides sufficient guarantee, so he claims, that, as language-users, we just *can't* be subject to 'total failure' or even (more remarkably) to 'partial failure' of mutual comprehension between different languages, cultures, paradigms, conceptual schemes or whatever. Thus, to repeat: '[g]iven the underlying methodology of interpretation, we could not be in a position to judge that other people had concepts or beliefs radically different from our own' (Davidson, p. 197). However the fact (if such it is) of our being 'in no position to judge' whether we and other people are on different doxastic, linguistic, conceptual or communicative wavelengths can scarcely be taken as offering support for a truth-based theory of interpretation unless one interprets 'truth' itself – as Davidson would surely be loath to admit – along Rortian-pragmatist lines, i.e. as what is currently and contingently 'good in the way of belief'.

This is how Rorty takes Davidson's point that if we can't make sense of their utterances in a way that that brings them out 'true' (or at any rate rationally motivated) according to those same, i.e. *our* accredited standards then they are just not candidates for interpretation on any (to us) comprehensible or rationally explicable terms.[72] However it ignores a very basic feature of all human communication, namely our ability to interpret what other people mean, intend, or believe *even though* we may sometimes consider their beliefs either false, misguided or downright irrational. In which case the principle of charity works out as something more complex and nuanced than a matter of always imputing maximal truth-content to whatever they say or whatever we 'charitably' take them to mean. Rather it functions as a general directive to make full allowance for the variety of ways in which beliefs may be either truth-tracking or subject to certain aberrations that we can best understand through an effort to see all around those various predicaments – of partial information, restricted epistemic access, fixed preconceptions, ideological bias, and so forth – whereby such erroneous beliefs become rationally or causally explicable. No doubt this involves sometimes counting them wrong and ourselves in the right with regard to both particular, small-scale, or localized differences of opinion or matters of a more fundamental character involving (say) a clash of scientific worldviews or a deep-laid disagreement over questions of historical fact. Still if one takes a truth-based and to that extent a realist view of these matters – as Davidson most often does – then logically there is no choice but to admit that, in such cases, the condition of one party's having got things right is that the other has got things wrong. Otherwise there is no stopping the slide to some version of the anti-realist argument according to which that condition, i.e. the logical axiom of bivalent truth/falsehood, extends no further than the range of statements for which we possess some means of proof or verification.

Davidson is generally keen to avoid this Dummettian way of posing the issue in metaphysical and logico-semantic terms, that is to say, as a question of whether or not we can conceive the existence of objective truth-values for statements of the disputed (unprovable or unverifiable) class.[73] Though concurring with Dummett that such questions are best framed in a linguistic mode he sees the main benefit of this approach as a matter of its clarifying issues in epistemology – what we can reasonably claim to know concerning (e.g.) the well-foundedness of our own and other peoples beliefs – rather than its raising the issue of truth as objectively determined or epistemically constrained. Still the success of Davidson's theory must be seen to rest on its capacity to find room for objective (recognition-transcendent) truth-values and also, crucially, on its managing to combine that standpoint with a due allowance for the various rationally explicable ways in which belief can fall short of epistemically warranted knowledge and present-best knowledge fall short of objective truth. This applies not only in the specialized contexts of epistemology and philosophy of science but also in matters of everyday linguistic understanding or communicative grasp where the truth-maximizing principle of charity needs to go along with a due allowance for the kinds and degrees of intelligibly motivated error. Thus we shall do much better *by them and ourselves* if we recognize the limits on truth-maximization and instead seek to explain what we take as erroneous beliefs on a principle that counts them not so much 'right in most matters' but as rationally justified within the limits of their own knowledge, understanding or access to the relevant information sources.

This argument often runs up against objections in so far as it invites us to treat other people's beliefs (where they differ from ours) as resulting from certain causal factors – factors external to the 'space of reasons' – and hence deny them any claim to genuine autonomy as thinking and judging agents.[74] It is a similar worry, as we have seen, that motivates Chomsky's outright rejection of externalist theories of reference-fixing such as that advanced by Kripke and early Putnam. However there is an equal and opposite risk of pressing too hard on this distinction between *reasons for* and *causes of* belief. That is, we can end up by holding people directly at fault for imputed failures – whether of reasoning on the evidence or acting on the basis of received moral and social values – which could better (more charitably) be put down to the intervention of just such causal or externally operative factors. Thus proponents of an ethical, social or legal philosophy based on the belief in absolute freedom of autonomous moral will are as likely to hail from the conservative or right-wing authoritarian quarter (since offenders or misfits can then be held fully to account) as from a 'left' libertarian standpoint, like Chomsky's, devoted to defending the unfettered exercise of individual conscience. On the other hand those who make the case for some more or less qualified determinist outlook can justifiably claim that it accords far better with the principles of justice and enlightened social policy.[75] From their point of view this allows for the manifold ways in which persons qua moral agents may be thought not to enjoy such a measure of free (hence potentially culpable or blameworthy) choice owing to the various causal factors that might be entered as legal pleas under the headings of 'diminished responsibility' or 'mitigatin circumstances'.

V

Clearly these are complex issues in moral philosophy as likewise in other current fields of interest – such as virtue-based epistemology – where questions of belief, knowledge and truth are conceived as involving certain ethical standards of well-conducted, responsible enquiry.[76] At any rate there seems good reason to think that a doctrine of unqualified doxastic voluntarism fails to take adequate stock of those causal factors, even though, just as plainly, a doctrine of unqualified determinism fails to explain how we could ever be justified in holding people to account for their morally repugnant actions or beliefs. Also it is worth noting that the distinction between reasons and causes is one that has been applied with particular emphasis by Wittgensteinian philosophers of action who derive from it the lesson that we always go wrong – merely demonstrate our own false claims to superior wisdom – when we presume to explain the beliefs of other (e.g. 'primitive') cultures in terms of their causal aetiology rather than the kinds of justification that the believers would produce if asked.[77] This position no doubt has the face-value appeal of a tolerant, pluralist, liberal-minded attitude which acknowledges the variety of human belief-systems and thus serves as a hedge against dogmatisms of whatever kind, not to mention the more doctrinaire versions of 'enlightened' progressivist thought. However, as critics have pointed out, it also has the marked disadvantage of opening the way to an outlook of extreme cognitive and cultural relativism that leaves us utterly bereft of arguments for rejecting any kind of irrational creed or condemning any instance of (to us) morally repugnant behaviour which nonetheless has its recognized place in some other value-system or cultural life-form.[78] So this principled veto on causal explanation when it comes to assessing the rationality of beliefs or the moral rightness of actions is one that ironically turns out to undermine any standards of rational or ethical accountability. Besides, it can easily be seen to rebound against the intentions of those who propose it, at least in so far as they seek to redress the asymmetrical relation between those whose beliefs are being explained in such reductive terms and those who purport to do the explaining. For if indeed one takes the view (following Wittgenstein) that what counts as 'rational or 'right' is a matter of conformity with this or that language-game or 'form of life' then we can have no choice – from our own cultural vantage-point – but to count other people wrong in so far as their doxastic commitments or principles of action fail to comply with our own. However this argument clearly backfires since it deprives both them and us of the jointly reason-ascribing and causal-explanatory resources that enable human beings to communicate across otherwise large divergences of language, culture and belief.

To be sure, Davidson comes close to acknowledging this point when he says that the 'guiding policy' in such matters is to optimize the truth-content of their utterances on the standard principle of charity, but always 'subject to considerations of simplicity, hunches about the effects of social conditioning, and of course our common-sense or scientific knowledge of explicable error' (Davidson, p. 196). In which case there would be plenty of room, after all, for what otherwise seems to drop out on Davidson's account, that is, for the fact that – in history and philosophy of science as well as in contexts of everyday communication – we are constantly making allowance for such 'explicable error' and doing so, moreover, in ways that involve some large-scale (even 'radical') differences of view on just the matters principally at issue. But we shall then have to reject, downplay or drastically reinterpret various passages of Davidson's essay that would seem, on the face of it, scarcely to support such a reading. Among them is his central and much-quoted assertion that '[c]harity is forced on us', since 'whether we like it or not, if we want to understand others, we must count them right in most matters' (p. 197). And again (to repeat): '[i]f we can produce a theory that reconciles charity and the formal conditions for a theory, we have done all that could be done to secure communication' (*ibid.*). Yet the main problems with Davidson's account can be seen to arise from just this combination of across-the-board, truth-maximizing 'charity' with a formal (Tarskian) truth-theoretic approach that lacks any definite, substantive content when applied to issues of natural-language understanding, or indeed to issues in epistemology and philosophy of science.

What is missing here, as likewise in Quine's case and in the case of those logical-empiricist theories that Quine set out to demolish, is any adequate means to explain just how we come by the kinds of improved knowledge or communicative uptake that can and do occur whatever doubts may be raised by sceptically inclined philosophers or even by those, like Davidson, who think them out of place but who argue in terms set by that same sceptical agenda. As I have said this involves a twofold deficit, firstly with regard to those normative values (of truth, rationality, explanatory power, and so forth) which provide an indispensable basis for the interpretation and evaluation of beliefs, and secondly as concerns that causal component that enters the process of belief-formation at every stage. Thus the rational allowance for such causal factors extends all the way from our own history of firsthand dealings with the physical world to our acquired knowledge of scientific laws and – crucially for matters of linguistic understanding – out grasp of how such dealings have affected the beliefs of others. In the latter case we may judge them to operate in ways that are reliably truth-conducive or (on occasion) in ways that are prone to produce certain kinds of erroneous, e.g. perceptually distorted or conceptually mistaken belief. To be sure, Davidson's truth-based, logico-semantic theory represents an improvement on Quine's radical-empiricist approach. That is to say, it offers a degree of rational assurance that we are not, after all, stuck with the notion of wholesale ontological relativity, or condemned to the hopeless situation of a 'radical translator' required to interpret the sentences of native informants with whom she has nothing in common – no linguistic or conceptual resources – bar a certain momentarily occurrent range of incoming sensory stimuli.[79] All the same Davidson's alternative account can be seen to swing back and forth between a formalized (Tarskian) truth-theoretic approach devoid of substantive empirical content and a radical-empiricist doctrine which effectively sides with Quine in treating epistemology as just another sub-branch of natural science or behavioural psychology.

Hence his famous concluding dictum that '[i]n giving up the dualism of scheme and world, we do not give up the world, but re-establish unmediated touch with the familiar objects whose antics make our sentences and opinions true or false' (Davidson, p. 198). Or again, to similar deflationary effect as regards any normative conception of epistemology:

> *[t]hat* experience takes a certain course, *that* our skin is warm or punctured, *that* the universe is finite, these facts, if we like to talk that way, make sentences and theories true. But the point is put better without mention of facts. The sentence 'My skin is warm' is true if and only if my skin is warm. Here there is no reference to a fact, a world, an experience, or a piece of evidence (p. 194).

Here as so often with Davidson one gets the impression that he has simply lost interest in philosophy, or at least in the sorts of philosophical issue – the 'problem of knowledge' as debated by thinkers from Descartes, Hume and Kant to the logical empiricists, Quine, Sellars and beyond – which after all constitute the chief focus and motivating interest of his own work. What this passage amounts to is effectively a vote of no confidence in the whole epistemological enterprise conceived as offering, potentially at least, a means of deliverance from the toils of sceptical doubt. Of course it is just the point of Davidson's extensive writings on truth, meaning and interpretation to offer such deliverance and do so moreover on terms that would count philosophically as meeting every form of sceptical-relativist challenge. Yet this desirable outcome is beyond reach of any theory – like Davidson's – that starts out from the assumed priority of formal (logico-linguistic) considerations over matters of causal-explanatory warrant conjoined with inference to the best, most rational understanding.

One problem concerns the applicability to natural languages in everyday communicative contexts of a Tarskian truth-theoretic approach – a formal definition of truth-in-L – whose original purpose was to specify terms for the analysis of logically 'perfect' languages, i.e. those that were capable of regimentation according to the first-order quantified predicate calculus.[80] Davidson puts up a case for the validity of just that move since, on his account, it is the logical components of a natural language – its quantifiers and stock of devices for conjunction, disjunction, negation, anaphora, and so forth – which provide the basic means of communicative grasp both for native speakers/interpreters and for translators out of some other (even if culturally remote) tongue. Such is, of course, the main plank of his argument *contra* Quine for the in-principle possibility of 'radical translation' and the mistake of supposing that it is somehow ruled out – or rendered deeply problematic – by the existence of disparate language-relative 'ontologies' or conceptual schemes. However this remains a highly formal and abstract line of approach that makes little contact with the detailed practicalities of natural-language understanding and which bears all the marks of its direct source in Tarski's more specialized logico-semantic programme. Hence the second problem, most directly addressed in Davidson's series of essays on 'The Structure and Content of Truth': that when it comes to matters of empirical content or 'truth' in a substantive, other than formally specified sense then any theory that banks so heavily on the Tarskian apparatus will not get us very far in that direction.[81] This is I think why Davidson is reduced to pre-empting such likely rejoinders by treating them as merely irrelevant – just products of the old epistemological mind-set – and opting instead for the straightforward belief that our 'sentences and opinions' are made 'true or false' by 'unmediated contact' with real-world objects and events. However his striking insouciance in this regard (as if the claim were wholly unproblematic) cannot disguise the lack of any reasoned or philosophically adequate justification for supposing that issues of truth and falsehood can be settled by appeal to the plain self-evidence of sensory-perceptual warrant. Indeed it offers no more in the way of normative or justificatory grounds than Quine's radical-empiricist notion of 'epistemology naturalized'.

Here we might recall Putnam's remark about the Quinean suggestion that psychology provides all that is needed for that particular purpose. Thus: '"[n]aturalized epistemology" in Quine's sense means the *abandonment* of epistemology. "Psychology"' (which for Quine always means Skinnerian psychology) is all the epistemology we want or need. This is evasion of the epistemological question with a vengeance![82] Despite Davidson's claim to have exposed and overcome the residual third dogma of empiricism in Quine's thought – i.e. the dualism of scheme and content – it seems to me that Davidson is himself still hooked on a version of that same dogma. At any rate this helps to explain his veering-about between (on the one hand) a formal or logically regimented theory of truth, meaning and interpretation and (on the other) a radical empiricist notion or direct or 'unmediated' sensory-perceptual content. According to Davidson the third (Quinean-Kuhnian) dogma – that of 'scheme and content' or 'organizing system and something waiting to be organized' – is probably the last which needs exposing, since 'if we give it up it is not clear that there is anything distinctive left to call empiricism' (Davidson, p. 189). At that stage it will make no sense – alter centuries of inconclusive debate – to think that there is some genuine (other than merely notional) dispute between rationalist and empiricist philosophies of mind, knowledge and language. Quite simply, we can push right through with Quine's revisionist programme (just as Quine claimed to push right through with the programme of those who had somehow stopped short on the same path) and thereby arrive at a point where these distinctions drop out since truth *just is* whatever counts as such by our best evidential lights.

Thus '[t]he totality of sensory evidence is what we want provided it is all the evidence there is; and all the evidence there is is just what it takes to make our sentences or theories true' (p. 194). However, one then has to ask what becomes of 'truth' when that concept is so directly linked to an empiricist notion of evidential warrant, and the 'evidence' in question is itself subject only to an abstract (Tarskian) conception of truth that offers no guidance in specific contexts of interpretative grasp or correct understanding. Once again, the lesson seems clear: that any adequate approach to such matters will have to incorporate a theory of reference that finds sufficient room for normative criteria beyond those envisaged by Davidson's idea of our somehow regaining 'unmediated touch' with the 'familiar objects' that fix the truth-conditions of our various candidate statements, hypotheses, predictions, and so forth. Also, as I have said, it will need to reconcile the otherwise conflicting claims of a truth-based, rationality-optimizing theory as to how meanings and beliefs can be best, most charitably construed and a causal-explanatory account which anchors them in certain objective features of the world and our own or other people's more or less adequate understanding of it.[83] That this is not to be had from any approach (whether logical-empiricist, Quinean, or Davidsonian) which conserves some remnant of the scheme/content or theory/evidence dichotomy is a case fully borne out by the past half-century of intensive debate on these issues of truth, knowledge and interpretation.

Notes

1 W. V. Quine, *Ontological Relativity and Other Essays* (New York: Columbia University Press, 1969), p. 72.
2 For further discussion from a range of viewpoints, see Tom L. Beauchamp and Alexander Rosenberg, *Hume and the Problem of Causation* (New York: Oxford University Press, 1981); H. O. Mounce, *Hume's Naturalism* (London: Routledge, 1999); David F. Norton (ed.), *The Cambridge Companion to Hume* (Cambridge: Cambridge University Press, 1993); Rupert Read and Kenneth A. Richman (eds), *The New Hume Debate* (London: Routledge, 2000); Galen Strawson, *The Secret Comnexion: Cansation, Realism, and David Hume* (Oxford: Clarendon Press, 1989).
3 See, for instance, J, Aronson, R. Harré and E. Way. *Realism Rescued: How Scientific Progress is Possible* (London: Duckworth, 1994); Roy Bhaskar, *A Realist Theory of Science* (Leeds: Leeds Books, 1975); Michael Devitt, *Realism and Truth,* 2nd edn (Oxford: Blackwell, 1986); R. Harré and E. H. Madden, *Causal Powers* (Oxford: Blackwell, 1975); Jarrett Leplin (ed.), *Scientific Realism* (Berkeley: University of California Press, 1984); Stathis Psillos, *Scientific Realism: How Science Tracks Truth* (London: Routledge, 1999); Wesley C. Salmon, *Scientific Realism and the Causal Structure of the World* (Princeton, NJ: Princeton University Press, 1984); M. Tooley, *Causation: A Realist Approach* (Oxford: Blackwell, 1988).
4 W. V. Quine, 'Two Dogmas of Empiricism', in *From a Logical Point of View,* 2nd edn (Cambridge, MA: Harvard University Press, 1961), pp. 20–46; also Quine, 'Epistemology Naturalized', in *Ontological Relativity and Other Essays* (op, cit.), pp. 69–90.
5 See also Peter Gibbins, *Particles and Paradoxes: The Limits of Quantum Logic* (Cambridge: Cambridge University Press, 1987); Susan Haack, *Deviant Logic: Some Philosophical Issues* (Cambridge University Press, 1974); Hilary Putnam, 'How to Think Quantum-Logically', *Synthèse*, Vol. 74 (1974), pp. 55–61.
6 See Sandra G. Harding (ed.), *Can Theories be Refuted? Essays on the Dubem-Quine Thesis* (Dordrecht: D. Reidel, 1976).
7 See especially Quine, *From a Logical Point of View* (*op. cit.*); also *Ontological Relativity and Other Essays* (New York: Columbia University Press, 1969); *Selected Logic Papers,* 2nd edn (Cambridge, MA: Harvard University Press, 1995); *The Ways of Paradox and Other Essays* (New York: Random House, 1966).
8 Quine, 'Reference and Modality', in Leonard Linsky (ed.), *Reference and Modality* (Oxford: Oxford University Press, 1971), pp. 17–34.
9 Quine, 'Epistemology Naturalized' (*op. cit.*).

10 See especially Wesley C. Salmon, *Hans Reichenbach: Logical Empiricist* (Dordrecht: D. Reidel, 1979) and *Four Decades of Scientific Explanation* (Minneapolis: University of Minnesota Press, 1989).

11 See Richard Boyd, 'The Current Status of Scientific Realism', in Leplin (ed.), *Scientific Realism* (*op. cit.*), pp. 41–82; also – for a similar statement of the case – Hilary Putnam, *Mathematics, Matter and Method* (Cambridge: Cambridge University Press, 1975), p. 73. For some sceptical counter-arguments see Larry Laudan, 'A Confutation of Convergent Realism', *Philosophy of Science*, Vol. 48 (1981), pp. 19–49.

12 Quine, 'Two Dogmas of Empiricism' (*op. cit.*).

13 John McDowell, *Mind and World* (Cambridge, MA: Harvard University Press, 1994).

14 Christopher Norris, 'McDowell on Kant: Redrawing the Bounds of Sense' and 'The Limits of Naturalism: Further Thoughts on McDowell's *Mind and World'*, in *Minding the Gap: Epistemology and Philosophy of Science in the Two Traditions* (Amherst, MA: University of Massachusetts Press, 2000), pp. 172–96, 197–230.

15 McDowell, *Mind and World* (*op. cit.*), p. 41.

16 Wilfrid Sellars, *Empiricism and the Philosophy of Mind* (Cambridge, MA; Harvard University Press, 1997).

17 See Notes 4 and 6 above; also Thomas S. Kuhn, *The Structure of Scientific Revolutions*, 2nd edn (Chicago: University of Chicago Press, 1970).

18 For further discussion see Michael Friedman, *A Parting of the Ways: Carnap. Cassirer, and Heidegger* (Chicago: Open Court, 2000).

19 See various contributions to Simon Glendinning (ed.), *The Ediuburgh Encyclopaedia of Continental Philosophy* (Edinburgh: Edinburgh University Press, 1999); also Norris, *Minding the Gap* (*op. cit.*) and *Resources of Realism: Prospects for 'Post-analytic' Philosophy* (London: Macmillan, 1997).

20 See, for instance, Joseph Rouse, *Knowledge and Power: Toward a Political Philosophy of Science* (Ithaca, NY; Cornell University Press, 1987); Richard Rorty, *Consequences of Pragmatism* (Brighton: Harvester, 1982) and *Objectivity, Relativism, and Truth* (Cambridge University Press, 1991); also Richard J. Bernstein, *Beyond Objectivism and Relativism: Science. Hermenentiss, and Praxis* (Philadelphia: University of Pennsylvania Press, 1983).

21 See Jaegwon Kim, *Supervenience and Mind: Selected Philosophical Essays* (Cambridge: Cambridge University Press, 1993).

22 Quine, 'Two Dogmas of Empiricism' (*op. cit.*), p. 43.

23 Kuhn, *The Structure of Scientific Revolutions* (*op. cit.*).

24 Quine, *Pursuit of Truth* (Cambridge, MA: Harvard University Press, 1990).

25 See Notes 3, 10 and 11 above; also Norris, *New Idols of the Cave: On the Limits of Anti-Realism* (Manchester: Manchester University Press, 1997) and *Philosophy of Language and the Challenge to Scientific Realism* (London: Routledge, 2004).

26 For early (causal-realist) Putnam, see especially the essays collected in his *Mind, Language and Reality* (Cambridge: Cambridge University Press, 1975). By the time of *Reason. Truth and History* (Cambridge University Press, 1981) he had adopted an 'internal' or framework-relative version of (quasi-)realism and has since explored a wide range of alternative pragmatist, naturalist, or 'commonsense' approaches. See *Realism and Reason* (Cambridge University Press, 1983); *Pragmatism: An Open Question* (Oxford: Blackwell, 1995); *The Many Faces of Realism* (La Salle, IL: Open Court, 1987); *Representation and Reality* (Cambridge University Press, 1988); *Realism With a Human Face* (Cambridge, MA: Harvard University Press, 1990); *Renewing Philosophy* (Harvard University Press, 1992).

27 Salmon, *Scientific Realism and the Causal Structure of the World* (*op. cit.*).

28 Norris, *Hilary Putnam: Reason, Realism, and the Uses of Uncertainty* (Manchester: Manchester University Press, 2002).

29 See Note 26, above; also Putnam, *Mathematics. Matter and Method* (Cambridge: Cambridge University Press, 1975).

30 Putnam, *The Collapse of the Fact/Value Dichotomy and Other Essays* (Cambridge, MA: Harvard University Press, 2002).

31 Putnam, *Reason, Truth and History* (*op. cit.*).

32 Putnam, *Mind, Language and Reality* (*op. cit.*); also Gregory McCulloch, *The Mind and Its World* (London: Routledge, 1995).

33 See, for instance, Amartya Sen, *On Ethics and Economics* (Oxford: Blackwell, 1987); *Inequality Reexamined* (Cambridge, MA: Harvard University Press, 1992); and *Development as Freedom* (New York: Anchor Books, 2000).

34 Cited by Putnam, *The Collapse of the Fact/Value, Dichotomy* (*op. cit.*), p. 30.

35 *Ibid.*, p. 31.

36 See Notes 1, 4, 7 and 24, above.

37 Noam Chomsky, 'Quine's Empirical Assumptions', *Synthèse*, Vol. 19 (1968), pp. 53–68.

38 Chomsky, 'A Review of B. F. Skinner's *Verbal Behavior*', *Language*, Vol. 35 (1959), pp. 126–58; also *Cartesian Linguistics* (New York: Harper & Row, 1966) and *Language and Mind* (New York: Harcourt, Brace, Jovanovich, 1972).

39 Putnam, *The Collapse of the Fact/Value Dichotomy* (*op. cit.*), p. 139.

40 Chomsky, *New Horizons in the Study of Language and Mind* (Cambridge: Cambridge University Press, 2000). See also James McGilvray, *Chomsky: Language, Mind, and Politics* (Cambridge: Polity Press, 1999).

41 See especially Chomsky, *Language and. Problems of Knowledge: The Managua Lectures* (Cambridge, MA: MIT Press, 1988).

42 Chomsky, 'Discussion of Putnam's Comments', in B. Beakley and P. Ludlow (eds), *The Philosophy of Mind: Classical Problems/Contemporary Issues* (Cambridge, MA: MIT Press, 1992), pp. 411–22.

43 Norris, 'Modularity, Nativism, and Reference-Fixing; On Chomsky's Internalist Assumptions', in *Language, Logic and Epistemology* (London: Macmillan, 2004), pp. 111–19.

44 See Edward Herman and Noam Chomsky, *Manufacturing Consent* (New York: Pantheon, 1988).

45 See Putnam, *Mind, Language and Reality* (*op. cit.*).

46 Putnam, *ibid.*; also Saul Kripke, *Naming and Necessity* (Oxford: Blackwell, 1980); David Lewis, *Counterfactuals* (Blackwell, 1973); M. Loux (ed.), *The Possible and the Actual* (Ithaca, NY: Cornell University Press, 1979); Stephen Schwartz (ed.), *Naming. Necessity, and Natural Kinds* (Ithaca, NY: Cornell University Press, 1977); R. C. Stalnaker, Inquiry (Cambridge, MA: MIT Press, 1987); David Wiggins, *Sameness and Substance* (Blackwell, 1980).

47 See Notes 3 and 11, above; also Gilbert Harman, 'Inference to the Best Explanation', *Philosophical Review*, Vol. 74 (1965), pp. 88–95; Peter Lipton, *Inference to the Best Explanation* (London: Routledge, 1993).

48 Quine, 'Two Dogmas of Empiricism' (*op. cit.*).

49 For further discussion see Norris, *Against Relativism: Philosophy of Science, Deconstruction and Critical Theory* (Oxford: Blackwell, 1997).

50 Donald Davidson, 'On the Very Idea of a Conceptual Scheme', in *Inquiries into Truth and Interpretation* (Oxford: Oxford University Press, 1984), pp. 183–98.

51 *Ibid.*, p. 198; see also Rudolf Carnap, *The Logical Structure of the World* (Berkeley: University of California Press, 1967).

52 Davidson, 'The Very Idea' (*op. cit.*), p. 197.

53 *Ibid.*, p. 197.

54 See especially Psillos, *Scientific Realism* (*op. cit.*) and other entries under Notes 3, 11 and 47, above.

55 See Hartry Field, 'Theory Change and the Indeterminacy of Reference', *Journal of Philosophy*, Vol. 70 (1973), pp. 462–81 and 'Quine and the Correspondence Theory', *Philosophical Review*, Vol. 83 (1974), pp. 200–28.

56 Putnam, *Mind, Language and Reality* (*op. cit.*).

57 For a different view of these matters, see Jerry Fodor, *The Elm and the Expert: Mentalese and Its Semantics* (Cambridge, MA: Bradford Books, 1995).

58 See, for instance, Schwartz (ed.), *Naming. Necessity and Natural Kinds* (*op. cit.*); also Gareth Evans, *The Varieties of Reference,* ed. J. McDowell (Oxford: Clarendon Press, 1982) and Gregory McCulloch, *The Game of the Name: Introducing Logic. Language and Mind* (Oxford: Clarendon, 1989).

59 Davidson, 'On the Very Idea' (*op. cit.*), p. 184.

60 See especially Michael Dummett, *Truth and Other Enigmas* (London; Duckworth, 1978), *The Logical Basis of Metaphysics* (Duckworth, 1991), and *The Seas of Language* (Oxford: Clarendon Press, 1993); also Michael Luntley, *Language, Logic and Experience: The Case for Anti-Realism* (Duckworth, 1988); Neil Tennant, *Anti-Realism and Logic* (Oxford: Clarendon Press, 1987) and *The Taming of the True* (Oxford: Oxford University Press, 1997).

61 My source for this particularly apt example is Scott Soames, *Understanding Truth* (Oxford: Oxford University Press, 1999).

62 See Bas van Fraassen, *The Scientific Image* (Oxford: Clarendon Press, 1980) and *Laws and Symmetry* (Clarendon, 1989).

63 van Fraassen, 'Empiricism in the Philosophy of Language', in Paul Churchland and Clifford Hooker (eds), *Images of Science: Essays on Realism and Empiricism, With a Reply from Bas C. van Fraassen* (Chicago: University of Chicago Press, 1985), p. 255.

64 *Ibid.*, p. 255.

65 Paul Churchland, 'The Ontological Status of Observables: In Praise of the Superempirical Virtues', in Churchland and Hooker (eds), *Images of Science* (*op. cit.*).

66 For a range of representative views, see William Bechtel and George Graham (eds), *A Companion to Cognitive Science* (Oxford: Blackwell, 1999); Alvin A. Goldman (ed.), *Readings in Philosophy and Cognitive. Science* (Cambridge, MA: MIT Press, 1993); Michael I. Posner (ed.), *Foundations of Cognitive Science* (MIT Press, 1989).

67 Kuhn, *The Structure of Scientific Revolutions* (*op. cit.*).

68 See Notes 1, 10 and 51 above.

69 Alfred Tarski 'The Concept of Truth in Formalised Languages', in *Logic, Semantics and Metamathmatics,* trans. J. H. Woodger (Oxford: Oxford University Press, 1956), pp. 152–278; also Davidson, 'In Defence of Convention T', in *Inquiries into Truth and Interpretation* (*op. cit.*), pp. 65–75; Simon Blackburn and Keith Simmons (eds), *Truth* (Oxford: Oxford University Press, 1999); Richard L. Kirkham, *Theories of Truth: A Critical Introduction* (Cambridge, MA: MIT Press, 1992).

70 See especially Davidson, 'The Structure and Content of Truth', *The Journal of Philosophy,* Vol. 87 (1990), pp. 279–328.

71 Davidson, 'A Coherence Theory of Truth and Knowledge', in Ernest LePore (ed.), *Truth and Interpretation: Perspectives on the Philosophy of Donald Davidson* (Oxford; Blackwell, 1986), pp. 307–19.

72 See Rorty, 'Pragmatism, Davidson and Truth', in *Objectivity. Relativism, and Truth* (Cambridge: Cambridge University Press, 1991), pp. 126–50 and 'Is Truth a Goal of Inquiry? Donald Davidson versus Crispin Wright', in *Truth and Progress* (Cambridge University Press, 1998), pp. 19–42; also Davidson, 'Afterthoughts, 1987', in Alan R. Malachowski (ed.), *Reading Rorty: Critical Responses to* Philosophy and the Mirror of Nature, *and Beyond* (Oxford; Blackwell, 1990), pp. 134–8.

73 See Note 60, above; also Norris, *Truth Matters: Realism, Anti realism and Response-Dependence* (Edinburgh: Edinburgh University Press, 2002).

74 See especially Davidson, *Essays on Actions and Events* (Oxford: Clarendon Press, 1980); also Kim, *Supervenience and Mind* (Note 21, above); G. II. von Wright, *Explanation and Understanding* (Ithaca, NY: Cornell University Press, 1971).

75 Sec, for instance, Ted Honderich, *Theory of Determinism: The Mind, Neuroscience and Life-Hopes* (Oxford; Clarendon Press, 1988) and *How Free Are You?: The Determinism Problem* (Oxford: Oxford University Press, 1993); also Honderich (ed.), *Essays on Freedom of Action* (London: Routledge & Kegan Paul, 1973).

76 See Lorraine Code, *Epistemic Responsibility* (Hanover, NH: University Press of New England, 1987); M. DePaul and L. Zagzebski (eds), *Intellectual Virtue: Perspectives from Ethics and Epistemology* (Oxford: Oxford University Press, 2002); A. Fairweather and L. Zagzebski (eds), *Virtue Epistemology: Essays on Epistemic Virtue and Responsibility* (Oxford: Oxford University Press, 2001); L. Zagzebski, *Virtues of the Mind: An Inquiry into the Nature of Virtue and the Ethical Foundations of Knowledge* (Cambridge: Cambridge University Press, 1996).

77 For the most widely influential statement of this view, see Peter Winch, *The Idea of a Social Science and Its Relation to Philosophy* (London: Routledge & Kegan Paul, 1958) and *Trying to Make Sense* (Oxford: Blackwell, 1987).

78 See, for instance, Alasdair MacIntyre, *Against the Self-Images of the Age: Essays on Ideology and Philosophy* (London: Duckworth, 1971) and Norris, *Against Relativism* (*op. cit.*).

79 See Notes 1 and 4 above; also Quine, *Word and Object* (Cambridge, MA: MIT Press, 1960).

80 See Note 69, above.

81 See Note 70, above.

82 Putnam, *The Collapse of the Fact/Value Dichotomy* (*op. cit.*), p. 139.

83 See, for instance, Alvin Goldman, *Epistemology and Cognition* (Cambridge, MA: Harvard University Press, 1986) and *Knowledge in a Social World* (Oxford: Clarendon Press, 1999); Hilary Kornblich (ed.), *Naturalizing Epistemology* (Cambridge, MA: MIT Press, 1985); David Papineau, *Philosophical Naturalism* (Oxford: Blackwell, 1993); Ernest Sosa, *Knowledge in Perspective: Selected Essays in Epistemology* (Cambridge: Cambridge University Press, 1991).

7 Aristotelian powers

Charlotte Witt

Aristotle's theory of causation has multiple threads, and his texts invite multiple interpretations. The variation in interpretation is, in part, a result of different perspectives and questions that are brought to the text. For instance, Aristotle's theory of the four causes has invited scrutiny from contemporary philosophers of science, who are interested in theories of explanation (van Fraassen 1977) as well as philosophers of biology, who are interested in teleology, taxonomy and other concepts (Gotthelf 1987). This chapter looks at Aristotle's theory of causal powers in relation to contemporary realist theories of causation in science and social science. Within this broad topic I focus on two aspects of Aristotle's ontology of causal powers that are crucial for an adequate understanding of his views and yet, unlike Aristotle's essentialism and theory of natural kinds, have not received the attention they deserve. I am thinking of the fact that Aristotle does not differentiate ontologically between rational and non-rational causal powers, and the fact that both types of power rest upon the ontological distinction between potentiality and actuality. The first topic should interest philosophers trying to extend a realist account of causation from the physical sciences to the social sciences. The second topic is of relevance to contemporary philosophers interested in exploring the metaphysical commitments of causal powers.

I devote particular attention to the ontology of causal powers as Aristotle develops it in *Metaphysics* IX (Witt 2004).[1] This focus will allow me to develop two points. First, Aristotle's realism about causal powers faces a challenge, which leads him to distinguish two ways of being for causal powers. Aristotle finds it necessary to defend the existence of inactive causal powers because of the challenge of Megarian actualism. The Megarians hold that a causal power exists only while and so long as it is active. A person can build a house only when she is actually building it; a fire can heat water only when it is actually heating it; an object is perceptible only when it is actually being perceived – and so on. But, it is part of the notion of a causal power that it exists whether or not it is active. In order to respond to this challenge Aristotle draws a distinction between two ways of being a power; when it is active the power exists actually; when it is inactive it exists potentially. Contemporary writers have noted that we need a way of understanding powers that includes their present but inactive existence (Harre 1970, p. 84), although Aristotle's ontological response to this difficulty might seem wrong-headed or unnecessary. One objectionable aspect to his solution is the inherently teleological relationship between being x potentially and being x actually. Aristotle's dispositional definition of causal powers rests upon a teleological footing.

Second, Aristotle does not draw an ontological distinction between those powers that operate with reason (e.g. crafts like house-building or arts like medicine), and those that do not. He does provide different conditions of realization for the two kinds of powers, but those conditions are variants within the same dispositional understanding of causal powers. In this regard, Aristotle offers one possible realist framework of causal powers that sees human action (and hence the social sciences) on a continuum with the natural sciences rather than as categorically (ontologically) different from them, and therefore requiring an entirely distinct explanatory framework. It is important to note, however, that Aristotle's paradigmatic natural science is biology and his framework for understanding natural living substances (organisms) is teleological. In contrast, contemporary philosophers take physics as the paradigmatic natural science. This difference raises the question of how relevant or useful Aristotle's unified framework of causal powers is today given that teleology fits well with a focus on biology but not with a focus on physics or chemistry.

The common theme that unites both of these aspects of Aristotle's ontology of causal powers is the central presence of teleology. It is because of the teleologically directed character of the potentiality–actuality framework that Aristotle can refute Megarian actualism. A dormant power is intrinsically dependent upon, and teleologically directed toward, activity, or actuality, and that is the character of its being; it exists potentially. And, Aristotle conceives of human activities as on a continuum with the behavior of non-rational animals because of the unifying role of teleology that is common to behavior at both ends of the spectrum. It may be the case that a realist ontology of powers that spans both natural and human activity must rest on a teleological footing, but I will not argue this point on Aristotle's behalf in this chapter. I *will* argue, however, that the central role of teleology in Aristotle's ontology of causal powers sets his views apart from many contemporary versions of realist theories of causal powers.

The discussion so far has concerned the ontological commitments of Aristotle's theory of causal powers. But how does Aristotle think that causal powers work? In the first section I introduce Aristotle's definition of a causal power as an origin of change in another thing, and his dispositional analysis of causal powers. Briefly, causal powers are defined in terms of their activation conditions. They are dispositions that a substance has to move or be moved by another substance in a particular way (the term "move" covers a wide range of possible changes and alterations including, but not limited to, locomotion). In the second section I explain how Aristotle's dispositional analysis is global, and, in particular, that it applies to both rational and non-rational powers. Aristotle draws no ontological distinction between the two kinds of powers. In the third section, I discuss the ontological challenge posed by Megarian actualism to Aristotle's theory of causal powers, and his response to it.

Aristotle's theory of causal powers

In ordinary Greek *dunamis* means "strength" or "power" and also "ability" or "faculty." The term occurs with this range of meaning in both philosophical and non-philosophical contexts. We say that fire has the power to heat other substances and we think that it has that power whether or not it is actually heating anything. We also speak of a person's abilities, like the ability to play the viola or to speak French. These abilities, we think, exist even when we are not using them, when we are asleep or engaged in other activities. One way to think about the powers or abilities of substances is as dispositional properties, which are exercised in certain circumstances but not in others. We can contrast the dispositional properties of a substance with its categorical properties, like height or weight. Since substances, like animals or plants, have both dispositional and categorical properties, it seems uncontroversial that powers and abilities exist. In *Metaphysics* IX, however, Aristotle tells us that some philosophers disputed the existence of *dunamis* and held, for example, that a person can play the viola or build a house only when she is actually or actively engaged in those activities. Actualists do not think that inactive powers or abilities exist. And, since it is part of the notion of a causal power that it exist even when inactive, the actualist argument is really an argument against causal powers. I return to the actualist challenge in the third section.

Aristotle's definition of the term *dunamis* builds on its use in ordinary language. For Aristotle the primary, or basic, meaning of *dunamis* is "the origin of change in another thing or in the thing itself as other" (*Metaph.* IX 1046a 10–11). A *dunamis*, in this sense, is a power to change another thing. As examples, Aristotle mentions the art of building and the power of heating. These powers are origins of changes, of building and of heating, respectively, that are located in an object separate from the building materials or the cold body. The act of building a house or heating a body has its beginning in a power or ability of the builder or heating agent. The primary meaning of *dunamis* centers on the idea of an agent or an active power. In the case of a builder, the power or ability to build originates in his knowledge of the art of building. A heating agent, in contrast, is able to heat by virtue of being hot. In one case, the power that originates the change is like the product (heat) and in the other case it is different (the art of building is not a building). Aristotle explains both human agency (house-building) and physical causal interactions (heating) by means of the notions of agent and passive powers. Although Aristotle distinguishes between the realization conditions of rational and non-rational powers, the distinction between rational agency and physical causation is not fundamental to his thought. I return to this point in the second section.

Corresponding to the idea of an agent power is a passive power, the power an object has to be changed in some respect. Each agent power or agent requires a corresponding receptivity to change in another object. "For the one is in the thing acted on; it is because it contains a certain motive principle, and because even the matter is a motive principle, that the thing acted on is acted on ... For that which is oily, can be burnt and that which yields in a particular way can be crushed" (1046a 20–25). These examples might give the impression that all agent powers originate in the form of a substance, while all passive powers originate in its matter. For example, the agent power of the doctor's art originates in her soul or form, and the passive power of an olive to be crushed is clearly a material feature. The correlation between agent power and form, and passive power and matter, does not hold in all cases, however. For example, the agent power of heat is material, and the ability to learn music is a passive power that originates in the form or soul of the student. Therefore, agent and passive powers cannot be systematically correlated with form and matter.

With one exception Aristotle insists on the separate location of agent and passive powers: in so far as an agent changes something, it changes another object, and not itself. The agent power and the passive power are in two different objects. If an object changes itself, as for example a doctor might cure herself, then Aristotle's different object requirement holds that we must divide the doctor into agent and patient. Aristotle adds "And so, in so far as a thing is an organic unity (*sumpephuken*), it cannot be acted upon by itself; for it is one and not two different things" (1046a 28–29). The different object requirement obviously does not govern changes which are internal to a natural substance, if that substance undergoes the change as a unified whole. So, for example, we cannot use agent and passive powers to explain the process of development a human being undergoes from baby through childhood to adulthood since that happens to the human organism as a whole. And, since every plant and animal is a natural unity that undergoes development, not all the changes that natural substances cause and undergo can be explained within the framework of agent and passive powers.

Towards the end of *Metaphysics* IX Aristotle tells us that he is particularly interested in a kind of *dunamis* or power that he calls "nature." Nature is an internal principle of change within a unified organism, which Aristotle explicitly distinguishes from agent and passive powers by invoking the different object requirement (1049b 5–9). Hence, Aristotle's understanding of *dunamis* is not restricted to the agent and passive powers of substances; it includes the internal origin or agent of their teleological development. Although it is fair to infer that nature is a power with different realization conditions from agent and passive powers, Aristotle does not explicitly spell out realization conditions for nature here. Of course, Books I and II of the *Physics* contain an extended discussion of nature and its principles.

In contrast, Aristotle's explanation of agent and passive powers strongly suggests that they can be given a dispositional analysis. To say that oil has the passive power of being flammable is to say that under certain conditions (which can be given a general or lawlike specification) oil will burn. Similarly, to say that fire has the agent power of heating is to say that under certain conditions (which can be given a general or lawlike specification) fire will heat another object. Absent the appropriate set of conditions, however, neither power will be activated or expressed. Hence, its agent and passive powers are dispositions that a substance has to act upon another substance or to be acted upon by another substance.

Aristotle's basic notion of a causal power is that of an agent, which is activated when it meets up with a correlative passive power (in the appropriate circumstances). These powers, together, achieve a single outcome: "the wholesome produces only health, and the calorific only heat, the frigorific only cold" (1046b 19–20). In *Metaphysics* IX chapter 5, Aristotle gives the conditions under which an agent power acts. "When the agent and the patient meet in a way appropriate to the power in question, the one must act and the other be acted upon" (1048a 5–7) Indeed, Aristotle proposes to define a power in terms of its realization or activation conditions: "that which is capable of something and at some time and in some way (with all the other qualifications which must be present in *the definition*)" (1047b 35–1048a 2). In order to act, an agent power like heat must meet up with something with the passive power to be heated, in the appropriate circumstances. And the agent power of heat can be defined by means of a specification of these activation conditions.

The operation of causal powers is necessary if and when all of the activation conditions have been met – "the one *must* act and the other be acted upon"– (1048a 7). While Aristotle maintains the reality of causal necessity throughout his discussion of causal powers (including, as we will see, those causal powers that underwrite human agency), Aristotle also recognizes that causal powers without reason differ from those that operate with reason with regard to their activation conditions. How does he describe the difference?

Aristotle on powers with reason

Not all agent powers have precisely the same kinds of realization conditions. Aristotle distinguishes powers that inhere in things without souls (non-living substances) from powers that inhere in things with soul (living substances). Living substances, in turn, are divided into those that have both rational (*meta logon*) and non-rational (*alogon*) agent powers and those that have only non-rational powers. For Aristotle the central cases of the rational powers of living beings are the arts or other productive understandings. Arts are "originative sources of change in another thing or in the artist himself considered as other" (1046b 2–4). The art of house-building is an example of a rational power that is the origin of change in another thing (the building materials) and the art of medicine is an example of a rational power that can originate a change in the object itself, in the case where the doctor heals herself. Although Aristotle is clearly thinking of human activities, and he believes that only human beings have rational soul, the centrality of productive (craft) activities might allow for an extension of rational powers to certain non-human animal species.

Agent powers that operate with a *logos* follow a slightly different pattern from those that do not. What does the word *logos* mean in this context? Some scholars argue that it should be understood to mean the power of reasoning, a part or function of the soul parallel to the power of growth or desire. Here the emphasis is on art as requiring reasoning; a doctor has to reason about the best means to achieve health in the patient. Others argue that "with a logos" means with a principle or rule.

Here the emphasis is on art as a rule-governed activity; a doctor has to follow the rules or principles of medicine. Pretty clearly Aristotle does think of arts, like medicine and house-building, as involving a means–end reasoning process. And, since Aristotle sometimes says that the active power in the doctor is the art of medicine, he might think of the doctor as following a medical rule or principle. Probably he incorporates both of these ideas in his phrase "with a logos."

Aristotle describes two differences between rational and non-rational agent powers. Both concern the effects of the causal power. A non-rational power or agent is capable of only one effect (in one set of circumstances); a heating agent heats. Non-rational powers are single outcome (1046b 19–20). A rational power like the art of medicine, in contrast, can produce either one of a pair of contrary effects (in one set of circumstances); a doctor can improve or cure the patient and a doctor can worsen or even kill the patient. Rational powers have multiple possible outcomes. Someone who knows what health is, and can bring it about, also knows what disease is, and can bring that about as well. And, even if the doctor has good motives, there is more than one possible outcome. Second, a rational power does not bring about an effect that is the same as itself in the way that a non-rational power can. A physician, whose knowledge of medicine is a rational agent power, cures a patient. She brings about the state of health in the patient rather than teaching him medicine. Similarly, a house-builder does not make the art of house-building or an object with that art (which is a rational power); he builds a house. In contrast, non-rational powers can convey the property they embody directly to the object. Heat makes the object hot (again, assuming a particular set of circumstances and conditions).

There is a kind of distance and flexibility between a rational power and what it brings about. Because it does not simply duplicate itself in another object, a rational power can bring about the full range of different effects that fall between the contraries that specify the range in question (e.g. health and illness for the doctor). Rational powers are not as limited in what they can cause as non-rational powers are. How does Aristotle explain the *flexibility* of rational powers?

Since the rational power of medicine could be the origin of a range of states in the patient from health to its opposite, it is clear that the power itself (the art of medicine) cannot be the sole origin of the change. If the art of medicine can produce either health or sickness (or some state in between the two), but cannot produce both at once, then some other factor must determine which of these will eventuate. Hence, Aristotle adds a realization condition to powers with reason – either desire or choice (*orexis, proairesis*) is the deciding principle. This is the third difference between rational and non-rational powers. Non-rational powers do not require any additional principle "when the agent and the patient meet in the way appropriate to the potency in question, the one must act and the other be acted on" (1048a 6–8).

Choice is a central concept in Aristotle's ethical theory; choice knits together the rational process of means–end deliberation to our actions. He defines choice as "a deliberative desire for things that are up to us" (*E.N.* 1113a 11). *Prohairesis* means "preference"; it is a choosing-before that incorporates desire into the process of reasoning. Does the addition of choice to the activation conditions of rational powers indicate an ontological distinction between human agency and natural change? In particular, does Aristotle think that the activity of rational powers is free in a metaphysical sense that would require a sharp ontological divide between the realm of human action and the realm of natural causation? How does Aristotle understand the voluntary character of human actions?

In different places Aristotle lists several conditions for voluntary actions. Voluntary actions are those that are "up to us" to perform or refrain from doing. If I were a divinity, a necessary being, then my actions would be necessary and not "up to me" to perform (*E.E.* II 6 1222b 20–23). Human actions are contingent and not necessary like divine action. The action must also have its causal origin in me. I am not responsible for what happens when my ship is blown off course by a typhoon. Finally, the agent must know the relevant facts concerning the circumstances surrounding the action. Oedipus did not kill his father voluntarily, since he did so in ignorance that the person he struck was his father. Although there are apparent tensions between what Aristotle says in different texts, it is clear that Aristotle's analysis of voluntary actions includes a causal condition and an epistemic condition. Actions that are "up to us" to perform or to refrain from performing are actions that are intentionally performed and whose origin is internal to the agent. However, the internal causal principle requirement does not require further that the internal origin itself is entirely unconditioned and a break in the causal order. On the contrary, Aristotle thinks both that a medical action like purging is up to the doctor to perform (or not), and that the action has an origin internal to the doctor. The internal origin in the case of a rational power like medicine is both the knowledge of medicine and the specific decision of the doctor to undertake one course of treatment rather than another.

Once choice or desire is added to tilt the scale, the activation of rational powers turns out to be no less necessitated than active powers like heat. "Therefore every agent, which has a rational power, when it desires that for which it has a power, and in the circumstances in which it has the power, *must* do this" (1048a 13–15). Rather than making an exception for rational powers, Aristotle wants to make the activity of agent powers all equally necessitated in the appropriate circumstances, which raises a problem for those powers which can result in opposites or multiple outcomes. Choice and desire are causal principles Aristotle uses to make rational powers *like* all other agent powers – as necessitated by their realization conditions – rather than to make them different. Hence, it is a mistake to interpret the Aristotle's distinction between rational and non-rational powers as ontological or as concerned with the issue of free will and determinism in the sphere of human action. For Aristotle both rational and non-rational powers can be given a dispositional analysis; both are to be defined in terms of their activation conditions. And both are necessarily activated when these conditions are met. With regard to the necessity governing causal powers, both rational and non-rational powers are the same. Aristotle's dispositional understanding of how causal powers operate and interact is unified, and does not support or require a sharp distinction between how we explain human activity and how we explain natural causation.

The ontology of powers in Aristotle

Intuitively, the existence of causal powers is obvious and uncontroversial. We often talk about the powers and abilities of substances – humans, plants, material stuffs. What could be less controversial than the idea that objects and materials have abilities and powers, which they exercise (or express) at certain times, but not at others? What could be more obvious than the idea that objects have the potential to do things other than they are doing at present or to be other than they are at present? Who could doubt the fact that human beings have a wide range of innate faculties – like perception – and acquired abilities for activities – like playing the viola or building a house?

No matter how uncontroversial the existence of powers and abilities might appear to us, there were (and are) philosophers who question their existence. According to Aristotle, "there are some who say, like the Megarians, that a thing can act only when it is acting" (1046b 29–30). If a thing can act only when it is acting, then there are no abilities and powers that the thing has even when it is not actually using them. Aristotle presents several arguments against the actualist position. It is important to see that what is at issue between Aristotle and the actualist is not the existence of *dunamis*, but the existence of inactive *dunamis*. The disagreement between Aristotle and the actualist turns on whether or not the idea of a *dunamis,* which can exist in two ways, as inactive *and* as active, is philosophically acceptable. Of course, if inactive *dunamis* does not exist, then we lose our ordinary view of powers, which exist both when active and when inactive.

Aristotle has two responses to the Megarians. First, he argues directly against the coherence and intelligibility of the Megarian account of powers. I have discussed the details of these arguments elsewhere (Witt 2004). Aristotle's second response is important for the purpose of understanding Aristotle's ontology of powers. Aristotle responds to the Megarian's position that inactive powers do not exist by reference to the ontological distinction between being x potentially (an inactive power) and being x actually (an active power). Notice that Aristotle does not think that a contrary to fact analysis of powers as dispositions is sufficient to account for the present existence of inactive powers (Harre 1970). To account for the present existence of inactive powers, Aristotle thinks, you need the concept of potentiality.

But the concept of potentiality is a relational concept, and must be understood in relation to actuality. To further complicate matters, Aristotle thinks that being x potentially and being x actually should be grasped by example, and that neither term can be defined. Aristotle's examples include that of the exercise of a power or capacity of a substance to the inactive capacity (e.g. someone actually seeing to someone who can see but has her eyes shut), and that of a completed substance to its matter. Aristotelian powers exemplify Aristotle's distinction between being x potentially and being x actually. When an agent power like house-building is inactive it exists potentially, and when it is active, it exists actually. Aristotle's distinction between two ways of being responds to the actualist claim that only active powers exist. In a sense, Aristotle splits the difference between his view and the Megarians. He denies the Megarian view that powers exist only when active; but he does not claim that inactive powers exist simpliciter. When they are inactive, they exist potentially; when active, they exist actually.

By applying the potentiality/actuality distinction to causal powers, Aristotle places them within a relational, teleological framework. Potentiality and actuality are relational terms in Aristotle because something that exists potentially only does so in relation to existing actually. Being x potentially is a relational way of being that is both teleologically directed toward, and ontologically dependent upon, being x actually. What is potentially is for the sake of an actuality, but actualities do not exist for the sake of potentialities. There is a one-way dependency that tracks the teleological directedness between what is potentially (the power of sight) and what is actually (seeing). In short, the priority of actuality in relation to potentiality is central to Aristotle's ontology of powers, and the basic structure that underlies this priority relation is teleological.

Conclusion

Aristotle's theory of causal powers is an important resource for contemporary philosophers interested in developing a non-Humean, realist theory of causation for the natural sciences and the social sciences. One positive aspect of Aristotle's view, I have argued here, is that he provides one model of what a unified theory of causal powers, applicable both to natural causation and human activity, might look like. As I remarked earlier, the centrality of biological organisms makes teleological explanations basic to Aristotelian science of the natural world. From this perspective it is easy to see human actions as explicable using the framework of causal powers appropriate to understanding the teleological activities of non-human natural beings – with just a little tweaking. But, if we restrict teleological action to the human realm (and to the exercise of rational powers), then the common thread that Aristotle finds between human action and nature is severed. Without the teleological thread it is unclear on what basis it makes sense to extend a realist theory of causal powers from natural causation to human activity. On the other hand, contemporary philosophers might be inspired by Aristotle to make biology the paradigmatic natural science and to find in biological explanations useful resources for a unitary theory of causal powers.

A deeper challenge facing contemporary readers is that Aristotle grounds his dispositional understanding of causal powers on the ontological bedrock of potentiality. And, as I have stressed, potentiality is a relational category that is teleologically directed toward, and ontologically dependent upon, actuality. And, the teleological directedness of potentiality is not (and cannot be) captured in a dispositional (counterfactual) analysis of causal powers. Although it provides a solution to the problem of the present existence of dormant causal powers, the metaphysical teleology associated with potentiality might be too high a price to pay for the ontologically parsimonious.

Notes

1 I am grateful to Cornell University Press for permission to use sections of my book, *Ways of Being: Potentiality and Actuality in Aristotle's Metaphysics*, in this essay.

References

Gotthelf, Alan (1987) "Aristotle's Conception of Final Causality." In *Philosophical issues in Aristotle's Biology*, eds. Gotthelf, Alan and Lennox, J. Cambridge: Cambridge University press.

Harre, R. (1970) "Powers." In *The British Journal for the Philosophy of Science* Vol. 21, No. 1:81–101.

Jaeger, W. (1957) *Aristotelis*. Metaphysica: Oxford.

Ross, W.D. (1950) *Aristotelis*. Physica: Oxford.

Van Fraassen, Bas (1977) "The Pragmatics of Explanation." In *American Philosophical Quarterly 14:*143–150.

Witt, Charlotte (2004) *Ways of Being: Potentiality and Actuality in Aristotle's Metaphysics*. Ithaca: Cornell University Press.

8   Powers, dispositions, properties or a causal realist manifesto

Stephen Mumford

Objects are powerful because properties are powerful

Particular objects and substances are causally powerful and causally responsive. They are able to do things and have things done to them. Dynamite is explosive: able to produce a dramatic bang, flash and flame when lit. A billiard ball is able to project other like objects when it strikes them and has sufficient momentum. Lysergic acid diethylamide is able to produce hallucinations in human beings but also able to turn litmus paper red.

In virtue of what do objects and substances have their powers? In general terms, all of these powers are attributable to the properties of the object or substance. The billiard ball is able to strike and propel another because of its hardness, shape, weight and momentum. A sponge is able to soak up water because it is porous. It is (has the property of being) full of pores, which have just the right size to take and hold water. Dynamite is made from volatile nitroglycerin but absorbed into an inert porous solid, meaning that an explosion is possible only through ignition. A knife cuts because it is hard and sharp. Ice cools because it has a lower temperature than its surroundings, which means that the kinetic energy of any adjacent substance will be transferred to the ice by conduction until the ice is melted.

In some causal transactions, one object appears more passive than another. Cloth is able to be cut with a knife but it seems slightly odd to speak of this as a power of the cloth rather than a power of the knife. But nothing would be able to cut if nothing were able to be cut. We have reciprocal powers here, as C. B. Martin put it (1993a: 516 and 1993b: 182). One can be thought of as an ability and the other perhaps as a liability. All of powers, abilities, liabilities, capacities, propensities, tendencies and aptnesses are among the rich dispositional family of concepts. The distinction between active and passive may not hold any real metaphysical importance. Is the disposition of a sponge to soak up and hold water an active or passive power? It is easy to think of it as either, which suggests that there is no ontological division in reality that mirrors the conceptual distinction we draw. Martin's phrase 'reciprocal mutual manifestation partners' keeps neutrality on this issue. The lemonade cools and the ice melts. Is the ice active or passive? Is the lemonade active or passive? Both are doing something to the other and yet at the same time are having something done to them. I will thus be taking the line that being able to do something and being able to have something done are both powers of an object, on a metaphysical par. Indeed, we will see in the fourth section that we have need of the causes of a property as much as we have need of its effects. It is important not just that things be powerful but also that they be responsive.

We have causal powers of objects, therefore, and I claim that objects have them in virtue of their properties. Some of the properties we have found are hardness, momentum, porosity, sharpness, temperature. Here are some further plausible claims about the connection between causal powers and properties:

1   Objects with all the same properties will have all the same causal powers.
2   To change the causal powers of an object, one will have to change its properties.
3   The same property always contributes the same causal power (even though there will be cases in which that power cannot be manifested because of its coinstantiation with other, counteracting powers).
4   Objects with the same causal powers will not necessarily have all the same properties: it's possible for the same power to come about in different ways. But properties with all the same causal powers will always be the same.

What relation between properties and powers would explain 1 to 4? In this chapter, I am going to defend a strong thesis. It is a thesis that some have considered attractive but usually too strong to hold. It is the thesis that what explains 1 to 4 is that properties just are powers. The relation between them is the closest relation: identity. The defence of this view is not my only aim, however.

Entangled concepts

A number of key concepts have been employed and they are often confused and conflated. My second aim in this chapter is to disentangle the concepts *power*, *disposition* and *property*. What is the problem? For a start, power and disposition are often taken to be equivalent. Hence just as we may speak of a disposition to explode, we can also speak of a power to explode. If it makes no difference whether we say power or disposition, then perhaps they mean one and the same. Something else suggests a difference, though. Dispositions are often thought of as properties, hence we have the phrase 'dispositional property' (usually opposed to 'categorical property'). But 'power property' seems inadmissible. We think of a property or of a power, but not both together as a single thing. Given how unnatural 'power property' seems, maybe powers and dispositions are not the same.

Are powers best thought of not as properties at all? Should they be considered linguistically and metaphysically as particulars rather than properties? We can indeed use power as a count noun, speaking of a power, two powers, a collection of powers. Perhaps, then, powers can be opposed to both dispositions and properties. If so, then how would powers contrast with and relate to dispositions? Couldn't dispositions also be understood as particulars? And, if so, how would these particulars (the powers and dispositions) relate to properties?

Note that powers and dispositions bear another mark of particularity: they can have/instantiate properties: for example, a power can be abundant or useful. But this is not decisive and does not compel the conclusion that powers and dispositions are particulars instead of properties. Being the subject of properties does not preclude something from being itself a property. Properties can bear further properties: higher-order properties. Squareness is symmetrical, where being symmetrical is a property of a property. That a power can instantiate a property is no guide, therefore, to whether it itself is a particular or a property.

We have three seemingly separate concepts, therefore, which appear to bear some relation. It is not clear exactly what this relation is. I hope to clarify this issue and, in so doing, make a substantial and interesting claim about the nature of properties. A correct understanding of powers and dispositions can reveal something about the very being of a property and establish the foundations of a causal realist metaphysic.

The early shoemaker theory

The claim I want to defend is based on Sydney Shoemaker's early theory of properties. The theory is blunt and simple: that properties *are* powers. I call this claim S:

S: 'properties are causal powers'.

(Shoemaker 1980: 210)

This theory trades on the intuition that I outlined at the beginning. There is a close relationship between the causal powers of an object and its properties, as described in the plausible claims 1–4. What is the exact nature of this relationship? Why does a change in an object's causal powers require a change in its properties? Shoemaker's view was that the close connection between powers and properties was actually the closest connection: identity itself. The idea was not new to Shoemaker. It can be found in Locke (1690: III, 8, viii). Popper has a related claim, that all properties are dispositional (1959: 424), but this is not quite the position that Shoemaker was defending and which I wish to revive. I will support S, though it should be noted that there are other claims in Shoemaker (1980) that I would wish to resist, for example, that the powers of a thing depend on its non-dispositional properties.

Shoemaker's position S undergoes a little revision to S1, which gives the position I will defend:

S1: 'properties are clusters of conditional powers'.

(1980: 213)

S1 introduces two refinements, each of which is significant for the theory of properties. First, properties are *clusters* of powers; hence there is not necessarily a one-to-one relation between properties and powers. Some properties will be complex in that having them involves having more than one power. Being acidic, for example, involves all sorts of powers to do different things in different situations and to different kinds of other object and substance. Being red and being spherical are also complex properties in the sense of involving a multiplicity of powers. Many properties, therefore, will be identical with a cluster or set of causal powers. But one need not rule out a property being identical with but a single power: a power in a singleton set or cluster of one. This would be a very simple property, perhaps something like spin, charge or mass, where there is a precise scientific account of what power this property involves or, on the S1 theory, what this property is. A cluster view might also have some unexpected advantages. For instance, the cluster view might explain why some properties are simple, some are complex, and why simplicity and complexity can come in degrees. A property is absolutely simple when it is a single power, complex when it is a cluster of many powers, and more complex than another when it is a cluster of more powers than that other. The cluster view also has an explanation of how some properties can resemble others. Resemblance, in at least some cases, could be accounted for in terms of common powers in two different clusters. This would be like two sets that had some common members. Just one difference in the membership is enough to make two different sets. Hence being round and being spherical have some resemblance because they have some powers in common. Among them is the power to cause a disc-shaped perception in human beings. Some of the powers of some of the properties will be powers to affect perceivers, though only idealists would think that this is so of all the powers of all the properties.

The second extra claim that S1 introduces is that properties are clusters of *conditional* powers. Here I would like to defend a slightly different emphasis to what I think is Shoemaker's. I take conditional to mean that a power may have its manifestation conditional on what other powers an object possesses. There is a power to cut in virtue of being knife-shaped though it can be manifested only if its bearer also has the property of being hard, rather than the property of being soft. A distinction can be made here between having a power whose manifestation is prevented and not having that power at all. I favour interpreting *conditional power* in the first sense. Shoemaker may prefer the second interpretation though what he says is sometimes ambiguous between the two (and I am not asserting that he definitely held one of these views rather than the other, see for example the discussion at 1980: 223). I prefer to say that a property involves powers, whose manifestations are conditional rather than possession of the power itself being conditional because otherwise the plausible claim 3, above – the same property always contributes the same causal power – would have to be relinquished. The following explains why.

S1 leaves us with a version of *dispositional essentialism*, though Shoemaker does not use that name to describe his position. Dispositional essentialism has been followed by Swoyer (1982) and Ellis (2001) has developed a wide-ranging version. In Shoemaker's account, such dispositional essentialism is restricted to the case of properties:

> … what makes a property the property it is, what determines its identity, is its potential for contributing to the causal powers of the things that have it. This means, among other things, that if under all possible circumstances properties X and Y make the same contribution to the causal powers of the things that have them, X and Y are the same property.
>
> (1980: 212)

In respect of properties, I will seek to retain dispositional essentialism. This does not commit me, I believe, to further forms of essentialism, extending the position to natural kinds (see Putnam 1975; Ellis 2001 and, for a non-essentialist account of kinds, Mumford 2005).

If X and Y make the same contribution to the powers of things that have them, then X and Y are the same property. But then Shoemaker went on immediately to say that while his knife has the power to cut because it is knife-shaped, a cloud could have the same shape property without having the power to cut. Shoemaker's explanation is that having the power is conditional on what other properties the object also instantiates. But if this means that having the power is conditional on other properties, then this compromises his dispositional essentialism. Some instances of a property do not have the usual power for that property. For this reason, I find it preferable to say that all instances of the same property involve the same power and what is conditional is that the power be manifested. Hence, a cloud does have the power to cut but its manifestation is conditional on there being something softer than itself to cut. Whether there is something softer will depend, in part, on how hard or soft it itself is. No object has just one property. Objects typically have many. What they are able to manifest will be in part a function of how the powers of the object's properties interrelate. Some may counteract others. Others may work together for a certain effect. The manifest behaviour will be the outcome of what J. S. Mill (1843: bk III, ch. vi) called the composition of causes. The theory is far neater, however, if we accept that the same property always contributes the same powers.

So far, S1 looks attractive. We will now see, however, that the matter is not so simple and is not helped by the fact that Shoemaker himself retracted the view and offered arguments against it.

Shoemaker retracts this view

Shoemaker backed away from the bold S1 form of the theory when he said:

> I would want to reject the formulation of the causal theory which says that a property *is* a cluster of conditional powers … We must make use of the notion of a property in explaining the notion of a conditional power, so there

is no question here of reducing properties to some more fundamental sort of entity.

(Shoemaker 1998: 412)

Properties are not equated with powers, so what other relation holds between them? We find this later:

properties are individuated by the contribution they make to the causal powers of their subjects – or, to put it another way, by the 'conditional powers' they *bestow* on their subjects.

(Shoemaker 1999: 297, my italics)

Hence we have an alternative view, which jettisons the metaphysical economy of S1:

S2: properties bestow conditional powers.

Note that the revised view preserves a commitment to dispositional essentialism:

the causal features of a property, both forward-looking and backward-looking, are essential to it. And ... properties having the same causal features are identical.

(1998:413)

The backward-looking causal features of a property are mentioned because of the possibility of two distinct properties having all the same types of effect or causal powers. I agree with Shoemaker that this is possible but I agree also with his response that distinct properties cannot have the same effects and causes (Shoemaker 1980: 233; see also Mumford 1998: 162). That is, a property is individuated not just by its power to affect other things but also by its power to be affected by other things. These are the forward-looking and backward-looking causal features respectively.

How significant is the move to S2? The switch from properties being (identical with) powers to bestowing distinct powers is a radical change of view in Shoemaker's basic ontology, I maintain. The theory that clusters of powers constitute a property could be a fundamental insight into the *being* of properties. This would tell us what a property actually is, and answer a very different metaphysical question to the traditional one of whether properties are universals, tropes or particulars (nominalism). The same question of identity (or constitution) or bestowal could be asked whether realism or nominalism or trope theory is true for properties. Hence we have a second, distinct and much neglected, question in the ontology of properties.

Shoemaker was attracted to the view that properties are identical with powers. Now he rejects it. Which account is the most attractive, S1 or S2?

Reasons to prefer S1 to S2

I want to support something like S1 and think that Shoemaker was wrong to move to S2. S2 requires a mixed ontology where there are powers in addition to properties, even though the same property always bestows the same powers and therefore powers purportedly can provide identity conditions for properties. The first advantage of S1 is, therefore, its relative economy. This is illustrated in Figures 8.1 and 8.2, representing the ontologies of S1 and S2 respectively.

It is not just that Shoemaker moves to an ontology of distinct properties and powers; in separating them he needs also to grant a relation of bestowing between them (represented by the arrows in Fig. 8.2). And given his retention of dispositional essentialism, he needs to explain why the same property always bestows the same power. This is not, of course, a problem for the S1 ontology.

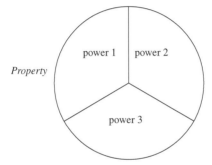

Figure 8.1 The S1 ontology.

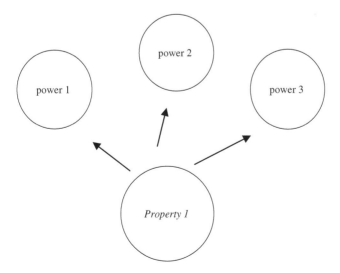

Figure 8.2 The S2 ontology.

Where the relation between a property and power cluster is one of identity, identity alone explains why the same property always brings the same powers. Instead of identity, Shoemaker seems to have in mind something like the laws of nature being responsible for the bestowing. In 1980: 222 and 233 and in 1998: 412 he mentions laws of nature governing which powers are bestowed by a property. He also states (1999: 298) that he is retaining his claim that a property's powers are essential to it but he is prepared to limit this to the actual world (I accept that this may be a mere rhetorical step in his presentation there). This threatens the thesis of dispositional essentialism: it suggests that it applies only in worlds with our laws of nature, which means that the powers of a property cannot be used to identify a property across possible worlds with different laws. But then how can we identify properties across worlds? Shoemaker would have to provide some other criterion of identity, so the extent of and justification for his dispositional essentialism is not clear.

Where the S1 ontology manages with just powers, therefore, the S2 ontology requires properties, laws of nature and powers, each with a distinct existence. Whereas we had an explanatory account of properties in terms of powers, S2 will need further explanations of the nature and being of three different types of entity. S1 will need an explanation of powers but once that is in place it needs no further explanation of properties and laws of nature (as I argue in my 2004). Shoemaker attempts to retain his dispositional essentialism in S2, and I am not saying that he cannot do this. But whereas S1 posits a *de re* necessary connection between a power and its manifestation, Shoemaker would need, as well as this, an additional *de re* necessary connection between a property and the powers it bestows. Otherwise, properties and their powers could vary and essentialism would not hold. S2 needs, therefore, two levels of *de re* necessity where S1 needs only one.

There is a second advantage to S1, as well as its economy. S2 makes a property unknowable. We know properties through their effects, including their effects on us, which S1 allows. Shoemaker made this very point: 'Only if some causal theory of properties is true, I believe, can it be explained how properties are capable of engaging our knowledge' (1980: 214). When he abandoned S1, Shoemaker tried to retain the causal element. But if properties and powers are now said to be distinct, and our knowledge can only be of that which affects us, then it is clear that what affects us is the causal powers. We know the powers but not the properties. In S2, a property is an unknown and unknowable. Following Black 2000, we can call it a *quidditas*, underlying the knowable powers.

There is more than simply an epistemic point to be found here. What this suggests is that the properties themselves are actually redundant according to S2. All that counts for the identity of a property, as Shoemaker still holds, is the forward- and backward-looking causal features. But if the identity of such clusters of causal powers is what really interests us, and the properties are distinct from such clusters, what purpose do those properties serve in our metaphysics? Why bother positing the further metaphysical necessity, from a property to its cluster of powers? It would seem to make no difference to anything at all if there was a different property underlying different tokens of the same causal power cluster.

Indeed, an apparently stable object, retaining the same cluster of powers, could on the S2 view be undergoing multiple changes in properties underneath the surface. A version of S2 that retains a necessary connection between a property and its powers would seem to have no practical difference from one that dispensed with such a necessary connection.

It is possible to use an inversion argument against this ontology. Locke (1690: II, 32, xv) suggested that words named private ideas in our heads. But he then realised that those ideas could be systematically inverted and yet our language use would continue unaffected. Hence, I could use the word 'blue' to name my idea of yellow and 'yellow' to name my idea of blue yet this need never show up in my behaviour. This is usually intended to show the redundancy of a supposition. In Locke's case, the redundancy is the inner ideas. The same can now be said of Shoemaker's properties in the S2 ontology. They could vary independently of causal powers, though it would make no other difference and things could look exactly the same to us. Such redundant suppositions were probably behind Wittgenstein's comment that 'a wheel that can be turned though nothing else moves with it, is not part of the mechanism (1953: §271).

S2 does not look attractive, therefore. Perhaps Shoemaker thought it was a relatively small and harmless adjustment to his theory of properties when he moved from S1 to S2. We have seen, however, that it is a major change of view and leaves him with a theory of properties that is problematic. Many of the arguments that were produced in defence of S1 will count against S2. But is S1 defensible? It should not be forgotten that Shoemaker abandoned S1 for a reason, which we should now examine.

The problem of S1

Shoemaker's avowed reason for rejecting S1 was that properties are not reducible. We have, said Shoemaker, to make use of the notion of properties to make sense of powers. The power of a solvent, for example, is a power to *dissolve* something. Making sense of the concept of a solvent requires sense in the notion of being dissolved. A power is always a power to ϕ. What will take the place of ϕ? If it is a further property then we have not succeeded in reducing properties to powers because powers themselves are made sense of in terms of the properties they are powers for. If, on the other hand, we try to give the same analysis of this further property, and say that it is a power (or cluster of powers), then a power is a power for a further power. It has been said of this view that we then have no sufficient idea of our original power. It is a power for a further power, and this second power would have to be a power for a third power, and so on. Another way of understanding this charge is that all is powerful but nothing is ever actual or manifested. The problem can be put in terms of a dilemma. A power must be either:

i   a power for a property

in which case properties are irreducible, or

  ii   a power for another power

in which case nothing is ever actual.

A causal realist manifesto

I argue that S1 can be defended as a theory of properties *qua* powers if one is prepared to accept certain features of the world. These features characterise a powers ontology.

First, necessity. There are metaphysical (necessary) connections between properties/powers that are not merely analytic. The position is anti-Humean, but so is the whole causal power metaphysic (see Molnar 2003). One property/power is a power for another property/power, indeed necessarily so. The Humean view takes distinct existences to be entirely loose and separate but then that allows the connection between being soluble and being dissolved is a metaphysically contingent one. The causal realist accepts that being soluble and being dissolved are distinct properties but metaphysically connected.

Second, this position has a relativistic nature. No property has an essence independent of the relations it bears to other properties. There are no primitive essences, no quiddities independent of the other properties. Hence, to be property F is just to bear certain relations to all the other properties, G, H, I, …, in virtue of the causal powers of F (and reciprocally the powers of G, H, I, …). A property/power F must be a property/power for a further property/power, partly because this is what it is to be a property. Without bearing such relations, F would not be a property. How could it be if it made no difference to what other properties something with F could have? How, otherwise, would the property F have any nature? This nature is relative to other properties, and each of those has its nature relative to the others. This might lead one to think that no property has any nature. We have seen, however, how a notion of absolute spatiotemporal location has become replaced by a notion of relative spatiotemporal location. A relative location is good enough and so too is a relative nature for properties. Given that the alternative is an absolute nature, a notion that seems hard to defend or even to conceptualise, we should accept relative natures.

Third, the power ontology has a holistic quality. Properties come in a holistic package. If the identity of G is in part determined by its causal power to F, then unless there is property F, there is no property G. At best, there might be a property similar to G but if the relation to F is absent then this is not exactly G. Therefore, a world is not possible that contains G but not F. No property would be possible, in this non-F-world, whose nature is related to F. If F has to go, then so too will G, H, I and all properties that are related to F. So too, we can have no property J, K, L, … that is related to any of G, H and I. It seems likely, extending this argument, that none of our properties could exist at a world that didn't have the property F. Another holistic set of interrelated properties might exist at that world, but they would not be our properties.

A fourth feature of the powers ontology, and perhaps the most important, is its realism. Powers have to be accepted as the basic building block of this metaphysic. If powers are accepted as actual and real then there is no objection from the charge that a power is always a power to a further power. Something will be actual because powers are actual. Causation may then turn out to be something like the shifting about of powers. But causal realists are often attracted to physical process accounts of causation in any case. Causation may be explicable in terms of energy transference (Fair 1979; also see Dowe 2000), for example, which looks exactly as if it should be understood as a shifting of powers from one object to another. Hence, object *a* may have the property F that, when appropriately stimulated, can cause object *b* to have property G, and so on. In such transference theories, the passing round of energy may be explicated as the passing round of causal powers. This means that in defending S1, and answering the dilemma of the previous section, we should accept ii, that a power is always a power to a further power, but reject the view that this is an unacceptable position to hold.

Apart from causal powers helping to explain and enlighten the nature of properties, it has also emerged that an account of causation could follow in terms of the exercise of powers, and further that laws of nature can fall out of the picture completely because no further additional element is required either to relate properties to their powers or powers to their manifestations. Again causal realists will see this as a welcome consequence. Laws were needed by an ontology that accepted distinct existences but then sought to impose some necessity from without. We saw an instance of this in Shoemaker's S2 theory, where there were relations of bestowing between properties and powers. If properties just are powers then there is necessity between a property and its powers and therefore the metaphysics does not require the addition of laws of nature. Such laws have historically raised more problems than they have solved (see Mumford 2004).

How it all comes together

I return now to the question of the second section to see whether an answer has been found. How do the three close concepts of power, disposition and property relate?

In the first place, the question was asked whether dispositions and whether powers should be considered properties, as when we speak of dispositional properties. It was noted, however, that 'power property' seemed an unnatural expression. After our investigation, however, we can conclude that disposition and power are indeed equivalents. Although there is the expression 'dispositional property', if the current analysis is close to the truth then dispositional property, if it means anything, would be pleonastic: all properties are dispositional in so far as all properties are powerful. Calling a property dispositional is an unnecessary qualification, rather like saying 'foot pedal'. Calling some properties dispositional was for a time thought to be significant because other properties were thought to be categorical (an expression which Armstrong 1968: 85–8 made popular). But if categorical properties are meant to be properties that are not powerful, then there is some doubt as to whether they exist. It was assumed that dispositions were in need of a defence (see Mellor 1974) but now categorical properties seem more an object of suspicion (for an attempt to make some sense of them see Mumford 1998: ch. 4).

Dispositions are not, therefore, a type of property. Rather, if the Shoemaker S1 theory is right after all, dispositions and powers are the same thing and they are constitutive of properties. We saw that this account of properties has considerable explanatory strength. Simple properties, the simplest, are constituted by single powers. Complex properties are complexes of multiple powers. Resemblance between properties is (sometimes) explained by common powers in the constitutive cluster.

There are also some important consequences of this account, which all seem defensible. Any two properties with exactly the same constituent powers are identical. The powers are essential to the properties, which follows from applying the axiom of extensionality in set theory. Powers are conditional in the sense that what something will cause is a result of many properties taken together.

Powers themselves can be understood as either universals or as particulars. This does not mean that they are properties, when they are universals. The distinction between particulars (tokens) and universals (types) cuts across many metaphysical categories, and is behind the contrasts between objects and kinds, tropes/property instances and universals, event tokens and event types, and power tokens and power types.

Our three concepts relate in the following way, therefore. Power and disposition are, for all metaphysical purposes, equivalents. Powers/dispositions are constitutive of properties. Clusters of them will be identical with properties. The relations defended in this account are simple. As has been shown, much of importance follows from them and, I hold, it constitutes the core of the causal realist ontology.

Acknowledgements

This chapter was previously presented at the University of Bilkent in Ankara, Turkey, and at the NAMICONA dispositions workshop held at Kolding in Denmark. I thank those who attended for their comments, in particular Bill Wringe, Lucas Thorpe, Joshua Cowley, Varol Akman, Johanna Seibt, Lars Binderup, Jacob Busch, Klemens Kappel and Lars Bo Gunderson.

References

Armstrong, D. M. (1968) *A Materialist Theory of the Mind*, London: Routledge.
Black, R. (2000) 'Against quidditism', *Australasian Journal of Philosophy*, 78: 87–104.
Dowe, P. (2000) *Physical Causation*, Cambridge: Cambridge University Press.
Ellis, B. (2001) *Scientific Essentialism*, Cambridge: Cambridge University Press.
Fair, D. (1979) 'Causation and the flow of energy', *Erkenntnis* 14: 219–50.
Locke, J. (1690) *An Essay Concerning Human Understanding*, P. H. Nidditch (ed.), Oxford: Clarendon Press, 1975.

Martin, C. B. (1993a) 'The need for ontology: some choices', *Philosophy* 68: 505–22.

Martin, C. B. (1993b) 'Power for realists', in J. Bacon, K. Campbell and L. Reinhardt (eds), *Ontology, Causality and Mind*, Cambridge: Cambridge University Press, 1993: 175–86.

Mellor, D. H. (1974) 'In defense of dispositions', *Philosophical Review* 83: 157–81.

Mill, J. S. (1843) *A System of Logic*, London: Parker.

Molnar, G. (2003) *Powers: A Study in Metaphysics*, S. Mumford (ed.), Oxford: Oxford University Press.

Mumford, S. (1998) *Dispositions*, Oxford: Oxford University Press.

Mumford, S. (2004) *Laws in Nature*, London: Routledge.

Mumford, S. (2005), 'Kinds, essences, powers', *Ratio* 18: 420–36.

Popper, K. R. (1959) *The Logic of Scientific Discovery*, revd. imp. 1980, London: Hutchinson.

Putnam, H. (1975) 'The meaning of "meaning"', in *Mind, Language and Reality, Philosophical Papers 2*, Cambridge: Cambridge University Press: 215–71.

Shoemaker, S. (1980) 'Causality and properties', in *Identity, Cause and Mind*, expanded edn, Oxford: Oxford University Press, 2003: 206–33.

Shoemaker, S. (1998) 'Causal and metaphysical necessity', in *Identity, Cause and Mind*, expanded edn, Oxford: Oxford University Press, 2003, 1984: 407–26.

Shoemaker, S. (1999) 'Self, body, and coincidence', *Proceedings of the Aristotelian Society*, supp. vol. 73: 287–306.

Swoyer, C. (1982) 'The nature of natural laws', *Australasian Journal of Philosophy*, 60: 203–23.

Wittgenstein, L. (1953) *Philosophical Investigations*, trans G. E. M. Anscombe, Oxford: Blackwell.

9 Inessential Aristotle

Powers without essences

Anjan Chakravartty

A groundswell of recent work in philosophy has sought to revitalize the analysis of causation by appealing to "active principles" such as powers, dispositions, capacities, tendencies, and propensities. These principles are described in a realist and rather Aristotelian fashion, in stark contrast to the deflationary and linguistic accounts of such principles characteristic of Humean thought and empiricist thinking more generally. Natures, essences, powers, and de re necessity are back in the analysis of causation. I do not argue in this chapter for the plausibility of the revitalization project in general; instead, I explain how I think one aspect of it must be understood if the project is to be plausible. I suggest that those who are moved to resist Humean austerity and embrace a realism about things such as causal powers should take care in how they formulate this realism. Some Aristotelian notions, such as the concept of a causal power, may well be useful to modern studies of causation. Others, such as the notion that causal powers are determined by essences which comprise the natures of things, are outmoded in many sciences today. This chapter focuses specifically on the notions of power and essence in the context of causation. Contra some of the most important recent proponents of the revitalization project, I contend that causal generalizations are not generally best understood as determined by the essential properties of natural kinds. How a member of a kind (natural or otherwise) behaves causally may be a function of its causal powers, but such powers need not constitute anything like the "essence" of a kind.

1   Revitalizing causation with dispositional essences.
2   Causal behaviour in kinds without essences.
3   Causal powers and inessential distributions.

Revitalizing causation with dispositional essences

After a renaissance in Aristotelian thought during the second to sixth centuries CE, and again after the twelfth to sixteenth centuries, declines in Aristotelianism were prompted in large measure, arguably, by overly conservative attempts to preserve it. It is doubtful, however, that it was *ever* reasonable to view the extraordinarily broad-ranging conception of the natural world typically associated with Aristotle as wholly internally consistent. Recent work in philosophy has appealed to distinctly Aristotelian-sounding concepts in order to make sense of the nature of causation in the context of the sciences. I believe this programme to be very promising, but I am also wary of invoking past ideas in an overly conservative manner. Some aspects of the Aristotelian worldview yield great explanatory resources with which to interpret scientific knowledge, but others are best consigned to the past. There comes a time to remove the baby from the bathwater. In this chapter I hope to do precisely this in connection with recent work on the nature of causation.

The Aristotelian world is replete with substances, forms, essences, natures, causal powers, natural kinds, *de re* necessity, and teleology. With the possible exception of teleological explanation, all of these elements are present to some degree in recent philosophical work concerning realist interpretations of scientific knowledge. My interest here, however, will be rather more specific. As part of this programme of invoking Aristotelian concepts in the context of the sciences, many authors have appealed to a realism about "active principles" or causal powers, variously described as dispositions, capacities, tendencies, and propensities. It is largely the rejection of such a realism that constitutes the heart of many empiricist critiques of metaphysical speculation, including Hume's. Several influential authors have recently situated their realism in an Aristotelian-sounding framework of natural kinds and essences, and it is this putative connection between causal powers and essences that will be my central concern here. I will argue that realists about powers are not generally well served by thinking that they constitute the essences of natural kinds. Consequently, causal generalizations about kinds of things are often not best understood as determined by essential properties. One may well account for causal behaviour in terms of causal powers, but, as we shall see, powers need not constitute anything resembling essences.

To be fair to those whose views I will dispute, it is important to acknowledge that they do not believe in essences as perhaps the common Aristotelian caricature describes them. According to this view, an essence is a unitary, fundamental feature of a thing that explains all of the other properties generally associated with things of that kind; it is the one feature that makes the thing the kind of thing that it is. (The requirement of a *unitary* essence may break down in Aristotle's biology, where it is arguable that the essences of biological taxa consist in more than one fundamental feature.) Furthermore, an essence is here associated with the *telos* of the relevant kind: the natural goal, aim or function of its members; having a particular essence facilitates its proper functioning. Neither the idea that essences are unitary nor the emphasis on teleology appear to be important to the authors I have in mind. The notion of an essence which either comprises or otherwise confers the causal powers characteristic of a kind, however, is crucial.

Consider Roy Bhaskar (1975), for example: "The ascription of powers ... presupposes a non-conventional distinction between those properties of the thing which are essential to it and those which are not" (p. 88); "The real essences of things are their intrinsic structures, atomic constitutions and so on which constitute the real basis of their natural tendencies and causal powers" (p. 174); "The importance of taxa in science may be expressed by saying what is non-accidentally true of a thing is true of a thing in virtue of its essential nature" (p. 212). Bhaskar here identifies kind essences with underlying properties, often called "categorical bases", of the causal powers of things. Along the same current but on a slightly different tack, consider the view of Brian Ellis (1999, p. 22), who dispenses with talk of categorical bases and identifies essences with causal powers even more directly[1]:

> ... the laws of action and interaction [laws describing causal processes] concerning natural kinds of things depend entirely upon the causal powers, capacities and propensities that these sorts of things have essentially. That is ... the properties and structures which constitute the real essences of a kind determine its laws of action and interaction.

Or again, in Ellis (2001, p. 1): "[causal] laws of nature depend on the essential properties of the things on which they are said to operate, and are therefore not independent of them". Despite the differences in formulation, authors such as Bhaskar and Ellis are united in opposing the Humean view according to which laws are "imposed" on otherwise passive, causally indifferent objects. This sort of empiricist understanding was commonly asserted in opposition to Aristotelianism, for example, by seventeenth-century natural philosophers, who held that the corpuscles out of which matter is composed are intrinsically inert, their behaviour being described and somehow determined from without by Boyle's and Newton's laws.

Before attempting to problematize the putative connection between causation and essences just described, let me clarify two matters of terminology. The first concerns the terms used to label what I earlier generically described as "active principles". "Causal power", "disposition", "capacity" and so on are terms of art; some authors use them synonymously and others make careful distinctions. I will use these terms synonymously, to refer to properties of things in virtue of which they behave in particular ways in particular circumstances. The second issue of terminology concerns the use of the term "causal law", as in the quotations above in which Ellis draws a link between causal powers and causal laws. Whether there are such things as laws let alone causal ones, and whether laws are relevant to all sciences, are matters of controversy. There are lively debates, for example, on the questions of whether there are laws in biology or the social sciences. I will use the term "causal law" in a relatively weak sense here, however, which I think renders it innocuous in application to almost all scientific disciplines. By "law" I mean any generalization about classes of things that functions effectively in scientific prediction or explanation, and by "causal law" I mean any law that can be used to give predictions or explanations regarding causal phenomena. This includes generalizations about mathematical relations between magnitudes of properties, such as that described by the ideal gas law, $PV = nRT$, relating magnitudes of pressure, volume, and temperature of gases. It also includes generalizations about how classes of things behave in causal processes, such as "all planets in solar systems move in approximately elliptical orbits".

Given that my present concern is the putative connection between the causal behaviours of things and the essences of members of their respective kinds, the latter sort of generalization will take centre stage in much of the discussion to follow. Relations involving quantitative properties, however, are also very important in this context. Behaviours such as orbitings of suns by planets are often indicative of causal processes, and causal processes generally involve relations of various quantitative properties. Behavioural generalizations usually do not mention the underlying relations of properties that yield the regularities they describe, but such relations are generally there nonetheless. I will not subject this claim to scrutiny here, however. Instead, let us proceed to confront the matter of essences. In the next section I argue that essences are really beside the point of describing causation in terms of powers. Scientific practices such as prediction and explanation regarding causal phenomena are concerned not merely with kinds having essences, but also with kinds lacking them. If one's account of the connection between classes of things and these epistemic practices is premised on the idea that the members of such classes have essences, it is unclear what connection there can be where essences are lacking. The solution to this difficulty, I will suggest, is to think of causal laws in terms of powers that may or may not be possessed essentially. Causal laws that describe the behaviours of members of kinds are useful, to the extent that they are, because of the ways in which powers are distributed within classes of things, whether "essentially" or inessentially.

Causal behaviour in kinds without essences

Let me define the concept of an essence more precisely. In the neo-Aristotelian sense in which most people understand the concept today, a kind essence is a set of intrinsic properties that are individually necessary and jointly sufficient for the membership of something in a class of things, or "kind". If a thing lacks any of these properties it is not a member of the relevant kind, and if it is not a member it lacks some one or more of the properties constituting the relevant essence. Armed with this definition, let me now make an observation about the kinds of objects described by contemporary sciences. The idea that scientific classes are ontologically distinguished by essences has a storied past, but many of the kinds we theorize about and experiment on today simply do not have essences. Indeed, many of these classes are groups whose members may have *no* distinguishing properties in common, let alone sets of properties that are necessary and jointly sufficient for membership. I will refer to kinds of things that appear to have essences and those that appear to lack them as *essence* kinds and *cluster* kinds respectively. The most familiar examples of essence kinds today come from physics and chemistry. The kind essence of an electron, for example, consists in a handful of determinate, state-independent properties – specific values of mass, charge, and spin – that are characteristic of all and only members of this kind. But many scientific classes do not fit this model.

The most common examples of cluster kinds today have come from attempts to give precision to the species concept in biological taxonomy. In this area it is generally agreed that the search for essences has failed. Despite their recent popularization by philosophers such as Saul Kripke and Hilary Putnam, intrinsic properties such as morphological and genetic features do not constitute species essences, because significant intra-species variation and overlap with other species generally entail that no one set of properties will distinguish all and only the members of a given species. Reproductive isolation is another frequently cited proposal for species essences. Let us suppose that one can analyze this sort of isolation in terms of sets of intrinsic properties shared by certain individuals that unite them reproductively and isolate them from others. This proposal also fails to specify essences, for several reasons: hybridization violates the requirement of reproductive isolation (and hybrid offspring are sometimes fertile, thus compounding the problem); some sub-populations within species mate successfully with others but not all; such reproductive criteria are irrelevant to asexual species. Furthermore these scientific facts jibe well, I think, with common sense. It is hard to imagine that morphological properties or reproductive features could be necessary conditions for species membership. After all, a sterile tiger with only three legs is still a tiger, and so is an albino, though lacking those famous, fearfully symmetrical stripes.[2]

Given that at least some things commonly regarded as kinds do not appear to have kind essences, many have chosen to relax the essence criterion in the demarcation of various, scientifically-sanctioned classes of things. Membership in kinds is generally described in these cases more loosely by means of suggestive metaphors: clusters, family resemblance, even "strands in a rope" (Hacking (1991, p. 115)). These are polythetic classes. The possession of a clustered subset of some set of properties, no one of which is necessary but which together are sufficiently many, entails membership. Now, consider the fact that the sciences that take such kinds as their subject matter are demonstrably interested in causal processes involving them. Animal behaviourists and ecologists trade in the causes and effects of the actions of organisms. Anatomists, physiologists, and cell biologists study causal processes involving organisms, organ systems, organs, and tissues. Immunologists spend their days worrying about kinds of proteins, which may be cluster kinds. Classes of things lacking essences, it seems, engage in causal processes and are described by causal generalizations.

What then of the idea that causal laws are somehow related to the essences of the kinds they describe? It seems to me that those who wish to connect causal powers and laws to essences now face a difficult task, prompted by the fact that scientific disciplines routinely theorize about and experiment on kinds without essences. Such a person may insist that only essence kinds are in some sense "genuine" kinds, but then they owes us an account of how cluster kinds are to be reasonably dismissed or otherwise explained away, despite the fact that the sciences appear to be interested in causal processes involving them. I believe there are at least two routes open to this person, but neither is compelling. Let us consider them in turn.

Wilkerson (1995, p. 132) and Ellis (2001, p. 21) take one route when they suggest that, in apparent cases of cluster kinds, essence kinds are generally lurking in the neighbourhood. For example, populations often regarded as biological species are not kinds *per se*, but rather groups of closely related kinds whose essences are composed of genetic constitutions. *Homo sapiens* are not all members of the same kind because different human beings have different genetic constitutions, but different human beings nonetheless have closely related genomes. Let me generalize this argumentative strategy: in the case of a cluster kind, simply refine the search for essences until acceptable candidates emerge, and explain the efficacy of causal generalizations regarding the cluster in terms of degrees of similarity between its members. In the case of biological taxa this search for essences is concluded in the genomes of individuals. This manoeuvre is no help, however. The possibility of formulating causal generalizations in such cases is not a function of the essence of the kind described (since *ex hypothesi* there is none), but rather a function of some high degree of similarity between the properties of vast numbers of kinds composed of individuals (or identical twins, clones, etc.) with unique genetic constitutions. Laws about causal behaviour are useful for prediction and explanation in such cases because of these similarity relations, *not* because of anything resembling an essence of the class of things these laws describe.

A second potential essentialist strategy for explaining cluster kinds away is to invoke the possibility of reductionism. One might think of certain basic essence kinds as the building blocks out of which cluster kinds are made, and then argue that causal generalizations concerning the behaviours of cluster kinds are reducible to causal generalizations concerning different combinations of their more basic essence kind constituents. One might thus contend that the challenge presented by the fact that some sciences appear to theorize about and experiment on classes of things lacking essences can be met. Again, however, I believe this response is misleading. The idea that causal generalizations about essence kind constituents might explain why causal generalizations about members of cluster kinds hold, to the extent that they do, suffers from the same sort of difficulty as the attempt to refine the search for essences just considered. The fact that members of some cluster kinds are subjects of causal generalizations reflects the degree to which they share causally efficacious properties, not the fact that they may be composed of essence kinds *per se*.

Let me spell this out in more detail. Different flavours of reductionism are debated in different philosophical contexts, but for present purposes it will suffice to consider a simple distinction between ontological and explanatory reduction. The sort of reductionism one might invoke so as to explain away cluster kinds is ontological in the first instance. Members of cluster kinds, it is said, are ontologically composed of arrangements of essence kinds parts. It is the next move that is crucial, however. Given ontological reduction, one might then suggest that the behaviours of clustered wholes are in principle explainable in terms of their essence kind parts. If this were the case it would be possible, in principle, to explain the behaviours of things like members of biological taxa in terms of the behaviours of the essence kinds out of which they are composed.

As it happens, the explanatory implications of ontological reduction are widely disputed. Some hold that properties of constituent parts are explanatorily complete in the sense that causal interactions of wholes can be explained in terms of the causal powers of their constituents, but others maintain that wholes are in some cases greater than the sums of their parts, and that organized systems have emergent properties that are not mere combinations of the properties of their constituents.[3] If the latter parties to this debate are correct about emergent, causally efficacious properties, then the causal behaviours of things are not in general explainable in terms of causal laws regarding more basic essence kind parts, even in principle.

I do not intend, though, to dwell on debates about the possibility of emergent properties here, for even if reductionists are right to deny this possibility, the idea that causal generalizations pertaining to cluster kinds are explanatorily reducible to causal generalizations pertaining to more basic essence kinds is still a non-starter. Let us grant for the sake of argument that in general, the behaviours of *individual* members of cluster kinds are explanatorily reducible to their essence kind constituents. Would this entail that causal generalizations about cluster kinds are likewise amenable to reduction, in principle if not in practice? It would not. For even assuming that token iguanas are exhaustively composed of some basic essence kinds, and that the causal powers of token iguanas can be explained in terms of the causal powers of these components, this would not by itself explain why causal generalizations about the kind iguana obtain, to the extent that they do. Explanatory reductionism concerning token things is incapable of yielding an explanation of why classes of things lacking essences admit of causal generalizations. The fact that the *kind* iguana is a cluster kind entails that its members may be composed of different essence kinds. Thus, the degree to which we may formulate causal generalizations about iguanas depends on the degree to which the members of this population have the same or similar causally efficacious properties, not anything having to do with properties possessed essentially. Explanatory reduction is no help to the essentialist.

Earlier I suggested that causal generalizations concerning scientific classes of things lacking essences present a serious challenge to those hoping to connect causal powers and laws to essences. Neither of the two strategies I have considered for meeting this challenge – refining the search for essences in cases of clusters, and reducing members of cluster kinds to essence kind components – is capable of dispelling this challenge. It is time to try something different. Essences were ineluctable for Aristotle, but they are not so for us. In the next and last section I propose an understanding of causal powers and causal generalizations that is applicable to the wide diversity of classes of things embraced by the sciences today, including both kinds with "essences", and those lacking them.

Causal powers and inessential distributions

If one were only ever concerned to formulate causal generalizations about classes of objects that can be identified with sets of properties, each of which is necessary for class membership, it might seem a simple matter to explain why these generalizations are true, or at least true enough to be useful. For in such a case, assuming that at least some of the properties composing the essence of the relevant kind are (or ground, or confer, as categorical bases) causal powers, all members of the kind will have these powers. Here the fact that membership requires the instantiation of a specific set of properties underwrites the causal behaviours described, and thus it is no surprise that in such cases, one might be tempted to say that causal laws are determined by essences. But in the case of cluster kinds there is no recourse to essences, so how is one to analyze the causal generalizations one formulates about them?

Let me begin to answer this question by setting the notion of essences to one side, and asking whether there is anything else here that might play the metaphysical role of underwriting causal generalizations. One might begin this investigation by considering first the classes I have called essence kinds. What explains the causal behaviours of their members? Well, to take physics as an example, our theories describe properties such as mass, charge, and spin, in virtue of which very small constituents of matter are thought to interact. The ambiguous phrase "in virtue of" here opens up the possibility of different interpretations of this claim, one of which has the distinctly Aristotelian flavour of the revitalization project: these properties confer causal powers on the things that have them. It is because subatomic particles have the properties and thus the powers that they do, that causal generalizations about them, where true, hold. So far so good, but now consider this: the same can be said about iguanas. Causal laws are determined by the causal powers of things regardless of whether they belong to essence kinds or cluster kinds. The attempt to ground causal laws in the essences of kinds is a red herring, for what explains why causal behaviours obtain is not the fact that some things are said to have essences – at least not in the first instance. Causal behaviours occur not merely as a consequence of the possession of essential properties by members of kinds with essences, but as a consequence of the possession of *any* causally efficacious property – a power or property that grounds or confers a power – by *any* sort of thing.

It should thus be clear that the question of whether a causally efficacious property is possessed essentially by a member of a kind is irrelevant to the causal behaviours of which it is capable as a consequence of having that property. Powers explain behaviours regardless of whether they are necessary for membership in a particular class of thing. With this understood, let me now propose a simple understanding of causal generalizations that is applicable to both essence kinds and cluster kinds. To introduce a metaphor of my own, it is a striking fact about things in the world that causally efficacious properties are systematically "sociable" in various ways. They seem to "like" each other's company. The highest degree of sociability is present in what I have called essence kinds, where particular sets of properties are always found together. In other circumstances, however, sociability is a looser affair, and in these cases we find cluster kinds. In all cases, it is the fact that there are shared, causally efficacious properties that underwrites the causal generalizations to which classes lend themselves. Kind essences are one kind of sociability giving rise to causal laws but, so to speak, they are not essential.

Sociability is just a metaphor, of course. It is intended to describe the metaphysical fact that wherever we recognize classes of things, whether within or outwith scientific contexts, property instances tend to cluster together. In the upper limit of sociability, the properties that compose the sets definitive of kinds are always present together, and we describe them as necessary and jointly sufficient for membership. In other words, we call them "essences". The metaphor of sociability is amenable to analysis on a case by case basis, but I doubt that any one analysis will apply to all classes of things. Richard Boyd (1999), for example, analyzes this phenomenon as arising in some circumstances from what he calls "homeostatic clustering". Homeostasis is understood here in terms of causal mechanisms that produce clusters of properties occurring together. These mechanisms may consist in causal relations between properties in a cluster that favour their co-instantiation, or underlying processes that favour co-instantiation, or both. This is an attractive idea, but it seems clear that sociability will not be analyzable in this way in many cases. Homeostatic mechanisms are not responsible for the co-instantiation of the mass, charge, and spin of an electron, for instance. Here, so far as we can tell, sociability is a brute fact admitting of no causal decomposition. The presence of homeostatic mechanisms is a special case of sociability, not an exhaustive account.

The preceding discussion suggests that the emphasis placed on essences by important proponents of the causal revitalization project is misplaced. In some cases it may well be that the causal powers typically manifested by the members of a class consist in (or are grounded in or conferred by) what we regard as their essential properties. In other cases, however, the causal powers typically manifested by the members of a class will have nothing to do with their essential properties, because there is simply no essence to be had. The important focal points of attention here are causally efficacious properties and their patterns of distribution within populations of interest, not whether they are possessed essentially. Causal laws often do not make reference to kinds of objects at all, but rather summarize relations between quantitative, causally efficacious properties of objects. Whether the kinds whose members have these properties are essence kinds or cluster kinds is another matter entirely. Dispositions for causal behaviour are present wherever such properties are found, and to the extent that they are found in members of the same kind, behaviours are subject to causal generalization. Members of classes that share such properties, whether strictly in the case of essence kinds, or loosely in the case of cluster kinds, can be expected to behave in similar ways in similar circumstances. How useful a causal generalization may be is purely a function of the strictness or looseness of the kind at issue, and the purpose or end to which the generalization is applied.

One of the most important features of the idea that causal powers are often inessentially distributed is that it respects the epistemic status of causal generalizations in the sciences. There are cases in which generalizations are strict, perhaps most likely in sciences whose subject matters are sufficiently fundamental or uncomplicated. In many cases, however, causal generalizations are susceptible to exceptions and *ceteris paribus* qualifications. Here the number of exceptions will vary according to the extent to which members of kinds figuring in the relevant generalizations share the same causally efficacious properties. The study of sociable properties and their relations distinguishes strict generalizations from weaker but nonetheless helpful ones, and the fact that one must often take causal generalizations about kinds as helpful rather than absolute guides is common not only in the social sciences, but also in the natural sciences. It is obvious why this is so in the case of cluster kinds, since their members need not possess any one of the properties associated with the set defining them. But even members of essence kinds can behave differently in exactly similar circumstances. Since the other, inessential properties of members of essence kinds may be causally efficacious as well, most causal laws concerning even these classes hold at best *ceteris paribus*. Consider a canonical example of essence kinds: atoms of particular elements. All atoms of a given element share an atomic number as their essence, but different ions (having different electric charge) and different isotopes (having different numbers of neutrons) of one and the same kind of atom may behave in very different ways in exactly similar conditions.

I began this chapter with the goal of considering whether a powers-based approach to understanding causation is properly associated with the concept of essences. Some who are keen to revitalize the analysis of causation in contemporary philosophy by appealing to certain Aristotelian-sounding notions take the concepts of power and essence to be appropriately and intimately connected, but I believe this is a mistake. It is misleading to say that causal generalizations are determined by the essential properties of classes of things. Some classes have what may be regarded as essences and others do not, but almost all admit of causal generalization to some extent. The behaviours of members of kinds may be a function of their causal powers, but only sometimes do powers constitute "essences". Indeed, the behaviour of any given thing is determined by its causally efficacious properties (together with others in its environment) whether these properties are essential or not. Upon careful investigation, scientific taxonomies yield many useful generalizations, including causal ones. These generalizations are useful insofar as they systematically describe sociable distributions of properties among the members of the taxa they concern. Thinking of these properties dispositionally, as powers, is a rich and fascinating non-Humean approach to the metaphysics of the sciences. But inspiration from past heroes will serve this project best when we discern the parts of their views that are inessential.

Notes

1 Ellis & Lierse (1994) give sustained arguments for the thesis that dispositions (powers) do not require categorical bases.

2 The most widely used species concept in contemporary evolutionary biology is the phylogenetic concept, which identifies species with historical lineages bounded by speciation and extinction events, over which time the intrinsic properties of organisms belonging to a species may change significantly.

3 See Beckermann *et al.* (eds) (1992) for discussions of emergence. See also Mellor and Crane (1991/1990, p. 87) for examples from physics that resist explanatory reduction; indeed, the authors note that physics is sometimes *macro*reductive.

References

Beckermann, A., H. Flohr and J. Kim (eds.) (1992) *Emergence or Reduction?: Essays on the Prospects of Nonreductive Physicalism*. Berlin: de Gruyter.

Bhaskar, R. (1975) *A Realist Theory of Science*. London: Verso.

Boyd, R. N. (1999) 'Homeostasis, species, and higher taxa', in R. A. Wilson (ed.), *Species: New Interdisciplinary Essays*, Cambridge: MIT Press, pp. 141– 185.

Ellis, B. (1999) 'Causal powers and laws of nature', in H. Sankey (ed.), *Causation and Laws of Nature*, pp. 19–34. Dordrecht: Kluwer.

Ellis, B. (2001) *Scientific Essentialism*. Cambridge: Cambridge University Press.

Ellis, B. and C. Lierse (1994) 'Dispositional essentialism', *Australasian Journal of Philosophy* 72, 27– 45.

Hacking, I. (1991) 'A tradition of natural kinds', *Philosophical Studies* 61, 109–126.

Mellor, D. H. and T. Crane (1991/1990) 'There is no question of physicalism', in D. H. Mellor, *Matters of Metaphysics*, pp. 82–103. Cambridge: Cambridge University Press. Originally published in *Mind* 99, 185–206.

Wilkerson, T. E. (1995) *Natural Kinds*. Aldershot: Avebury.

10 Causal exclusion and evolved emergent properties

Alexander Bird

Emergent properties are intended to be genuine, natural higher level causally efficacious properties irreducible to physical ones. At the same time they are somehow dependent on or 'emergent from' complexes of physical properties, so that the doctrine of emergent properties is not supposed to be a return to dualism. The doctrine faces two challenges: (i) to explain precisely how it is that such properties emerge—what is *emergence*; (ii) to explain how they sidestep the exclusion problem—how it is that there is room for these properties to be causally efficacious, given the causal completeness of the physical. In this paper I explain how evolved functional properties can meet both challenges.

1 Introduction

1.1 The exclusion problem for higher level properties

A fragile vase is struck with only a moderate amount of force and breaks. It may be possible to describe its breaking in terms of some micro-structural property of the vase, B. Thus the breaking of the glass is caused by the combination of its being B and its being struck. In explaining the breaking we have not yet mentioned the vase's fragility. It possesses the fragility in virtue of its possessing B. Its fragility supervenes, relative to the laws of nature, on its being B, which is to say that in all possible worlds that share the laws of the actual world, objects with B are fragile. May we also explain the vase's breaking by reference to the combination of its being fragile and its being struck?

Although it seems perfectly natural to explain the behaviour of things in terms of their being fragile or sturdy, irascible or docile, conducting or non-conducting, and so forth, such explanations, regarded as causal, face a well-known objection. It seems as if we have two combinations that cause the breaking: (the micro-structure B, the striking) and (the fragility, the striking). So it looks as if the breaking is over-determined. Given the striking, B is sufficient to bring about the breaking. But so is the vase's fragility. Which is the real cause? This is the causal exclusion problem. The completeness of a causal explanation seems to leave no room for any further causal explanation—complete causal explanations exclude one another. Hence it looks as if we are forced to choose between the supposed causes. And if we are forced to choose, then B wins. Clearly, the vase is fragile in virtue of its being B. B is doing the work if anything is, and so it rather than fragility is the real cause of the breaking. More generally, we think that a final physics will provide all the explanations of events (or explanations of their chances of occurring) if anything can. While physics may leave some gaps (e.g. in the explanation of why some particular fissile nucleus decayed when it did), it leaves no gaps of a kind that can be filled by other kinds of cause. Thus causal explanations framed in a vocabulary other than that of physics seem to be otiose, excluded by the sufficiency of physical explanation.

Are we forced to choose between B and fragility? We would not be if one of the following were true:

i   B and fragility are identical. If they are one and the same, then there is no genuine choice;
ii B is causally downwind of fragility or vice-versa. The throwing of the cricket ball and its striking the vase are both causes of its breaking. But that's no over-determination since the throwing of the ball is itself a cause of its striking the vase—the throwing causes the vase to break via the striking.

But neither of these is the case. B and fragility are not identical. Take a piece of very old and dry paper. It too is fragile. But it doesn't possess B. The causal basis of its fragility is something else altogether. So B and fragility cannot be identical. Perhaps fragility is identical with some disjunction combining B and the various other possible causes bases of fragility. But that does not help. That looks to be a very gerrymandered, disjunctive property and far from the sort of property that can be said to be a cause. And even if it could be, that does not dissolve the problem, since that disjunctive property is clearly not identical to any of its disjuncts alone. And so the over-determination problem remains.

Nor can we regard one of B and fragility as causally downwind of the other. Some have argued that B is a cause of fragility. But this will not do. For on the one hand it raises its own problems and on the other it does not answer the question posed. It is problematic since we must suppose the cause and effect are simultaneous, rather than, as in the throwing of the ball and its striking the vase, the cause preceding the effect. The same relationship as that between B and fragility holds between Aloysius being 2m and his being tall. The latter is true in virtue of the former. It supervenes upon it, but is not identical to it. But we would not say that being 2m is a cause of being tall. Consequently it is difficult to see being B and being fragile as distinct links in a chain leading to the vase's breaking. And so even if we were to grant that being B causes fragility, we do not regard B as causing the breaking via its causing the fragility. From the mirco-structural point of view, B causes the breaking directly. The fact that it also causes the vase to be fragile is an epiphenomenal effect.

1.2 Is overdetermination a problem?

What forces the choice on us is the presumption that overdetermination is impermissible—effects can have more than one set of synchronic complete causes. A common response is that we should not be worried about overdetermination when B and fragility have the sort of relationship that they do have. For example, let us imagine that the counterfactual account of causation is correct. Thus the fragility of the vase is a cause of its breaking, for if it had not been fragile, it would not have broken. But notice that had the vase not been fragile, it would not have had B. Hence we do not have the sort of overdetermination that is worrying. Overdetermination is worrying when X and Y are both held to be causes and were X not to have existed Y would still have existed and caused the effect on its own. If X and Y are fully independent in this way, then there is something worrying about the supposition that they both cause the effect. It is tempting to think that only one of them is the real cause whereas the other is not actually the cause but is merely a backup, something that would have been the cause in the absence of the first.[1] But this sort of worry cannot arise when X and Y are not independent. Clearly there is no worry in the case where X and Y are identical. In that case X cannot be a mere backup to Y's real cause: had Y not occurred neither would X have. The worry also seems to fail to arise when there is a relationship of supervenience. As we saw, had the vase not been fragile, it would not have been B. Being B cannot be a mere backup to the real cause, the fragility. Such is the sort of response articulated by Barry Loewer (2002: 656–657).

The principal reason given by Jaegwon Kim (2002b) for being suspicious of this response is that we should not be too quick to adopt the counterfactual account of causation. As is well known it suffers from numerous objections, and even its repairs do not seem immune from counterexamples.[2] That fact suggests what one might have suspected in the first place, which is that the counterfactual account is insufficient to capture our intuitive notion of causation. Causation is what makes things happen, or, in Kim's terms, is 'production', or 'generation' (2002b: 674). But a counterfactual relationship does not seem enough to capture those ideas. A counterfactual relationship might be a symptom of causation, but should not be mistaken for it. Thus if B is what causes the breaking, then fragility cannot. The relationship between fragility and the breaking is a shadow of the real causal (productive) relationship between B and the breaking. As a shadow it inherits some of the form of the real thing, viz. the counterfactual relationship with the breaking, but that isn't causation itself.

There is a further reason that one may adduce from Kim for employing a counterfactual account of causation to deflate overdetermination worries. Kim thinks, in effect, that the overdetermination worry is rather more like the two assassins case. Let us imagine that in the actual world a neurophysiological state or event N realizes a mental state or event, M. Both N and M cause a physical event E. According to Kim, had N been absent, M would have still caused the physical effect, E. Loewer's response is that this suggests that compared to the actual world, world w_2, where M occurs and E occurs, but E has no physical cause, is closer than w_1, where M occurs and is realized by some different neurophysiological state, N*, which causes E. Loewer think that this is wrong, and that since we accept 'if M had occurred but had not been realized by N it would have been realized by another neural state', we regard w_1 as closer.

I think, however, that Kim's view has more going for it than has been appreciated. Let us distinguish as Lewis does between sparse and abundant properties. The sparse properties are the *natural* properties of the world whereas abundant properties are mere reflections of our predicates. There is an ontological difference. Sparse properties are parts of the world, and the most straightforward reflection of this is to regard them as universals, whereas merely abundant properties are not genuine entities at all. We may ask then, is M (or the property of being in state M) a universal, a natural, sparse property, that has ontological being? Let us first consider the response that it is not. Then 'S is M' is a mere predication of S rather than the attribution of a universal to S. The properties we are considering here are either dispositional ones (such as fragility) or, possibly, higher order functional role properties (the property of possessing some physical property that has the causal role ...). Either way, Loewer is right that w_1 is closer than w_2. The nearest world in which the same functional role predication is true of S, but S is not N, is (trivially) a world in which some other physical state, N*, realizes the functional role. Similarly, if the dispositional predication is true, we may ask in virtue of what the predication is true. *Ex hypothesi* it is not a dispositional universal. The only suitable candidate would seem to be some new physical state (N* again) that realizes the dispositional predication. But that success is hollow for the non-reductive physicalist, since this response, that M is a merely abundant property, is equivalent to eliminativism. It permits mental predications alright, but denies that there are genuine mental properties. So we must consider the other option, according to which M really is a genuine property (a universal). We are now asked to consider the nearest world in which S is still M but is not N. The question now is whether we should expect that world to contain N*? It is at least rather less clear, since neither of the reasons given above hold. We asked, in virtue of what it is true that S is M? Now we have the straightforward answer 'S instantiates the universal M', and so we are not obligated to find the answer in N*. It may yet be that the nearest world where S is M but not N is one where S is N*. That would mean that there M has the characteristic that it may be instantiated only when some other kind of property is instantiated. What kind of relationship between universals would require that? The obvious answer would be when one or other of the universals is complex and the other is a part of it. But M is clearly not a conjunctive universal of which N, N* etc. are parts—if it were, M would always be realized by all its (incompatible) realizers simultaneously. Nor can we regard each N, N* etc. as possessing M as a part—and even if we did that would not show that we could not have M without one of its realizers. What would work if M is a disjunctive universal, the disjunction of all its possible realizers. However, there are good reasons (Armstrong 1978:19–22) for denying the possibility of disjunctive universals.[3] We need therefore some other reason for thinking that the universal M can be instantiated without having some realizer. Loewer does not provide such a reason. (I shall later argue that for *some* higher level properties, such a reason can be given.)

It looks therefore as if we can talk about causation at a higher level of description (the level of familiar objects and their properties) only when there is the strongest kind of reduction to a lower level, viz. identity. In the absence of identity there is causation at the level of the causal bases, but not at the level of macroscopic properties. Furthermore, the macroscopic properties are not genuine natural, sparse properties. This fits with (but does not entail) a view according to which our macro-level descriptions reflect a view of the world that although not entirely divorced from its natural processes, is nonetheless in many respects shaped by human interests and perspectives.

Such a conclusion may not be too disturbing when it comes to questions of whether the fragility of the vase really caused it to break.[4] Indeed, I accept for many higher level dispositions, such as fragility, the conclusion of Elizabeth Prior, and Prior, Pargetter and Jackson, that they are causally inert. But that conclusion is more disturbing when it comes to other macro-properties and their causal roles. When it comes to mental states and properties, it is very difficult to give up the idea that they are causally effective (not least because philosophers find it so natural to gives accounts of mental concepts in causal terms). The only way to avoid the problem would be to adhere to a type-identity theory of mind. But that is now almost universally rejected also, for reasons already discussed.

In what follows I wish to promote a view which argues that under certain circumstances the higher level property can be regarded as natural and causally efficacious while admitting the strength of the forgoing arguments. The idea is that where the higher level properties have been selected for by a natural process, they can be regarded as natural themselves and causally efficacious. In Agustin Vicente's words, that process converts dispositions into teleological functions (Vicente 2002, 2004).

2 Evolved emergent properties

Consider an old, dry, brittle leaf, which crumbles underfoot. The discussion so far leads to the conclusion that the brittleness plays no part in the causal explanation of its crumbling. This is not to say that the leaf is not brittle—it clearly is. Rather it is to say that brittleness is not the sort of natural property that can play a part in causal explanation. Brittleness is thus somewhat like grueness. Things can be grue or not grue. But grueness is not itself a cause of anything, because grueness is not a natural property. If we were ever tempted to say that *x*'s being grue caused something, it would really be *x*'s being green, or *x*'s having the causal basis of green, that is the true cause (or, *mutatis mutandis*, *x*'s being blue etc.).

A natural way to think of what is going on is to say that there is no universal of grueness or of brittleness. Natural properties are real entities—universals—but unnatural, constructed properties are not real entities. The former, being real, can be elements in causal and nomic explanations; the latter, not being real, cannot explain anything. While the realist about universals has a clear way of explaining why natural properties are causally efficacious and unnatural ones are not, any other acceptable view of properties ought to be able to make a similar distinction.

2.1 Emergent properties

The problem we face is that of finding a way of regarding mental and other higher level properties as genuinely natural and hence causally efficacious. Such properties will be distinct from lower level properties—if they were identical there would not be a problem to face, but as we have seen, the properties we are interested in are not identical to any lower level properties. Genuinely natural, causally efficacious higher level properties that are not identical nor reducible to lower level properties are *emergent* properties. More precisely I take emergent properties to have in common the following features:

i   they are genuine, natural properties, with the causal or nomic efficacy that non-emergent properties have;
ii   they are not identical with nor composed out of the fundamental properties of physics;
iii they are properties of physical entities;
iv   they nomically supervene on the distribution of physical properties.[5]

The role of (iii) is to rule out Cartesian dualism about substances as a form of emergentism. If there were immaterial substances such as minds, their properties would satisfy (i) and (ii). Feature (iv) rules out dualism about properties, the view that in addition to physical properties of things (their charge, mass, etc.) there are further properties (e.g. mental ones) that although possessed by physical entities (e.g. human bodies) are nonetheless fully causally efficacious and not dependent on the physical ones, offering a parallel sources of causal influence. I do not wish to count such properties as emergent, although this is contentious.[6] (In any case I do not see how there could be properties satisfying (i)–(iii) but not (iv).)

There are two challenges for emergent properties. The first is to explain how they arise: how do they 'emerge' from physical properties? We should note that there may be more than one kind of emergent property—more than one way to be emergent. Even so it is difficult to find *any* convincing way of being emergent. The second challenge is to explain how is it possible for emergent properties to exist at all. For as long as physical supervenience holds, viz. (iv), it looks as if whatever the emergent property claims to be doing is really being done by something else at a lower level.

Emergent properties are sometimes thought to arise from the complexity of certain systems in which higher level patterns arise (such as, in chaotic systems, the patterns that arise over the longer term around Lorenz attractors). But that fact alone does not justify a belief in emergent properties. The fact that the patterns are not to be found at the lower level does not mean that they are truly causally efficacious at the higher level. They may be mere epiphenomena, and indeed it seems that they are, for there is no good reason to suppose that they have a causal status of their own of a kind different from the brittleness of the leaf, which is also a property that arises only at the higher level.

So mere complexity is not enough. Other have suggested that emergence is to be related to biological phenomena, and this I think is correct. But the important thing is to explain *how* it is that biological phenomena can lead to emergence.

2.2 Evolved properties

Phenotypic properties are clear examples of higher level properties that supervene on lower level properties. And among the phenotypic properties we can include the mental properties of animals, including humans. Being bipedal, having the capacity to see, and being able to engage in abstract thought, are all phenotypic traits of normal adult humans. Such capacities supervene on lower level traits that are the musculo-skeletal, visual, and cerebral structures of man. These are also multiply realizable capacities. Flamingoes are bipedal in a different way from humans, bees see, but employing very different structures, and Martians probably engage in abstract thought employing a different kind of brain. So the arguments above ought to come to the conclusion that these are not genuine natural properties. Such a conclusion would be less easy to accept than the conclusion that fragility is not a natural property.

Consider a bee which flies around a tree trunk and a cat which walks around it. In both cases we want to explain the behaviour by saying that the creature sees the tree. We are inclined to think that this is a more unifying kind of explanation than that which says that the vase and the ancient manuscript were easily destroyed because of their fragility. The unity does not come from an unity in the underlying causal basis—there is none, since the mechanism of vision in bees is very different from the mechanism of vision in mammals. Nor does it come from the fact that both cases can be subsumed under a single disposition or capacity, since the two instances of fragility can also be thus subsumed. The unity comes, I suggest, from the similarity of the causal stories behind the existence of the capacity. The causes of the fragility of the various instances of fragility of fragile items are various and are typically merely the different causes of their causal bases. However, when it comes to vision, we think otherwise. The immediate causes of vision in that bee and in that cat are different—the differing genotypes of the two creatures. But the more distal cause, which is the same as the general cause of the presence of vision in bees and cats, is much the same. It is the selective advantage that vision gives creatures that possess it over those that do not. The crucial thing about selection is that it selects for dispositions, not for their causal bases, or, as Alexander Rosenberg (1994: 25) puts it, 'selection for function is blind to structure'.[7] Individual instances of a predator catching its prey may depend on the causal bases of their individual speeds, acuity in hearing and vision, possession of claws or camouflage; many such cases at a certain time may be considered as just so many cases of fragile things breaking, with no especial underlying unity. But when we consider the prevalence of the trait in subsequent generations it is no longer possible to explain matters in terms of the causal bases alone. For the existence of the trait has only its function to thank. The process of selection would have selected the same trait even if underwritten by a different causal basis. Indeed, it does in fact happen that the same trait in a single species is underwritten by more than one causal basis. Codons (sequences of three bases in a strand of DNA) code for the creation of amino acids. Each codon codes for a single amino acid. But since there are more codons than are needed, one and the same amino acid is coded for by several distinct codons. Consequently, the same protein can be coded for by different sequences of bases, and so natural selection is indifferent to such differences in the DNA. At a larger scale differences in protein brought about by more significant differences in the DNA may nonetheless fulfil the same function equally well. Consequently both proteins (and both kinds of genetic material) may be found in a population.[8]

It should be remembered that selection processes do not take place only on genetic material. Neural networks also evolve by selection processes. The animal brain has a high degree of innate structure. But that structure is modified by stimuli under a regime of selection. Those modifications include the development of general capacities (e.g. the capacity for abstract thought) and the results of their exercise (e.g. the belief that root two is irrational). Thus for the same reasons we should not expect the structures underlying the same mental capacities and mental states to be constant across different individuals. (Such properties (the capacities and states) are thus doubly evolved, in that they have developed by a selection process from an innate structure that is itself an evolved entity.)[9]

2.3 Evolved properties are emergent

The proposal I am making is that such properties should be regarded as emergent. Let us consider such properties against the criteria for emergence I specified above:

i   Emergent properties must be genuine, natural, nomically or causally efficacious properties. It is *prima facie* highly plausible that evolved capacities and states are indeed natural properties that are causally efficacious. The properties are generated by a natural process. This is what distinguishes them from non-natural properties such as fragility. Of course, it is contended whether they can be causally efficacious—that is the thrust of the exclusion problem. I shall return to this below.

ii Emergent properties are not reducible to the properties of physics. The conclusion of the preceding section is just this. We knew all along that mental and (other) biological properties are multiply realizable. The point of the evolutionary story is to remind us why this is so while at the same time making the case for their being natural.

iii Emergent properties are properties of physical things. Emergentism is not a form of substance dualism. And the properties in question are properties of physical objects—creatures made of non-vitalistic molecules and nothing more.

iv The distribution of emergent properties nomically supervenes on the distribution of physical properties. Strictly, this account may not satisfy a synchronic supervenience claim. For I have characterized evolved emergent properties in aetiological terms—how they have evolved. An evolved biological system could have a molecule-for-molecule duplicate that has not evolved, but has come about by accident (e.g. swampman). On an aetiological account of emergence this duplicate system would not have emergent properties. Thus supervenience fails. However, the point of the supervenience claim was to rule out entirely parallel non-physical causal properties, and the current proposal does not introduce them. The supervenience claim can be interpreted more locally: there is no possibility of changing *this* system's distribution of emergent properties without changing its physical properties. Or it can be given a diachronic element: no two extended histories can differ in their final distribution of emergent properties without differing in their physical properties at some point.

A different approach to reconciling supervenience with a evolutionary account of emergent properties would be to provide an alternative to the aetiological account of emergent properties. What is important for the current story is that emergent properties are functional. The accounts of biological function are typically aetiological, which is why this story is aeatiological also. However, we may account for biological function in terms not of historical evolutionary benefit but in terms of current fitness provision (Walsh 1996). Thus we may argue that swampman does have organs with functions precisely because *he can* reproduce and those organs help him do so. Swampman may thus also be attributed with emergent properties. On this picture emergence is a synchronic product of a very particular kind of complexity, the degree of complexity that permits reproduction and evolution. Such complexity has itself hitherto only ever been the product of evolution, but in principle need not be (and recent developments in bio-engineering suggest that the first purely artificial bacterium is not far off).

2.4 The structure of emergent properties

It is worth noting that when we ascribe causal efficacy to emergent properties, we do so in relation to one another as well as to purely physical, non-emergent properties. Emergent properties do not emerge singly but in relation to one another. Not only are the functional properties of our bodies and their parts causally related to one another, they are related to the functional properties and capacities of other organisms (most obviously in the case of symbiosis). Equally, our mental properties are responsive to one another—and to the mental properties of other creatures. If prey is faced with a predator and is selecting between fight or flight it is the other's capacities, the ability to fight or to run fast, that is being assessed, as is also the other's mental state (e.g. willingness to fight). Language gives us the ability to respond (mentally) in a highly sensitive manner to the mental states of others. Just as physical capacities have co-evolved, so have mental ones.

The picture of the structure of natural properties we should have is this. At the bottom are the fundamental physical properties. Built out of these are the non-fundamental physical and chemical properties, to which strict type-reductionism applies. However, once we get to biological properties, we find a new level of quasi-fundamental properties, the emergent properties. They are fundamental to the extent that they are irreducible, but non-fundamental in that some supervenience thesis holds of them. If there is more than one fundamental physical property, then those fundamental properties form an interrelated family which are responsible in concert for the non-fundamental (but reducible) physical properties. Similarly, the quasi-fundamental emergent properties form a family that can potentially form the basis of further properties, reducible to them.

Another way of looking at this is in terms of the Ramsey sentences required to describe truly a certain area of science. We might describe some area of chemistry or non-fundamental physics. If so we will describe the relevant properties in functional terms—a property is characterized in terms of its causal relations to other properties. However, we need not regard the functional characterization as describing the property's essence. For investigations at a deeper level will show how the relevant property is reducible to those at that deeper level. However, when we get to the fundamental level, there will be no further reduction. The fundamental properties will have a functional characterization, and that is all that there is to be said about them. According to the dispositional essentialist, in the special case of a fundamental property, its functional characterization *does* describe its essence (for the other properties, their reduction via type-identities describes their essence). Now let us consider the properties quantified over in a true biological or psychological theory. In such cases, there may be some such properties that are reducible to further biological and psychological properties. But just as in the chemical-physical case, we reach a fundamental level whose properties are not type-reducible. As in the physical case, those properties have functional (or dispositional) essences. Only in this case the properties are emergent, not 'utterly' fundamental. But their quasi-fundamentality does mean that they could supervene on an entirely different base, and in that sense, they are an independent set of properties.

3 The causal efficacy of emergent properties

So far it looks as if biological, including mental properties are emergent. While they look to be causally efficacious, the challenge remains to show how they really can be, in the light of the causal exclusion problem.

I shall take as the key to causal efficacy the ability of a property to raise the chances of the supposed effect. In general, events or facts are causes of other events or facts when they raise their chances of occurring: smoking causes cancer because it raises the chance of cancer, hard work is a cause of success because it raises the chance of success. When we analyze the antecedent facts in question, the complex or simple properties we find will be causally efficacious properties.

3.1 Emergent properties as chance-raisers

Biological and mental properties have this chance raising character: the mottled colouring of a moth raises its chance of survival; infection with *Cryptosporidium* raises the chances of diarrhoea; desire for X raises the chances of actions that bring about X, and so forth. That much seems clear. However, our problem is to show on the one hand that the causal work is not really being done elsewhere and on the other hand it is not either overdetermining or, worse, in conflict with chance-fixing determined elsewhere.

Thus one proposal would be that in each case of alleged biological or mental causation there is a physical event doing the causing. In the case of desire raising the chance of action, it is some physical state of the individual that raises the chance. Note first that we do not need to think of these as being in competition, since many factors can raise the chance of the same event: S's smoking raises the chance of S's getting cancer. But then so does S's being exposed to high doses of radiation. Secondly, we note that facts about chance-raising relate, usually implicitly, to a reference class. There is a certain class of people who are disposed such that if they were to take up smoking (perhaps under duress) that they would so compensate in leading healthier lives in other respects, that for them the chances of cancer are reduced. But when we say that smoking causes cancer we are not thinking about that reference class but about the class of normal adult humans. Now let us consider the claim that the chance-raising (of action A) achieved by S's mental property, M, of desiring X, is really achieved by some relevant physical property P of S. We know that not only is M multiply realizable but also that P need not correspond to M in other individuals. Consequently the reference class for which P is a chance-raiser for A may be very small, perhaps limited to S alone. By contrast, M is a chance-raiser for a much wider reference class, that of all adult humans. That shows that S's being M is a distinct chance-raising fact from S's being P. Furthermore, the class consisting of S alone is not a natural reference class. Bogus chance-raising can be achieved by considering unnatural classes (consider the class consisting of (a) non-smokers who are obese, take no exercise, suffer from many infections, and are exposed to high doses of radiation; and (b) light smokers who lead an otherwise very healthy life).

One might instead take the physical state in question to be a disjunctive state, the disjunction of the relevant physical states for all people with M. This seems to give us a large and natural reference class—all humans. This proposal faces an obvious problem, that we should not regard the disjunctive property as a genuine natural property. Gerrymandered disjunctive properties can be made to be chance-raisers even in large natural classes.

So the causal work of emergent properties is not done by anything else. Does that not mean that it duplicates the work of the physical properties or even potentially conflicts with it? That there is no potential conflict is ensured by the fact of supervenience. There will be some *apparent* conflict, since the chances of some physical outcome (the result of an action) may differ when conditional on S's being in M and S's being in P. But that will be because we are implicitly using different reference classes (all humans when considering M, a much smaller class when considering P, perhaps S alone). As the classes converge, the chances will converge. As we may have expected, the real challenge is that the emergent and the physical properties overdetermine their effects.

3.2 Causal exclusion

The concern presented by the challenge is that the complete causal efficacy of the physical properties excludes any genuine causal role for the emergent properties. The attraction of reductionism is that it just eliminates the exclusion problem. Other views that are not manifestly reductionistic may nonetheless trade on its attractions. Thus one might claim to be non-reductionistic by virtue of denying type identity between the mental and physical yet gain the benefits of reductionism by admitting token identity. But this is misleading. The identity of facts, states-of-affairs, depends on the individuals and properties composing them. If S's having mental property M is the same fact or state-or-affairs as S's having physical property P, then if M and P are genuine natural properties, they must be the same natural property. Conversely, if M and P are distinct properties, then S's having M and S's having P are distinct states of affairs. Such a problem does not arise if the term 'M' does not name a natural property. The proposition 'S has M' then may pick out the state-of-affairs that is S's having P, even though M and P are not identical. But in that case there are no genuine, natural mental properties at all. Compare s's being grue. If grueness were a genuine natural property it would be different from the natural property of being green, a's being grue and a's being green would be distinct states-of-affairs. However, as it is grueness is not a genuine natural property, and if we think of 'a's being grue' as picking out a state-of-affairs, or being made true by a state-of-affairs (before the switching time *t*) then that state-of-affairs is just a's being green. That does not amount to a non-reductive view of grueness. If anything, it is a species of eliminativism, since grueness is eliminated from the catalogue of genuine properties. The only difference between 'grue' and 'M' on this picture would be that 'grue' has a straightforward definition, whereas we suppose that 'M' need not. But that is a ground only for denying conceptual reduction, not ontological reduction (or elimination).

Similar remarks may be made about the claim that mental properties are higher order functional properties—the property of having some physical property with the causal role …. This is supposed to be physicalistic since the instantiation of the high order property just is the instantiation of some physical property. But if that is right, then there is no genuine higher-order property in existence. To be sure, we can introduce a higher-order functional *predicate*. But that provides no guarantee that the predicate corresponds to a property any more than defining 'grue' does. As it stands, such a view is physicalistic alright, but it has done nothing to show that there are any higher order properties that fail to be reduced. Its attractions are therefore the real attractions of reductionism plus the deceptive attractions of the fallacy that conceptual non-reduction is the same as ontological non-reduction.

Thus a genuinely non-reductivist view must be explicit that the emergent properties are genuine natural properties. This Fodor does, for example, by appealing to the role of mental properties in genuine natural laws. That, as O'Connor and Wong (2006) point out leads to a true property dualism, but at the price of overdetermining causes. This, they concede, is softened by 'the usual appeal to an asymmetrical supervenience of the mental on the physical', but, as they go on 'supervenience here will be inexplicable'. (This they contrast with the grounding in causal relations that there is in their brand of emergentism.)

Thus the challenge is not so much overdetermination, but rather overdetermination in the absence of a satisfactorily grounded supervenience. How is it that irreducible higher level (biological, mental) properties can get to supervene on the physical? I have assumed all along that in some way other that they do so supervene; but *why* do they supervene? In the absence of a satisfactory explanation it looks as the if alignment of the mental with the physical could be just a fluke. In which case the exclusion problem begins to bite: why isn't it that the causal efficacy of the physical excludes the mental from having a role? And couldn't the mental and the physical come apart so that they compete, perhaps interfering with one another's causal processes? In which case the causal closure of the physical looks like an accidental feature of the world.

The benefit of the evolutionary emergentism being proposed here is that it both allows the existence of genuinely natural, quasi-fundamental emergent properties and explains their supervenience on the physical, fully fundamental properties. The story of evolutionary emergence in section 2 shows how emergent properties are functional/dis-positional properties that have physical realizers. Once a physical system has reached a certain degree and kind of complexity, its (complex) parts will interact so that certain macro-features, functions are selected for in a manner that is blind to structure. The blindness to structure is what means that emergent properties are irreducible properties. But blindness to structure doesn't mean entirely independent of structure—there has to be some structure supporting the function. And thus we won't have difference in function without difference in structure.[10]

Furthermore, we can see why we can appeal to supervenience for emergent properties to avoid the exclusion problem despite the earlier criticism of Loewer's similar appeal. The problem there was that we had no reason for thinking that the higher level universal should always be accompanied by a realizer—why in the nearest world where S is (higher level) M but not (lower level) N, S is N* (some other lower level realizer). Now we do have an explanation for emergent properties, one which will not carry across to non-emergent dispositions (such as fragility). For the nature of such properties is that they are instantiated precisely by the selection of some physical property to realize them. This is the significance of the idea of Vicente and van Gulick that the brain selectively recruits and activates neural structures according to their function. The nearest world in which the higher level, in this case mental, state is present (but not N), is one in which the same selection processes are at work and which thus select some other state (N*) according to its possessing the same functional capacity.

4 Conclusion

The causal completeness of the physical seems to leave little room for genuine causation at higher levels, and in particular within the realm of the special sciences. Whatever causation is to be found there would seem really to be just physical causation, and correspondingly the properties of the special sciences can be causally efficacious only if identical to physical properties or complexes thereof. Thus we can accept causation in the special sciences only at the cost of adhering to reductionism. But reductionism is widely rejected, precisely because there is a failure of type-type identity between higher level and physical properties. At the same time, eliminativism, which concludes that there are no higher level properties at all, is widely resisted. The possibility of *emergent* properties is supposed to square this apparent circle.

The claim of this paper is that the complexity of systems that show selection for functional properties is an answer to what (at least some, more predominant) emergent properties are. In such a system, it is such functional properties that have causal power, because the development of the system (the interactions of its parts) are sensitive to them in a way that they are not sensitive to the physical causal basis. They are not sensitive to the causal basis, since the causal basis exists precisely to fulfil the role of basis to the function. Had matters been different, the same higher level properties would have been present but with a different causal basis. This is the reverse of the relationship between a causally inert higher level ('abundant') property, such as fragility. In such cases the higher level property is merely a disposition possessed solely in virtue of the object's causal micro-structure, whose presence cannot be explained in terms of the disposition it confers. A fragile snowflake does not have the causal basis for fragility in virtue of its conferring fragility on the snowflake. Nonetheless, emergent properties do have their instantiation explained in terms of their functional character. They are instantiated precisely because a selection process ensures that some physical state fulfilling the appropriate role is instantiated too, thereby ensuring that—and so explaining why—some version of the supervenience thesis holds.

5 Notes

1 Some philosophers think that such cases are not worrying in unusual cases, such as the two assassins case, but do regard ubiquitous overdetermination of this sort as objectionable. (In the two assassins case, two assassins independently fire at the intended victim.)
2 Kim's particular objections are that the counterfactual account does not distinguish causation from epiphenomenal relations and pseudo-processes.

3 Kim's (2002a: 642) view is that M is a disjunctive property. He remarks that 'If you would rather reserve "property" for causally/nomologically homogenous properties, that would be all right—we could call M and other such disjunctions something else. But this is too weak a response. For the issue is whether M is a genuinely natural, sparse property, a universal. If it is not, then we have eliminativism, not reductionism, and calling it something else will not help.

4 There are others who reject the causal claim in any case because of Molière's 'dormitive power' objection. I do not.

5 This is a characterization of *ontological* emergence. There are also doctrines of epistemological emergence, e.g. Batterman (2001), Clark (1996, 2001). There may well be epistemological emergence without ontological emergence, and maybe also vice-versa.

6 My reason for rejecting parallel non-physical properties as emergent is that they and physical properties would not show the asymmetry that is implicit in the term 'emergent'.

7 Agustin Vicente (2004: 305) makes a similar point, concerning explanations of the existence of an organ, such as the heart, in terms of its function: 'The process of selection did not take its intrinsic properties into account, only their effects'.

8 Such cases are the exception rather than the rule since beneficial mutations are rare and so the chances of two or more mutations at the same locus that are equally beneficial are very small.

9 Robert van Gulick's (van Gulick 1993) approach to mental causation (cited in this context by Vicente (2004: 307)) develops just this feature of the mind. As Vicente puts it, 'the brain ... recruits physical structures according to their causal capacities, and because they have such causal capacities, and then *selectively activates* them'.

10 This is assuming that function can be fixed synchronically, as on the current contribution to fitness view. But if we adopt the diachronic, aetiological view of function, we have to say that we cannot have a difference in function without a difference in *the history of* the structure.

References

Armstrong, D. M. 1978. *A Theory of Universals. Universals and Scientific Realism Volume II*. Cambridge: Cambridge University Press.

Batterman, R. 2001. *The Devil in the Details: Asymptotic Reasoning in Explanation, Reduction, and Emergence*. Oxford: Oxford University Press.

Clark, A. 1996. *Being There*. Cambridge, Mass.: MIT Press.

Clark, A. 2001. *Mindware*. Oxford: Oxford University Press.

Kim, J. 2002a. Précis *of Mind in a Physical World. Philosophy and Phenomenological Research 65:* 639–642.

Kim, J. 2002b. Responses to critics. *Philosophy and Phenomenological Research 65:* 670–679.

Loewer, B. 2002. Comments on Jaegwon Kim's *Mind in a Physical World. Philosophy and Phenomenological Research 65:* 654–661.

O'Connor, T. and H. Y. Wong 2006. The metaphysics of emergence. *Noûs*.

Rosenberg, A. 1994. *Instrumental Biology. Or the Disunity of Science*. Chicago: University of Chicago Press.

van Gulick, R. 1993. Who's in charge here? And who's doing all the work? In Heil and Mele (Eds.), *Mental Causation*. Oxford: Clarendon Press.

Vicente, A. 2002. How dispositions can be causally relevant. *Erkenntnis 56:* 329–344.

Vicente, A. 2004. The role of dispositions in explanation. *Theoria 19:* 301–310.

Walsh, D. 1996. Fitness and function. *British Journal for the Philosophy of Science 47:* 553–574.

11 Are there natural kinds in psychology?

Rachel Cooper

> When are the patterns of explanation and theory development that are characteristic of the physical sciences appropriate in a given area of study, and when are they inappropriate? When is it reasonable to assume that a general theory of causation in an area of study is possible? The answer that will be given here is: it is reasonable to believe that a general theory of causation in an area is possible only if the kinds of entities under investigation can reasonably be assumed to belong to natural kinds.
>
> Brian Ellis (2002) *The Philosophy of Nature*, p. 161

Prototypical examples of natural kinds are chemical elements and types of fundamental physical particles. Natural kinds are objective – the differences between them are fixed by the structure of the world, rather than being imposed by human minds – and they are theoretically important. Whether the kinds investigated by a discipline are natural kinds is a question of key importance to New Essentialists and other causal realists. Causal realists claim that the world is full of powerful particulars. These particulars fall into natural kinds, and each particular behaves in ways characteristic of its kind. Thus, where there are natural kinds there will also be real causal powers, and, as members of a natural kind behave predictably, there will also be natural laws. This in turn implies that where there are natural kinds it will be possible to make sound inductive inferences. For example, as oxygen is a natural kind, we are justified in concluding that the flame will burn brightly in this test-tube of oxygen, as it has in all the other test-tubes of oxygen. Where there are kinds we can also explain the behaviour of individuals by reference to the kind to which it belongs (so, for example, we can explain that the key is attracted to the magnet because it is made of iron). In short, whether a domain consists of natural kinds matters, because with natural kinds come natural laws, and the possibility of explanations and sound inductive inferences.[1]

In this chapter I argue that at least some psychological kinds are natural kinds. This implies that within psychology there are at least some laws, and can be at least some explanations and inductive inferences that are scientific in the same sort of way as those found in, say, chemistry. To put it mildly, this is a controversial claim. Most new essentialists think that while chemistry is a good science with neat natural kinds, biology is a slightly disreputable science with kinds that only approximate to natural kinds. That psychology will be in a yet worse state is assumed, but to many seems too obvious to even be worth stating.[2] Against such views I will here argue that although biological species are plausibly not natural kinds (at least not on the essentialist notion of "natural kind" at issue here),[3] there can still be natural kinds in psychology.

I will argue that there are natural kinds in psychology in a somewhat roundabout way. I will examine the reasons why many people have thought that there are not natural kinds in psychology, one by one, and show why each reason is inadequate. My argument that there are psychological natural kinds then follows: there are plausible candidates for such kinds, and no good reason to deny them natural kind status. There are four main reasons why people claim that psychological kinds cannot be natural kinds. First, many are convinced that human psychology varies so greatly across cultures and historical periods that there can be no natural kinds in psychology (the variation objection). Second, some claim that there can be no natural kinds in psychology because biological species are not natural kinds (the objection from biology). Third, some argue that one should not claim that there are psychological natural kinds because this would have problematic ethical and political implications (the political objection). Fourth, Colin McGinn has claimed that functionalism about the mind implies that psychological kinds cannot be natural kinds (the functionalist's objection). In this chapter I shall show that all these objections can be overcome, and that there are plausibly psychological natural kinds.

The remainder of the chapter falls into the following sections:

1   The place of natural kinds and psychological causation within the causal realist tradition.
2   The variation objection.
3   The objection from biology.
4   The political objection.
5   The functionalist's objection.
6   Conclusions.

1   The place of natural kinds and psychological causation within the causal realist tradition

Contemporary causal realism can be traced back to Harré and Madden's *Causal Powers* (1975). From this starting point, the tradition splits in two, to yield on the one hand a body of work in analytic philosophy of science, and on the other the movement known as Critical Realism. The extent to which causal realism in analytic philosophy of science and Critical Realism have become separate movements cannot be over-emphasised. Analytic philosophers of science neither cite nor discuss critical realists, and critical realists tend similarly to ignore work in analytic philosophy of science. I suggest that this mutual disinterest is best taken as a symptom of the fragmentation of the academy, rather than as a reflection of any deep disagreement. Critical realists and analytic philosophers of science don't hate each other, maybe they don't even disagree, rather they simply don't know about each other's work because they are in different academic departments and go to different conferences.

Given this fragmentation, it is best to return to the beginning and start by considering how Harré and Madden deal with natural kinds and psychological causation in *Causal Powers*. Harré and Madden's central claim is that the world is full of things with particular natures. The nature of a thing dictates that it will act in particular ways. Thus a daffodil is the kind of thing that grows up towards the light. It couldn't be the kind of thing that it is and act differently. In contrast to the Humean, Harré and Madden think that causal powers are accessible to us – we can see and feel them, and science explains their action. While agent causation is not discussed in any depth, cases where people cause things are accepted as paradigm cases of causation, amongst other cases. Harré and Madden say, "When we think of causality and action we look to such images as a springtime plant forcing its way upwards towards the light, ... of a flash of radiation as a positron and an electron meet, ... of the mobility and imaginative control of his own actions exercised by a human being, of the potent configuration of a magnetic field".[4] Harré and Madden clearly accept that there will be wide variety of causal powers – and that the powers of human agents will be amongst them.

While Harré and Madden consider psychological causation alongside other causes, in work on causal realism in contemporary analytic philosophy of science, psychological causation is seldom mentioned. Writers in this tradition take their paradigm cases from physics and chemistry.[5] It is assumed that it is here, if anywhere, that the claim that there are natural kinds, such that all members of a kind possess some essence, is most plausible. All electrons, or all samples of gold, really are alike in important respects. Thus, it can be claimed, for example, that gold essentially has an atomic number of 79, and therefore must melt at 1064.18°C. In contrast, the biological and human sciences seem messy and uncertain. Harré and Madden assumed that the nature of an organism would be determined by its genotype.[6] But in more recent work in the philosophy of biology it has become commonplace to suggest that members of a species may share no essential property – genetic and morphological properties of members of a species can both vary.[7] Scepticism about the existence of essentialist natural kinds in biology has led causal realist philosophers of science to shy away from considering biological and human examples, and to stick to worrying about what they know best – mainly electrons, salt and gold.[8] This retreat, though disappointing to those interested in the human sciences, is justified given that such examples prove problematic enough, and that these philosophers are principally interested in basic metaphysics.

In contrast, critical realists tend to be fundamentally concerned with causation in the social realm.[9] For many critical realists the aim is to provide both a philosophy of science and a theoretical framework for emancipatory projects. Thus, it is not enough to claim that some entities in the world have real causal powers. It needs to be the case that the entities that have natures and powers include people and social structures. The idea that social structures have real, but possibly hidden natures, that agents might seek to change, is fundamental to such projects.

REASONS FOR THINKING THERE ARE NO NATURAL KINDS IN PSYCHOLOGY

2 The variation objection

Probably the major reason why people are sceptical about there being natural kinds in psychology is that human psychology has plausibly varied greatly in different places and at different times.[10] Many assume that variation is incompatible with the existence of natural kinds. Thus, in his book *Against Essentialism* (2001)Stephan Fuchs states "Natural kinds always exist, or seem to exist, independent of relationships, context, time, or observer", and goes on "Allowing for variation means dissolving natural kinds".[11] The idea that where there is variation there cannot be natural kinds is widespread, but wrong-headed. Psychological variation is in fact consistent with there being psychological natural kinds, for two reasons.

First, we must remember that members of a natural kind need not be found everywhere. It is quite normal for members of a kind to only be found in certain places. Thus, many radioactive elements can be artificially manufactured, but are not found naturally, yet there is nothing metaphysically suspect about them. It is simply the case that their half lives are so short that the quantities of element created early in the history of the universe have long ago decayed. As another example, Bendetti *et al.* (1999) experimentally demonstrated that methane breaks down to form diamond under conditions similar to those expected on Uranus and Neptune. They say that, "Once these diamonds form, they fall like raindrops or hailstones toward the center of the planet".[12] If they are right, there will be showers of diamonds on Neptune, though there are none on earth. Differing environmental conditions mean that members of a kind are found in some places but not in others.

As with chemical kinds, some psychological natural kinds are not found at all times and places because the environment that they require is not found everywhere. The most obvious examples are psychological states caused by drugs or nutritional deficiencies. So, cretinism is only found in places where people's diet lacks iodine, and L.S.D. hallucinations only occur when people take L.S.D. Such examples may be too "biological" for some. But more purely psychological kinds may also require particular environments. For example, many theorists believe that Multiple Personality Disorder is caused by childhood trauma, often sexual abuse. If this is the case then the incidence of M.P.D. will vary with the incidence of such causes.

The second reason for variation is that the superficial properties of members of a natural kind can vary with environment. As a consequence, members of the same natural kind can look different in different conditions. Thus, in areas where people polish bronze door-knobs, they look shiny, while where no one polishes the door-knobs, they look dull. Similarly the superficial properties of psychological kinds can be expected to vary in different environments. Thus, Westerners suffer from depression, while Chinese people suffer from neurasthenia, but many hold that the underlying condition is the same in both cases.[13] Or to take another example, suppose that "affect programs" form natural kinds, as argued by Paul Griffiths (1997). It is consistent with such a claim to think that the expression of emotions is culturally shaped. Thus Ekman and Friesen (1971) found that Japanese students tend to suppress emotional expressions in the presence of authority figures, and present only a polite smile. In contrast the emotions of U.S. students are more transparent. Still, the same affect programs might underlie the responses of both groups. I conclude that, as the incidence and superficial properties of members of a kind commonly vary with environment, the perceived variation in human psychology is compatible with there being psychological natural kinds.

It would be amiss to end this section without mentioning a well-known modification of the variation objection proposed by Ian Hacking. In a series of papers, Hacking has argued that what he calls "human kinds", which would include any kinds in psychology, cannot be natural kinds.[14] Human kinds are altered by "looping effects" that occur when people change their behaviour in response to the ways in which they are classified. Thus obese people, for example, may diet because obesity is stigmatised and they know this. Such looping results in human kinds having histories unlike prototypical kinds, leading Hacking to conclude that human kinds cannot be natural kinds. There is not space here to deal adequately with Hacking's argument, but I have argued elsewhere that it fails (Cooper, 2004). The gist of my response to Hacking is that his feedback, though complicated, has no magical effects. Human kinds can indeed be affected by people's ideas, because ideas can cause changes in people's behaviour, but this does not show that human kinds cannot be natural kinds.

3 The objection from biology

Some are resistant to the idea that there might be natural kinds in psychology because they think there are no natural kinds in biology and assume that psychology will be in a yet worse state.[15] Those who think that there are no natural kinds in biology generally think this because they think that biological species are not natural kinds. However, even if this is the case, to conclude that there can be no natural kinds in psychology is a mistake.

Those who hold that biological species are not natural kinds stress that the members of a species are frequently morphologically and genetically diverse. There may well be no essential property that they all share. However, it is consistent to think that biological species will often not be natural kinds, while thinking that there can be other natural kinds in biology. For example, although genetic variation amongst members of a sexually reproducing species is the norm, the off-spring of a member of an asexual species will be clones of the parent (so long as no mutation arises). This means that there are groups of organisms that are all genetically identical. Such groups form natural kinds.[16] In addition, many of the kinds of microbiology and biochemistry are natural kinds – types of enzyme, haemoglobin and phagocyte would be plausible candidates here. Even if biological species are not natural kinds, natural kinds will still be bountiful within the biological sciences. There will still be natural kinds that are dealt with by the biological sciences, and, I claim, there are natural kinds within psychology too.

4 The political objection

Many are repulsed by the claim that there are natural kinds in psychology because they think that such a stance commits one to reactionary political beliefs. In *The Disorder of Things*, for example, John Dupré claims that when types of people are considered to form distinct natural kinds "it is inevitable that any systematic differences that are found will be taken to be explained, or explicable, in terms of the intrinsic differences between members of the two kinds".[17] This leads to the "legitimation of conservative politics and to the discouragement of proposals for significant social change".[18] The basic thought seems to be that if some group of disadvantaged people form a natural kind, then this implies that their state is natural and thus unalterable.[19]

I have two responses to such claims: First, the political implications of there being psychological natural kinds are limited. It must be remembered that the superficial properties of natural kinds can be changed, and that members of a natural kind can also be destroyed. Suppose, as seems to me plausible, that heroin addicts form a natural kind. The drug does something to their brains, producing characteristic effects when they have taken heroin, and withdrawal symptoms when they have not. This does not imply that I think that heroin addicts are beyond help. Heroin addicts can stop being heroin addicts. While addicted to heroin their brains are a certain way and they are members of the kind "heroin addict", but once drug-free for long enough, their brains recover, and they cease to be members of the kind. Similarly, one can hold that heroin addicts form a natural kind, and yet think it possible that a drug might be discovered that blocks their cravings for heroin. In this case the causal powers of the heroin would be counteracted by another agent. The superficial properties of the heroin addict would have been altered by changes in the environment in which the heroin acted. Thus, one can consistently hold that some disadvantaged group form a natural kind, and also think that their situation could be improved by social changes.

In addition, it should be remembered that even if unfortunate political implications were to follow, this is not a reason for denying that there are natural kinds in psychology. Politics cannot drive metaphysics, as the world is often not as we might like it to be.

5 The functionalist's objection

The functionalist's objection is somewhat complicated and so this section will be split into two. Part (a) outlines the functionalist's objection. Part (b) outlines my response to it.

5.1 (a) The objection

Harré and Madden claim that the entities in the world fall into natural kinds with particular natures. If an individual belongs to a kind then it must behave as things of its kind do. If a piece of "salt" behaves in an unsalty way then it simply isn't salt at all, rather it's some other substance, Fool's Salt, say. This style of reasoning can be applied to all natural kinds. But when we try to apply it to cases of psychological causation a worry emerges. In "Mental states, natural kinds and psychophysical laws" (1991) Colin McGinn argues that if a functionalist account of mind is adopted, mental or psychological kinds cannot be considered natural kinds.[20] If he is correct, then insofar as functionalism is an attractive account of mind, it looks as if psychological causation may fall outside the remit of causal realism.

Functionally defined entities are entities that can be characterised in terms of what they do – mouse-traps, kitchen utensils and computer programs are classic examples. Functionalists about the mind hold that mental states can be defined wholly in functional terms, that is by how they are causally connected to sensory inputs, behavioural outputs and other mental states. So, for example, beliefs that it is about to rain are characteristically produced by seeing dark clouds, and lead people to put on waterproof coats, if they want to stay dry.

If mental states are functionally defined, this implies that they can be multiply realised – the same mental state can be realised by multiple physical, or even possibly non-physical, systems. So, while my belief that it is about to rain is realised by some configuration of neurons in my brain, a Martian's belief that it is about to rain would be realised by some configuration of the green slime that fills Martian heads. Both states would count as beliefs that it about to rain so long as they behave appropriately (in the right circumstances, the state must prompt raincoat wearing and so on). Multiple realisation implies that tokens of a mental state can be physically dissimilar.

Members of prototypical natural kinds are physically alike because they share some physical essential property. All samples of gold are similar in having an atomic number of 79, all diamonds are made of similarly structured carbon. In contrast, at the physical level, members of a psychological kind can be completely different. This means that if members of a psychological kind share essential properties these properties cannot be physical properties.

What about the possibility that members of a psychological state instead possess essential properties that are functionally defined – that the essential property of a belief that it is about to rain is having a particular causal role? McGinn gives three reasons for rejecting this possibility.

First, McGinn suggests that, as mental states operate holistically, there will be no particular causal role that can be taken to be characteristic of a type of mental state. To say that mental states operate holistically is to say that the effects of a particular mental state will depend on the other mental states possessed by an agent. If you know that I like Jaffa Cakes, for example, you cannot simply conclude that when offered a selection of biscuits I will choose those. Maybe I am in an unusually generous mood, and decide to leave the best biscuits for others. Maybe I believe that Rich Tea biscuits contain more vitamins, and so even though I think they are horrible, I go for those instead. As what a mental state does depends so radically on circumstances, McGinn concludes that there may well be no particular causal role that can be used to identify a mental state.

Second, McGinn reminds us, the essential properties of paradigmatic natural kinds are properties linked to their internal constitution. In contrast, functionally defined properties are specifically not linked to the internal constitution of entities.

Third, McGinn claims that any specification of a mental state's causal role would be definitional and a priori. It is not an empirical discovery that those who want to stay dry take action to ensure this result, rather that they do this is true by definition. In contrast, the properties that characterise natural kinds can only be specified a posteriori. Empirical work was required before we knew that all samples of gold have an atomic number of 79, or that water is H_2O.

If functionalism is correct, and many philosophers find it an attractive view, then functionally defined psychological kinds cannot be characterised in terms of the physical properties they possess. However, claims McGinn, kinds characterised by functionally defined properties would differ so much from prototypical natural kinds that they would not be natural kinds at all. It follows, he thinks, that psychological kinds cannot be natural kinds.

5.2 (b) A response

Here I shall argue that McGinn's argument fails as not all psychological kinds are functionally defined. Rather, some psychological kinds are natural kinds. In arguing against McGinn, I shall restrict my attention to mental states other than the propositional attitudes. In other words, I will not be considering mental states like beliefs, desires and intentions, but rather will be worrying about mental states like emotions, pains and character traits. Some will suspect that this is cheating. Surely everyone knows that the propositional attitudes are more problematic and more interesting! I accept that the propositional attitudes are more problematic (that's why I'm avoiding them), but deny they are more important (which is why I think my choice is justified).

In discussing the possibility of there being psychological natural kinds, or of there being mental causation, the propositional attitudes are more problematic than other mental states because they have content. Content causes problems on two counts. First content appears to make a difference to the causal powers of a mental state – it makes a difference whether one's desire is for beer, or gin and tonic, say – but content is abstract, and so appears to be the wrong sort of thing to enter into causal relations. Second, Putnam/Burge style arguments suggest that the content of a mental state can be at least partially determined by things that may be far distant in space and time from the thinker (i.e. the content of a mental state might depend on far-away features of the world, or linguistic conventions).[21] If content is not fixed by facts about the thinker's brain (or at least by fairly local states of affairs) it's hard to see how it can make a difference causally.[22] Propositional attitudes are thus especially problematic and the discussion here will steer well clear of them.

This strategy is justified in part because propositional attitudes have already received a lot of attention,[23] while non-propositional mental states remain comparatively neglected. Furthermore, though one might not guess it from the philosophical literature, non-propositional mental states are of key importance in both folk and academic psychology. Let's consider folk psychology first. In the philosophical literature it is often assumed that folk psychological explanations focus on the propositional attitudes – we are supposed to posit that an agent possesses appropriate beliefs and desires, and then conclude that he will act as is reasonable (or, on the simulation view, we assume that the agent will act as we would if we had his beliefs and desires). However, a little reflection will show that many of our folk psychological explanations are not like this. Many of our predictions and explanations rely on the attribution of character traits, rather than on the attribution of beliefs and desires. Suppose I predict that colleague X will be at the meeting. I don't think to myself, "X desires to go to the meeting, and knows it is in room B13 at 1pm, so X will be there". Rather, I think that X is diligent and so will be at the meeting. Similarly, I can predict that Y will not be able to make small talk with strangers at a party because Y is shy. Z, on the other hand, will be fine, because Z is friendly (note, in this case Y and Z may have identical beliefs and desires, both may think it would be nice to talk – but still Y is shy and says nothing, while Z chats away – it is the attribution of character traits that does all the predictive work in such cases).

In academic psychology too non-propositional mental states play an important role in explanation and prediction. Psychologists divide people into extroverts and introverts, or risk-averse and risk-takers, or those who tend to express emotions and those who don't. Categories such as these figure in their theories to as great an extent as do attributions of beliefs and desires. I conclude that non-propositional mental states are important and neglected, and so examining whether they fall into natural kinds is a worthwhile project. With this restriction on my argument noted, we can return to McGinn's worries.

As McGinn argues, multiple realisation causes problems for the idea that psychological kinds are natural kinds because it implies that mental states of the same type need not be physically similar. If Martians can be in pain, and they lack C-fibres, then the essential property of pain cannot be C-fibre activation.

There may, however, be a way of getting round such concerns. Multiple realisation implies that not all pain is C-fibre activation. But it is consistent with this to think that normal human pain may be C-fibre activation, while Martian pain may be something else.[24] While the functionalist is committed to the claim that pain might be realised by all sorts of odd physical systems, they can still claim that normal human pain may well be a natural kind. Indeed, this is the most plausible line to take. Pain-killers work. And, they don't work via reprogramming our "software". This suggests that normal human pain is produced by some natural kind of biological process that can be reliably interfered with by chemical means.

Of course it might turn out that multiple realisation occurs even in normal humans – maybe in the same way that some people have A-type blood and others O-type blood, some people have C-fibre type pain and others D-fibre type pain. If this turned out to be the case, then further retreat would be required, one would have to say that human pain came in two varieties – a C-fibre type and a D-fibre type. There might turn out to be two, or four, or six physically distinct pain-types, and, I suggest, these might be considered natural kinds.

What, however, if at the physical level there turns out to be just utter complexity? I suggest that with psychological kinds such as pain and affect programs this is unlikely to happen. Humans are evolved biological organisms, and such mental states depend on the brain. There is thus no more reason to expect complete confusion at the psychological level than at the biological level.

What kinds of human mental states might fall into natural kinds? Candidates include not only pain and affect programs, but also character traits, and some types of mental illness. Although I wouldn't bet big money that any one of these actually will turn out to be natural kinds, at present they seem likely examples. In all these cases one can imagine that scientific evidence might show that the psychological state is produced by some specific physical cause. Already, for example, we have discovered that the mental disorder Huntington's Chorea is caused by a single dominant gene on chromosome four. More controversially, depression might be caused by low serotonin levels, and fear linked to activity in the amygdala.

As these examples show, two of McGinn's concerns can easily be dealt with. If the essential property of cases of human depression is an abnormality in neurotransmitter levels, then all cases of depression will be physically similar. Furthermore, as McGinn requires, the essential property of depression would have been discovered by science, not by definition.

What of McGinn's worry about the holism of the mental? It turns out that sticking to non-propositional mental states helps deal with this. I accept that the holism of the mental implies that propositional mental states cannot be matched up with a characteristic causal role. However, I suggest that at least some non-propositional mental states are different. States such as the basic emotions, or pain, tend to produce characteristic effects regardless of an agent's other mental states. So, if an agent finds something funny they will tend to giggle, no matter what else may be going on. Of course, in some cases, the giggling must be suppressed. If something seems funny at a funeral, my desire to be respectful will mean I will try not to giggle. But, still, the urge to giggle is there, and has to be overcome by other forces. This situation is no different from that with physical forces. Being amused tends to produce giggling, although some giggling is suppressed. In the same kind of way, gravity tends to make apples fall to the ground, although some apples are caught. It appears that some non-propositional mental states do have characteristic effects, although as is usual in other domains, these effects only become visible all things being equal.

I conclude that functionalism about the mind is an attractive position, but that it is possible to be a sort of functionalist and yet to think that at least some normal human psychological kinds are not functionally defined. Martians might feel pain or fear, and these states be realised by some system quite different from a human brain. However, it can still be the case that some of the psychological states of normal human beings fall into natural kinds.

6 Conclusions

In this chapter I have examined arguments that purport to show that psychological kinds cannot be natural kinds and found them wanting. Given that there are plausible candidates for psychological natural kinds, we should thus accept that there are natural kinds in psychology. Possible examples would be normal human pain, and normal human affect programs. Any such psychological natural kinds will be able to support laws, explanations and sound inductive inferences. Thus, if I am right, certain areas of psychology can be scientific in the same way as chemistry.

However, it should be borne in mind that the conclusions of this chapter are limited. In particular I have not considered problems related to propositional mental states. Propositional mental states are more difficult to deal with, both because it is hard to see how content can enter into causal relations, and because problems linked to the holism of the mental primarily affect propositional mental states. As I have not considered propositional mental states, and propositional mental states are important in both folk and academic psychology, my conclusions here can only be limited. I have argued that *some* of psychology (that relating to those non-propositional mental states that fall into natural kinds) is a science more like, say chemistry, than many have thought. It may still be the case, however, that models of causation, explanation and law drawn from the natural sciences cannot be appropriately applied to those areas of psychology that deal with propositional mental states.

7 Acknowledgements

I am very grateful to John Cromby, Ruth Groff and Alison Stone who read and commented on earlier drafts of this Chapter.

Notes

1 That there are links between natural kinds, natural laws, explanations and inductive inferences is brought out very clearly in Bird (1998), ch. 3.
2 See, for example, Ellis (2002), pp. 28–32. Ellis explains that biological species are unlikely to be natural kinds and then continues, "As we move up to yet more complex systems, from biological organisms up to ecological or social systems, natural kind analyses become much less interesting" (p. 32).
3 Various writers have proposed non-essentialist accounts of kinds, on which biological species plausibly are natural kinds. See, for example, Boyd (1991, 1999); Dupré (1981); Millikan (1997).
4 Harré and Madden (1975), p. 7.

5 Thus, Ellis (2002), mainly discusses chemical kinds.
6 Harré and Madden (1975), p. 18.
7 Dupré (1981).
8 Ellis (2001), contains some discussion of psychological and social kinds, but Ellis is mainly concerned with kinds in the physical sciences.
9 Agent causation is a fundamental concern in Bhaskar (1979), for example.
10 For example, Harré (ed.) 1986, and Harré and Parrott (eds) (1996), use case studies that illustrate how emotions vary with culture to argue that emotions are largely socially constructed, and that biological accounts of emotions have little to offer – i.e. they argue that cultural variation indicates that emotions do not fall into natural kinds.
11 Fuchs (2001), p. 13.
12 Quote from University of California, Berkeley New Release 30.9.99.
13 Parker *et al.* (2001).
14 Hacking(1986, 1988, 1992, 1995a, 1995b).
15 See, for example, Ellis(2002), pp. 28–32. Ellis explains that biological species are unlikely to be natural kinds and then continues, "As we move up to yet more complex systems, from biological organisms up to ecological or social systems, natural kind analyses become much less interesting".
16 This is noted by Ellis (2002), p. 30, though Ellis claims (falsely in my view) that "these microspecies are the only genuine natural kinds in the domain of living organisms".
17 Dupré (1993), p. 253.
18 Dupré (1993), p. 256.
19 As another example, Hayes (1995), claims that positions that are "reductionist" (by which she means positions that claim that there are psychological natural kinds) "tell us to accept things as given and do nothing" and that this is "one reason for their popularity among the very right-wing sectors of society" (p. 17).
20 McGinn himself is not a functionalist, but he presents these arguments from a functionalist's perspective. G. Botterill and P. Carruthers (1999), p. 39 also suggest that the multiple realisability of psychological kinds means that they cannot be natural kinds.
21 Putnam (1975); Burge (1979).
22 For discussion of these problems see Heil and Mele (1995), Part III.
23 Most of the contributions to Heil and Mele (1995), are concerned with propositional mental states.
24 Kim (1993), pp. 309–335 also argues that multiple realisation may be compatible with species-level reductions.

References

Beneditti, J. Nguyen, W. Caldwell *et al.* (1999) Dissociation of CH$_4$ at high pressures and temperatures: Diamond formation in giant planet interiors? *Science*, (1 Oct 1999), 286: 100–102.
Bird, A. (1998) *Philosophy of Science.* London: UCL Press.
Bhaskar, R. ([1979], 1998) *The Possibility of Naturalism* (3rd edn). London: Routledge.
Botterill, G. and P. Carruthers (1999) *The Philosophy of Psychology.* Cambridge: Cambridge University Press.
Boyd, R. (1991) Realism, anti-foundationalism and the enthusiasm for natural kinds. *Philosophical Studies*, 61, 127–148.

Boyd, R. (1999) Homoestatis, species and higher taxa. In R. Wilson (ed.) *Species.* MIT Press: Cambridge, Massachusetts.

Burge, T. (1979) Individualism and the mental. In P. French, T. Uehling and H. Wettstein (eds) *Midwest Studies in Philosophy. Vol. 4.* Minneapolis: University of Minnesota Press.

Cooper, R. (2004) Why Hacking is wrong about human kinds. *British Journal for the Philosophy of Science,* 55: 73–85.

Dupré, J. (1981) Natural kinds and biological taxa. *The Philosophical Review,* XC, pp. 66–90.

Dupré, J. (1993) *The Disorder of Things.* Cambridge, Massachusetts: Harvard University Press.

Ekman, P. and W. Friesen (1971) Constants across culture in the face and emotion. *Journal of Personality and Social Psychology,* 17: 124–129.

Ellis, B. (2001) *Scientific Essentialism.* Cambridge: Cambridge University Press.

Ellis, B. (2002) *The Philosophy of Nature.* Chesham: Acumen.

Fuchs, S. (2001) *Against Essentialism.* Cambridge, Massachusetts: Harvard University Press.

Griffiths, P. (1997) *What Emotions Really Are.* Chicago: University of Chicago Press.

Hacking, I. (1986) Making up people. In T. Heller, M. Sosna and D. Wellberry (eds) *Reconstructing Individualism.* Stanford, California: Stanford University Press, pp. 222–236.

Hacking, I. (1988) The sociology of knowledge about child abuse. *Nous,* 22, 53–63.

Hacking, I. (1992) World-making by kind-making: Child abuse for example. In M. Douglas and D. Hull (eds) *How Classification Works.* Edinburgh: Edinburgh University Press, pp. 180–238.

Hacking, I. (1995a) *Rewriting the Soul.* Princeton: Princeton University Press.

Hacking, I. (1995b) The looping effects of human kinds. In D. Sperber and A. Premark (eds) *Causal Cognition.* Oxford: Clarendon Press, pp. 351–394.

Harré, R. and E. Madden (1975) *Causal Powers.* Oxford: Basil Blackwell.

Harré, R. (ed.) (1986) *The Social Construction of Emotions.* Oxford: Basil Blackwell.

Harré, R. and W. Parrott (eds) (1996) *The Emotions.* London: Sage.

Hayes, N. (1995) *Psychology in Perspective.* Basingstoke: Macmillan.

Heil, J. and A. Mele (eds) (1995) *Mental Causation.* Oxford: Clarendon Press.

Kim, J. (1993) *Supervenience and Mind.* Cambridge: Cambridge University Press.

McGinn, C. (1991) Mental states, natural kinds and psychophysical laws. In his *The Problem of Consciousness.* Oxford: Basil Blackwell, pp. 126–152.

Millikan, R. (1997) On cognitive luck: Externalism in an evolutionary frame. In M. Carrier and P. Machamer (eds) *Mindscapes: Philosophy, Science and the Mind.* Konstanz: Universitätsverlag Konstanz GmbH, pp. 207–219.

Parker, G., G. Gladstone and K. Tsee Chee (2001) Depression in the planet's largest ethnic group: The Chinese. *American Journal of Psychiatry,* 158: 857–864.

Putnam, H. (1975) The meaning of "meaning". Reprinted in his (1979) *Philosophical Papers, Vol. 2. Mind, Language and Reality.* Cambridge: Cambridge University Press.

University of California, Berkeley (30.9.99) New Release: UC Berkeley researchers report experimental evidence for diamond showers on Neptune and Uranus. Available at http://www.berkeley.edu/news/media/releases/99legacy/9-30-1999a.html

Part III

Realism about causality in social science

12 Sociology's causal confusion

Douglas V. Porpora

Sociology – or at least American sociology, which will be the focus of this paper – remains confused about causality. It remains confused because American sociology, like American culture more broadly, is deeply empiricist. That empiricism, this paper will show, stifles conceptual thought about causality, yielding in the end only the most meager understanding of causality, an understanding shared ironically enough by both supporters and critics of an enduring positivism.

In saying that American culture and American sociology are empiricist, I mean that both tend to privilege observation over contemplation. Empirical observation seems active – one goes out and looks – whereas contemplation is something one does while sitting in one's chair. Thus, empirical work accords much better with action-oriented, American pragmatism than conceptual labor, which seems like and often is dismissed as idle speculation.

The continuity between the general American culture and its sociology in the prejudice favoring the empirical over the conceptual shows up in any class in social research methods. It does not matter whether the class is at the graduate or undergraduate level. Just make the distinction between empirical questions and conceptual questions and ask your novice sociologists which ones can be answered with absolute certainty. Clearly considering conceptual questions next to worthless, the budding scientists will enthusiastically respond that it is empirical questions that can be answered with certainty.

This is the moment to inform your charges that, sadly, no empirical claim can be proven with the certainty of a mathematical proof, that the most we can do is establish a preponderance of evidence, sometimes perhaps beyond a reasonable doubt. Speaking of mathematics, however, therein lie conceptual claims the truth of which can be established with absolute certainty once and for all. The Pythagorean Theorem, for example, is a conceptual claim, established not by empirically examining sample triangles but by the logical deductions one can perform while musing in one's chair. Yet, given a Euclidian geometry, the truth of the Pythagorean Theorem is more certain than any empirical claim.

Although we Americans, including American sociologists, are more comfortable with empirical than with conceptual questions, many of the basic questions that interest us are of course conceptual: What is social structure? What is democracy?

What is causality? None of these definitional questions is answered principally by the collection of data.

Because Americans are impatient with the collective work it takes to reach clarity on conceptual questions, we typically cannot think clearly about such basic ideas as democracy, social structure, or causality. Thus it is that in the nation that fancies itself the bastion of democracy, very few Americans can adequately say what democracy is beyond voting, freedom, or rule by the people. Similarly, few sociologists could be very articulate if asked point blank what sociology means by social action or social structure. American sociologists would rather get on with the important work of data collection than sit around too long figuring out what their concepts can defensibly mean.

It is no different with the concept of causality. Although virtually all sociologists have a tacit understanding of causality, how that tacit understanding is articulated in practice is not the product of much care. Consider two of our best-selling texts on research methods, W. Lawrence Neuman's (2000) *Social Research Methods* (4th edn), and Earl Babbie's (2004) *The Practice of Social Research* (10th edn). The two books are similar in several regards. Both spend a lot of time on the concept of "concepts," and in both their indexes under "Concepts," there are entries labeled "defined" (Babbie) or "definition of" (Neuman). Concepts are evidently important to social scientific research methods. By contrast, in neither index under "Causality" is there any entry telling us where we might find causality defined.

Both texts offer a glossary of important terms where we might expect to see causality listed. Babbie's glossary contains no such listing. Neuman's does contain a listing labeled "Causal Explanation," which tells us edifyingly that a causal explanation is "a statement in social theory about why events occur that is expressed in terms of causes and effects" (Neuman 2000: 505). There is no follow-up entry for either "cause" or "effect," although, revealingly, there is an entry for "Causal Laws," which simply tells us, rather unrevealingly, that causal laws are associations in the empirical world that positivists use to describe causal relations.

The treatment of causality in these texts is peculiar. Why should "causality" be treated more cavalierly than "concepts"? Presumably, not because causality is so much less important than concepts to the enterprise of research methods. A more likely explanation of the differential treatment of the two terms is that the concept of "concepts" is uncontroversial whereas the concept of "causality" is, and sociology seeks to avoid any conceptual controversy that might detain us from data collection. Thus, the meaning of causality is brushed over so as to get quickly to the more usable "criteria of causality." Consider, for example, how Neuman makes this transition:

> Philosophers have long debated the idea of cause. It has been controversial since the writings of the eighteenth century Scottish philosopher David Hume ... Without entering into the philosophical debate, many sociologists pursue causal relationships. You need three things to establish causality: temporal order, association, and elimination of plausible alternatives ... An

implicit fourth condition is an assumption that a causal relationship makes sense or fits with broader assumptions or a theoretical framework.

(Neuman 2000: 52)

Evident in Neuman's treatment is the typical sociological hurry to be done with anything smacking of philosophy; the result is not the absence of philosophy but, rather, by default the philosophy of Hume. Babbie likewise is eager to get to the criteria of causality without much ado about causality itself. Babbie arrives there by first distinguishing idiographic and nomothetic explanation, the difference between explanations focusing on the particular and explanations focusing on the general. With this distinction established, Babbie simply announces the three criteria for what he calls nomothetic causality, which coincide with the three explicit criteria Neuman identifies.

It does not follow from anything either Neuman or Babbie says that the criteria of causality are what they are. Instead, Neuman and Babbie each rely on the reader's own tacit, pre-scientific sense of causality to comprehend that whereas it makes sense to say, for example, that gender may affect a person's attitudes toward marijuana use, it makes no sense to suggest that attitudes toward marijuana use may affect a person's gender. In these texts, the tacit understanding that allows appreciation of such a point always remains tacit.

Because our tacit pre-scientific understanding of causality is never made articulate in these texts, the texts can further – illicitly – privilege the empirical over the conceptual when it comes to the criteria of causality. The three explicit criteria of causality Neuman mentions above – the only ones mentioned by Babbie – are all empirical in nature. Whether or not they are met is a matter of observation. The inference is thereby fostered that what causality is is largely if not entirely an empirical matter.

Neuman at least acknowledges another criterion of causality, if only "implicit," that any putative causal connection make sense or fit a theoretical framework. Neuman (2000: 47, 55) even says a complete explanation must elaborate a causal mechanism, and the phrase "causal mechanism" actually appears in his index. Of course, Neuman does not tell us much about causal mechanisms. All he tells us is that "a *causal mechanism* is a statement of how things work, such as: When people fear a loss, they strike out at those they believe to be their direct competitors and who have less social and political power" (Neuman 2000: 47).

Neuman is not a philosopher, so leave aside the infelicity of his equating causal mechanisms with statements (statements after all about the causes of cancer do not themselves cause cancer). Ignore as well that the causal mechanism Neuman cites is not so clear. The real problem is Neuman's subordination of causal mechanism as an implicit afterthought to the criteria of causality. Of course, this is infinitely more than Babbie allows. Babbie says nothing about causal mechanisms, implicit or otherwise.

Why do the methods textbooks so deemphasize causal mechanisms? Because in contrast with the three criteria of causality that the texts emphasize, the elaboration of a causal mechanism – detailing how things work – is a conceptual matter not an empirical one. Consider, for example, how our conception of an atom has changed: from a point particle, to a mini solar system, to some kind of inscrutable cloud. These models are what has progressively driven practical success in dealing with atomic realities. To be sure, empirical observation has been needed to refine and shape these models, but the models themselves are complex conceptions. They are not just lists of deductive propositions or statements as sociology's research textbooks tend to describe theory.

It begins to become clear that a profound evasion is at work in sociology, a kind of bad faith. To privilege the empirical, sociology must mutilate its understanding of causality. In the process sociology distorts its understanding of theory as well.

Although we are not supposed to notice, the resulting problems are already apparent in the methods texts. Consider the criterion that there is a causal connection – as opposed to a merely "spurious" correlation – only when other possible causes have been ruled out. In terms of sociology's favored talk of variables, this criterion means that the association between some putative independent and dependent variables remains even after controlling for some third variable. Sociologists have all been reared on a number of familiar stories to illustrate this point. Babbie relates some of them.

> There is a correlation between ice cream sales and deaths due to drowning: the more ice cream sold the more drowning, and vice versa. There is, however, no direct link between ice cream sales and drowning. The third variable at work here is season or temperature. Most drownings occur during summer – the peak period for ice cream sales.
>
> (Babbie 2004: 91)

> Areas with many storks have high birth rates. Those with few storks have low birth rates. Do storks really deliver babies? Birth rates are higher in the country than in the city; more storks live in the country than in the city. The third variable here is urban/rural areas.
>
> (Babbie 2004: 92)

Contrary to the whole thrust of the methods texts, these stories of spurious correlation work only because of conceptual rather than empirical considerations. In each case, we are presented with a correlation between two variables that are supposed to be amusingly silly to think of as causally connected. We are then told how the two variables correlate with a third, which makes more sense as the cause of both, thus explaining why the other two are correlated without one's causing the other.

The first question is how the reader is expected to grasp right away the absurdity of supposing that the initial correlations signify causality. Appealed to is not the reader's vast background with enduring empirical regularities. Instead, although it goes unsaid, what makes the prospect of a causal connection immediately ludicrous is the lack of any plausible mechanism linking the two initially introduced, correlated variables of the story. As no one today thinks storks deliver babies, there is no causal connection imaginable between the two variables.

The situation is a bit more complicated with ice cream sales and drownings. For some reason, Babbie has altered the canonical story. The usual account posits a correlation between ice cream sales and the murder rate with season again being the common cause of both. Although there is no imaginable causal connection between ice cream sales and the murder rate, there actually is a plausible mechanism linking ice cream sales and drownings: the old warning against entering the water within a half hour after eating, lest one cramp and drown. For this reason, Babbie must explicitly say there is no "direct" link between ice cream sales and drownings. Of course, there may yet be an indirect link, which makes Babbie's version of the story work less well than it should.

In any case, it is on conceptual grounds that we immediately recognize that the two variables initially presented in these stories are not likely to be connected causally. We do not even need the introduction of some specific third variable to make this determination. It is not as if, should the correlation between storks and births remain even after the introduction of all likely third variables, that we would finally conclude storks and births are causally connected after all. The reason, again, is conceptual.

The second question to ask of these stories is how we know which third variables to consider introducing. It is not as if we can control for all possible variables, and in fact we never do. So what determines which variables we do control for? Babbie cannot answer this question because he has introduced nothing that can answer it; thus, in his text, the question is not even considered.

Neuman at least tells us that "eliminating alternatives is an ideal because eliminating all possible alternatives is impossible" (Neuman 2000: 54). What the researcher should try to do, Neuman says, is eliminate the major alternatives. How do we know which of the alternatives are major? Neuman does not directly raise or answer this question, but he does at least speak of "plausible" alternatives – a conceptual distinction – and as he next proceeds to speak of control variables, he makes use of a resource he, unlike Babbie, allowed himself. He invokes the implicit criterion of causal mechanisms.

So far, we have found that a conceptual consideration – the one concerning plausible mechanisms – plays two important but un- or under-acknowledged roles in the instructional stories of the methods texts. This conceptual consideration begins the stories, and it makes sense of how we go about applying the second empirical criterion of causality – the elimination of plausible alternatives.

Finally, the same conceptual consideration is needed to end the stories. The stories are all meant to end with an "Aha!" response upon the introduction of the third variable. We are meant to see right away that of course the third variable explains everything. Why should this be the expected response? Why are we not expected to continue asking whether the final correlation too is spurious? The unacknowledged reason is that in all stories, the causal mechanisms operating through the finally introduced third variables are much clearer. Thus, what is satisfied finally is not a need for more data but a need for conceptual closure. The more clearly discerned causal mechanisms provides it.

It becomes evident that in the case of causality, conceptual considerations – and, thus, theory – matter even more decisively than empirical considerations. This is a revelation that an empiricist sociology must repress, which is perhaps another reason why the methods texts so rush past causality itself to the indicators of causality.

The cost to sociology of this rush is a highly atomized view of causality – atomized, that is, in the antiquated sense of an atom as a point particle. Sociology has little patience for the kind of elaboration of causal mechanisms as characterize more sophisticated models of the atom or, on the social plane, the structural mechanism, for example, through which Adam Smith accounts for the market's "invisible hand." Instead, sociology prefers causal mechanisms that fit comfortably within a variable. Thus, the causal mechanisms associated with the third variables in Babbie's stories – season and place – are themselves little more than associations, the descriptions of which require nothing more than one-liners.

If sociology prefers causal mechanisms that can be described by a single line, it is because such compact causality most conveniently fits into causal laws, which in turn are central to the old positivist covering law model of causal explanation. The fact is that even now in the twenty-first century, the covering law model remains American sociology's only articulated understanding of causal explanation.

The covering law model conceives of causal explanation as a species of deductive argument in which the explanandum (that which is to be explained) is logically deduced from the explanans (that which does the explaining). According to the covering law model, the key part of the explanans is a covering law, which relates two types of events: an antecedent event (A) – which may be a compound event – and a consequent event (B). Taking the form "If A, then B," the covering law simply stipulates that if an event of type A occurs, then an event of type B will occur. To explain any particular event B, the full explanans consists of the covering law "If A then B" and the observation that an event of the antecedent type A has in fact occurred. Event B follows as a logical deduction.

The covering law model conceives of a cause exclusively as an event rather than a structure. Thus, a covering law is exactly what Bhaskar (1975, 1979) referred to as an "event-regularity." The covering law simply links events: If one thing happens, then another thing happens. Thus, all that remains of causality is a conceptually thin empirical regularity, itself not much more than a covariation.

Such a meager conceptual residue is ideal if the objective is a thorough-going empiricism. The extra benefit to empiricism of such a thin understanding of causality is that causal connections can now be fully expressed mathematically. That mathematical formulation is the ideal expression of sociological theory was the central idea behind Herbert Blalock's (1969) highly influential *Theory Construction: From Verbal to Mathematical Formulation*. In consequence, sociology came to elevate statistics from technique to theoretical language. In other words, statistical formulations – a regression equation, for example – became not just a way of determining which explanation is correct but the explanation itself.

What gets distorted when causality is so thinned out for mathematical formulation is not just causality but theory as well. Theory on this view is a series of logically connected, one-liners, each of which can be tested as an empirical hypothesis. Thus, does Blalock describe theory circa 1969:

> It has been noted that theories do not consist entirely of conceptual schemes or typologies but must contain lawlike propositions that interrelate concepts of variables two or more at a time. Furthermore these propositions must themselves be interrelated. For example, if one proposition relates variables A and B, a second C and D, and a third E and F, then there must be additional propositions enabling one to make deductive statements connecting these three propositions. Ideally, one might hope to achieve a completely closed deductive theoretical system in which there would be a minimal set of propositions taken as axioms, from which all other propositions could be deduced by purely mathematical or logical reasoning. More realistically, we might take the model of the completely closed deductive system as an ideal which in practice can only be approximated.
>
> (Blalock 1969: 2)

Around the same time, Peter Blau (1969) described theory almost identically. Three features of the description are worthy of note. First is the call for "lawlike" propositions that can fit the covering law model. Second is the equation of theory with an interrelated string of such propositions. Finally, there is the ideal of theory as a completely closed deductive or "axiomatic" system.

This positivist understanding of theory and causality privileges a narrow range of empirical research. In fact, empirical research becomes equated with quantitative, statistical research. If causal explanation must follow the covering law model, then all causal explanation must be "nomothetic" or general. "Idiographic" explanation, which does not invoke general laws but rather the particularities of the individual case, does not count at all as causal explanation. It is instead mere description. Thus, not only is theory marginalized but so is all qualitative research that adopts, for example, historical or ethnographic methods.

The problem with the covering law model is that it is a chimera to which sociologists only pretend to commit themselves. It survives only because, again eschewing conceptual reflection, sociologists do not consider it too closely. Already in Blalock's description, there is the characteristic hedge. Departing from the canonical version of the covering law model, the propositions for which Blalock calls are not actually laws but only lawlike.

How far from actual laws can propositions depart before the covering law model ceases to work? If the covering model is to work at all, then the propositions must specify either deterministic or, at minimum statistical laws; the mere statistical generalizations sociology normally offers up will not suffice at all (Porpora 1983). Yet, despite all its empirical efforts, sociology has not only failed to identify any deterministic laws, it has likewise failed to identify even any statistical laws. No one pretends otherwise. What is pretended is that it still somehow makes sense to call for "lawlike" theoretical propositions (Blau 1983; Mayhew 1983; Turner 2003).

That call survives to this day. Leading sociologists like Rodney Stark and Roger Finke (2000) continue to trot out as theory sets of deductively related, "testable" propositions. Highly sophisticated, quantitative, positivist analysis is what continues to be produced at the top graduate departments in sociology and is what fills the two major American journals of sociology: *The American Journal of Sociology* and the *American Sociological Review*.

Even in the latest issue of the newsletter of the theory section of the American Sociological Association, a polemic by Stephen K. Sanderson (2005) argues that sociological theory has an "excessive concern with classical theorists," particularly " 'chic' European theorists" and that sociological theory has become extremely politicized, representing more social commentary than scientific theory. Some theorists, Sanderson further complains, specifically the postmodernists, reject science altogether in favor of literary criticism and epistemological relativism. Altogether, he claims, theorists have isolated themselves "hermetically" from the rest of sociology.

What does Sanderson propose? Citing Blau, Turner, and Stark and Finke, Sanderson (2005: 2) wants "the formulation of more modest sets of propositions that are focused on specific substantive phenomena and that can be subjected to empirical tests." What Sanderson wants, in other words, is for even the minority of sociologists holding out in the theory section to adopt the more mainstream view of theory as a string of testable, propositional one-liners.

Sanderson gets two things absolutely right. First, Sanderson is correct that sociological theory remains in "hermetic isolation" from the empirical sociology practiced by the rest of the field. This isolation, however, is less the fault of the theorists than of American sociology's refusal to heed any kind of philosophical self-reflection. Largely because it just has not thought much about it, the sociological mainstream retains the positivist view of causality, theory, and science that Sanderson upholds. Worse, the view is retained even by those who oppose it. Thus, Sanderson is also correct that often even the sociological opponents of positivism cede causality, theory, and science to the positivists, declaring themselves against causality, theory, science, or all three. It becomes evident that the positivists have managed to confuse more than themselves. They have also generally confused many of their opponents, provoking them to various sorts of ill-conceived overreactions.

Among the most pervasive of such overreactions has been the embrace by a considerable number of sociologists of post-Wittgensteinian philosophy, especially as elaborated by Peter Winch (1958). The central idea here certainly makes sense: Human action, motivated by reasons – wants, beliefs, emotions, and so forth – hardly seems to fit the determinism – absolute or stochastic – of the covering law model of causality. The post-Wittgensteinian conclusion was that explanations by reasons is not a species of causal explanation but a distinct sort of explanation in its own right.

Following the distinction between explanation by reasons and explanation by causes, a sharp distinction is still sometimes erected between interpretative understanding and causal analysis (although outside of sociology proper, see, for example, Hollis and Smith 1990 for an important statement of this position). Reprising the Weberian distinction between the natural and human sciences, human behavior is then deemed non-causal. Instead, interpretative understanding is considered the proper provenance of sociology.

Two important consequences of this move have followed. If causality in the human sphere is rejected, then so is any firm kind of social structural analysis, not just of the Durkheimian variety but of the Marxian variety as well. If causality is inherently deterministic, then to speak of social structural causality is necessarily to speak of structural determinism. Any mention of structural causality thereby becomes equivalent to structural reductionism. Since the 1980s, accordingly, there has been a pervasive abandonment of social structural analysis in favor of exclusively cultural approaches (see Porpora 2002).

Oddly, at the same time as the post-Wittgensteinian view led to an abandonment of social structure, it likewise led to a deprived understanding of the human actor. If actors' mental states are not in some sense internal causes of actors' behavior then what are they? Mental states soon were expropriated from the actor to become the property of the enveloping culture (Blum and McHugh 1971; Coulter 1989; Harre 1986). On this view, mental states are not states of or within actors but external rules cultural observers utilize to make sense of or interpret actors' behavior. Such a view leaves actors themselves ontologically depleted of internal life and sociologists unable to explain why those actors choose to follow one cultural convention rather than another (Porpora 1997).

The post-Wittgensteinian view is an excessive reaction to the covering law model and was eventually abandoned by philosophers of mind (see Hyman and Steward 2004). By that time of course, sociology was no longer listening. Nor has American sociology been listening to any word of critical realism, which has been developing over the past quarter century. Thus, American sociology has little awareness of a post-positivist conception of causality that links not events but generative structures with forces, tendencies, powers, and capacities. It has little awareness of a concept of causal theory that consists not of a string of one-liners but of the elaboration of mechanisms or of what Harre and Madden (1975) call "powerful particulars." It knows little of the interaction of such mechanisms, structures, and particulars, which interfere with each other in historically particular ways that preclude any kind of lawlike generalizations. American sociology has little grasp of a non-Humean concept of causality that can encompass the distinctly non-random indeterminacy associated with social action.

References

Babbie, Earl 2004 *The Practice of Social Research*. (10th edn) Belmont, CA: Wadsworth.

Bhaskar, Roy 1975 *A Realist Theory of Science*. Leeds. Leeds Books.

Bhaskar, Roy 1979 *The Possibility of Naturalism: A Philosophical Critique of the Contemporary Human Sciences*. Sussex: Harvester.

Blalock, Hubert M. 1969 *Theory Construction: From Verbal to Mathematical Formulation*. Englewood Cliffs, NJ: Prentice-Hall.

Blau, Peter M. 1969 "Objectives of Sociology," pp. 43–71 in Robert Bierstedt (ed.) *A Design for Sociology: Scope, Objectives, and Method*. Philadelphia: American Academy of Political and Social Science.

Blau, Peter M. 1983 "Comments on the Prospects for a Namothetic Theory of Social Structures," *Journal for the Theory of Social Behaviour* 13: 265–272.

Blum, Alan and Peter McHugh 1971 "The Social Ascription of Motives," *American Sociological Review* 36: 98–109.

Coulter, Jeff 1989 *Mind in Action*. Atlantic Highlands, NJ: Humanities Press.

Harre, Rom 1986 (ed.) *The Social Construction of the Emotions*. Oxford: Blackwell.

Harre, Rom and E. Madden 1975 *Causal Powers*. Totowa, NJ: Rowman & Littlefield.

Hyman, John and Helen Steward 2004 *Agency and Action*. Cambridge: Cambridge University Press.

Hollis, Martin and Steven Smith 1990 *Explaining and Understanding International Relations*. Oxford: Oxford University Press.

Mayhew, Bruce. 1983 "Causality, Historical Particularism, and Other Errors in Sociological Discourse," *Journal for the Theory of Social Behaviour* 13: 285–300.

Neuman, W. Lawrence 2000 *Social Research Methods: Qualitative and Quantitative Approaches* (4th edn). Boston: Allyn and Bacon.

Porpora, Douglas V. 1983 "On the Prospects for a Nomothetic Theory of Social Structure," *Journal for the Theory of Social Behaviour* 13: 243–264.

Porpora, Douglas V. 1997 "The Caterpillar's Question: Contesting Anti-Humanism's Contestations," *Journal for the Theory of Social Behaviour* 27.

Porpora, Douglas V. 2002 "Social Structure: The Future of a Concept." pp. 43–59 in Sing C. Chew and J. David Knottnerus (eds.) *Structure, Culture, and History: Recent Issues in Social Theory*. New York: Rowman & Littlefield.

Sanderson, Stephen K. 2005 "Reforming Theoretical Work in Sociology: A Modest Proposal," Perspectives: *Newsletter of the ASA Theory Section* 28 (2): 1–4.

Stark, Rodney and Roger Finke 2000 *Acts of Faith: Explaining the Human Side of Religion*. Berkeley: University of California Press.

Turner, Jonathan H. 2003 *Human Institutions: A Theory of Societal Evolution*. Lanham, MD: Rowman & Littlefield.

Winch, Peter 1958 *The Idea of a Social Science and its Relation to Philosophy*. New York: Humanities Press.

13 The mother of all "isms"

Organizing political science around causal mechanisms

Andrew Bennett

The field of political science is currently undergoing a new variation of its perennial debates on whether and in what sense it is a "science," how it should organize its inquiry into political life, and how it should build and justify its theories. On one side of this renewed debate, many political scientists have focused their work on championing one grand "ism" or another. The subfield of international relations as it is studied in the United States, for example, is largely organized around realpolitik "neorealism," institution-centered "neoliberalism," and sociologically informed "constructivism," grand schools of thought that scholars have often modeled either implicitly or explicitly in the style of either Kuhnian paradigms or Lakatosian research programs.[1] On the other side, political scientists who focus on causal explanation via reference to causal mechanisms critique the paradigmatic "isms" as a constraint on understanding complex social and political phenomena.[2] In this view, no single grand theory can capture political life, and the real explanatory weight is carried by more finely grained and contextual causal mechanisms. Political scientists increasingly theorize about path dependencies and complex interactions among the mechanisms emphasized by each grand "ism," but we are still struggling to develop appropriate methods for making valid and cumulative inferences about such complex phenomena in settings that are in most instances observational rather than experimental. As Peter Hall has argued, the ontologies that political scientists posit in their theorizing about complexity have become disconnected from their methodologies.[3]

In this chapter I focus on the epistemological level of this debate. While critiques of the grand "isms" style of theorizing are compelling and the call for focusing on causal mechanisms fruitfully draws on contemporary developments in the philosophy of science, four fundamental issues regarding causal mechanisms demand attention if the other social sciences are to focus on explanatory theories that reference causal mechanisms. First, how should we define "causal mechanisms?" Second, in what ways are the discussions of causal mechanisms that developed with a focus on the natural sciences relevant to the social sciences? Third, does explanation via reference to causal mechanisms have implications for debates over "emergent properties," or the idea that systems may have properties that are not strictly the sum of the units that comprise them? Does explanation via causal mechanisms require a commitment to methodological individualism?

Finally, does emphasis on causal mechanisms necessarily give up the ability of the grand "isms" to provide a focus and a language for social science research communities to achieve cumulative theoretical progress and communicate their findings to scholars, students, political actors, and the public? This chapter addresses each of these issues in turn. It concludes that the field of political science and the social sciences more generally will progress more rapidly and effectively if they adopt a more self-conscious focus on causal mechanisms. The social sciences can build from individual-level mechanisms, to mechanisms on relations between and among individuals, to mechanisms between individuals and social and material structures, and finally to more complex typological theories that address combinations of causal mechanisms. Such theories can be usefully applied to "issue areas" or recurrent contexts of political activity, and to "problem-driven" research, to improve historical explanations and develop theoretical generalizations that can inform political actors as well as social scientists of the likely consequences of alternative policies.

Defining causal mechanisms[4]

Many social scientists and philosophers of science, even those who disagree with one another on important theoretical and methodological issues, have placed increasing emphasis on explaining phenomena via reference to causal mechanisms.[5] Fundamental disagreements remain about how to define "causal mechanisms," however.[6] A key distinction among the many definitions that have been offered concerns whether causal mechanisms are to be defined as ontological entities, whose reality is separate from the minds of observers, or as theoretical entities bound up in the thinking of theorists. This distinction is particularly important for the social sciences, where the reflexivity of social subjects and of theorists are central concerns. Some have defined causal mechanisms as being essentially indistinguishable from theories; Peter Hedstrom and Richard Swedburg, for example, define causal mechanisms as "analytical constructs that provide hypothetical links between observable events" (my emphasis).[7]

The problem with such definitions is that they do not add anything to earlier discussions by Karl Hempel and others of explanation via reference to laws or theories, and they are subject to all the well-known limitations of these approaches. Hempel, for example, sought to explain "theories" by reference to "laws," but he never fulfilled his promise, delivered in a famous footnote in a paper with Paul Oppenheim, to develop an explanation of laws themselves.[8]

I prefer instead a scientific realist definition that places causal mechanisms on the ontological level. In this view, theories are hypotheses that invoke or attempt to refer to ontological mechanisms that are themselves in some ultimate sense unobservable. Theories, in other words, are hypothesized models of how underlying mechanisms work, and explanations apply theories in particular contexts to indicate why the observed outcome was to be expected under the circumstances. Roy Bhaskar, for example, states that "the construction of an explanation for ... some identified phenomenon will involve the building of a model ... which *if* it were to exist and act in the postulated way would account for the phenomenon in question."[9] Similarly, James Mahoney has defined a causal mechanism as "an unobservable entity that – when activated – generates an outcome of interest."[10] Wesley Salmon also defines causal mechanisms on the ontological level, stating that "an intersection of two processes is a *causal interaction* if both processes are modified in the intersection in ways that persist beyond the point of intersection ... causal processes are capable of transmitting energy, information, and causal influence from one part of spacetime to another."[11]

Building on these definitions, I define causal mechanisms as ultimately unobservable physical, social, or psychological processes through which agents with causal capacities operate in specific contexts to transfer energy, information, or matter to other entities. In so doing, the causal agent changes the affected entity's characteristics, capacities, or propensities in ways that persist unless and until subsequent causal mechanisms act upon it. If we were able to measure changes in the entity being acted upon after the intervention of the causal mechanism and in temporal or spatial isolation from other mechanisms – that is to say, if we could conduct a perfect experiment – then we could say the causal mechanism generated the observed change in this entity.

This definition addresses the question of how explanation via reference to causal mechanisms is different from explanation via Hempel's Deductive-Nomological (D-N) model. In the D-N model, an outcome is explained if it is shown that it should have been expected under the circumstances. This model invokes only one aspect of causality, the outcomes or effects of causal processes, and it builds on only two of the sources of causal inference that Hume discussed, those of constant conjunction and congruity in magnitude between purported causes and observed effects. D-N explanations are satisfied by statements of regularity, and they black-box the mechanisms and processes that generate outcomes.

Milton Friedman, for example, famously argued that:

> ... truly important and significant hypotheses will be found to have 'assumptions' that are wildly inaccurate representations of reality ... the relevant question to ask about the 'assumptions' of a theory is not whether they are descriptively 'realistic,' for they never are, but whether they are sufficiently good approximations for the purpose in hand. And this question can be answered only by seeing whether the theory works, which means whether it yields sufficiently accurate predictions.[12]

Friedman maintains that all theories simplify reality by making *as if* assumptions, that is, assumptions that the entities under study behave as if the theory were true, even if the theory is not literally true as stated. A theory built on the assumption that actors make choices based on complex calculations involving backwards induction, for example, need not this view show that actors actually go through such calculations. Rather, it must only demonstrate that they behave as if they make such calculations.

While it is true that all theories are simplifications of reality, Friedman's approach and the related logic of the D-N model fail to distinguish between a predictive relationship and a causal explanation. In an often-used counter-example to the D-N model, a barometer gives readings that are highly correlated with the weather, but it does not give a causal explanation of the weather. An explanation of the weather would invoke air pressure, temperature, topography, and other factors and discuss how they contribute to the formation of weather patterns as well as influencing the readings on a barometer. Yet the D-N model and Friedman would admit the movement of the barometer itself as an explanation of the weather.

How is stating that outcomes are generated by causal mechanisms and are explicable and perhaps predictable in terms of these mechanisms different from stating that laws or theories made a certain outcome predictable in a given context? After all, covering laws can be re-stated in narrower and more contingent terms to look very much like hypotheses about causal mechanisms. Where the two approaches differ is in their willingness to posit "as if" assumptions. In contrast to Friedman's view, researchers seeking to explain phenomena via causal mechanisms must frankly acknowledge that their theories are cast into doubt if it can be shown that the mechanisms their theories posit are not consistent with the observed processes at the next level of analysis down. As Renate Mayntz notes:[13]

> The main difference between a mechanism approach and a covering-law approach is not that mechanism statements are less general than the propositions in a nomological-deductive explanation but that in the analytical theory of science (e.g. Nagel 1961, Hempel 1965), 'laws' are basically general statements about covariation; that is, 'laws' point out causal *factors* and not processes.

Explanation via causal mechanisms draws not just on the sources of inference that Hume emphasized most, regularity of association and congruity of magnitude as sources of causal inference, but also on two additional sources of inference that Hume discussed in less detail, spatial contiguity and temporal succession. Causal mechanisms work through spatial and temporal causal processes. Hume ultimately gave limited attention to these aspects of causation, but for more contemporary philosophers, such as Wesley Salmon, causal mechanisms provide the causal link that Hume sought but despaired of attaining.[14] In particular, *explanation via causal mechanisms involves a commitment in principle to making our explanations and models consistent with the most continuous spatial–temporal sequences we can describe at the finest level of detail that we can observe*. In this regard, the barometer cannot be characterized as having "explained" the weather, as we are confident from our observations at more micro levels that there are processes involving air pressure, temperature, and so on which, through their continual interaction, account for both the barometer readings and the weather. More generally, in this view an adequate explanation is not provided merely by correlations, but requires also the specification of or hypotheses about a causal process that brought about the observed correlation.

Mechanism-based explanations are committed to realism and to continuousness and contiguity in causal processes.[15] In principle, mechanism-based explanations of social phenomena entail commitments even to microfoundational mechanisms beneath the level of individual behavior, that is, looking beyond individuals to the chemical, electrical, and biological interactions within their brains and bodies that generate their behavior, and making sure that our theories of individual behavior are consistent with what we understand of these micromechanisms. D-N explanations, in contrast, admit "as if" assumptions that are demonstrably untrue at lower levels of analysis.

Causal mechanisms provide more detailed and in a sense more fundamental explanations than general laws do. The difference between a law and a mechanism is that between a static correlation ("if x, then y") and a "process" ("x leads to y through steps a, b, c"). As Jon Elster notes:

> Generally speaking, the scientific practice is to seek explanation at a lower level than the explanandum. If we want to understand the pathology of the liver, we look to cellular biology for explanation. ... To explain is to provide a causal mechanism, to open up the black box and show the nuts and bolts. ... The role of mechanisms is two-fold. First, they enable us to go from the larger to the smaller: from molecules to atoms, from societies to individuals. Secondly, and more fundamentally, they reduce the time lag between the explanans and explanandum. A mechanism provides a continuous and contiguous chain of causal or intentional links; a black box is a gap in the chain. ... The success of the reduction is constrained by the extent to which macro-variables are simultaneously replaced by micro-variables. ... The search for micro-foundations ... is in reality a pervasive and omnipresent feature of science.[16]

Does reflexivity make causal mechanisms irrelevant to the social sciences?

One potential objection to the definition of causal mechanisms offered above is that it draws too heavily on concepts developed primarily with a focus on the natural sciences, and that its physicalist nature is therefore less relevant to the social sciences. In this view, philosophies of science developed for the natural sciences, including many discussions of causal mechanisms, are not necessarily appropriate for the social sciences because in the social sciences both scientists themselves and the human subjects they study are reflexive. In other words, individuals interpret the social and physical world around them and attempt to change this world to achieve long-term intentions rather than merely to satisfy immediate wants.

This provides the basis for post-modern and hermeneutic critiques of the social sciences. Post-modernists argue that language, a key medium of both science and society, is open to multiple interpretations, and that definitive explanatory theories, especially those about social life, are unattainable. Hermeneuticists argue that scientists are themselves socialized into certain theories and conceptions of science and society that they cannot entirely transcend, and that the social sciences face an additional hermeneutic loop since the theories social scientists devise can change the thinking and behavior of the individuals or groups that they study. Additionally, social, political, and economic structures change over time independent of the activities of social scientist, so "social kinds" or "social facts," and the mechanisms that underly them, are not immutable subjects of study in the same sense as the physical entities that are the focus of some of the natural sciences.

These considerations do indeed distinguish the social sciences from the natural sciences. Social science theories are necessarily more contingent and time-bound than natural science theories. This does not mean that the social and the natural sciences do not share some common features, however. Some of the natural sciences, such as evolutionary biology, study changing subjects, and even the natural sciences are subject to some elements of reflexivity, as natural scientists' ideas are shaped by society and their theories are human interpretations. As Philip Kitcher has argued, science is "a process in which cognitively limited biological entities combine their efforts in a social contest," and he argues for "placing the knowing subject firmly back into the discussion of epistemological problems." This is applicable to both the social and the natural sciences. At the same time, Kitcher agrees that scientists probe a world that exists independently of human cognition.[17] This, too, is applicable to the social as well as the natural sciences. Observations may be theory-laden, but they are not theory-determined. Social realities, such as the beliefs and preferences of other actors, lead to social surprises for the observer if they are improperly understood, just as misunderstandings of causal mechanisms in the natural world lead to unexpected observations.

There is also an evident tension among post-modern critiques of the social sciences. Some post-modern social theorists decry inequalities of social, political, and economic power that they see as pervasive and strongly self-reproducing. Others emphasize the ever-changing and open-ended nature of language and the many different interpretations that can be given for any particular text or symbol. But society cannot at the same time be both strongly self-reproducing and continually undergoing wholesale change or being open to infinite interpretations. Sometimes the rich do get richer, and sometimes, to borrow from President Clinton's famous circumlocution on the Lewinsky scandal, "is" means "is." It is in fact clear that social structures, including language, capitalism, the state, and many others are sufficiently self-reproducing to remain recognizable for long periods of time. These social structures are thus stable enough for social scientists to theorize about them in ways that are cumulative, albeit not timeless, and that are useful for social actors.

Moreover, the mechanisms behind reflexivity and human agency themselves are suitable subjects for study by scientists at the intersection of the natural and the social sciences, including psychologists, neurologists, and other clinical and laboratory researchers. Social scientists need to keep apprised of developments in the understanding of individual behavior, as findings on the mechanisms behind individual decision-making can substantiate or call into question the microfoundational assumptions of social theories. The 2002 Nobel prize in economics, for example, was awarded to Daniel Kahneman for his work in identifying common psychological heuristics and biases in individual decision-making that depart from the assumptions of rational decision-making models, and many economists are now engaged in building new theories based on these non-rational mechanisms of decision and choice.

Mechanisms, social structure, and "emergent phenomena"

A second possible objection to my definition of causal mechanisms is that it is too microfoundational. Must all mechanism-based explanations necessarily delve into the most micro level of processes that is observable? Does an approach to explanation based on causal mechanisms necessarily reject claims that emergent phenomena exist? These are perhaps the most sharply contested issues raised by discussions of social mechanisms.

Several of the contributors to a June 2004 symposium on causal mechanisms in the journal *Philosophy of Social Science,* for example, argue that mechanism-based explanations do not rule out emergent properties and macro-level mechanisms. Mario Bunge develops an approach to causal mechanisms that he argues, rather ambiguously, is an alternative to both individualism and holism but in his view "invites us to analyze wholes into their constituents." [18] Colin Wight argues more forcefully that social structures "possess powers and liabilities that neither reside at lower levels nor are explainable in terms of the lower level."[19] Renate Mayntz argues that as a pragmatic matter it is often impossible to go down to the individual level to explain macro-level phenomena, and she adds that "it would be a fateful misunderstanding to believe that macro-phenomena follow *directly* from motivated individual behavior."[20]

The main thrust of my argument, in contrast, is microfoundational, as I maintain that in principle social explanations must be consistent with the finest level of detail that we can observe. Yet I concur with Mayntz that this does not mean that in practice this level of detail is always or even usually the most fruitful level of analysis for social theorizing. My definition still allows for the possibility that theorizing and explanation can at times most usefully take place at the macro level. Macro-social mechanisms can be tested at the macro level, as is common in the field of economics. It is not necessary or possible in every research project to explain or study macro-level processes at the individual level, and the acceptable level of generality of hypotheses on causal mechanisms will vary depending on the particular research question and research objectives under investigation. If all units that comprise a system behave in predictable ways within the context of that system, and in predictable but different ways in another systemic context, then the interesting variation may be that in the systemic context, not the units.

There is an important caveat here, however, one that might lead me to disagree with Mayntz, depending on how we interpret how *directly* individual behavior must contribute to macro effects.[21] The caveat is that macro-causal social mechanisms in my view have to be based in principle on hypotheses that model the micro-level processes that explain individual behavior, and these hypotheses must be consistent with evidence at this level of behavior. Some simplification of the micro-foundations of macro theories is tolerable for the purposes of parsimony or pedagogy, but at the frontiers of research social scientists need to relax stylized assumptions and build upon the most accurate micro-level mechanisms that can be discerned. Theories positing "emergent phenomena," in other words, should at least not be inconsistent with the observable micro-level processes that are hypothesized to contribute to them, and at best they should be consistent with all the relevant micro-level processes that we can observe.

David Dessler gives a good example of this process from physics:

> ... in the ideal gas model, the gas is said to behave *as if* the molecules occupy no volume and have no interactions. These are idealizations. They are useful because they lay bare the essential workings of a gas ... the idealizations also restrict the model's range of applicability ... the theory's explanatory power increases as its false assumptions are 'relaxed' – that is, as the assumptions distorting, idealizing, or simplifying effects are removed. At each step in the process, *it is the assumptions that are true that carry the explanatory burden.* To the extent the theory remains false, its range and power are restricted.[22]

Thus, while our theories rely on simplifying assumptions that are helpful for the purposes of communicating or teaching them to others, at the frontiers of our knowledge we work to make our assumptions as accurate as possible.

The commitment to consistency with microfoundations raises the "infinite regress" question: does a causal mechanism involve the irreducibly smallest link between one entity and another, and at what point does inquiry into causal mechanisms stop? It is useful on this question to think of the frontiers of research as involving a potentially movable border between the observable world and the unobservable ontological level on which causal mechanisms reside. This is most evident in the natural sciences: at one point, our instruments of observation did not allow examination of "molecules" or their observable implications, so it would not at that time have been unreasonable to question the existence of "molecules." Later, as new instruments enabled the observation of molecules and their implications, it became unreasonable to disbelieve the broad outlines of the "molecule" model but it remained reasonable to question the nature of atoms. As new instruments made possible observations of the implications of different models of atomic particles, one could still question the nature of sub-atomic particles. Now that models of some sub-atomic particles are fairly well established because of observations from linear accelerators, debate has shifted to whether it is reasonable to believe in the esoteric mathematics of string theory, which posits the existence of additional dimensions for which there are as yet no readily observable implications. This progression is less obvious in the social sciences, but we do continue to develop instruments of observation, from public opinion surveys and focus groups to brain-scanning technologies, that render more elements of social mechanisms observable. At some point, social scientists "hand off" inquiry to neurologists or psychologists who are more adept at probing the biochemical and psychological processes that generate individual behavior, but this is a hand-off between sciences, not between fundamentally different approaches to "science."

Explanations that are at one point and for some purposes satisfactory later come to be considered insufficiently precise as new evidence becomes available at lower levels of analysis. For example, correlational evidence alone was for a long time sufficient for many intents and purposes to support the argument that smoking "causes" cancer, but it is only recently that a better understanding has emerged of the micro-level biological processes that account for this relationship. This may lead to better understanding of and prediction of what kind and level of smoking, among what kind of individuals, leads to what kind of cancers.

No matter how far down we push the border between the observable and unobservable worlds, some irreducibly unobservable aspect of causal mechanisms remains. At the frontier of our knowledge at any given point of time, our theoretical commitment to "molecules" or "Duverger's Law" (which relates the number of political parties to whether electoral systems are winner-take-all or proportional representation) resembles an "as if" assumption about the underlying mechanisms at the next level down. In this sense, the causal mechanism view, like the D-N model, ultimately does not offer an explanation of laws themselves at the frontiers of our knowledge. At every point up to the border of the unobservable, however, hypotheses or laws are explained via reference to observations on underlying processes at a more micro level of analysis. The commitment to explanation via mechanisms differs in this respect from more general "as if" assumptions in that it pushes inquiry to the outer boundaries of what is observable and urges us to keep trying to expand those boundaries, rather than stopping with "as if" assumptions at higher levels of analysis that are demonstrably false.

Cumulating and communicating complex combinations of mechanisms: typological theorizing

The above definition of causal mechanisms recognizes that these mechanisms operate within specific contexts or causal fields, and their effects depend on interactions with the other mechanisms that constitute these contexts. Indeed, as David Dessler has argued, rather than focusing our efforts solely on nomological generalization, the social sciences rightly focus as well on the theoretically informed historical explanation of individual cases. Dessler notes that there are two approaches to the explanation of events: a generalizing strategy, to show the event as an instance of a certain *type* of event, and particularization, detailing the sequence of happenings leading up to an event, without necessarily placing it into a larger class. The particularizing or historical explanation relies on laws to explain each step toward an historical outcome, but laws are used only in piecemeal fashion on each "segment of the pathway leading up to the event." Dessler notes that much explanatory progress in the social sciences but also in such natural and medical sciences as paleontology, evolutionary biology, epidemiology, and pathology, consists of improving historical rather than theoretical explanations.

Progress in historical explanation consists of "*using* existing theories and laws and acquiring a more precise characterization of the initial conditions and the event itself." At the same time, there is a feedback loop from improved historical explanations to improved theories. We may change our theories or limit their scope if, for example, we find that they do not explain a "most-likely" case that they should be able to easily explain.

In this regard, causal mechanisms are consonant with what Paul Humphreys has termed his "aleatory theory" of explanation. Effects are brought about by bundles or configurations of mechanisms, some of which contribute to the effect and some of which push toward counteracting the effect or reducing its magnitude. Aleatory explanations take the form of "Y occurred because of A, despite B," where A is a set of contributing causes and B is a (potentially empty) set of counteracting causes (the set A cannot be empty or we would not have an explanation for the occurrence of Y). Salmon gives an example, modified from Humphreys, in which we might say that a car went off a road at a curve because of excessive speed and the presence of sand on the road and despite clear visibility and an alert driver. He notes that the addition of another mechanism or contextual factor can change a contributing cause to a counteracting one or viceversa: sand on a dry road decreases traction, but sand increases traction when there is ice on a road.[23]

Similarly, Jon Elster discusses a number of psychological theories which posit mechanisms that are in tension with one another – e.g. the "sour grapes syndrome" in which one's desires are adjusted in accordance with the means of achieving them, and "the opposite mechanism" when one wants what one cannot have, precisely because one cannot have it.[24] Elster recognizes the challenge presented by the existence of many such "contradictory" mechanisms and suggests that this raises the need for identifying the different conditions under which each applies:

> Moving from a plurality of mechanisms to a unified theory would mean that we should be able to identify in advance the conditions in which one or the other mechanism would be triggered. ... My own view is that the social sciences are currently unable to identify such conditions and are likely to remain so forever.[25]

Elster adds that the goal of establishing general and invariant propositions in the social sciences "is and will always remain an illusory dream. Despite a widespread belief to the contrary, the alternative to nomological thinking is not a mere description or narrative ideographic method. Between the two extremes there is a place and need for the study of mechanisms."[26]

Elster is right on the usefulness of thinking in terms of causal mechanisms and on the elusiveness of general and timeless laws of social behavior, but it may still be possible to model in contingent ways and for significant periods of time the conditions under which particular social mechanisms, or combinations thereof, are operative. It is useful here to focus not only on the causal mechanisms that generate individual behavior, but those that affect relations between individuals and those that link individuals to social and material structures. For present purposes, no more than a brief and illustrative cataloguing of such mechanism-based theories is possible. Individual-level mechanisms include not only rational choice dynamics, but also other cognitive mechanisms modeled by such theories as prospect theory, schema theory, the representative-ness and availability heuristics, and framing theories. At the second level of agent-agent mechanisms, relevant theories include those on persuasive communication, emulation, strategic interaction, collective action, and principle-agent relations. These might be categorized into groups of mechanisms where the actions of one agent make similar or aligned behavior by other agents more likely, including mechanisms of power, socialization, and persuasion, and groups of mechanisms that make opposite or offsetting behavior by other agents more likely, such as provision of public goods that leads to free-riding by others. Theories on mechanisms leading from individual agents to changes in social or material structures include those on agenda-setting, issue entrepreneurs, and revolutionaries. Theories on mechanisms leading from structural constraints or opportunities to individual behavior include those on evolutionary selection and socialization.[27] From a mechanism-based perspective, although theories can model changes from one macro state to another, there are no mechanisms leading directly from one social structure to another, as all relations between macro structures must work through individual behaviors and mechanisms, even if these individual behaviors are invariant with respect to the structures in question.

With theories on each of these types of mechanisms as building blocks, scholars can develop "typological theories" on how mechanisms interact with one another in recurrent combinations. This addresses Elster's challenge of outlining in a structured and cumulative way the conditions under which different mechanisms prevail, and it constitutes a middle ground between Dessler's two poles of nomological generalization and historical explanation. Similarly, typological theories are consonant with Robert Merton's emphasis on the need to develop "middle-range" theories that are situated between the micro level of individual causal mechanisms and the highly abstract level of macro theories.[28]

Typological theories model complex interactions of causal mechanisms by including recurrent combinations of hypothesized mechanisms as distinct types or configurations.[29] Typological theorizing can provide an avenue for transcending traditional arguments among the "isms" by including mechanisms from various approaches and focusing upon the conditions under which they interact in characteristic ways. Instead of asking whether institutional, cultural, or agent-based variables matter "more," we can ask how different kinds of institutions (hierarchical, decentralized, etc.) interact with different cultural contexts (such as strong or weak civil societies) and various kinds of agents (status quo seekers versus revisionists or revolutionaries). Typological theorizing can also cumulate by focusing on certain issue areas, where the actors and their interests, beliefs, and resources are fairly constant or strongly self-reproducing.

To take an example, the causal mechanisms of collective action theory, which posits that individuals or units will attempt to "free ride" on the efforts of the most powerful and capable actors to attain public goods, play out across many issue areas, including environmental cleanups, burden-sharing in alliances, mobilization of rebellious groups, preservation of fishing stocks, and so on. Within each of these issue areas, the mechanisms of collective action theory may operate in characteristic ways that relate to the issue area context itself, such as the prior allocation of property rights, the relative transparency of actors' behavior, and historical sets of expectations that actors have of one another. At the same time, collective action dynamics work in different ways within each issue area depending on contextual factors that vary within issue areas (the number of relevant actors, the distribution of power among them, and so on). Hypotheses on how collective action mechanisms work provide a generalizable form of knowledge that helps unravel variance within issue areas, while the fairly stable contextual variables that are evident in particular issue areas provide a relatively bounded domain for issue-specific generalizations of how collective action dynamics work. Mark Lichbach, for example, has analyzed how collective action dynamics play a role in social mobilization efforts among rebellious groups and government efforts to suppress rebellions. Elsewhere, I have written with colleagues about how collective action dynamics and other mechanisms come together in theories about burden-sharing in ad hoc international security coalitions.[30]

Conclusions

Paradoxically, the best way to organize the study of politics is around the seemingly least organized path of all: building from the ground up from causal mechanisms. It is thus important to maintain a broad view on what forms scientific progress takes. Paradigms or "isms" are not the only way, nor necessarily the best way, for judging theoretical progress. Problem- or puzzle-driven research and the historical explanation of individual cases deserve increased attention in assessing progress.

Although new insights about underlying mechanisms ideally take the form of simple and widely generalizable models, as is sometimes the case in the natural sciences, often in the social sciences improved models built on more detailed observations take the form of more complex and contingent generalizations that describe a smaller subset of a phenomenon with a higher degree of precision or probability. In particular, historical explanation of individual cases helps to direct our attention away from grand "isms" and toward causal explanation, as it naturally encourages the use of variables from different schools of thought and levels of analysis. Even political scientists whose careers are largely identified with developing and defending one grand theory readily borrow from other schools of thought when they attempt to explain particular historical cases.

The challenge is to allow for complexity and eclecticism at the level of causal explanation of cases and populations while still maintaining a sufficiently simple set of common concepts and terms for teaching our students and communicating within and across subfields. Such a discourse can indeed be achieved even while moving away from research organized around grand paradigmatic "isms" to more localized and contextual causal mechanisms. Fortunately, we already have well-developed theories on causal mechanisms. Collective action theory, rational choice theory, socialization theory, cognitive theory, evolutionary selection theory, and many other theories addressing individual and social behavior already provide a context for research and communication not just within political science, but across the social sciences. To a large degree, organizing the social sciences around causal mechanisms does not require creating vast new theories; rather, it demands only that we recognize the extent to which existing theories on causal mechanisms are already doing the real explanatory work behind all other isms.

Notes

1 These examples are drawn from the subfield of international relations, where the emphasis on grand "isms" has been greatest. On neorealism, see Kenneth Waltz, *Theory of International Politics* (McGraw-Hill, 1979); on neoliberalism, see Robert Keohane, *After Hegemony: Cooperation and Discord in the World Economy* (Princeton University Press, 1984); on constructivism, see Ted Hopf, "The Promise of Constructivism in International Relations Theory," *International Security*, Vol. 23, No. 1 (Summer, 1998), pp. 171–200; Hopf and Waltz both cite Lakatos in these works.
2 See, for example, Peter Katzenstein and Nobuo Okawara, "Japan and Asian-Pacific Security: Analytical Eclecticism, not Parsimony," with Nobuo Okawara, *International Security* 26, 2 (Winter 2001/02): 153–185.
3 Peter Hall, "Aligning Ontology and Methodology in Comparative Poltics," in James Mahoney and Dietrich Rueschemeyer, eds., *Comparative Historical Analysis in the Social Sciences* (Cambridge University Press, 2003).
4 This section and those that follow draw upon Alexander L. George and Andrew Bennett, *Case Studies and Theory Development in the Social Sciences* (MIT Press, 2005), chapter 7.
5 Often these scholars have associated their interest in causal mechanisms with the "scientific realist" school of thought in the philosophy of science. See David Dessler, "Beyond Correlations: Toward a Causal Theory of War," *International Studies Quarterly,* Vol. 35, 1991, pp. 337–355; Jon Elster *Nuts and Bolts for the Social Sciences* (Cambridge University Press, 1989); Daniel Little, *Microfoundations, Method, and Causation: On the Philosophy of the Social Sciences* (New Jersey, Transactions Press, 1998); and Peter Hedstrom and Richard Swedburg, eds., *Social Mechanisms: An Analytical Approach to Social Theory* (Cambridge University Press, 1998).
6 For a listing and analysis of two dozen definitions of causal mechanisms, see James Mahoney, "Beyond Correlational Analysis: Recent Innovations in Theory Method" Sociological Forum; Sept.2001 Vol .16, Issue 3, pp. 575–594.
7 Hedstrom and Swedburg, *Social Mechanisms*, p. 13.
8 On this point, see Wesley Salmon, "Scientific Explanation: Causation and Unification," in Salmon, *Causality and Explanation* (New York, Oxford University Press, 1998), p. 69.
9 Roy Bhaskar, *The Possibility of Naturalism: A Philosophical Critique of the Contemporary Human Sciences* (Atlantic Highlands, N.J: Humanities Press, 1979), p. 15.
10 Mahoney, "Beyond Correlational Analysis." For other scientific realist views on causal mechanisms, see Roy Bhaskar, *The Possibility of Naturalism: A Philosophical Critique*

218   *Andrew Bennett*

of the Contemporary Human Sciences (Atlantic Highlands, "NJ: Humanities Press, 1979), and Rom Harre, *The Principles of Scientific Thinking* (Chicago: University of Chicago Press, 1970).

11 Salmon, "Scientific Explanation," p. 71.

12 Milton Friedman, "The Methodology of Positive Economics," in Daniel Hausman, ed., *The Philosophy of Economics* (Cambridge University Press, 1984) p. 218.

13 Renate Mayntz, "Mechanisms in the Analysis of Social-Macro Phenomena," *Philosophy of the Social Sciences* Vol. 34, No. 2 (June, 2004) pp. 240–241, her emphasis.

14 Salmon, "Scientific Explanation," p. 71.

15 As Martin Hollis notes, Friedman's version of the "as if" assumption "lets Positive science dabble in unobservables, provided they are not thought more than useful fictions ... I call this dabbling because there is no concession to the idea of unobservables existing in nature, as opposed to the model." Martin Hollis, *The Philosophy of Social Science: An Introduction* (Cambridge University Press, 1994) p. 56.

16 Jon Elster, *Explaining Technical Change: A Case Study in the Philosophy of Science* (Cambridge: Cambridge University Press, 1983), pp. 23–24.

17 Philip Kitcher, *The Advancement of Science: Science without Legend, Objectivity without Illusions* (New York: Oxford University Press, 1993), pp. 9, 127.

18 Mario Bunge, "How Does it Work? The Search for Explanatory Mechanisms," *Philosophy of the Social Sciences* Vol. 34, No. 2 (June, 2004) p. 191.

19 Colin Wight, "Theorizing the Mechanisms of Conceptual and Semiotic Space," *Philosophy of the Social Sciences* Vol. 34, No. 2 (June, 2004) p. 283.

20 2004, 248–249, her emphasis.

21 I agree with Mayntz's apparent implication that unintended and unconscious as well as motivated behavior by individuals can have macro effects. It is also possible that my disagreement with Mayntz and others on these issues is partly semantic, as they focus on "relational" mechanisms between and among individuals as a kind of emergent mechanism, whereas I would model many relational mechanisms, such as those in the literature on social psychology, as working through individuals' perceptions of the social environment.

22 David Dessler, "Explanation and Scientific Progress," in Colin Elman and Miriam Fendius Elman, eds., *Progress in International Relations Theory: Appraising the Field* (MIT Press, 2003), pp. 398–399.

23 Wesley Salmon, *Four Decades of Scientific Explanation* (University of Minnesota Press, 1990), pp. 166–167, citing Paul Humphreys, "Aleatory Explanations," *Synthese 48*: 225–232, 1981, and "Aleatory Explanations Expanded." In P. D. Asquith and T. Nickles, (eds.) (1983), *PSA 1982*, Vol. 2. Philosophy of Science Association, East Lansing, Michigan.

24 Jon Elster, *Political Psychology* (Cambridge: Cambridge University Press, 1993), p. 2.

25 *Ibid.*, p. 5. Elster also notes that while his examples of mechanisms are essentially psychological, the construction of sociological causal mechanisms is also possible (pp. 6–7).

26 Jon Elster, *Political Psychology* (Cambridge: Cambridge University Press, 1993), p. 2.

27 Similarly, Hedstrom and Swedburg discuss situational (macro-micro), individual/agency (micro-micro) and transformational (micro-macro) mechanisms (1996: 296–298) and McAdam, Tarrow, and Tilly distinguish environmental, cognitive, and relational mechanisms (2001).

28 Robert Merton, *Social Theory and Social Structure*, Revised Edition (New York: Free Press of Glencoe, 1957), pp. 36, 41, 45–46, 51–53, 68–69.

29 This is similar to the notion of theories as "repertoires of causal mechanisms" (cf. David Dessler, "Beyond Correlations: Toward a Causal Theory of War," *International Studies Quarterly*, Vol. 35, 1991. p. 343. Dessler cites R. W. Miller, *Fact and Method: Explanation, Confirmation and Reality in the Natural and Social Sciences* (Princeton: Princeton University Press, 1987), p. 139. For more on typological theorizing, see Alexander L. George and Andrew Bennett, *Case Studies and Theory Development.*
30 Mark Irving Lichbach, *The Rebel's Dilemma* (University of Michigan Press, 1998); Andrew Bennett, Joseph Lepgold, and Danny Unger, eds., *Friends in Need: Alliance Burden-Sharing in the Persian Gulf War* (New York, St. Martin's, 1997).

14 Marxian crisis theory and causality[1]

Robert Albritton

The newborn's mind gropes for primordial understanding of the causal links between reaching out and human touch, crying and a mother's soothing voice, sucking and the relief from hunger. Causal inquiry drives children's endless why questions as they try to make sense of life. While scientists try to limit themselves to the how of phenomena, an ultimate why lies behind all their observations and experiments. The concept of causality grounds physicists' study of subatomic events and astronomers' probing of the cosmos.... Psychiatrists struggle to discover why their patients become ill, just as historians investigate why wars break out and why civilizations rise and fall.... Causality is thus a centerpiece of the inquiring human mind....[2]

I believe that there are several important contributions made by Bhaskar's work to thinking about causality in the social sciences. First is the renewed emphasis that it places on ontology. As he puts it in *Reclaiming Reality*, 'it is the nature of objects that determines their cognitive possibilities'.[3] It follows that different objects of knowledge may have distinctive cognitive possibilities because of how they differ ontologically. Second, and closely related to the first, is the emphasis on distinct levels or strata of theory in relation to the ontological distinctiveness of what is being studied. Thus it is possible that a causal power at one level of theory may be diverted, blocked, or transformed at another level. According to Bhaskar, then, the aim of social science is to 'designate tendencies (like rates of profit to be equalized) which may never be manifested, but which are nevertheless essential to understanding (and the changing) of the different forms of social life, just because they are really productive of them'.[4]

What I want to argue in this chapter is that neither Bhaskar nor any of his followers has adequately thought through the unique ontology of capital and therefore its 'cognitive possibilities' including some rather distinctive forms of causality. And, it seems to me that a principal reason for this is a tendency to focus too much on the vertical relations between the theory of deep structures and history and not enough on the horizontal relations amongst categories at the most abstract level of analysis. For example, instead of carefully studying what is implied by theorizing the most fundamental economic categories as different forms of value with necessary inner connections or what is implied in theorizing capital as 'self-valorizing value', critical realists tend to map Marxian political economy on to Bhaskar's distinction between the real, the actual, and the empirical, or they do not get much beyond general claims about causes as tendencies.[5] In short, I have seen very little creative work that in rethinking capital would expand the horizons of critical realism. As a result, not enough attention is given to Marx's use of 'inner' as in 'inner logic', 'inner structure' or 'necessary inner connections'; and hence, the precise sense in which the 'inner' is inner and how, because of this, it might relate to the 'outer'. In what follows I shall attempt to stretch and even alter the categories of critical realism by presenting an account of crisis theory in Marxian political economy based on a brief account of capital's unique ontology, three levels of analysis, and three types of causality: dialectical causality, structural causality overdetermined by dialectical and historical causality, and historical causality overdetermined by dialectical and structural causality.

Since I (1999) have written a great deal about capital's unique ontology elsewhere, what I present here will be highly condensed. In my view Marx's *Capital* is primarily a theory about economic power relations that has 'disappeared' into quantitative categories by the complete hegemony of the commodity form. Marx theorizes the power relations that stem from capitalist property relations, and he shows how these relations can be maintained by capital acting through the commodity form to maximize profits. And it is Marx's theory of the commodity form that by thinking of the basic economic categories of capitalism in terms of commodification places him head and shoulders above all other economists.

It is only when commodification is complete that the economic categories can be thought at the same time both dialectically (i.e. as a set of necessary inner connections) and quantitatively. And while the capitalist commodity form both expands and deepens itself in capitalist history (especially after the advent of the factory), thus giving an historical basis for theorizing its completion, this completion is never attained in any historical society much less globally. This means that by letting the commodity form objectify us in thought, we can achieve an objective theory to guide our thinking about actual history which is only ever partially commodified. But if actual economic relations are only partially commodified and if this partial commodification is typically supported or resisted by qualitatively distinct human practices that cannot be reduced to numbers, then purely quantitative economic theory only has a very limited role to play. And that limited role is to present the ways in which all the central economic variables of completely commodified society necessarily vary in relation to each other. What is crucial here is that purely mathematical economics can only think horizontally and even this only in the context of complete commodification. It cannot successfully think vertically all the way down from complete commodification to historical capitalism, because at more concrete levels of analysis non-capitalist qualitative economic structures, non-economic (e.g. political and ideological) qualitative structures, and human agency must be taken into account.

According to Bhaskar, Marx's *Capital* as a 'setting out, as it were, a pure schema for the understanding of economic phenomena under capitalism, specifying the categories that must be employed in any concrete investigation'.[6] In contrast, I would argue that Marx's *Capital* does not 'set out' (this is too voluntaristic) at all, but rather thinks through a situation in which the commodity-form is allowed to complete itself. What is thought through is not simply a 'pure schema', but is a set of necessary inner connections amongst the basic economic categories of capital. What is understood is not 'economic phenomena under capitalism', but economic phenomena in a context of complete commodification or the economic phenomena of capital's deep structures. And finally, the categories may be utilized to inform our analysis of concrete investigations without being utilized directly. For example, in a society where the commodity-form rules completely, capitalist money must be a particular commodity that has been set aside and transformed into a universal equivalent or universal value reflector in relation to all other commodities. And while reflecting on this may be useful in considering the nature of capitalist money in the abstract and in general, the gold standard only acts as a kind of background norm of which the monetary authorities may have little or no cognisance in the current world economy. Both political manipulation and speculation play their roles in influencing the current international monetary regime.

Next to his incomparable and even astounding theory of the commodity-form, it is his theory of surplus value that also places Marx head and shoulders above all other economists when it comes to understanding capitalism. Prices exist wherever there is money so that a theory of price determination may not tell us anything about the specificity of capitalism.[7] What is central to capital is profit as its single driving force; and hence, any theory that aims to understand capital must centrally theorize the source of profit.[8] And I am not aware of any other theory that does this nearly so well as Marx's theory of surplus value. His theory that the profits of individual units of capital should be conceived as a redistribution of total surplus value extracted from the total working class by total capital is brilliant and unparalleled. Finally, any theory of capitalist profit worth considering must utilize a labour theory of value since what we want to know ultimately is how economic numbers, particularly profits, relate to the expenditure of one's life *time*, a large part of which for most people is *labour* time. And it is this that connects economic theory with ethics, a connection that should be made whenever possible because of the deep relations between how economic life is organized and the possibilities for human flourishing.[9]

It may be the aim of experimentation in the natural sciences to control all causal mechanisms but one in order to assess its causal powers. The dialectical theory of capital's inner logic is also a kind of experiment, but much different from the typical case of natural science.[10] In this case the necessary inner connections of all the basic generative mechanisms (economic categories) is theorized. To leave one out, say the category 'interest' would make the theory incomplete, and to leave out the category 'money' would make the theory impossible. The aim of the theory is to expose the fundamental nature of capitalist economic categories and the structural dynamic that must occur amongst them given this nature. The thought experiment is not simply an 'artificial construct' or 'model', for it is based on letting the historically apparent self-reifying force of capitalism complete itself in theory, with a little help from Marx and from us. In some ways the thought experiment in this case is superior to experimentation in the natural sciences because it enables us to think the necessary inner connections amongst *all* the generative mechanisms of capital in the abstract and in general. And this is possible because capitalism objectifies us to such an extent that it enables us to think the situation where the commodity form is in charge. While commodification is always more or less in history, the progressive development of the more or less can enable us to theorize the most: the situation of complete commodification, and thereby maximally clarify capital's inner logic.

Complete commodification implies that all production is the production of capitalistically produced commodities by simple, average, abstract labour. Second, it implies that all extra-economic force is bracketed and all exchanges are therefore voluntary exchanges that average out to be equal exchanges. Third, it implies the secure and complete commodification of all inputs and outputs of capitalist production, including that most crucial commodification of labour-power. Fourth, it implies that there are no obstacles to competition such that capital and labour are freely mobile. Fifth, it implies that capital is self-expanding value based on the exploitation of labour-power. And sixth, it implies a capitalist economy whose pretensions towards indefinite expansion are periodically brought down to earth as a result of periodic crises.

In the theory of capital's deep structural dynamics the rate of profit will fall. It is not a tendency, it is a necessity. This is because even though a rising rate of surplus value can to some extent offset a decline in the rate of profit, the advance of productivity for the mass of the means of production increases more rapidly than the mass of labour-power causing the rate of profit to fall in the long run. In actual capitalist history, there are many ways to prevent the rate of profit from falling (Marx was most concerned with the centralization of capital). Indeed if it did fall very much for very long, capitalism, having lost its motivating force, could not continue. Thus the fact that according to capital's inner logic the rate of profit will fall, suggests that capitalism is mortal, and that some day it will run out of ways of maintaining its profit rate or it may come to an end for other reasons long before any real prolonged fall in the rate of profit. It does not offer any explanation of the periodicity of crises. It is obvious that the short-term rate of profit will fall when a crisis occurs, but this may be the result of the crisis such that we need to find out what suddenly caused the rate of profit to fall.

Going back at least to the dawn of the twentieth century, Marxists have debated whether or not capitalist crises are caused primarily by a declining rate of profit, a profit squeeze, a rising organic composition of capital, underconsumption, overaccumulation or disproportionality. I believe that these debates were not theoretically very productive because their conceptions of causality were too simple. Each position strove to prove that its favoured cause was always the ultimate cause behind all or at least most crises actually occurring in capitalist history. The result was the sort of reductionism that becomes manifest when the effort is made to explain large and complex historical events by a single causal factor. I would go further and argue that even a consideration of numerous economic causes could not be adequate since such causes would always be mixed with political and ideological causes. In order to develop the sort of complex conception of causality required to move the debate forward, I shall extract from Marx's *Capital* a layered theory of capital and capitalism.[11]

Within the three volumes of Marx's *Capital*, there is a great deal of textual evidence indicating that Marx was continually struggling with the issue of levels of abstraction. Some of the terms that he uses to indicate the highest level of abstraction are: 'the laws as such'(1968, 106); 'the phenomenon in its pure shape' (1976, 203); 'immanent laws of capitalist production' (1976, 381); 'the laws of political economy in their purity (1976, 1014); 'inner necessary relationship' (1981, 138); 'the general nature of capital' (1981, 205); 'the laws ... in their pure form' (1981, 275); 'inner core' (1981, 311); 'the general analysis of capital' (1981, 342); 'basic inner structure' (1981, 379); 'society, viewed according to its economic structure' (1981, 957); 'internal organization of the capitalist mode of production' (1981, 970). And terms that he uses to refer to more concrete levels of analysis that lie outside of his theory of capital's inner logic or necessary inner connections are: 'a scientific analysis of competition is possible only if we can grasp the inner nature of capital'(1976, 433); 'We simply make an empirical reference to this point here, as, like many other things that might be brought in, it has nothing to do with the general analysis of capital, but has its place in an account of competition, which is not dealt with in this work'(1981, 342); 'An exposition of all these forms [wage forms] belongs to the special study of wage labour, and not, therefore, to this work'(1976, 683); 'These concrete forms ["the credit system and competition on the world market"] [are] therefore outside the scope of this work ... they belong to a possible continuation' (1981, 205); 'The analysis of landed property in its various historical forms lies outside the scope of the present work' (1981, 751); 'This is because the actual movement of competition lies outside our plan. ...' (1981, 970). While Marx (1981, 205, 426) occasionally refers to 'a possible continuation', suggesting that he intended to develop his theory at more concrete levels of analysis, he in fact never did this, leaving us to sort out the problems that this raises. Indeed, there has been confusion on this issue because of three quite different senses that he gives to the concept 'competition' in the three volumes of *Capital*: the competition that is a fundamental necessary condition for a purely capitalist society, the competition amongst capitals in Volume III where capital is no longer homogeneous, and the competition that refers to theories that are more concrete than the theory of capital's inner logic. In other words, there is the competition basic to the commodity-economic logic of pure capitalism, the competition that differentiates levels of abstraction within this theory, and the competition that refers to levels of abstraction outside this theory. Furthermore, since during his lifetime, he mostly witnessed a world in which competitive capitalism was spreading, and since he saw the early manifestations of monopoly as pre-figuring the end of capitalism (1981, 569), Marx would not have felt a pressing need to carry out the programme implied by the third meaning of 'competition', despite his explicit statements that he intended to.

Throughout the three volumes of *Capital*, Marx occasionally discusses actual crises in capitalist history. Marx (1976, 802) claims that the years between 1846 and 1866 in England are ideal for the study of capital accumulation because of the advent of free trade from 1846. But when he discusses the proximate causes of the depression of 1847 they turn out to be quite complex. Because the Opium War of 1843 supposedly opened the Chinese market to English cottons, in anticipation of this huge new market the cotton industry expanded rapidly. However, trade with China was undermined by the British government's failure to lower its tariffs on Chinese tea, no doubt in part because of the huge amount of British capital being poured into India to develop the tea industry there. At the same time, in anticipation of the China trade, there was also a huge expansion of railway building from manufacturing towns to ports. This industrial activity required significant credit expansion. Then in 1846 there was a devastating harvest failure in England and Ireland, requiring that gold reserves be spent to import food from abroad. All of this contributed to a paralysingly high interest rate that was exacerbated by the restrictions of the Bank Act of 1844 (1981, 533–4, 550, 618). In short, when we consider the complexity of factors that produced or exacerbated the crisis of 1847, it would seem that a mixture of natural, economic, political, and ideological causes were involved.

How does Marx mediate between his consideration of the causes of crises in pure capitalism (i.e. causes that are purely economic) and of the causes of a particular historical crisis where capitalist economic causes may be mixed with relatively autonomous non-capitalist economic causes and non-economic causes? The answer is that he never fully problematizes this set of issues nor does he attempt to deal with it in systematic theory. And yet, because his concept 'commodification' admits of more or less, it lends itself to theorizing levels of analysis.

Today it is a pressing theoretical need to develop these more concrete levels of analysis given that capitalism still exists, that it has developed extremely unevenly, and that it has become increasingly politically manipulated. Indeed, given the historical extension of capitalism far beyond what Marx imagined, I shall argue that the complexity of that history requires at least three levels of analysis (and of causality) rather than the two usually implied by Marx's distinction between inner connections and external competition.[12] The most abstract level theorizes the interrelations amongst the most basic capitalist economic categories and can be referred to as Capital's 'inner logic', 'necessary inner connections', or 'general structures' (expressions used repeatedly by Marx). A mid-range theory sets forth the dominant patterns of capital accumulation characteristic of different phases in the development of capitalism. And at the level of historical analysis, it is possible to weigh the causal factors that interact in producing historical change. At each level the problems of causality are different.

A purely capitalist society is one in which social relations have become so reified or commodified that they become structures that can interact entirely numerically through price mechanisms. Indeed, it is only at this high level of abstraction that power relations can be thought purely quantitatively such that all basic social relations can be thought in subsumption to 'self-valorizing value'.[13] For example, in order for the basic circulation form of capital (M-C-M': buying cheap and selling dear) to make sense, it must subsume the labour and production process because it is only labour-power that in a system of equal exchanges can create more value than it costs. Thus it is the productive consumption of a particular 'C' (labour-power) that is necessary in order to explain how the second M could be larger than the first.

How does dialectical reasoning work in the theory of capital's inner logic? First, it emphasizes what is most opposing between two categories, as between commodity as use-value and commodity as value. The commodity form has two sides which are at the same time mutually exclusive and mutually condition each other.[14] Value is what makes all commodities the same, differing only quantitatively as members of the community of number. It constitutes a commodity's sociality or interconnection or indeed sameness with all other commodities. Use-value represents a commodity's materiality or its qualitative difference from other commodities. In the ideal of apologists for capitalism, the motion of value ensures that use-values are distributed so as to maximally meet social needs. In sharp opposition to such apologetics, Marx demonstrates that while in capitalism the motion of value can subsume the fundamental use-values of economic life, its accomplishment of this is at a great social cost. This is because it creates an economy where social needs are systematically sacrificed if they do not fit the requirements of short-term profit considerations, where one class is systematically dominated and exploited by another, and where all are dominated by the violence of things. And all of this is mapped out theoretically by a logic that moves forward because of the contradictions between value and use-value.

Since it is commodity as form of value that is central to unfolding capital's inner logic, for the dialectic to proceed, it must generate a new category by which value can subsume use-value. For example, the dialectic proceeds to find a logical way to show that the money-form is always already-contained in the commodity-form as necessary to its development towards becoming a fully filled-in capitalist commodity-form. In short, dialectical reasoning demonstrates that for the commodity-form to evolve into self-valorizing value, it presupposes the money-form from the beginning, but we cannot thereby simply posit money, rather we must derive it logically from the commodity-form such that the money-form becomes a qualitative differentiation that takes place within the commodity-form.

A dialectic is a kind of theoretical bootstrap operation.[15] The further development of a more abstract category requires a more concrete category, such that though capitalist commodities finally presuppose the entire theory, as the most abstract category with fewest presuppositions they constitute the beginning. Thus while in order to be a commodity, a product must always exchange for money, we cannot theoretically generate the money-form without first starting with the commodity-form.[16] The dialectical movement from commodity-form to money-form is one of the most important for the entire theory because it liberates value from its enclosure in the commodity, giving it the externalized form as money – a palpable object that as universal equivalent is hyper mobile (as in liquid funds) and relatively autonomous from the commodity.[17] Indeed, in order for us to reach a conceptualization of capital as self-valorizing value, value must first achieve the 'independent selfhood' that becomes a potential with the money-form.[18] Marx (1976, 152–3) derives the money-form from the commodity-form by showing the necessity for a particular commodity to be set aside from all others in order to serve as universal value reflector. Or to put it otherwise, money is a commodity whose use-value serves to express value so that all other use-values can be subsumed to the motion of value. All use-values are material properties that are wanted for some purpose; whereas since money can buy any use-value, it is wanted for all purposes.[19]

Reification invests the movement of commodities and money in markets with the characteristics of subjectivity while investing the actions of persons with the characteristics of being objectified.[20] In other words, M-C ... P ... C′-M′ exactly maps the circuit that capital must take, setting in advance the paths individuals must follow in order to participate in this circuit. If the profit M′ for an individual capitalist turns into a deficit, bankruptcy will soon follow, forcing that person out of the circuit. If a depression ensues, not only will many capitalists cease operating, but many workers will not be able to sell their labour-power, and those who do will have to accept lower wages. It is this that Marx means to emphasize when he refers to capitalists and workers as 'personifications of economic categories'.[21] The course of economic life and the path of individual wills is dictated by price signals generated in markets, or in other words, socio-economic life is market-governed and profit-driven. Thus, when the commodity-form subsumes the labour-and-production process, it finds within itself the well-spring of value expansion which makes it possible for a commodity-economic logic to encompass the material reproduction of a society and for capital to become self-valorizing value. When Marx refers to the 'immanent laws'[22] of capital or to capital as an 'independent force',[23] he is referring to its reifying force.

Dialectical reason continually returns to the initial commodity-form to deepen our understanding of it as it moves forward. At first it focuses primarily on circulation forms. Then it shifts to the basic production relations between capital and labour as these are subsumed to the circulation forms. Finally, it shifts to distribution relations which examine the distribution of the surplus value resulting from the marriage of circulation forms and production relations. According to Marx (1971, 56) 'the relations of distribution are only the relations of production seen from a different aspect'. He can make this claim because all of the categories involved are different transformations of value and thus connected inwardly. All the forms of profit and rent are thus surplus value expressed in more concrete and externalized forms, but still interconnected. And we proceed this way until capital itself, as interest-bearing capital, is subsumed to the commodity-form.

Marx always attempts in so far as possible to present the inner connections amongst value categories as necessary connections.[24] Thus the money-form is necessary to the commodity-form and these two forms are necessary to the capital-form.[25] Similarly the commodification of labour-power is necessary to the further development of the capital-form as self-valorizing value. And the theory of relative surplus population and periodic crises are necessary to understand how the commodification of labour-power is maintained relative to the needs of self-valorizing value. Inner necessary connections are often contrasted by Marx with outward appearances, which may mislead. Sometimes Marx utilizes the term 'competition' to refer to the realm of empirical appearances, and this needs to be kept in mind in order not to get confused with his use of 'competition' to refer to one of the basic conditions of pure capitalism. In the empirical world of competition economic phenomena appear as discrete perceptions without any connections other than constant conjunction. For Marx, one of the main tasks of theory is to clarify the inner connections that stand behind these outward appearances.

From the point of view of capital, the cost-price for producing a commodity is a very important category, because profit appears as the difference between cost-price and selling-price. And yet cost-price makes it appear as if profit arises equally from total cost-price. By breaking down this category into c+v, Marx makes it clear that profits arise totally from v and not at all from c.[26] Economists see the appearance of capital 'in its mere material existence, independently of its social relation to labour … an autonomous source of surplus value alongside labour and independent of it'(Marx, 1981, 135). The specificity of the capital/labour relation is further obscured by the wage-form, which makes it appear that what is being paid for is a quantity of labour rather than the use of labour-power for a certain amount of time (Marx, 1976, 682). With the category 'profit' *'capital appears as a relationship to itself'* and with this appearance the source of all profit in surplus value cannot be thought. And the extreme of this appears with interest-bearing capital represented as M-M'.

I have above presented some of the reasons for considering the theory of capital's deep structures to be a dialectic.[27] In such a theory, the sort of causal question that I would pose for purposes of this chapter would be: what causes periodic crises in a purely capitalist society? At the level of mid-range theory, capital's commodity economic logic is both supported and disrupted by relatively autonomous non-capitalist economic processes, and by relatively autonomous political and ideological practices. This is because at different phases of capitalist development, value expansion must cope with historically specific use-value resistances (i.e. qualitatively distinct forms of materiality including human institutions) such as particular organizational forms of capital and labour, particular technologies, and particular disciplinary practices. For example, a putting-out system producing woollen cloth may require laws preventing workers from embezzling the product and selling it on the side, whereas this would largely be unnecessary where production takes place in factories. Or, economies of scale associated with steel production as opposed to textile production may lead to oligopolistic practices in a phase of history where steel production becomes a leading and characteristic sector of the economy.

Furthermore, the various inputs of capitalist production may not be fully com-modified, and even maintaining this partial commodification may require phase specific political and ideological supports. For example, labour-power always resists total commodification. Land and money also tend to be politically regulated, though the degree and types of regulation vary historically. Finally, while state intervention always plays an important role in capital accumulation, in the phase of liberalism most typified by British capital accumulation between 1840 and 1870, it would not be possible for the state to utilize Keynesian monetary and fiscal policies, nor were the dominant 'free trade' ideologies compatible with high degrees of protectionism and national chauvinism. It is clear that at this level of abstraction causality becomes complex in a particular sense. The structural dynamics that are theorized exist between relatively autonomous practices whose distinct temporalities thwart theorizing narrow time slices as simple synchronies. While causality becomes significantly more complex at the level of mid-range theory, it is made manageable by focusing on a dominant type of capital accumulation with its accompanying political and ideological resistances and supports abstracted from a 'a golden age' whose twenty to thirty year time span enables a theoretical time compression even though relatively autonomous practices may be temporally out of phase with each other. Finally, our thought about causality at this level is continually informed by the theory of pure capitalism, where capitalistic rationality operates without outside supports, and by historical analysis, which in turn can be continually improved by being informed by both of the more abstract levels.

Causal relations at the theoretical level of pure capitalism are essentially relations of reciprocity amongst interrelated economic variables whose very meaning as well as range of variability stems from their specific interconnectedness (as Marx repeatedly argues, they are 'inner connections'). Thus, for example, money in its fundamental capitalist form must be a qualitative distinct commodity that serves to reflect the values of all other commodities. And capital in its fundamental form is the use of money to expand value through the exploitation of labour. And finally, while wages may rise above or fall below the value of labour-power, through a complete business cycle they will equal the value of labour-power.

Capital's inner logic

In Volume II of *Theories of Surplus Value*, Marx (1968, 507–13) makes it clear that it is the commodity-form itself with its contradiction between value (sociality quantified) and use-value (qualitative materiality) that sets the stage for the possibility of periodic capitalist crises. Marx argues that value and use-value are both dependent and relatively independent, such that a crises occurs when their relative independence stretches their dependency to the breaking point. In other words, at some point they become so disjointed from each other that their mutual dependence is reasserted through a crisis. Thus, the first abstract possibility of crises appears with the separation that may occur between the effort to sell and the actual purchase of a commodity. If the entire society produces too much, the product will not sell and capital will spiral down into a crisis. The dialectic of capital's necessary inner connections can be read as an ever deepening of the value/use-value contradiction,[28] until all the basic socio-economic forms required for capital in the abstract and in general to reproduce and expand are subsumed to the commodity form. Each step in the deepening dialectic can be considered as yet another possibility for value to become sufficiently disconnected from use-value for a crisis to be necessary precisely in order to maintain the essential connectedness between value and use-value. This is the reason why Marx (1968, 507, 534) sometimes claims that in a crisis all the contradictions of capital come to a head. It is important to add, however, that the theory of capital's inner logic assumes the full commodification of the economy, so that the disconnectednesses causing crises cannot at this level of abstraction result from incomplete commodification, but only from the workings of a fully commodified economic logic.

In Volume III of *Capital* Marx (1981, 317–18) discusses the tendency for the rate of profit to fall. He argues that in the formula for the rate of profit $s/c+v$ (s=surplus value; c=constant capital; v=variable capital), with rate of surplus value s/v remaining constant and with the material volume of c increasing relative to v, the rate of profit will fall. Or in other words, as each worker processes hugely increasing amounts of fixed and circulating constant capital per unit time as will be the case with increasing productivity, the rate of profit will tend to fall. In Marx's discussion of countertendencies to this tendency, it is clear that the only ones that are internal to the law of value are increasing the rate of exploitation and cheapening the constant capital. Marx (1981, 342) makes this particularly clear in his discussion of 'reduction of wages below their value' of which he writes: 'We simply make an empirical reference to this point here, as, like many things that might be brought in, it has nothing to do with the general analysis of capital, but has its place in an account of competition, which is not dealt with in this work'.

A general falling rate of profit might suggest why capital is not immortal, but it cannot explain in commodity-economic terms why capital would pass through periodic crises (1981, 350). Of course, should the rate of profit suddenly fall, one would expect a crisis to result, but a general tendency cannot explain its sudden fall. Elsewhere, however, Marx (1981, 365) makes it clear that as the industrial reserve army shrinks with the expansion of capital during its phase of prosperity, the demand for labour-power will eventually push wages above the value of labour-power. Further, he argues (1981, 419) that the relative independence of commercial capital from industrial capital, can encourage further expansion of industrial capital before the final market demand for the product is known. The need for more liquid funds to pay an expanding labour force a higher wage on a weekly basis drives up the rate of interest. As commercial capital has difficulty selling the product at the expected price, creditors begin to call in their debts and this further demand for liquidity further raises the interest rate at the same time that the rate of profit is declining because of higher wages and saturated markets. At the point when the rate of interest approaches the level of the rate of profit, productive investment begins to shrink and values and prices collapse (1981, 483).

Assuming the approximate accuracy of this very condensed account, what can we say about the causes of crises at this level of abstraction? Since the entire theory is simply an actualization that moves the commodity-form along until it subsumes the entire expanded reproduction of capital in the context of complete commodification, we could say that the cause is the commodity-form with its contradiction between value and use-value. But while this may be the moving force of the entire inner dialectical logic of capital, it is not entirely accurate to say that the commodity-form is the primary cause of periodic crises, though it may be accurate to refer to it as the primary necessary condition. And for reasons already given, it does not make sense to derive periodic crises from a general tendency such as the falling rate of profit. Indeed, the theory of capital's inner logic suggests many abstract possibilities for periodic crises to occur, and therefore, many possible causes (1968, 570). But as the movement of the dialectic increases the concrete content of the theory, the triggering mechanisms become clarified.

It thus becomes possible to say something definite about the causes of crises in a purely capitalist society. In such a society, it is clearly the commodification of labour-power that is the most tenuous part of value's commodity-economic logic. Labour-power cannot be capitalistically produced in response to increased demand, and, consequently an industrial reserve army is a necessary condition for capital to be able to expand. And yet, increasing the demand for labour as the supply shrinks, will ultimately drive wages up and hence cut into profits. The situation is further exacerbated by activities of both commercial capital that drive capital towards further expansion at precisely the time it should be contracting and by interest-bearing capital that demands payment when least possible. Thus we might conclude that in the theory of capital's necessary inner connections, periodic crises are caused by the difficulties posed by the commodity-economic management of labour power that causes a sudden decline in profit rates in conjunction with the overproduction fostered by commercial capital and the sudden sharp discipline imposed by higher interest rates and demands for payment of debts. As the falling profit rate and rising interest rate approach each other, new capital investment would halt (Sekine, 1997, Vol. II, 61–70). While these would be the causes of crises in a purely capitalist society, it is not necessarily the case that any actual historical capitalist crisis would have precisely this causal structure. At the same time, this theory explains why periodic crises would occur even in the most perfect capitalism where the commodity-form is totally secured. In any actual capitalism, where the commodity-form is never totally secure, the possible causes of crises would multiply. Indeed, any significant labour shortage would give labour too much power, and hence is avoided like the plague by capital. In history, the radical uneven development of capitalism always assures that labour-power is available either internally from the rural sector or the unemployed or internationally through immigration or various forms of forced labour. Furthermore, both political (e.g. class struggle or war) and natural causes (crop failures due to bad weather or the depletion of resources) could play a prominent role. And yet the clearer case of pure capitalism should help us clarify and explain actual less clear capitalist crises by helping to distinguish causes that flow from the deep structure of capital as opposed to other causes and to alert us to the particular problems associated with maintaining the commodification of labour-power in the face of on-going exploitation, oppression, and unemployment.

Mid-range theory (theory of phases or stages)

One purpose of mid-range theory is to help us theorize the causes of crises in the context of a dominant mode of capital accumulation characteristic of a specific phase of capitalism. At this more concrete level of analysis different types of commodities may exhibit different degrees of commodification, and whatever degree they exhibit may be partially the result of a variety of political or ideological extra-economic forces that support the commodification in question. Thus besides the causal factors discussed above we need to consider causal factors that stem from incomplete commodification, from the relative effectiveness/ineffectiveness of major political or ideological supports of commodification, or from the uneven development of capitalism on a global scale.

As an example of mid-range theory, I shall consider the phase of imperialism in which capital accumulation reached its most classical structural dynamics in the US and Germany between 1890 and 1914. At this level of analysis, instead of studying actual crises, we study the likely fault lines of crisis in a phase specific mode of accumulation whether or not a deep crisis actually occurs in history. Because this is a more concrete level of analysis, the most likely causes of crises multiply to the extent that the account given here can only be a sketch indicating the kinds of causes that would most likely need to be accounted for.

The most important features of capital accumulation in the phase of imperialism are the following:[29]

1　The shift of the centre of capital accumulation to heavy industry, most typically steel.
2　The development of the limited-liability joint-stock company (corporation).
3　The growth of banks, stock markets, and debt expansion (finance capital).
4　An international monetary system based on a gold standard and managed by the Bank of England.
5　Oligopoly and monopoly become widespread in the leading sectors of the economy.
6　Adult male workers get the vote. Workers and farmers increasingly try to form trade unions, political movements, or political parties and as a result class tensions increase.
7　Prairie grain production undermines European agriculture, resulting in massive migration.
8　Efforts to hypersubsume labour-power to capital through ideological indoctrination, welfare, paternalism, scientific management, and repression.
9　Increased state revenues from custom duties and some debt expansion.
10　A growing state repressive apparatus. (Police, army, courts, prisons, etc.)
11　A significant state-funded armaments industry.
12　Strong national capitalisms and nationalism.

13 Aggressive expansionism and inter-imperialist rivalry.
14 Colonialism and unequal exchange.
15 Universal primary education and technical education.

In such a mode of accumulation, it is unlikely that a crisis would be caused by rising wages, a falling rate of profit, and a rising rate of interest as in pure capitalism because massive migration could replenish the industrial reserve army of labour, because monopolies could maintain profits even if wages were to rise, and because finance capital could often prevent a rising interest rate through its effective mobilization of savings and through debt expansion. In my understanding, the most likely possible causes of a crisis in such a mode of accumulation would be:

1 The surplus profits of monopoly capital which could lead to underconsumption problems by shifting income from the competitive sector and from consumers to the monopoly sector.
2 A large balance of payments deficit could force lower wages triggering off significant class struggle.
3 A high interest rate imposed by the Bank of England through its hegemony within the International Monetary System.
4 A stock market collapse or series of bank failures.
5 A working class powerful enough to effectively resist having a potential crisis resolved at its cost.

These causes could be counteracted by:

1 Government spending on infrastructure and the military, which would stimulate heavy industry.
2 Protectionism that would facilitate dumping (selling below the international price in order to capture markets abroad) and a whole range of 'beggar thy neighbour' policies.
3 The creation of new products and the capturing of new markets at home and abroad.
4 The effective countering of efforts of workers and farmers to organize.
5 Unequal exchange in foreign trade that would cheapen industrial inputs.
6 Increased wages that might mollify workers or reduce underconsumption tendencies.
7 Population increase through migration and increased fertility rates that might increase the work force and effective demand even if wages remain the same.
8 Technological advances that would require large investments in fixed capital that would have long depreciation periods, again reducing underconsumption pressures.
9 Maintaining a positive balance of payments surplus through protectionism and aggressive expansionism. This would be important given the disciplining character of the international monetary system.

10 Debt expansion might be of some significance, but nothing like the importance that it assumes in the post-World War II economy.
11 Lowering prices in the monopoly sector to expand markets and drain off surplus profits.
12 New industries that would increase the consumption of the outputs of heavy industry.
13 Foreign investment in infrastructure that would stimulate heavy industry at home.

This list of possible causes and ways of counteracting them is meant to be indicative and not exhaustive.

A well worked out mid-range theory could further discuss the relative weightiness of these various causes by considering, for example, constraints on state taxing and spending power during this phase and hence the relative significance of state fiscal policies in maintaining monopoly profits. Or one could explore the extremely limited control that states had over monetary policy given the type of international monetary system that existed. Also it would be necessary to explore how counteracting one possible cause of crisis could exacerbate another cause. For example, it is no doubt possible that some means of avoiding a balance of payments deficit could contribute to monopoly surplus profits and underconsumption.

Historical analysis

It is at the level of historical analysis that we can explore the causes of actual historical events, and it is therefore at this level that we can speak of causality in its most common usage as attempting to account for the occurrence of an event in a particular time and place by considering its causes. With a large and complex human event like an economic crisis, even a list of the most important causes can be quite large. And moving beyond a list to the interaction of causes and their relative weightiness is enormously challenging. And yet there is little doubt that the more sophisticated our theories and the more we explore the causes of an event, the closer we are likely to get to understanding its causes in their full complexity. And to the extent that future events have similarities to past events, the understanding of the past can be utilized to shape a future that is more in accord with human aspirations

At this level I shall focus on the case of Germany between 1890 and 1914, and I shall consider specific reasons why Germany did not experience a deep crisis (though it was not without economic downturns), but why its avoidance strategies contributed to the ground swell that ultimately plunged Europe into World War I.

The Great Depression of 1873 and the large economies of scale associated with heavy industry more or less forced German capital to centralize rapidly in the late nineteenth century, whereas the new corporate form coupled with large banks certainly facilitated the processes of centralization. Further, since monopoly prices tended to be higher than competitive prices, large cartels were encouraged by this to vertically integrate in order to cheapen inputs. Thus, for example, by 1900 twenty per cent of the coal production in the Ruhr was controlled by steel cartels (Spencer, 1984, 21). The largest of these cartels was Krupp, which just prior to World War I had 70,127 workers, making it the largest steel producer in Germany (*ibid.* 22).

Since monopoly surplus profits tend to shift profit away from the competitive sector and income away from consumers, such profits are always haunted by the spectre of underconsumption. A number of factors staved off severe underconsumption crises.

1 The main consumers of the centrally important heavy industries were other industries, and with the exception of Russia, which started with very low figures, Germany had the most rapidly growing economy in the world between 1890 and 1905 (Barkin, 1970,127).

2 High protective tariffs for both the products of industry and agriculture united the politically dominant landed Junker class with big industry. The high agricultural tariffs saved this sector from the international competition of prairie wheat farming which was undermining much of Europe's agricultural sector. And the industrial tariffs protected high domestic monopoly prices from international competition while facilitating the capture of foreign markets through dumping. Approximately 25 per cent of German steel was exported over the period between 1890 and 1914, and the foreign price was at times as much as 19 per cent lower than the domestic price (Milward and Saul, 1977, 28).

3 In 1898 the German government decided to build a huge navy that would compete with Britain's: 80 per cent of the taxes came from customs duties and excise taxes, while the rest came from low income and inheritance taxes (Webber and Wildavsky, 1986, 344). Unlike the United States and Britain, Germany did not adhere to a balanced budget; and hence, a portion of military spending also came from debt expansion.

4 The large size of German industrial and banking cartels and the high degree of integration between banking and industrial capital (Deutsche Bank representatives played an active role on the boards of 159 major firms) (Milward and Saul, 1977, 48) facilitated paying the costs of applying science to industry and of the long-term fixed capital investments required by the new heavy industries: steel, chemicals, electronics, etc.

5 Depression in the Eastern European agrarian sector (mainly as a result of prairie grain production in the new world) led to migration to the industrial areas of Germany where there were jobs, thus increasing effective demand by increasing the population in Germany.

6 German foreign investment in infrastructure often meant more orders directed to German heavy industry.

7 Increased wages were not a counteracting factor. There were no effective unions, with the result that industrialists simply set wages at the lowest possible level that would still enable them to get sufficient workers. Indeed, between

1890 and 1914 there were large productivity increases in German industry and almost no wage increases (Spencer, 1984, 82, 143).

Even more than a possible underconsumption crisis, the greatest threat to German capital during this period was posed by the Social Democratic Party which presented itself as a revolutionary socialist party. Despite Bismarck's effort to co-opt some SPD support by introducing social insurance, and despite actually outlawing the SPD for a period of time, support for it continually grew. Long before the outbreak of World War I, it was already by far the largest single party in Germany's multi-party system. Such electoral success for a revolutionary socialist party was truly terrifying to German financial capital and the politically dominant Junkers. With such a party waiting in the wings, any mass strike could easily escalate into a generalized revolutionary insurrection. Countering the influence of the SPD thus became a significant preoccupation of the dominant classes. And it was not simply a question of preventing severe economic downturns, but also of combating economically, politically, and ideologically the SPD's efforts to mobilize the working class.

In order to diminish the influence of the SPD in the steel industry, it was considered absolutely essential to prevent unionization from occurring. Unions would not only be inconsistent with 'scientific management', but work stoppages would be disastrous to many of the around-the-clock continuous processes of heavy industry given the huge start-up costs. Moreover, work stoppages would result in the enormous investments in fixed capital lying idle. Following are some of the obstacles faced by union organizers in the German Steel Industry:

1 Workers worked 12 hour shifts, 365 days a year, leaving them little time or energy for organization. Also, given the exhausting nature of the work and the high rate of injury, there was a high rate of worker turnover, making organization difficult.
2 Many workers were recent immigrants from the agrarian sector lacking German citizenship, workplace experience or a sense of solidarity. Religious, ethnic, and language differences further complicated organization.
3 Steel cartels often offered low rental housing for workers and other paternalistic benefits in order to buy their loyalty.
4 Workers could be fired without notice for being late, low quality work, inattentiveness or any form of insubordination, not to mention something so heinous as meeting together or organizing.
5 The use of piece-rate wages to institute competition amongst workers discouraged solidarity on the shop floor.
6 Extreme state repression (calling out the troops) would be threatened at the first rumblings of a mass strike.
7 A deeply entrenched status-based order attempted to instil deference to authority.
8 An ideology of national chauvinism suppressed class struggle by uniting the classes into a nation against external enemies.

All of this added up to what I have called the 'hypersubsumption of labour-power' (Albritton, 1991, 182). It might be thought that the electoral power of the SPD would result in legislation more favourable to union organizing, but such was not the case. While a large proportion of adult male citizens could vote, increasingly power shifted from the legislature to the executive as the state became more bureaucratic. Further, by astutely designing electoral constituencies ('gerrymandering'), the right-wing parties ensured that the SPD got far fewer deputies than their popular vote would lead one to expect.

In order to stem the growing class consciousness in the working classes, the dominant classes relied heavily on a continual promotion of intense national chauvinism in order to unite all classes against a variety of possible foreign enemies (increasingly Britain). And there were new institutions such as newspapers and schools that aided the efforts of ideological indoctrination. Further, the aggressive expansionism of German capital backed by the state tended to make the emphasis on foreign enemies a kind of self-fulfilling prophecy. At a very general level, one might claim that in order to avoid class war, dominant capitalist powers generated a world war. Or one might claim that the effort to avoid a serious capitalist economic crisis fuelled the inter-imperialist rivalry that played a significant role in generating World War I. And these two statements are not contradictory since the avoidance of class war and of crises were arguably in this case closely connected.

My whole analysis of causality might suggest that this is a greatly exaggerated conclusion that falls back into an overly simplified single-factor analysis. But such is not the case. I make these statements as a kind of provocation to suggest that even where causality is very complex, there may be certain deep causes that ultimately carry the most weight.[30] Of course, in a short essay, it is not possible to present the kind of analysis that might convince the sceptical reader.[31]

Levels of analysis and types of causality

Marx's theory of capital's inner logic attempts to trace the necessary inner connections amongst the basic economic categories of capital. In other words, he tries to show that it is possible to theorize capital as a coherent self-expanding commodity-economic logic. In his presentation of the theory each category is the necessary condition for the category that follows and all the categories are necessary in order for the capitalistic commodity form to subsume economic life. The result is a theory of capital's deep structure presented as a tightly knit possible world, and the theory as a whole presents a picture of many possible crises points even with a fully commodified and fully capitalist economy. But it is primarily because of the use-value characteristics of labour-power, that the competitive movement of prices cannot ensure balanced growth without crises. Indeed, periodic crises are perhaps most necessary precisely in order to maintain the commodification of labour-power. Ironically, then, crises function in the short term to preserve the capitalist system, but at the same time they reveal the system's deep contradictions. Causality at this level of analysis presents itself in purely commodity-economic terms because human agency only serves to energize the motion of commodities which ultimately provide the price signals that direct all economic behaviour. This means that crises are not traceable to anyone's specific agency, but instead result from the very commodity-economic logic of self-expanding value, which is in this case the overriding 'agency'. The cause of crises stems ultimately from the fact that labour-power is not a commodity that can be capitalistically produced as a supply adequate to demand in response to market price signals. But this is the cause that occurs even when all inputs and outputs of capitalist production are securely commodified, when all markets are competitive, and when there is no state intervention in the economy. I refer to this kind of causality as dialectical because it consists of necessary inner connections amongst all the basic economic categories of capitalism that can be unfolded from the commodity form.

At the level of mid-range theory when it is not the case that all inputs and outputs of capitalist production are securely and completely commodified and when even non-capitalist or semi-capitalist economic practices may interact with the more capitalist practices, the possible causes of crises multiply dramatically. At the same time, the possible interventions that might avoid crises also multiply. Thus, at this level of theory, it is not possible to determine if or what kinds of crises will occur amongst the dominant capitalist accumulators during the golden age of a phase-specific type of accumulation. Instead, the aim is to explore the most likely causes of crises given the dominant type of capital accumulation. In other words, mid-range theory examines the dominant type of structural dynamics of capital-accumulation characteristic of a particular phase in order to shed light on its weakest points and the capacities of the structures to effectively respond to the crisis tendencies associated with these various points. And it must be strongly emphasized that the more abstract level of theory plays a crucial role in both theorizing dominant types of phase-specific capital accumulation and their crisis possibilities, even though there may be no phase where labour shortages play the role that they do in triggering crises in pure capitalism. Similarly historical analysis helps in the construction of the material type concepts characteristic of mid-range theory. For these reasons I refer to causality at this level as structural causality (causality of relatively autonomous interrelated institutions constituting the most typical patterns of capital accumulation) overdetermined by both dialectical causality and historical causality.

These two more abstract levels of analysis help to shape the extensive historical analysis required to weigh actual historical causes (or forces) that result in economic crisis or political crisis. Causes at this level of analysis are essentially those of collective human agency conditioned by various degrees of reification or structuration. Economic causes are typically more reified while political and ideological causes are less so. Powerful forms of collective agency may in some cases resist or alter even some of the most reified economic social relations. Indeed causes at the level of historical analysis may be considered practices of mobilization and demobilization as they are conditioned by and alter the structures that they act through, and structures themselves are simply practices that have hardened to become more or less difficult to alter.

In the case study briefly outlined above severe economic crises were avoided (as, for example, the great depression of 1873), but at the same time the avoidance strategies created pressures that resulted in the severe political crises that triggered World War I. From the point of view of the capitalist class this was clearly a desirable outcome since it effectively utilized national chauvinism to defuse the appeal of a class-based opposition that threatened to bring capitalism to an end. And while the working class would be decimated by World War I, the capitalist class would emerge from it far less damaged.

Notes

1 I would like to thank Tom Sekine, Ken Kawashima, and John Bell for their helpful comments.
2 Stephen Kern, *A Cultural History of Causality*, Princeton: Princeton University Press, 2004, p. 1.
3 Roy Bhaskar, *Reclaiming Reality*, London: Verso, 1989, p.25.
4 Bhaskar, *The Possibility of Naturalism*, New Jersey: Humanities Press, 1979, p. 68.
5 See Collier (1994) and Brown *et al,*(2002).
6 Bhaskar, *The Possibility of Naturalism*, New Jersey: Humanities Press, 1979,. p. 65.
7 The 'theory of price determination' is all too often the *sine qua non* of bourgeois economic theory.
8 Most bourgeois economic theory has almost nothing to say about profits except for some version of abstinence theory, the uselessness of which, Marx demonstrated more than a century ago.
9 For a fuller discussion of human flourishing in connection with Marxian political economy see Albritton (2007).
10 For a good analysis of the sense in which the theory of capital's inner logic is dialectical see Kourkoulakos (2003).
11 See Sekine (1997) for a strong theory of pure capitalism, and see Albritton (1991) for mid-range theory. While there is a lack of extended historical analyses using this approach see Albritton (1991); Albritton in Albritton *et al.* (2001); Albritton in Westra and Zuege (eds) (2003); Albritton (2003b); Albritton (2004); and Albritton (2005).
12 These three levels of analysis were first developed by Japanese Political Economist Kozo Uno, and continued to be important in the work of his student Tom Sekine. While most modern Marxist thinkers employ some notion of levels of analysis, it is this Japanese approach that takes it furthest. At the same time, it is this idea that has most divided Japanese Unoists.
13 Marx uses this term hundreds of times in *Capital* and *Theories of Surplus Value* as his primary conceptualization of the nature of capital.
14 For example, Marx (1976, 140) writes: 'The relative form of value [the commodity form as value form] and the equivalent form [ultimately the money form] are two inseparable moments, which belong to and mutually condition each other; but, at the same time they are mutually exclusive or opposed extremes....'
15 'Money and commodities as such are therefore latent capital, potential capital; this applies to all commodities insofar as they are convertible into money, and to money insofar as it is convertible into those commodities which constitute the elements of the capitalist process of production. Thus money – as the pure expression of the value of

commodities and of the conditions of labour – is itself as capital antecendent to capitalist production' (Marx, 1971, 475).

16 In criticizing Proudhon (it could just as well be Ricardo) Marx writes: 'he has never understood that money is a necessary aspect of the commodity' (Marx, 1971, 523).

17 'Exchange, however, produces a differentiation of the commodity into two elements, commodity and money, an external opposition which expresses the opposition between use-value and value which is inherent in it' (Marx, 1976, 199).

18 According to Marx money '... is the first form of appearance of capital'. (1976, 247) '... all new capital, in the first instance, steps onto the stage – i.e. the market, whether it is the commodity-market, the labour-market or the money-market – in the shape of money, money which has to be transformed into capital by definite processes'. (1976, 247). See also (1976, 255)

19 'This contradiction between the quantitative limitation and the qualitative lack of limitation of money keeps driving the hoarder back to his Sisyphean task: accumulation. He is in the same situation as a world conqueror, who discovers a new boundary with each country he annexes'. (Marx, 1976, 231).

20 'What is also implied already in the commodity, and still more so in the commodity as the product of capital, is the reification of the social determinations of production and the subjectification [*Versubjektifierung*] of the material bases of production which characterize the entire capitalist mode of production'. (Marx, 1981, 1020).

21 Marx 1976, 92, 179, 254, 342, 424, 739, 991, 1003, 1015, 1058; 1978, 196–7, 207, 550; 1981, 403, 727, 958.

22 (1976, 381; 1981, 298).

23 (1978, 195; 1981, 753).

24 '... the simple form of value automatically passes over into the more complete form'. (Marx, 1976, 154).

25 'Money as a measure of value is the necessary form of appearance of the measure of value which is immanent in commodities, namely labour-time' (Marx, 1976, 188).

26 '... cost price does ... in the economy of capital, present the false semblance of an actual category of value production' (Marx, 1981, 119). 'Capital runs through the cycle of its transformations, and finally steps as it were from its inner organic life into its external relations, relations where it is not capital and labour that confront one another, but on the one hand capital and capital, and on the other hand individuals as simple buyers and sellers once again ... surplus-value itself does not appear as having been produced by the appropriation of labour-time, but as the excess of the sale price of commodities over their cost price ...' (Marx, 1981, 135). Sekine (1997) utilizes the contrast between widening and deepening phases of accumulation in connection with periodic crises to show how a commodity-economic logic can assure that all fixed capital on average cannot pass on more value than its original cost.

27 Using Colletti's (1975) language capital's inner logic moves by 'dialectical contradiction' and not 'real opposition'.

28 See Bhaskar (1989, 120): 'Ultimately, for Marx, all the contradictions of capitalism derive from the structurally fundamental contradictions between use-value and the value of the commodity, and between the concrete useful and abstract social aspects of the labour it embodies'.

29 For a more developed theory of the stage of imperialism see Albritton (1991).

30 See Hobsbawm (1987) for an introduction to some of the debates on the more proximate causes of World War I.

31 Much that Lenin and other Marxists have written on this is quite convincing.

References

Albritton, R. (1991) *A Japanese Approach to Stages of Capitalist Development*, London: Macmillan.

Albritton, R. (1999) *Dialectics and Deconstruction in Political Economy*, London: Palgrave.

Albritton, R., Itoh, M., Westra, R., Zuege, A.(eds) (2001) *Phases of Capitalist Development: Booms, Crises and Globalizations*, Houndmills, Basingstoke: Palgrave.

Albritton, R. and Simoulidis, J. (2003a) *New Dialectics and Political Economy*, Houndmills Basingstoke: Palgrave.

Albritton, R. (2003b) 'Returning to Marx's *Capital:* A Critique of Lebowitz's *Beyond Capital*', in *History of Economic Ideas*, XI, No. 3.

Albritton, R. (2004) 'Theorising Capital's Deep Structure and the Transformation of Capitalism', *Historical Materialism*, 12.3.

Albritton, R. (2005) 'How Dialectics Runs Aground: The Antinomies of Arthur's Dialectic of Capital', *Historical Materialism*, 13.3.

Albritton, R. (2007) *Economics Transformed: Discovering the Brilliance of Marx*, London: Pluto Press.

Barkin, K. (1970) *The Controversy Over German Industrialization 1890–1902*, Chicago: University of Chicago Press.

Bhaskar, R. (1979) *The Possibility of Naturalism*, New Jersey: Humanities Press.

Bhaskar, R. (1989) *Reclaiming Reality*, London: Verso.

Brown, A., Fleetwood, S., Roberts, J. M. (2002) *Critical Realism and Marxism*, London: Routledge.

Colletti, L. (1975) 'Contradiction and Contrariety', in *New Left Review* No. 93.

Collier, A. (1994) *Critical Realism*, London: Verso.

Hobsbawm, E.J. (1987) *The Age of Empire*, London: Weidenfeld and Nicolson.

Kern, S. (2004) *A Cultural History of Causality*, Princeton: Princeton University Press.

Kourkoulakos, S. (2003) 'The Specificity of Dialectical Reason', in Albritton and Simoulidis (2003a) *New Dialectics and Political Economy,* Houndmills, Basingstoke: Palgrave.

Marx, K. (1963) *Theories of Surplus Value*, Vol. I, Moscow: Progess.

Marx, K. (1968) *Theories of Surplus Value*, Vol. II, Moscow: Progress.

Marx, K. (1971) *Theories of Surplus Value*, Vol. III, Moscow: Progress.

Marx, K. (1976) *Capital*, Vol. I, New York: Penguin.

Marx, K. (1978) *Capital*, Vol. II, New York: Penguin.

Marx, K. (1981) *Capital*, Vol. III, New York: Penguin.

Milward, A. and Saul, S. B. (1977) *The Development of the Economies of Continental Europe 1850–1914*, Massachusetts: Harvard University Press.

Sekine, T. (1997) *An Outline of The Dialectic of Capital*, two volumes, London: Macmillan.

Spencer, E. G. (1984) *Management and Labour in Imperial Germany*, Rutgers University Press.

Westra, R. and Zuege, A. (eds) (2003) *Value and the World Economy Today*, Basingstoke: Palgrave.

Webber and Wildavsky (1986) *A History of Taxation and Expenditure in the Western World*, New York: Simon & Schuster.

15 On the clear comprehension of political economy

Social kinds and the significance of Section 2 of Marx's Capital[1]

Howard Engelskirchen

Since Quine's essay, "Natural Kinds," in 1969, there has been a small explosion of attention to the use of natural kinds in science (Rieppel 2004, 2005a, 2005b; Keller *et al*. 2003; Boyd 1999, 1991, 1989; Psillos 1999; Wilson 1999; Bhaskar 1998, 1997; Platts 1997; Pessin and Goldberg 1996; Dupre 1993; Kornblith 1993; Hacking 1991a, 1991b; Schwartz 1979, 1977). In this chapter I survey briefly a few of the essential features that make natural kind investigations important today and then explore their extension to social life. In "Realism, Anti-Foundationalism, and the Enthusiasm for Natural Kinds," Richard Boyd (1991) argues that the core conceptions of our current understanding of natural kinds are fully applicable to the study of social phenomena. I will test this proposal by showing the way natural kind analysis contributes to understanding Marx's presentation of the commodity in the early pages of *Capital*. I conclude that Marx's analysis may be understood to foreshadow today's sophisticated scientific realism.

The enthusiasm for natural kinds

As part of our struggle to know the world, we fashion categories in science to refer to things. The use of such categories in scientific practice requires that their content be determined by the causal structures of the world (Boyd 1991). That is, the properties or mechanisms a definition picks out will be causal ones and when we get it right the categories we use make it possible for us to accommodate the world's causal structures and relations to the demands of our practice (Boyd 1999, 1991). The causal structures to which such categories refer fall under natural kinds and the terms we use to refer to them are natural kind terms. Always our identification and understanding of natural kinds is an *a posteriori* product of observation, investigation and our background theories.

The emphasis on understanding kinds in terms of the causal structure of the world is fairly new. This was not made explicit even in the essay which effectively initiated modern attention to the problem of kinds, Quine's 1969 article, though it was certainly implicit in important threads of his account. Quine underscored how critical were judgments of similarity, of sorting things into kinds, not only to thought and language but also to the inductive practices of science. And he took pains also to insist that our judgments of similarity were judgments about the world, not about our theories or beliefs. For that reason he considered that the progress of science required development beyond reliance on surface judgments of similarity. A mature science like chemistry would offer explanations in terms of underlying chemical compositions and atomic or molecular structure. This reduction, he thought, would supersede the need for resort to similarity relations.

Experience, however, does not bear out Quine's suggestion – deference to judgments of similarity remains very much a part of scientific practice all would characterize as mature.[2] Still we would emphasize today that "to be significant, similarity needs to be causally grounded," and therefore attention to kinds reflects an effort to reach out to the causal structure of the world (Rieppel 2004, 1). That is, the goal of scientific investigation "[remains] definitions that have explanatory power in that they establish the link to the underlying causal powers of the object being defined" (Rieppel 2005b, 19), a theme significantly developed by the critical realist Roy Bhaskar.[3] Hilary Kornblith sums up how this emphasis has evolved as follows:

> Indeed it was the application of the causal theory of reference to natural kinds which allowed for the elaboration of a sophisticated scientific realism. ... On the account of science which began to emerge ... , it is the business of science to discover the real causal structure of the world; what this means, in a word, is the discovery of natural kinds and the causal relations among them ... natural kinds make inductive knowledge of the world possible because the clustering of properties characteristic of natural kinds makes inferences from the presence of some of these properties to the presence of others reliable.
>
> (Kornblith 1993, 6–7)

Our demand for causal explanation, in other words, drives us to organize our understanding of the world by means of kinds (Rieppel 2004; Platts 1997).

Significantly, this contemporary emphasis suggests that Quine's (1994) ultimate suspicion of kinds – he thought they were, from a scientific point of view, "dubious," (159) "disreputable," (170) and not the mark of a mature science (161, 174), was misplaced. Quine understood that in investigating the world we can't make do with nominal kinds – the way we fashion categories in science has to fit the world, not just what we think logically convenient. But he argued that definition of kinds in terms of the similarity relation implied was unreduced. For example, he suggested that to define the set of all things that "actually did or will dissolve in water" [not also "could"?] as a water soluble kind was unsatisfactory for this reason – the concept of kind used was "unreduced" (168). Any reference to properties that are the "same" or "common" to members of the kind is just another way of evoking similarities among them, and, according to Quine, "definition of kind in terms of similarity is unknown" (160).

The impasse seems very much a residue of traditional thinking of kinds in terms of sets and classes rather than in terms of the causal structures of the world (Rieppel 2005a; Keller *et al.* 2003). And, as far as the logic of the matter goes, perhaps today's scientific realism can learn something from Marx's emphasis on contradiction. Consider Boyd's "accommodation thesis," for example, in light of Marx's invocation of Spinoza – "to determine is to negate." We need reference to kinds in science, Boyd argues, in order to accommodate our causal engagement with the world to the world's own causal structures (1999, 1991). Surely this is an evolutionary trait long in the making – a rattlesnake adjusts its lunge to a source of heat. That is, the things of the world demand a causal response from us and we will call instances of a thing the same when we are incapable of making a relevant distinction among the causal responses they evoke. Plainly our ability to discriminate will depend on experience – different soils that you or I might call indifferently "dirt" a farmer will sort into kinds, and a layperson will find a blob under a microscope where a biologist will recognize the component parts of a cell. Thus we can reduce "same" to our ability to differentiate, in the accommodations we make to the causal structures of the world, between what a thing is and what it is not. "Similarity," in turn, is just a relation of more or less with respect to the "same."

If membership in a kind consists in the possession of the same cluster of dispositional properties as are shared by other members of the kind, then there is nothing unreduced about the definition. A natural kind is just a collection of things that possess the same or a similar cluster of homeostatic dispositional properties (Boyd 1999, 1988).

Now social and many other natural kinds – biological kinds are a prime example – simply do not show the same kind of unambiguous sorting into necessary and sufficient properties that sometimes occurs in the physical sciences; in consequence, traditional definitions of kinds in terms of the vocabularies of sciences like chemistry and physics, as Quine preferred, have tended to make the concept of natural kinds a poor fit for all but such sciences. As a result, the idea that a kind may instead be defined in terms of a cluster of homeostatic causal properties or mechanisms rather than unvarying membership conditions (Boyd 1999, 1988) has opened a path to much broader applications. "Homeostasis" is a concept borrowed from biology and refers to the means an organism uses to maintain itself in a dynamically stable relationship to its environment. As used in the context of kinds, three things seem particularly important. First, homeostasis recalls a distinction going back to Aristotle between those causal properties that are essential to a thing's persistence and those properties which may or may not be associated with it without the thing ceasing to be what it is. Thus in a particular environment, water may never take the form of a solid, but it can never not be H_2O. In Boyd's terms it is the underlying cluster of an entity's essential properties that assures the aptness of a kind for use in the practices of induction and explanation.

Second, traditional examples drawn from chemistry and physics, like H_2O, useful though they can be for simple illustration, cannot lock us into thinking that natural kinds depend on properties that are unvarying. The concept of homeostasis we use in our definitions of kinds is a cluster concept that looks to the gathering of causal properties that tend to co-occur. But there is no demand that each such property be found always present in every member of a kind in order for it to figure in our definition – again recalling Aristotle, kind properties are "all or for the most part." In the last analysis, whether the features we use to pick out a causal structure co-occur in a unity nature has produced depends (in a reminder of Quine) on the world, not our theories or the demands of logic.

Finally, since for living things homeostasis requires always the selection from the enormous mass of stimuli otherwise constantly present in the environment to those specific few causally relevant to a thing's persistence as the kind of thing it is, accommodation to the causal structures of the world would appear to be a quite general feature of natural selection. The recent way we have learned to think about natural kinds adds to this, on the argument Boyd offers, an understanding of the way the capacity to use language may contribute, by means of causally determined reference, to facilitating that accommodation.

Nominal and real essences

Before turning to a consideration of the way kinds figure in *Capital*, it is worth recalling Locke's famous distinction between nominal and real essences in order to situate the way Marx might have approached such problems. Locke thought real essences, the microstructures of the objects of the world, determined how things behaved, but he also thought that we had no way to know such "insensible parts" because we could not observe them. Instead, we were left to sort things according to the more or less arbitrary ideas of our understanding, gathered, such as seemed convenient, from properties we did observe.

> the *nominal Essence* of *Gold*, is that complex *Idea* the word *Gold* stands for, let it be, for instance, a Body yellow, of a certain weight, malleable, fusible, and fixed. But the *real Essence* is the constitution of the insensible parts of that Body, on which those Qualities, and all other Properties of *Gold* depend.
> (Bk.III, vi, Section2, p. 439)

The problem is that if the properties associated with a thing depend on a microstructure we have no understanding of, then we have no reason to suppose that what we observe today will hold true tomorrow. Quine remarked that induction is our hope that similar causes have similar effects, but if we lack knowledge of causes, then we have no hope that the effects we observe on different occasions will correspond. That is, induction is unjustified (Boyd 1991).

It is easy to imagine Marx studying this passage from Locke, but with an understanding of the significance of the developments of the physical sciences of the nineteenth century. In effect he could know then what we surely know now – that the success of science has proven Locke wrong: we are able to know (approximately, revisably) the insensible parts of things.[4] Thus in "Notes on Wagner," Marx (1975) suggests the connection between this advance in science and his own analysis of the commodity form. He referred to the alchemists before the science of chemistry who classified zinc chloride and antimony trichloride as "butters" – the butter of zinc and the butter of antimony – because they were soft and malleable (201). But classifying on the basis of the common malleability of things tells us little about their nature or how they can be expected to behave. This was Quine's point. More, the similarity identified lacks causal ground. Thus Marx, anticipating contemporary scientific realism, invites us to look for underlying structural relations in the analysis of social things and to reject explanations that do not move beyond surface similarities. Both in "Notes on Wagner" and in his famous "Letter to Kugelmann" (July 11, 1868) (Marx 1965), he emphasized that his own method needed to be understood in just that way.

Value as cause

In turning to the analysis of Section 2 of *Capital*, I can effectively frame my task by summarizing what I take to be an important misreading of Marx's analysis, one I hope to correct. In a seminal essay, also dating back to 1969, Hans-Georg Backhaus, a student of Adorno, offered a critique of the first two sections of *Capital* (Backhaus 1980). The argument goes like this: Backhaus argued that there was a "defectiveness of the presentation" reflected above all in a "break" or "gap" between the first two sections and the third. According to Backhaus, the whole importance of Marx's critique of political economy was the line of demarcation drawn with Ricardo. Ricardo, unconcerned with social form, had dissolved value into labor, the substance of value. But he had offered no analysis of value's forms. By contrast, Marx's attention to the value form in Section 3 of *Capital* showed the possibility for a decisive rupture with classical political economy. Nonetheless, Backhaus thought there was a problem. Enormously sensitive to the difficulty of his opening analysis, Marx had taken such pains to popularize the first two sections that he had compromised the methodological structure of his problematic. There was a capitulation to Ricardian analysis: specifically labor presented in Sections 1 and 2 as the substance of value, is developed as nothing more than the bare physiological expenditure of human effort. There is no concern for an explanation that either shows or will prepare the way for a consideration of social form. The transition from Section 2 to Section 3 is therefore unmediated and "pseudo-dialectical." We are left with an incomplete break with classical political economy that has undermined not only the dialectic of Marx's presentation, but also its critical bite.

Backhaus's essay, together with renewed attention to Marx's debt to Hegel, has led to an influential trend of contemporary Marxism called "Value Form Theory" (e.g. Arthur 2002, 1979; Taylor 2000; Reuten 1993; Reuten and Williams 1989; Williams 1988; Eldred and Hanlon 1981). The work of Christopher Arthur offers one important example. For almost three decades Arthur has continued and deepened the core argument of Backhaus in an effort to bring out more fully the implications a coherent understanding of the value form might have for the critique of capitalism. He argues that Marx's introduction of the subject of labor into the first sections of *Capital* is done "far too hastily" (2002: 87) and he offers instead an analysis of the value form without any consideration of labor at all. Labor does enter, but only after the logic of capital has been developed and as a result of contradictions presented in that connection. In his analysis of commodity exchange, Arthur treats value as an expression of "pure form" (155), abstracted from all materiality, which, by analogy to Hegel's concept of pure Being, becomes the source of all subsequent development of the logic of *Capital*.

The question is whether Value Form Theory's rejections of Marx's presentation in the first sections of *Capital* can be sustained. I argue that it can't. Ironically, the reason for this is that Value Form theorists have ignored precisely the social form of labor presented in Section 2. By claiming that Marx there reduces value to the bare physiological expenditure of labor, Value Form Theory, like Schumpeter and others, does indeed make Marx into a Ricardian, but only because they miss the underlying causal structure he has located, the thing that allows us to characterize labor's form as a social kind. In this early stage of the analysis of the commodity, Value Form theorists tend to consider social form only in connection with the forms of manifestation of value presented by Marx in Section 3 of *Capital's* first chapter. They bypass the *constitutive* form of value presented in Section 2, a causal structure capable of accounting for value's forms of manifestation.[5] This leads quite explicitly to an inversion whereby value is instead constituted by its forms of manifestation, in particular, money, and Marx's political economy gets reconstructed accordingly. By focusing on the analysis of the forms value takes in exchange, Marx's insistence on the social forms of production is lost.

A remarkable claim

To understand how Marx analyzed the social form of commodity producing labor is to understand value as a social kind.

Marx begins Section 2 by reminding us that the commodity presents itself as something useful and as something that has value in exchange. He remarks immediately that Section 1 also established that the labor that produced commodities has a two-fold nature – labor insofar as it found expression in value and labor insofar as it was the creator of use values. He then adds quite a remarkable claim: "I was the first to point out and to examine critically this two-fold nature of labour contained in commodities. As this point is the pivot on which a clear comprehension of Political Economy turns, we must go into more detail" (1967: 49).

Now the group to which Marx has reference in claiming that he has moved to the front of the line includes William Petty, Ben Franklin, Adam Smith, Jean Baptiste Say, and David Ricardo, and others, not to speak of Hegel, who while not a political economist, nonetheless found an important place for the study of the political economy of value in the *Philosophy of Right*. This suggests it is time to pay attention. Marx is either puffing or something important is going on.

The fifth paragraph following this first one, that is, the sixth paragraph of the section, begins, "To resume, then." Plausibly the detail we're invited by the first paragraph to consider has been presented in the intervening four paragraphs. We need to track the argument in them.

The first of these paragraphs is a single sentence. A commodity, Marx established in Section 1, is a use value offered in exchange. That is, a commodity must be a useful object, but it is not just a useful object. For one thing, if it is useful but not produced by labor, it is not a commodity. For another, if it is consumed directly by its producer it is not a commodity. Instead, in order to be a commodity a useful object must be exchanged. Moreover, it is exchanged in some or another proportion with another commodity, and, roughly, this is its exchange value. So a commodity is a useful thing that is a bearer of exchange value; that is, it stands in a variety of exchange relations with other things. The single sentence of the second paragraph of Section 2 offers a simple example of two commodities, 10 yards of linen and a coat, standing in a 2 to 1 relation to each other – the coat has twice the value of 10 yards of linen.

In the next paragraph, the third, Marx notices that the coat is the result of a particular kind of useful activity, tailoring. He adds that labor, considered from the perspective of the way in which it manifests itself in a useful product, is called "useful labor." This is one aspect of the two-fold character of labor.

In the fourth paragraph Marx observes that just as two use values, the linen and the coat, are qualitatively different, so is the labor which produced them. But it is just this qualitative difference that drives their producers to exchange and thus makes it possible for the results of useful labor to function as commodities. "Coats are not exchanged for coats," he writes. The commodity form, in other words, requires the distribution by means of exchange of the products of aggregate social labor to need.

In the fifth paragraph Marx considers labor insofar as it is productive of value, the other aspect of the two-fold character of labor. This is a point of detail not yet developed either in the preceding paragraphs of Section 2 or in Section 1. We learn here that because the useful labors expended in producing goods offered for exchange are qualitatively diverse, these labors are part of the social division of labor. But Marx immediately emphasizes that while the division of labor is necessary for the production of commodities, the converse is not true – there can be a division of labor in society without the production of commodities. Ancient communities that divided work among the members of a community without resorting to exchange offer one example. A factory offers another – labor is specialized within a factory and the object of production passes from hand to hand without the intervention of market exchange. Markets emerge when production is carried on by persons or groups of persons producing independently as part of the social division of labor. Thus, Marx concludes, "Only such products can become commodities with regard to each other, as result from different kinds of labour, each kind being carried on independently and for the account of private individuals" (49).

It should not escape our attention that this is the pivot on which a clear comprehension of political economy turns.

That is, if we're following the text, the next sentence begins the sixth paragraph: "To resume, then" (49).

What Marx has presented here is a structure of social labor, a social form that generates value. We can ask whether the features identified constitute the kind of homeostatic dispositional properties that characterize a social kind.

By returning to Section 1 we get a better sense of the significance of the point in the flow of the analysis. In Section 1 Marx explains that exchange value, the proportion in which values of one product exchange for values of another, is constantly changing. A book worth $10 today is worth $20 tomorrow and $30 in another town. The phenomena that characterize exchange value seem relative and accidental. As such, assuming nothing more, exchange value is a poor candidate for a social kind.

But since the similarity commodities share in exchange does place them in relation to one another in determined proportions, Marx concludes that exchange value must express something common to the use values exchanged. Long ago, however, Aristotle noticed that use values offered for exchange are incommensurable (1962: 127). Marx therefore concludes that the act of exchange must take place in total abstraction from use value in the following sense: use value motivates the exchange, but it does not explain the ratio of exchange; in fact, any given use value can exchange for any conceivable other so long as they are presented in the right quantitative proportions. Marx adds also that if we abstract from all consideration of use, we abstract from every material element of the product that determines use. Use value must become then simply the bearer of the one feature that commodities still have in common – labor. Each commodity is a product of labor. Insofar as this labor has been expended on a product, transforming it to use, it is value. While this labor, because expended, is not the living labor located in the actual process of production that constitutes the value relation, still, expended labor, like living labor, can be quantitatively measured by duration and can thus serve as a measure of the value each product of labor represents.

An early criticism of Marx's analysis here, one that has persisted, is that commodities share in common an infinite number of properties – they all exist under the stars, they all exist at some specific distance from London, they all are the object of need, and so forth. Most of these alternatives are trivial and fail because we know intuitively they do not causally regulate exchange – distance from London is an example. And the problem with need, despite the heroic efforts of mainstream economics, is this: to regulate the exchange of incommensurables, needs would have to be commensurable, but they are not.

So we're left with labor. Labor is the thing products have in common that may plausibly be understood to regulate exchange. But we're stuck still. The concrete useful labors that produce useful objects for exchange are themselves incommensurable. The tailor who goes to market demanding 30 yards of linen for a coat because 10 yards are produced in a half day and the coat took him a day and a half to produce may be as likely to wind up with a quarrel as with linen.

It is this problem that provokes us to look not just for labor as the source of value – the limitation of Ricardo's analysis – but also to consider the *form* of social labor. In fact it is the causal structure of commodity producing labor that both generates the problem of commensurability in exchange and the solution to it. Recall how we have characterized that structure: independent producers produce use values useless to them. We are immediately presented with the problem of finding an appropriate ratio for goods to exchange. In order to distribute aggregate social labor to need, goods must change hands.

But by generating the need for exchange, the causal structure that I have elsewhere called "interdependent autonomy" (Engelskirchen 1997, 2003) generates also the solution to the problem. Use values are not use values unless they are consumed. That means they must be exchanged in order to be used. Since any product whatsoever can be exchanged for any other as long as each exists in an appropriate quantity, the total amount of productive labor devoted to the production of commodities can be considered an aggregate. That is, when products exchange, as they must, they are equated practically by the act of exchange and thus the entire mass of aggregate concrete labors that produced them can be considered one mass to be distributed to social need. Each product then represents a proportion of this mass.

An analogy from the physical sciences making news while Marx was working through his analysis of the commodity may contribute to understanding. In 1857 the German physicist Rudolph Clausius for the first time explained the kinetic theory of gases in a satisfactory way.[6] A container filled with gas of any sort consists mostly of empty space. The molecules that make up the gas exist there in a condition of random motion. Collisions, which are also random, affect the speed of the molecules. Some go faster than average, some less. This means that the kinetic energy of individual molecules, which is an expression of their mass and speed, will vary. Nonetheless, the temperature of a gas, whatever its chemical composition, is proportional to the average kinetic energy of its molecules.

Now there is a point worth emphasizing here: it makes no difference what gas or gases are mixed in the container. Heavier molecules will move more slowly than lighter ones, but at the same temperature, their average kinetic energy will be the same. In this respect we can abstract from the chemical composition of the molecules.[7] We can even call this, legitimately, a "real" abstraction.

Much ink has been spilled over "real" abstraction in Marx and the concept has become something of a *deux ex machina* in a good deal of recent literature. In the case of a gas, we're entitled to call what we're left with when we abstract from chemical composition "real" because the average kinetic energy we now take as our exclusive focus remains fully present and causally effective. What do we mean by real abstraction then?

This can have no other meaning than that the features rendered irrelevant by the process we investigate have lost their causal significance for our inquiry. They are causally irrelevant to explanation and understanding. In natural kind terms, they do not serve induction or explanation by helping to accommodate our practice to the causal structures of the world.

The meaning of "real" abstraction in Marx is the same. Consideration of the material and useful properties of objects produced as commodities *are* casually relevant to exchange – as we have seen they are what drive people to exchange. But these same properties make no relevant contribution to establishing the commensurable ratios in which goods exchange.

Labor expended is different. Far from abstracting from the different concrete labors that contribute to exchange, these labor expenditures constitute value. Reference to the kinetic theory of gases may once again be helpful. For any gas, temperature is proportional to the average kinetic energy of the molecules, but this does not at all mean that the speed or actual kinetic energy of every molecule is the same. Instead, the total kinetic energy of a system depends on the different masses and random speeds of the individual molecules. When distributed over the number of molecules in the system, average kinetic energy is proportional to temperature, and thus as temperature increases the average speed of the individual molecules will increase. The speed of any particular molecule will deviate from average, but, at constant pressure and volume, average kinetic energy is a causal composition of these particular speeds taken together with their molecular mass, not an abstraction from them.

In commodity exchange we abstract from the useful effects of labor, but we do not abstract from the different concrete expenditures of labor conducted all with varying intensities deviating from any average of them. Just as at a given temperature the chemical composition of a gas does not affect the average kinetic energy of its molecules, so too for commodity exchange the useful effect of labor is irrelevant to establishing value. But just as kinetic energy depends on the actual mass and speed of the different molecules of a gas, value depends on the concrete labor expenditures of different units of production. Temperature is an expression of average kinetic energy jointly produced by the random motions of all molecules. So too, value is an expression of the average of all the different concrete labor expenditures of which a market is made. We can only conceptually abstract from these different concrete expenditures by thinking of the value of a product as a causal composition of them.

Think of it this way. The different speeds of gas molecules are the product of random collisions. Goods taken to market are reduced to expended labor that can be considered homogeneous by the collisions of exchange. We noticed above Marx's observation that any two products can be equated practically in the market in some specific ratio – some given proportion of the one for the other regulates the exchange of potatoes, say, for widgets. But for this to happen, widgets and potatoes must be, each one respectively, homogeneous in kind. Suppose four people each produce a widget and all the widgets produced are effectively identical in their features and qualities. One does this in two hours, the other in four, the third in six, and the last in eight. As a result of competition, and because they are the same, the widgets will tend to sell for the same price. This means that competition will reduce all different expenditures of widget labor to homogeneity. The labor time contributed by the production of widgets to aggregate social labor is 20 hours. Since each widget, no matter who produced it or how efficient the process of production was, is rendered equal by competition to every other, each tends to represent five hours contributed to this total, though no one actually produced a widget in five hours. But this deviation of the actual labor expenditure from the social average for producing widgets does not mean that those specific expenditures are causally irrelevant to the constitution of value. On the contrary, value is the causal result of them. The expended labor that is the source of value is abstract because the useful effects of labor are causally irrelevant, not because the duration of labor expenditure is causally irrelevant.

There is one more lesson we can draw from the foregoing analogy. The development of the causal theory of reference in the relatively recent past has had the effect of clarifying a distinction that earlier attention to the philosophy of language often confused. We call Hesperus the evening star and Phosphorus the morning star, but they refer to the same thing – the planet Venus. Since reference is the same but meaning different we're forced to recognize a distinction between the thing referred to and our meaning – meaning which may very well, as in this case, be context specific. So too we can see that temperature and average kinetic energy refer to the same thing – we reduce them both to the motion of molecules in a gas – but can recognize also that they are used in different contexts to mean quite different things.

On the analysis just given we can make a comparable distinction between Marx's use of the concepts of abstract labor and value. Like temperature and average kinetic energy, both terms refer to the same thing – a quantitative relationship of the respective expended labors socially required to produce the commodities brought to market – but these two terms do not mean the same thing. Value connotes the relative weight such labor expenditures give the products of labor in exchange. Abstract labor, by contrast, is paired with and understood in relation to concrete labor – it connotes the way expended labor is reduced to a homogeneous and common measure by the random collisions of exchange.

Once again on the "defectiveness" of Marx's presentation

Does this specification of the social form of commodity producing labor respond to the critique offered by Value Form Theory? I think it does. First, the idea that there is a defectiveness of presentation in the first section of *Capital* is the result of ignoring exactly the point Marx emphasizes and on which a clear comprehension of political economy turns – the social form of labor. As we have seen, it is the social form of commodity producing labor that gives rise to the problem of commensurability in exchange – producers are independent and produce use values that are useless to them. But this same social form also gives rise to the means for the problem's solution. Because any product may exchange for any other in an appropriate proportion, producers entering exchange abstract necessarily from the concrete usefulness of their labors and each product is a bearer of value to the extent of its contribution, as a result of exchange, to the aggregate total of labor distributed to need.

By ignoring the social form of labor specified in Section 2, Value Form theorists have been led to argue that abstraction from use in exchange means abstraction from all materiality in the process. Value could thus better be understood at this early stage of the analysis as "pure form" and "without content" (Arthur 2002, 155; Reuten and Williams 1989: 65). But there is a philosophical mistake here as well as a mistake in reading Section 2. The quantitative relations expressed by numbers are necessarily the quantitative relations of something. Quantity is the predicate of a subject. You can abstract from any particular subject, but $1 + 2 = 3$ is one of a thing and two more of it making three of such things. Arthur recognizes this (2002: 91), but the point gets lost, nonetheless, insofar as value as pure form is thought to abstract from all materiality.[8]

It is clear, also, that this approach misreads Section 2. In the act of exchange abstraction is made from all consideration of use and of all material properties of goods that account for their use. But there is no abstraction either from the duration of labor expenditure or from the materiality of the *social form of labor* that causes exchange! Exchange does not abstract from, but depends on, the material division of labor in society; equally exchange does not abstract from but is a causal consequence of the separation of units of production one from the other.

In sum, the labor that produces the product in the commodity form is itself form determined in two ways: it is produced independently and it is produced as part of the social division of labor. These causal features of labor's social form offer a real definition of the form of commodity producing labor as a social kind.

Labor as the substance of value

No doubt Value Form theorists would respond to the criticisms I've made by noticing an omission – I've said nothing about Backhaus's claim that in the first sections of *Capital* Marx reduces value to the bare physiological expenditure of labor. However it be with your analysis, they might argue, this reduction has nothing to do with social form. Consider the way Marx concludes Section 2:

> On the one hand all labour is, speaking physiologically, an expenditure of human labor power, and in its character of identical abstract human labour, it creates and forms the value of commodities. On the other hand, all labour is the expenditure of human labour power in a special form and with a definite aim, and in this, its character of concrete useful labour, it produces use-values.
>
> (53)

On a quick reading of this passage we could conclude that the bare physiological expenditure of labor explained the source of value and the special form of labor explained what made labor useful. But we can read more carefully. First, there are not two different labors here, of course, and attention to labor's useful form does not efface the social form presupposed by labor expenditures that produce commodities. That is, the labor that produces a commodity must count as one labor with distinct causal consequences, each of which realizes different causal results. When we focus on its definite aim – weaving or tailoring is meant here – we consider its useful form. When we focus on it as an expenditure of independent labor functioning as a part of a complex social division of labor, we consider its social form or value.

To consider the labor expended on commodities from the point of view of its social form, we consider its character as "identical abstract human labor." But the abstract, identical character of human labor is not something that belongs to the bare expenditure of human effort in all times and all places as such. In the "Introduction" to the *Grundrisse*, Marx observes that "there is no production in general" (1973: 86) only production in specific social and historical circumstances. In the same sense there is no "labor in general." The particular social form in which the physiological expenditure of labor takes an abstract and identical character consists in the separation of units of production that produce goods useful to others but useless to themselves. As a direct causal consequence producers exchange and the process of exchange then renders causally irrelevant the useful effects of their labor to the regulation of the exchange; instead, all labor is reduced by exchange to commensurability in terms of labor time.

Nor in the study of labor's social forms throughout history do we disregard useful effects in all times and all places. Quite the contrary. There is no labor in general and if the bare expenditure of labor is to be considered without regard to its useful effects this necessarily presupposes a historically determined social form of labor in the actual activity of production. Marx presented the essential features of this in the first paragraphs of Section 2. Backhaus's argument that in Sections 1 and 2 Marx presents the substance of value as the mere bare physiological expenditure of human effort misreads by ignoring this. It is only in virtue of Marx's explicit specification of the social form required that labor's product can appear in the commodity form as a manifestation of abstract and identical human labor.

Value's substance and primary substance

There is another way to approach this question. As we've seen, Marx calls labor expenditure, objectified labor, the "substance of value," and he is consistent in this throughout *Capital* and its drafts – the substance of value refers to labor expended in producing a product and objectified there in virtue of the transformation accomplished in the material worked on. But just as we can never ignore the context within which the bare physiological expenditure of labor takes place if we are to understand the social form of labor, neither can we ignore that context if we are to understand the social form of the product. If it is value that objectified labor is the substance of, then this substance presupposes the social form of value: both the independence of producers and their production of use values as part of the social division of labor provide the material context for the appearance of the product as a commodity.

In effect, Marx's use of the word "substance" as an expression of the social form of value needs to be understood with an appreciation of the much more far-reaching meaning of "primary substance" that I'm convinced he has taken over from the middle books of Aristotle's *Metaphysics* (1960). Marx was a close student of Aristotle and his understanding of social form seems importantly informed by Aristotle's search for the primary substance of things. Because Marx's use of

Aristotle on this point accounts for the way in which he foreshadows today's scientific realism, I need to make my meaning clear.

Aristotle was after an understanding of the primary stuff that constituted the world. He called this *ousia*, a term that has been translated as "substance" – that which is underlying. But *ousia* is far from meaning "substance" in the modern sense of "matter." For Aristotle matter could not be a candidate for primary substance because if matter were to be considered for itself alone, as undifferentiated and without form, it would remain then unspecific and as such could not ground explanation. Bare form too could not serve because unless this were materially grounded it recalled Plato's forms, the Ideas; moreover, unless one were to give mystical potency to such forms, form alone could not explain the causal power of things. But if the form of a thing were instantiated in the matter of it, then that structure could account for its causal potency and, as a consequence, account for what it was, how it behaved, and how it tended to maintain itself as what it was. And in this respect, it bears emphasizing, Aristotle approached what we now mean when we say that a natural kind can be characterized by a cluster of homeostatic dispositional properties.

How might Marx have appropriated these lessons to inform his study of social life? For one thing, Marx's analysis of the social forms of labor may best be considered a kind of hylomorphic composite of labor and form. "Hylomorphic" comes from the Greek roots for matter, "hylo," and form, "morphe," and was used by Aristotle to refer to how the things of the world were constituted as composites of matter and form. On this reading, the concept of a physiological expenditure of labor, considered in abstraction from social form, would be like the concept of bare matter for Aristotle: without considering its form, without considering it as *enformed*, it would be no more than the undifferentiated possibility of productive social life. But it could not ground social explanation. For that we need a constitutive form actually embedded in material activity – that is, the causal potency of labor depends on its being instantiated in a specific social form. Otherwise stated, we cannot understand how a bare expenditure of labor could present itself in the character of identical and abstract human labor without knowing how such labor, as creative of value, is structured or enformed. Nor can we understand objectified labor as the substance of value except insofar as that "substance" is the product of living labor expended within a specific, underlying and primary social form.

Marx's characterization of that social form in Section 2 is clear – the physiological expenditure of labor that is the source of value occurs as living labor actually located in the process of production in a historically specific social form: a form of productive autonomy as part of the social division of labor. Consider, for example, the observation offered in Section 2 immediately following the "To resume, then" of the sixth paragraph. Marx sums up the point he's just made, but now in a way that situates it in the two-fold character of labor:

> In a community, the produce of which in general takes the form of commodities, i.e., in a community of commodity producers, this qualitative

difference between the useful forms of labour that are carried on independently by individual producers, each on their own account, develops into a complex system, a social division of labour.

(49–50)

That is, the double character of labor is instantiated in a specific social form: useful labors carried on independently for private exchange presuppose and in turn generate the social division of labor. It is labor expended within this underlying social form, and no other, that forms the substance of value.

Marx's drafts for *Capital* make clear that he was devoted to investigating the forms of social labor. He sought to give a structural and causal account that would serve to anchor the study of social life – he wanted to show how social life was "form determined." But this makes sense only if labor's forms are understood as a social composites of Aristotelian inspiration: a physiological expenditure of labor must be considered always as embodied in the social form within which such expenditure was actualized. In the manuscript *Pre-Capitalist Economic Formations* (Marx 1964) we find this presented across the canvas of history as the form in which the working individual, actually engaged in labor, is related to nature and to others. Such causal structures, Marx argued, hold the key to social understanding. That is, for Marx, understanding the form of the product of labor, the immense accumulation of commodities of the first sentence of *Capital*, for example, was hardly decisive. The form of the product of labor was not the economic cell form that could ground an understanding of political economy. Instead, the product of labor and how it stood in relation to other products was merely a starting point to the search for a causal structure of living labor that could account for the form of the product's appearance.

Conclusion

As part of our struggle to know social life, we fashion categories in social science to refer to social things. The reference to and use of such categories in scientific and political practice require that their content be determined by causally efficacious social structures. That is, the social mechanisms a definition picks out will embody those properties that make it possible for us to accommodate the causal structures of social life to the demands of our practice. "Economic categories," Marx writes, "are only the theoretical expressions, the abstractions of the social relations of production" (1978: 102). Generalizing, we call the material relations of production social kinds and the theoretical categories that give expression to them we characterize by the use of social kind terms.

In his analysis of the commodity Marx moves from a similarity relation, a relation of commensurability that appears on the surface of social life as the exchangeability of products, to the source of commensurability in expended labor, and then to the source of expended labor in a historically specific causal structure of living labor, commodity producing labor's social form. The expended labor that is the substance of value is form determined by this causal structure. Moreover, the causal structure of living labor Marx has specified – independent production for private exchange – depends on each producer producing a product, not for her own use, but for others. Plainly this exhausts her resources of raw materials, instruments of production and means of subsistence. So viewed exchange appears as a homeostatic mechanism by means of which the producer is able to alienate her own product and receive in return the value equivalent in commodities she needs to renew the process of production on which she depends. That is, by means of independent production and exchange she is able to obtain and reproduce the conditions of her own reproduction. In this way each unit of production contributes to the continuation of the process of labor in the value form. As so understood, the social relation given expression by value is a relation of production – not a mode of production, which is a way we characterize a social totality such as feudalism or capitalism, but a social relation which forms a constituent element of some such larger social organism.

We can refer to the relation of production identified in Section 2 of *Capital* as a social kind because it is constituted by a causal structure, the essential features of which account for its own persistence. It is a social form to which we can accommodate the demands of our transformative practice.

Finally, there is a qualification to make. I have shown very briefly how different concrete labors may be averaged to make exchange possible. I have not shown how different producers succeed in communicating with one another about this. This more difficult problem is taken up by Section 3 of the first chapter of Marx's *Capital*. Its analysis will show not only the forms by which value becomes manifest but also how and why they must become so.

Notes

1 I have benefited from important suggestions by Richard Boyd, Anthony Preus, Herb Shore, and John Milios; errors that persist are my own.
2 Thanks to Richard Boyd for insisting on this point.
3 See e.g. "The Logic of Scientific Discovery," excerpted from Bhaskar (1997), in Archer *et al.* eds.(1998). Groff (2004) evaluates Bhaskar's emphasis on science's search for the generative mechanisms of nature and society.
4 See Groff (2004) for a discussion of Bhaskar's appropriation of Locke's categories.
5 I develop the concept of value's constitutive form in Engelskirchen (forthcoming).
6 Clausius' papers on kinetic energy, published in German in 1857 and 1858, were quickly translated into English and appeared in *The Philosophical Magazine* in 1857 and 1859. Maxwell's work on kinetic theory began with his reading of Clausius' second paper, On the Mean Length of the Paths Described by the Separate Molecules of Gaseous Bodies, in 1859. Thereafter the two of them carried on what has been described as a "scientific correspondence" in print for the next 15 years and this contributed to the rapid advance of understanding (Purrington 1997, 135–136). Clausius' papers are reprinted in Brush 1965.
7 The abstraction does not hold for gases under either high pressure or as they approach temperatures cool enough to liquefy. As a gas cools, the forces of attraction and repulsion among molecules can no longer be disregarded nor at high pressure can we disregard the

space occupied by the molecules. But where no such extremes are presented deviations in the actual behavior of different gases are negligible.

8 His resort to the "The Spectral Ontology of Value" (2001, 2002: 153–174) is a consequence.

References

Archer, M., Bhaskar, R., Collier, A., *et al.* (1998) *Critical Realism: Essential Readings.* London, New York: Routledge.

Aristotle (1962) *The Nicomachean Ethics* (trans. M. Ostwald). Indianapolis IN: Bobbs-Merrill.

Aristotle (1960) *The Metaphysics* (trans. R. Hope). Ann Arbor: The University of Michigan Press.

Arthur, C. J. (2002) *The New Dialectic and Marx's Capital.* Leiden, Boston, Koln: Brill.

Arthur, C. J. (2001) The Spectral Ontology of Value. *Radical Philosophy* 107, May/June 2001, pp. 32–42.

Arthur, C. J. (1979) Dialectic of the Value Form. In D. Elson (ed.), *Value: The Representation of Labour in Capitalism* (pp. 67–81). London: CSE Books.

Backhaus, Hans-Georg (1980) On the Dialectics of the Value–Form. *Thesis Eleven* 1, 94–120. Originally written in 1969; published as 'Zur Dialektik der Wertform' in A. Schmidt (ed.), *Beitraege zur marxistischen Erkenntnistheorie* Frankfurt a.M. (1980).

Bettelheim, C. (1975) *Economic Calculation and Forms of Property.* New York: Monthly Review Press.

Bhaskar, R. (1998) *The Possibility of Naturalism* (3rd edn) London: Routledge (first published 1979).

Bhaskar, R. (1997) *A Realist Theory of Science.* London, New York: Verso (first published 1975).

Boyd, R. (1999) Kinds as the 'Workmanship of Men': Realism, Constructivism, and Natural Kinds. In J. Nida-Rumelin (ed.), *Rationality, Realism, Revision, (Perspectives in Analytical Philosophy,* v. 23, pp. 52–89). Berlin, New York: Walter de Gruyter.

Boyd, R. (1991) Realism, Anti-Foundationalism, and the Enthusiasm for Natural Kinds. *Philosophical Studies,* 61: 127–148.

Boyd, R. (1988) How to Be a Moral Realist. In G. Sayre-McCord (ed.), *Moral Realism.* Ithaca: Cornell University Press.

Brush, S. G. (1965) *Kinetic Theory, v. 1.* London, New York: Pergamon Press.

Dupre, J. (1993) *The Disorder of Things. Metaphysical Foundations of the Disunity of Science.* Cambridge, MA: Harvard.

Eldred, M. and Hanlon, M. (1981) Reconstructing Value-Form Analysis. *Capital and Class,* 13: 24–60.

Engelskirchen, H. (2003) Value and Contract Formation. In J. Joseph and J. M. Roberts (eds), *Realism, Discourse and Deconstruction* (111–134). New York, London: Routledge.

Engelskirchen, H. (2005) "Why Is This Labor Value" (unpublished manuscript).

Engelskirchen, H. (1997) Consideration as the Commitment to Relinquish Autonomy. *Seton Hall L. Rev.* 27: 490–573.

Groff, R. (2004) *Critical Realism, Post-positivism and the Problem of Knowledge.* New York, London: Routledge.

Hacking, I. (1991a) A Tradition of Natural Kinds. *Philos. Stud.,* 61: 109–126.

Hacking, I. (1991b) On Boyd. *Philos. Stud.,* 61: 149–154.

Keller, R., Boyd, R. and Wheeler, Q. (2003) The Illogical Basis of Phylogenetic Nomenclature. *Bot. Rev.* 69(1): 93–110.

Kornblith, H. (1993) *Inductive Inference and its Natural Ground: An Essay in Naturalistic Epistemology.* Cambridge MA: MIT.

Locke, J. (1975) *An Essay Concerning Human Understanding,* Nidditch, P. H. (ed.) Oxford, New York: Oxford.

Marx, K. (1978) *The Poverty of Philosophy.* Peking: Foreign Languages Press.

Marx, K. (1975) Notes on Wagner. In T. Carver (ed.), *Texts on Method.* New York: Harper & Row.

Marx, K. (1973) *Grundrisse* (trans. M. Nicolaus). Harmondsworth: Penguin, NLB.

Marx, K. (1967) *Capital,* v. 1. New York: International Publishers.

Marx, K. (1965) Letter to L. Kugelmann, July 11, 1868. In *Marx Engels: Selected Correspondence* (2nd edn, 209–211). Moscow: Progress Publishers.

Marx, K. (1964) *Pre-Capitalist Economic Formations* (Hobsbawm, E., ed.). London: Lawrence & Wishart.

Pessin, A. and Goldberg, S. (1996) *The Twin Earth Chronicles. Twenty Years of Reflection on Hilary Putnam's 'The Meaning of Meaning',* Armonk, NY: M.E. Sharpe.

Platts, M. (1997) *Ways of Meaning: An Introduction to the Philosophy of Langugage* (2nd edn), Cambridge, MA: MIT.

Psillos, S. (1999) *Scientific Realism: How Science Tracks Truth.* London, New York: Routledge.

Purrington, R. (1997) *Physics in the Nineteenth Century.* New Brunswick, NJ, London: Rutgers Univ. Press.

Quine, W. V. (1994) Natural Kinds. In S. Schwartz (ed.), *Naming, Necessity and Natural Kinds,* 155–175. Ithaca, NY: Cornell.

Reuten, G. (1993) The Difficult Labor of a Theory of Social Value: Metaphors and Systematic Dialectics at the Beginning of Marx's *Capital.* In F. Moseley (ed.), *Marx's Method in Capital: A Reexamination* (pp. 89–113). Atlantic Highlands, NJ: Humanities Press.

Reuten, G. and Williams, M. (1989) *Value-Form and the State,* London, New York: Routledge.

Rieppel, O. (2004) Monophyly, Paraphyly, and Natural Kinds, *Bio. and Phil.,* 19: 1–23.

Rieppel, O. (2005a) "Proper names in twin worlds: Monophyly, Paraphyly, and the World Around Us," *Organisms, Diversity & Evolution,* 5: 89–100.

Rieppel, O. (2005b) "Modules, Kinds, and Homology," *J. of Experimental Zoology,* 304B: 18–27.

Schwartz, S. (1979) "Natural Kind Terms," *Cognition,* 7: 301–315.

Schwartz, S. (1977) *Naming, Necessity and Natural Kinds.* Ithaca, NY: Cornell.

Taylor, Nicola (2000) "Abstract Labour and Social Mediation in Marxian Value Theory," unpublished Bachelor's thesis, Murdoch University School of Economics, Western Australia.

Williams, M. 1988 *Value, Social Form and the State.* New York: St. Martin's.

Wilson, R. A. 1999 *Species: New Interdisciplinary Essays* (ed.) Cambridge, MA: MIT.

Index